25

VELLEIUS PATERCULUS:
THE CAESARIAN AND AUGUSTAN
NARRATIVE
(2.41–93)

VELLEIUS
PATERCULUS

THE CAESARIAN
AND AUGUSTAN NARRATIVE
(2.41–93)

EDITED WITH A COMMENTARY

BY

A. J. WOODMAN

University of Leeds

CAMBRIDGE UNIVERSITY PRESS

CAMBRIDGE

LONDON   NEW YORK   NEW ROCHELLE

MELBOURNE   SYDNEY

PUBLISHED BY THE PRESS SYNDICATE OF THE UNIVERSITY OF CAMBRIDGE
The Pitt Building, Trumpington Street, Cambridge, United Kingdom

CAMBRIDGE UNIVERSITY PRESS
The Edinburgh Building, Cambridge CB2 2RU, UK
40 West 20th Street, New York NY 10011–4211, USA
477 Williamstown Road, Port Melbourne, VIC 3207, Australia
Ruiz de Alarcón 13, 28014 Madrid, Spain
Dock House, The Waterfront, Cape Town 8001, South Africa

http://www.cambridge.org

First published 1983
First paperback edition 2004

A catalogue record for this book is available from the British Library

Library of Congress catalogue card number: 83-1988

ISBN 0 521 25639 9 hardback
ISBN 0 521 60702 7 paperback

CONTENTS

TO G.B.A. FLETCHER AND DAVID WEST
uterque amicus magister Nouocastrensis

PREFACE

This volume covers Velleius' narrative of Caesar and Augustus down to the point at which my commentary on his Tiberian narrative, published in 1977, began. As before, my aims have been to try to establish what Velleius wrote and to explain the nature and meaning of his narrative. I very much regret that I have not been able to take anything more than a token account of the Budé edition of Velleius by Professor J. Hellegouarc'h, the very welcome appearance of which coincided with the virtual completion of my typescript.

During the preparation of this volume I have again benefited from John Prater's bibliographical notes on Velleius, kindly passed on to me by his father and mother. Mr R. W. Lamb has engaged me in a fascinating correspondence about the publication of the *editio princeps*, for which I am most grateful, and Mr J. J. Paterson has made me realise that 'at-a-distance' teaching is not necessarily a meaningless concept. My colleagues and friends in Leeds, especially Professor R. H. Martin, have allowed me to pester them with various questions; and I am also most grateful to Dr G. von der Gönna, Professor J. Hellegouarc'h, Professor P. Santini and Dr R. J. Starr for sending me copies of their various writings on Velleius.

By far my greatest debts are to Mr I. M. LeM. DuQuesnay, Professor G. B. A. Fletcher, Professor F. R. D. Goodyear and Mr R. J. Seager, each of whom has read my entire typescript and expended a great deal of time and energy in correcting errors and in supplying me with copious notes and suggestions. Many of these suggestions have been adopted with acknowledgement, others have been tacitly incorporated where appropriate. Without the scholarship and erudition of these four friends, among whom Professors Fletcher and Goodyear are conspicuous for having served a second term, the present volume would have been greatly impoverished.

Finally, it is a pleasure to express my gratitude to the Cambridge University Press for undertaking to publish, with their customary friendliness and efficiency, another volume of commentary on Velleius.

University of Leeds   A. J. W.
September 1982

REFERENCES AND ABBREVIATIONS

References to Book 1 and to chapters 1–18 of Book 2 of Velleius are always given in full; other references to Book 2 omit the book number. In the commentary I often omit also the chapter number when reference is being made to a different section of the same chapter.

When referring to Cicero's letters and to Appian's *Bellum Ciuile*, I usually place in brackets the numeration used by their respective editors D. R. Shackleton Bailey and E. Gabba.

A. ABBREVIATIONS

Note. This list includes neither current periodical abbreviations, for which I generally follow the system used in *L'Année philologique*, nor the familiar abbreviations of certain standard works.

ALL	*Archiv für lateinische Lexikographie und Grammatik*
ANRW	Temporini, H.–Haase, W. (1972–). *Aufstieg und Niedergang der römischen Welt.* Vols. 1– . Berlin–New York
BMC Emp.	Mattingly, H.–Carson, R. A. G. (1923–62). *Coins of the Roman Empire in the British Museum.* Vols. 1–6. London
CAH	Cook, S. A.–Adcock, F. E.–Charlesworth, M. P. (1923–39). *Cambridge Ancient History.* 1st edn. Cambridge
CRR	Sydenham, E. A. (1952). *The Coinage of the Roman Republic.* London
EJ	Ehrenberg, V.–Jones, A. H. M. (1955). *Documents Illustrating the Reigns of Augustus and Tiberius.* 2nd edn. Oxford [references are to entries unless otherwise stated]
F.	Fletcher, G. B. A. [notes privately communicated: see p. ix]
H–W	Hainsselin, P.–Watelet, H. (1932). *Velleius Paterculus et Florus. Texte revu et traduit.* Paris
K–S	Kühner, R.–Stegmann, C. (1971). *Ausführliche Grammatik der lateinischen Sprache.* Vol. 2 *Satzlehre.* Parts 1 and 2. 4th edn. Repr. Hanover
L–H–S	Leumann, M.–Hofmann, J. B.–Szantyr, A. (1972). *Lateinische Grammatik.* Vol. 2 *Syntax und Stilistik.* Revised edn. Munich
L&S	Lewis, C. T. & Short, C. (1879). *A Latin Dictionary.* Oxford

xi

REFERENCES AND ABBREVIATIONS

MRR   Broughton, T. R. S. (1951–60). *The Magistrates of the Roman Republic.* Vols. 1 and 2 (with Supplement). New York

OLD   *Oxford Latin Dictionary* (1968–82). Oxford

PIR²   Groag, E.–Stein, A.–Petersen, L. (1933–). *Prosopographia Imperii Romani.* Vols. 1– . 2nd edn. Berlin

RG   *Res Gestae Diui Augusti*

RIC   Mattingly, H.–Sydenham, E. A. *et al.* (1923–67). *Roman Imperial Coinage.* Vols. 1–9. London

RRC   Crawford, M. (1974). *Roman Republican Coinage.* Vols. 1–2. Cambridge

TLL   *Thesaurus Linguae Latinae*

TN   Woodman, A. J. (1977). *Velleius Paterculus: The Tiberian Narrative (2.94–131).* Cambridge Classical Texts and Commentaries 19. Cambridge

B. CRITICAL EDITIONS AND COMMENTARIES

Note. I always refer to critical editions etc. of Velleius by the name of the editor or commentator. This list includes only those works to which I refer in this volume; more complete inventories will be found in Krause 61–104, Kritz cxxviii–cxxxvi, Stegmann viii–xii.

Acidalius, V. (1590). Padua
Aldus [see Manutius, A.]
editio Bipontina (1780). Zweibrücken
Boeclerus, J. H. (1642). Strasbourg
Bolaffi, E. (1930). Turin
Bonhomme, A. (1532). Avignon
Bothe, F. H. (1837). Zürich
Burman, P. (1719). Leyden [the elder Burman]
Cludius, A. H. (1815). Hanover
Ellis, R. (1898). Oxford
Gelenius, S. (1546). Basel
Gruner, J. F. (1762). Coburg
Gruter, J. (1607). Frankfurt
Haase, F. (1884). Leipzig [the first edn appeared in 1851]
Halm, C. (1909). Leipzig [a reprint of the first edn of 1876]
Heinsius, N. (1678). Amsterdam
Hellegouarc'h, J. (1982). Paris
Krause, J. C. H. (1800). Leipzig
Kreyssig, J. T. (1836). Meissen
Kritz, F. (1840). Leipzig
Lipsius, J. (1591). Leyden

REFERENCES AND ABBREVIATIONS

Manutius, A. (1571). Venice [grandson of the 'great' Aldus Manutius, hence often called Aldus Nepos]

Orelli, J. C. (1835). Leipzig

Popma, A. (1620). Franeker

Puteanus, C. (1608). Paris

Rhenanus, B. (1520). Basel [the *editio princeps*]

Ruhnken, D. (1779). Leyden

Schegk, J. (1589). Frankfurt

Stegmann de Pritzwald, C. (1965). Stuttgart [a reprint of the first edn (1933), with some recent bibliographical material added by H.-D. Blume]

Sylburg, F. (1588). Frankfurt

Vascosanus, M. (1538). Paris

Vossius, G. (1703). Frankfurt [this edn, by the third son of G. F. Vossius, first appeared in 1639]

C. OTHER WORKS

Note. This list includes only those works of which I do not give full details elsewhere or to which I refer by author's name: where an author is responsible for several works, these are distinguished either by a date or by an abbreviation, as indicated below. This list is not a bibliography of all the works cited in this volume; nor is it a bibliography of modern work on Velleius, for which at the time of writing we still await the contribution to *ANRW* by J. Hellegouarc'h.

Achard, G. (1981). *Pratique rhétorique et idéologie politique dans les discours 'Optimates' de Cicéron. Mnem.* Suppl. 68. Leyden

Adams, J. N. (1972). 'The language of the later books of Tacitus' *Annals*', *CQ* 22.350–73

   (1973). 'The vocabulary of the speeches in Tacitus' historical works', *BICS* 20.124–44

   (1974). 'The vocabulary of the later decades of Livy', *Antichthon* 8.54–62

André, J. (1949). *La vie et l'oeuvre d'Asinius Pollion.* Paris

Avenarius, G. (1956). *Lukians Schrift zur Geschichtsschreibung.* Meisenheim am Glan

Baehrens, W. A. (1912). 'Beiträge zur lateinischen Syntax', *Philologus* Suppl. 12.233–556

Balsdon, J. P. V. D. (1979). *Romans and Aliens.* London

Barnes, T. D. (1974). 'The victories of Augustus', *JRS* 64.21–6

Bell, A. J. (1923). *The Latin dual and poetic diction.* Oxford

Bengtson, H. (1974). *Zum Partherfeldzug des Antonius. SBAW* 1. Munich

REFERENCES AND ABBREVIATIONS

Béranger, J. (1953). *Recherches sur l'aspect idéologique du principat.* Basel

Bernays = J. Bernays' Velleian emendations in Haase vii–xii

Bosworth, A. B. (1972). 'Asinius Pollio and Augustus', *Historia* 21.441–73

Botermann, H. (1968). *Die Soldaten und die römische Politik in der Zeit von Caesars Tod bis zur Begründung des Zweiten Triumvirats. Zetemata* 46. Munich

Bramble, J. C. (1974). *Persius and the Programmatic Satire.* Cambridge

Brunt, *IM* = Brunt, P. A. (1971). *Italian Manpower 225 B.C.–A.D. 14.* Oxford

Cairns, F. (1972). *Generic Composition in Greek and Roman Poetry.* Edinburgh

Canfora, L. (1972). *Totalità e selezione nella storiografia classica.* Bari

Carter, J. M. (1970). *The Battle of Actium.* London

Castiglioni, L. (1931). 'Alcune osservazioni a V.P.', *RAL* 7.268–84

Chausserie-Laprée, J.-P. (1969). *L'expression narrative chez les historiens latins.* Paris

Christ, K. (1976). *Römische Geschichte: eine Bibliographie.* Darmstadt

Cornelissen, J. J. (1877). 'Coniecturae Velleianae', *Mnem.* 5.47–55
    (1887). 'Kritische Aanteekeningen op V.P.', Verslagen en Mededeelingen der Kon. Akad. van Wetenschappen. Afdeeling Letterkunde 3.4.102–50

Dahlmann, H. (1975). *Cornelius Severus. AAWM* 6. Wiesbaden

Damsté, P. H. (1905). 'Ad Vell. Pat.', *Mnem.* 33.398–420

Degrassi, A. (1947). *Inscriptiones Italiae.* Vol. 13, fasc. 1. Rome

Delbenius = P. Delbenius' Velleian emendations in Manutius' edn

Dihle, A. (1955). 'C. Vell. Pat.', *RE* 8A.1.637–59

DuQuesnay, I. M. LeM. (1977). 'Vergil's fourth *Eclogue*', *Papers of the Liverpool Latin Seminar 1976. Arca* 2. Liverpool

Earl = Earl, D. C. (1961). *The Political Thought of Sallust.* Cambridge

Earl, *Aug.* = Earl, D. C. (1968). *The Age of Augustus.* London

Ehrenwirth, U. (1971). *Kritisch-chronologische Untersuchungen für die Zeit vom 1. Juni bis zum 9. Oktober 44 v. Chr.* Diss. Munich

Esteve-Forriol, J. (1962). *Die Trauer- und Trostgedichte in der röm. Literatur.* Diss. Munich

Fletcher (1964) = Fletcher, G. B. A. (1964). *Annotations on Tacitus.* Brussels

Fraenkel, E. (1957). *Horace.* Oxford

Freitag, P. (1942). *Stilistische Beiträge zu V.P.: Pleonasmus und Parenthese.* Unpubl. diss. Vienna

Friebel, C. (1937). 'Emendationes in V.P. Hist. Rom.' in *Graecorum Satyrographorum Fragmenta* (ed. F. Larsow), 146–53. Berlin

Frisch, H. (1946). *Cicero's Fight for the Republic.* Copenhagen

Gagé, J. (1977). *Res Gestae Diui Augusti.* 3rd edn. Paris

Gelzer, *Caes.* = Gelzer, M. (1969). *Caesar: Politician and Statesman.* Eng. trans. by P. Needham. Oxford

xiv

REFERENCES AND ABBREVIATIONS

Georges, H. (1877). *De Elocutione V.P.* Diss. Leipzig

Gesche, H. (1976). *Caesar.* Darmstadt

Gönna, G. von der (1977). 'Beatus Rhenanus und die editio princeps des Vell. Pat.', *Würzb. Jahrb. f. d. Altertumsw.* N.F. 3.231–42

Goodyear, *Comm. Tac.* = Goodyear, F. R. D. (1972–). *The Annals of Tacitus: Books 1–6.* Vols. 1– . Cambridge

Grant, *Cleo.* = Grant, M. (1974). *Cleopatra.* St Albans

RAI = Grant, M. (1950). *Roman Anniversary Issues.* Cambridge

Grenade, P. (1961). *Essai sur les origines du principat.* Paris

Gruen, E. S. (1974). *The Last Generation of the Roman Republic.* Berkeley–Los Angeles–London

Gutzwiller, H. (1942). *Die Neujchrsrede des Konsuls Claudius Mamertinus vor dem Kaiser Julian* [= *Pan. Lat.* 3]. Basel

Hadas, M. (1930). *Sextus Pompey.* New York

Häussler, *Nachträge* = Häussler, R. (1968). *Nachträge zu A. Otto: Die Sprichwörter und sprichwörtlichen Redensarten der Römer.* Hildesheim

   Tac. = Häussler, R. (1965). *Tacitus und das historische Bewusstsein.* Heidelberg

Haller = Haller, B. (1967). *C. Asinius Pollio als Politiker und zeitkritischer Historiker.* Diss. Münster

Haller, B. (1975). 'Augustus-Bibliographie' [to 1972], *ANRW* 2.2.55–74

Hand, *Turs.* = Hand, F. (1969). *Tursellinus seu de particulis latinis commentarii.* Repr. Amsterdam

Harris, W. V. (1979). *War and Imperialism in Republican Rome 327–70 B.C.* Oxford

Haupt, M. (1875). 'Kritische Bemerkungen über V.P.' in *Opuscula* 1.265–76. Leipzig

Heinen, H. (1966). *Rom und Ägypten von 51 bis 47 v. Chr.* Diss. Tübingen

Hellegouarc'h = J. Hellegouarc'h's Budé edn of Velleius [see above, p. xii]

Hellegouarc'h, *VL* = Hellegouarc'h, J. (1963). *Le vocabulaire latin des relations et des partis politiques sous la république.* Paris

Hellegouarc'h, J. (1964). 'Les buts de l'oeuvre historique de V.P.', *Latomus* 23.669–84

   (1976). 'Lire et comprendre. Quelques remarques sur le texte de . . . V.P.', *REL* 54.239–56

Hellegouarc'h, J.–Jodry, Cl. (1980). 'Les *Res Gestae* et l'*Historia Romana* de V.P.', *Latomus* 39.803–16

Herel, J. F. (1800). 'Adnotationes criticae ad V.' in Krause 559–78

Herkommer, E. (1968). *Die topoi in den Proömien der römischen Geschichtswerke.* Diss. Tübingen

Housman, *CP* = Housman, A. E. (1972). *Classical Papers* (ed. J. Diggle and F. R. D. Goodyear). Cambridge

REFERENCES AND ABBREVIATIONS

Huth, J. E. (1833). *Quaestiones Criticae de locis nonnullis V.P.* Altenburg

Huzar, E. G. (1978). *Mark Antony: a biography.* Minneapolis

Jal, P. (1963). *La guerre civile à Rome.* Paris

Jeep, I. W. L. (1839). *Emendationes Velleianae.* Wolfenbüttel

Jones, *Aug.* = Jones, A. H. M. (1970). *Augustus.* London

   Studies = Jones, A. H. M. (1960). *Studies in Roman Government and Law.* Oxford

Klebs, E. (1890). 'Entlehnungen aus V.', *Philologus* 49.285–312

Kloft, H. (1970). *Liberalitas Principis.* Kölner Historische Abhandlungen 18. Vienna

Koch, G. A. (1866). *Quaestiones Velleianae.* Leipzig

Kohl, R. (1915). *De scholasticarum declamationum argumentis ex historia petitis.* Paderborn

Krebs, J. P.–Schmalz, J. H. (1905–7). *Antibarbarus der lateinischen Sprache.* Vols. 1–2. Basel

Kuntz, F. (1962). *Die Sprache des Tacitus.* Diss. Weisenheim am Berg

Lana, I. (1952). *V.P. o della propaganda.* Turin

Latte, K. (1960). *Römische Religionsgeschichte.* Munich

Laurent, J. C. M. (1836). *Loci Velleiani.* Altona

Lausberg, H. (1966). *Manual de retórica literaria.* Spanish trans. by J. P. Riesco. Vols. 1–3. Madrid

Lebek, W. D. (1970). *Verba Prisca.* Göttingen

Leroux, J. (1968). *Les problèmes stratégiques de la bataille d'Actium.* Recherches de philologie et de linguistique, Faculté de Lettres de l'Université de Louvain, Section de philologie classique, 2. Louvain

Liebeschuetz, J. H. W. G. (1979). *Continuity and Change in Roman Religion.* Oxford

Lintott, A. W. (1971). 'Lucan and the history of the civil war', *CQ* 21.488–505

Löfstedt, *Synt.* = Löfstedt, E. (1942, 1933). *Syntactica.* Vols. 1^2 and 2. Lund

Luce, T. J. (1977). *Livy: the Composition of his History.* Princeton

Madvig, J. N. (1871–3). *Adversaria Critica.* Vols. 1–3. Copenhagen

Manuwald, B. (1979). *Cassius Dio und Augustus. Palingenesia* 14. Wiesbaden

Massauer, B. (1968). *Historisch–antiquarischer Kommentar zur Augustus-Partie des V.P. (II.90–123).* Unpubl. diss. Vienna

Michel, D. (1967). *Alexander als Vorbild für Pompeius, Caesar und Marcus Antonius.* Brussels

Milkau, F. (1888). *De V.P. genere dicendi quaest. selectae.* Diss. Königsberg

Millar, *CD* = Millar, F. G. B. (1964). *A Study of Cassius Dio.* Oxford

Millar, F. G. B. (1973). 'Triumvirate and principate', *JRS* 63.50–67

Mommsen = T. Mommsen's Velleian emendations in Haase vii–xii

Mommsen, *Staatsr.* = Mommsen, T. (1887). *Römisches Staatsrecht.* Vols. 1^3, 2^3, 3. Leipzig

REFERENCES AND ABBREVIATIONS

Neue, F.–Wagener, C. (1892–1905). *Formenlehre der lateinischen Sprache.* Leipzig–Berlin

Nicolet, C. (1966, 1974). *L'ordre équestre à l'époque républicaine.* Vols. 1–2. Paris

Nisbet, R. G. M. (1961). *Cicero: In Pisonem.* Oxford

Nock, A. D. (1972). *Essays on Religion and the Ancient World* (ed. Z. Stewart). Oxford

Novák, R. (1892). *Grammatická, lexikalní a kritická pozorování u V.P.* Abhandl. der czechischen Akad., Jahrg. 1, Klasse 3 (4). Prague (1906). 'Zur Kritik des V.P. I ', *WS* 28.283–305 (1907). 'Zur Kritik des V.P. II ', *WS* 29.130–49

Ogilvie, R. M. (1965). *A Commentary on Livy Books 1–5.* Oxford

Opelt, I. (1965). *Die lateinischen Schimpfwörter und verwandte sprachliche Erscheinungen.* Heidelberg

Otto, A. (1890). *Die Sprichwörter und sprichwörtlichen Redensarten der Römer.* Leipzig

Pluygers, W. G. (1881). 'ἀπομνημονεύματα Gul. Geo. Pluygers' (ed. C. G. Cobet), *Mnem.* 9.21–32

Pöschl, V. (1964). *Bibliographie zur antiken Bildersprache.* Heidelberg

Postgate, J. P. (1917). *M. Annaei Lucani De Bello Ciuili Liber VIII.* Cambridge

Premerstein, A. von (1937). *Vom Werden und Wesen des Prinzipats.* Munich

Purser, L. C. (1897–9). 'Professor Ellis's edition of V.', *Hermathena* 10.369–96

Raaflaub, K. (1974). *Dignitatis contentio.* Munich

Reinhold, M. (1933). *Marcus Agrippa: a Biography.* Geneva–New York

Rice Holmes, *Arch.* = Rice Holmes, T. (1928). *The Architect of the Roman Empire.* Oxford

Rep. = Rice Holmes, T. (1923). *The Roman Republic.* Vols. 1–3. Oxford

Rockwood, F. E. (1893). *Velleius Paterculus. Book II, chapters xli–cxxxi. Edited with Introduction and Notes.* Boston–New York–Chicago

Rosenheyn, J. S. (1810). *Lectionum Velleianarum Specimen.* Berlin

Sattler, P. (1960). *Augustus und der Senat.* Göttingen

Sauppe, H. (1896). 'M. Vell. Pat.' in *Ausgewählte Schriften* 39–72. Berlin

Schmitthenner, *Test.* = Schmitthenner, W. (1973). *Oktavian und das Testament Cäsars. Zetemata* 4. 2nd edn. Munich

Scott, K. (1933). 'The political propaganda of 44–30 B.C.', *Mem. Amer. Acad. Rome* 11.7–49

Scriner, P. J. (1879). *Quaestiones Velleianae.* Utrecht

Seager, *Pomp.* = Seager, R. (1979). *Pompey: a Political Biography.* Oxford

Shackleton Bailey, D. R. (1956). *Propertiana.* Cambridge

Shipley, F. W. (1924). *Velleius Paterculus: Res Gestae Diui Augusti, with an English Translation.* (Loeb edn) London–Cambridge, Mass.

REFERENCES AND ABBREVIATIONS

Sigonius, C. (1732). *Fasti consulares Capitolini*. Milan

Stanger, J. (1863). *De M. Vell. Pat. fide*. Munich

Starr, R. J. (1978). *A Literary Introduction to V.P.* Unpubl. diss. Princeton
(1981). 'The scope and genre of V.'s history', *CQ* 31.162–74

Strasburger, H. (1966). *Caesars Eintritt in die Geschichte*. Repr. Darmstadt

Sumner = Sumner, G. V. (1970). 'The truth about V.P.: prolegomena',
HSCP 74.257–97

Sumner, *Orators* = Sumner, G. V. (1973). *The Orators in Cicero's Brutus*.
Toronto

Syme, *DP* = Syme, R. (1971). *Danubian Papers*. Bucharest
HO = Syme, R. (1978). *History in Ovid*. Oxford
RP = Syme, R. (1979). *Roman Papers*. Vols. 1–2. Oxford
RR = Syme, R. (1939). *The Roman Revolution*. Oxford
Sall. = Syme, R. (1964). *Sallust*. Berkeley–Los Angeles
TST = Syme, R. (1970). *Ten Studies in Tacitus*. Oxford
Tac. = Syme, R. (1958). *Tacitus*. Oxford

Syme, R. (1970). 'The conquest of north-west Spain' in *Legio VII Gemina*
83–107. León
(1978). 'Mendacity in Vell.', *AJPh* 99.45–63

Taylor, L. R. (1931). *The Divinity of the Roman Emperor*. Middletown,
Conn.

Thomas, E. (1893). *De Vell. voluminis condicione aliquot capita*. Berlin

Thomas, P. (1921). 'Observationes ad scriptores latinos', *Mnem.*
49.17–21

Ungewitter, J. (n.d. [1904]). *De V.P. et Val. Max. genere dicendi quaest.*
selectae. Diss. Donauwörth

Ursinus, F. (1595). *Fragmenta Historicorum Romanorum*. Antwerp

Verhaak, H. J. W. (1954). *V.P. en de rhetoriek van zijn tijd*. Grave

Vogt, J. (1960). *Orbis: Ausgewählte Schriften*. Freiburg im Breisgau

Watson, J. S. (1852). *Sallust, Florus and Vell. Pat. Literally Translated*.
London

Weber, W. (1936). *Princeps*. Vol. 1. Stuttgart–Berlin

Weinstock, S. (1971). *Divus Julius*. Oxford

Weippert, O. (1972). *Alexander-Imitatio und römische Politik in republikanischer
Zeit*. Augsburg

Wickert, L. (1974). 'Neue Forschungen zum römischen Principat',
ANRW 2.1.3–76

Wilhelm, E. (1866). *Quaestiones Velleianae*. Jena

Wilkes, J. J. (1969). *Dalmatia*. London

Williams, G. (1968). *Tradition and Originality in Roman Poetry*. Oxford

Winterbottom, *Sen.* = Winterbottom, M. (1974). *The Elder Seneca*. (Loeb
edn) Cambridge, Mass.–London

Wirszubski, C. (1950). *Libertas as a Political Idea at Rome*. Cambridge

REFERENCES AND ABBREVIATIONS

Wiseman, T. P. (1971). *New Men in the Roman Senate 139 B.C.–A.D. 14.* Oxford

Wistrand, E. (1958). *Horace's Ninth Epode and its Historical Background.* Göteborg

Wölfflin, E. (1933). *Ausgewählte Schriften* (ed. G. Meyer). Leipzig

Woodman, *EA* = Woodman, A. J. (1975). 'Vell. Pat.' in *Empire and Aftermath: Silver Latin II* (ed. T. A. Dorey) 1–25. London

Woodman, A. J. (1968). 'Sallustian influence on V.P.' in *Hommages à M. Renard* 1.785–99. Brussels

   (1975). 'Questions of date, genre and style in V.: some literary answers', *CQ* 25.272–306

Yavetz, Z. (1969). '*Plebs*' and '*Princeps*'. Oxford

Note on emendations. Almost every emendation recorded in this volume may be traced to its original source by using the works listed under B and C above. However, some early emendations were originally proposed in works which are now almost inaccessible and for which reference should be made to the editions of Krause and Kritz: in the main such emendations have long since been assimilated into the common stock of Velleian scholarship.

NOTE ON THE TEXT

The purposes of this brief note are, first, to recapitulate my editorial position and, secondly, to correct some errors which I committed in my discussion of the text in my previous volume.

V.'s text ultimately depends upon the lost Murbach codex (M) which Beatus Rhenanus discovered between the end of March and the month of August 1515 (see von der Gönna 231). Rhenanus arranged for (M) to be copied by an anonymous friend: this copy, known as (R), is now also lost. In 1516 another friend, Bonifacius Amerbach, made another copy of V.'s text which is known as A: in my opinion this was a copy of (R) and not, as most editors have believed, a direct copy of (M) (see *TN* 11–25 for the detailed arguments on which this opinion is based). Within a further two or three years Rhenanus began to prepare the *editio princeps*, known as P: the text was printed by Froben in Basel, was based on (R), and was completed by 15 November 1520 (the date of Rhenanus' epilogue to his readers on p. 70 of the *ed. pr.*). Six days later Rhenanus' father died at Sélestat (see von der Gönna 237): he had no doubt been ill for some time, and Rhenanus had presumably been commuting between there and Basel during his illness. During the same month one of Rhenanus' scribes, J. A. Burer, noticed a discrepancy between P and (M) which led him to collate the one with the other: this collation, known as B, is printed as an appendix to P. The relationship between these various authorities can be summed up schematically as follows:

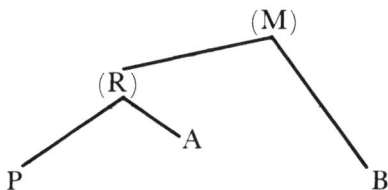

Although the latest date to appear in P is 13 December 1520, the book was not published during the following day or two, as I stated at *TN* 7; it has been shown by von der Gönna (238) that the book was still not published by 13 January of the following year, and that the earliest reference to its appearance is 11 March 1521. Two final points need to be made about P. First, in some places different copies of the *ed. pr.* exhibit different readings, a phenomenon which I have indicated by *uel* in my apparatus criticus and discussed at 67.1n. and 83.2n. Secondly, Rhenanus' personal copy of the *ed. pr.* may still be consulted at Sélestat, and it reveals that he continued to emend V.'s text in his own hand in its margins (see von der Gönna 238–40), thereby anticipating some of the emendations which other scholars were to make later on. I have naturally reattributed such emendations to Rhenanus where appropriate.

TEXT

SIGLA

P   editio princeps quam Rhenanus imprimendam curauit
     anno 1520

B   lectiones quas Burer e codice Murbacensi se testatur
     hausisse anno 1520

A   apographon quod Amerbach scripsit anno 1516

Coniecturae quas Rhenanus in marginibus editionis principis, Burer in eiusdem appendice fecit, ipsorum nominibus
in apparatu critico indicantur.

VELLEII PATERCVLI
HISTORIARVM AD
M. VINICIVM CONSVLEM

LIBER SECVNDVS

41 Secutus deinde est consulatus C. Caesaris, qui scribenti manum iniicit et quamlibet festinantem in se morari cogit. hic nobilissima Iuliorum genitus familia et (quod inter omnes antiquissimos constabat) ab Anchise ac Venere deducens genus, forma omnium ciuium excellentissimus, 5 uigore animi acerrimus, munificentia effusissimus, animo super humanam et naturam et fidem euectus, magnitudine cogitationum, celeritate bellandi, patientia periculorum Magno illi Alexandro (sed sobrio neque·iracundo) simil- **2** limus, qui denique semper et somno et cibo in uitam non in 10 uoluptatem uteretur, cum fuisset C. Mario sanguine coniunctissimus atque idem Cinnae gener (cuius filiam ut repudiaret nullo metu compelli potuit, cum M. Piso consularis Anniam, quae Cinnae uxor fuerat, in Sullae dimisisset gratiam) habuissetque fere XVIII annos eo tempore quo 15 Sulla rerum potitus est, magis ministris Sullae adiutoribusque partium quam ipso conquirentibus eum ad necem mutata ueste dissimilemque fortunae suae indutus habitum nocte urbe elapsus est. **3** Idem postea admodum iuuenis, cum a piratis captus esset, 20 ita se·per omne spatium, quo ab his retentus est, apud eos gessit ut pariter his terrori uenerationique esset neque

---

1 COS C. Caesar[is] *A*   2 quamlibet *A*: queml- *P*: 'alias ... quamlibet' *Burer*   4 antiquitatis studiosos *Halm*: quod i. omnes constat, antiquissima *Acidalius: alii alia*   6 munificentia *Gelenius*: -ae *PA*   10 et cibo et somno *A*   21 se per *B*: semper *PA*   21–2 iis *Orelli* (*bis*)   22 horroriq (*del.*) terrori *A*

umquam aut nocte aut die (cur enim quod uel maximum
est, si narrari uerbis speciosis non potest, omittatur?) aut
excalcearetur aut discingeretur, in hoc scilicet ne, si quando
aliquid ex solito uariaret, suspectus his, qui oculis tantum-
42 modo eum custodiebant, foret. longum est narrare quid et 5
quoties ausus sit; quanto opere conata eius qui obtinebat
Asiam magistratus populi Romani motu suo destituerit,
2 illud referatur, documentum tanti mox euasuri uiri. quae
nox eam diem secuta est qua publica ciuitatium pecunia
redemptus est, ita tamen ut cogeret ante obsides a piratis 10
ciuitatibus dari, contracta classe et priuatus et tumultuaria
⟨manu⟩ inuectus in eum locum in quo ipsi praedones erant,
partem classis fugauit, partem mersit, aliquot naues mul-
3 tosque mortales cepit; laetusque nocturnae expeditionis triumpho ad suos reuersus est, mandatisque custodiae quos 15
ceperat, in Bithyniam perrexit ad proconsulem Iunium
⟨Iun⟩cum (idem enim Asiam eamque obtinebat), petens ut
auctor fieret sumendi de captiuis supplicii. quod cum ille se
facturum negasset uenditurumque captiuos dixisset (quippe
sequebatur inuidia inertiam), incredibili celeritate reuectus 20
ad mare, priusquam de ea re ulli proconsulis redderetur epistula, omnes, quos ceperat, suffixit cruci.
43   Idem mox ad sacerdotium ineundum (quippe absens
pontifex factus erat in Cottae consularis locum, ⟨cum⟩
paene puer a Mario Cinnaque flamen Dialis creatus uictoria 25
Sullae, qui omnia ab iis acta fecerat irrita, amisisset id

1 aut die aut nocte *A*   re maximum *Pluygers*   4 hiis *A*   6 quotiens
A   *post* sit *interpunxit Kritz*: ante quanto *lacunam posuit Krause*   7 motu
PA: metu *Gelenius*   destituerit *Rhenanus*: -uere *PA*   9 quam p. ciuita-
tum *A*   10 est *BA, om. P*   12 ⟨manu⟩ *Halm*: et priuata et tum.
Oudendorp: et priuatim et tumultuarie *Cludius*: tumultuaria priuatus (et . . .
et *secl.*) *Rühl*   ubi (*del., suprascr.* in quo) *A*   15 custodia equos
A   16 Bythiniam *A*   17 ⟨Iun⟩cum *Nipperdey*   Asiam eamque
Lipsius: A. eam quam *PA*: eam Asiamque *Stegmann*   19 negauit (*del.*)
negasset *A*   20 inuidiam inertia *olim Haase*: inuidiam auaritia *E.*
Wilhelm   21 redderetur epistola *P*: -erentur epistula *B*: -eretur epla *A*:
-erentur epistulae *Burer*   24 ⟨cum⟩ *Lipsius*   26 iis facta (*del.*)
accepat (*del.*) acta *A*   id *Gelenius*: ad *PA*

sacerdotium) festinans in Italiam, ne conspiceretur a prae-
donibus omnia tunc obtinentibus maria et merito iam
infestis sibi, quattuor scalmorum nauem una cum duobus
amicis decemque seruis ingressus effusissimum Adriatici
2 maris traiecit sinum. quo quidem in cursu conspectis (ut 5
putabat) piratarum nauibus, cum exuisset uestem alligass-
etque pugionem ad femur alterutri se fortunae parans, mox
intellexit frustratum esse uisum suum arborumque ex
longinquo ordinem antemnarum praebuisse imaginem.
3   Reliqua eius acta in urbe – nobilissimaque Dolabellae 10
accusatio et maior ciuitatis in ea fauor quam reis praestari
solet; contentionesque ciuiles cum Q. Catulo atque aliis
eminentissimis uiris celeberrimae et ante praeturam uictus
⟨in⟩ maximi pontificatus petitione Q. Catulus, omnium
4 confessione senatus princeps, et restituta in aedilitate aduer- 15
sante quidem nobilitate monumenta C. Marii; simulque
reuocati ad ius dignitatis proscriptorum liberi; et praetura
quaesturaque mirabili uirtute atque industria obita in
Hispania (cum esset quaestor sub Vetere Antistio, auo huius
Veteris consularis atque pontificis, duorum consularium et 20
sacerdotium patris, uiri in tantum boni in quantum humana
simplicitas intellegi potest) – quo notiora sunt, minus egent
stilo.
44   Hoc igitur consule inter eum et Cn. Pompeium et M.
Crassum inita potentiae societas, quae urbi orbique ter- 25
rarum nec minus diuerso cuique tempore ipsis exitiabilis
2 fuit. hoc consilium sequendi Pompeius causam habuerat ut
tandem acta in transmarinis prouinciis, quibus (ut
praediximus) multi obtrectabant, per Caesarem confir-
marentur consulem; Caesar autem quod animaduertebat 30

2 iam ed. Bipont.: tam PA   4 effusissimam A   8 se (del.) frus.
A   10 nobilissima Gn. Dol. Haase   Dolob- PA   11 in eo
Heinsius   praestare A   12 q. Cat- A   14 ⟨in⟩ Halm   q
(suprascr. Q.) A   20 atque P: ac A   26 cuique Laurent: quoque PA,
quod post ipsis transpos. Haase: quoique Acidalius   29 praedixi A

7

se cedendo Pompeii gloriae aucturum suam et inuidia communis potentiae in illum relegata confirmaturum uires suas;
Crassus ut, quem principatum solus adsequi non poterat,
3 auctoritate Pompeii, uiribus teneret Caesaris. adfinitas
etiam inter Caesarem Pompeiumque contracta nuptiis: 5
4 quippe filiam C. Caesaris Cn. Magnus duxit uxorem. in hoc
consulatu Caesar legem tulit ut ager Campanus plebei diuideretur, suasore legis Pompeio. ita circiter XX ⟨milia⟩
ciuium eo deducta et ius ab his restitutum post annos circiter
CLII quam bello Punico ab Romanis Capua in formam 10
5 praefecturae redacta erat. Bibulus, collega Caesaris, cum
actiones eius magis uellet impedire quam posset, maiore
parte anni domi se tenuit; quo facto dum augere uult
inuidiam collegae, auxit potentiam. tum Caesari decretae in
quinquennium Galliae. 15

45 Per idem tempus P. Clodius, homo nobilis, disertus,
audax, qui ⟨ne⟩que dicendi neque faciendi ullum nisi quem
uellet nosset modum, malorum propositorum executor acerrimus, infamis etiam sororis stupro et actus incesti reus ob
initum inter religiosissima populi Romani sacra adulterium, 20
cum graues inimicitias cum M. Cicerone exerceret (quid
enim inter tam dissimiles amicum esse poterat?) et a
patribus ad plebem transisset, legem in tribunatu tulit ⟨ut⟩
qui ciuem Romanum ⟨in⟩demnatum interemisset, ei aqua
et igni interdiceretur; cuius uerbis etsi non nominabatur, 25
2 Cicero tamen solus petebatur. ita uir optime meritus de re
publica conseruatae patriae pretium calamitate⟨m⟩ exilii
tulit. non caruerunt suspicione oppressi Ciceronis Caesar et
Pompeius; hoc sibi contraxisse uidebatur Cicero quod inter
3 XX uiros diuidendo agro Campano esse noluisset. idem 30

---

1 secedendo A   3 quem BA: qui P   4 uiri uiribus BA   6
⟨Iuliam⟩ filiam Orelli   7 aut ager A   8 ⟨milia⟩ uulgo   9 ab his
PA: his Lipsius: a II uiris G. A. Koch: urbis Heinsius: ciuitatis
Puteanus   11 erat om. A   17 ⟨ne⟩que Vascosanus: quique PA   23
⟨ut⟩ Novák (1906)   24 ⟨in⟩demnatum Puteanus: damn- PA   ei Gel-
enius: et PA   25 quibus uerbis Burman   27 calamitate PA, em.
Gelenius   30 uidendo A

8

intra biennium sera Cn. Pompeii cura uerum (ut cupi⟨i⟩t) intenta, uotisque Italiae ac decretis senatus, uirtute atque actione Annii Milonis tribuni plebis dignitati patriaeque re- stitutus est. neque post Numidici exilium aut reditum quis- quam aut expulsus inuidiosius aut receptus est laetius; cuius 5 domus quam infeste a Clodio disiecta erat, tam speciose a senatu restituta est.

4   Idem P. Clodius in senatu sub honorificentissimo minis- terii titulo M. Catonem a re publica relegauit: quippe legem tulit ut is quaestor cum iure praetorio, adiecto etiam quaes- 10 tore, mitteretur in insulam Cyprum ad spoliandum regno Ptolemaeum, omnibus morum uitiis eam contumeliam 5 meritum. sed ille sub aduentum Catonis uitae suae uim intulit: unde pecuniam longe sperata maiorem Cato Romam rettulit. cuius integritatem laudari nefas est, inso- 15 lentia paene argui potest, quod una cum consulibus ac senatu effusa ciuitate obuiam cum per Tiberim subiret, nauibus non ante is egressus est quam ad eum locum per- uenit ubi erat exponenda pecunia.

46   Cum deinde immanes res uix multis uoluminibus expli- 20 candas C. Caesar in Gallia ageret nec contentus plurimis ac felicissimis uictoriis innumerabilibusque caesis et captis hostium milibus etiam in Britanniam traiecisset exercitum, alterum paene imperio nostro (ac suo) quaerens orbem, †uictus pars† consulum, Cn. Pompeius et M. Crassus, 25 alterum iniere consulatum, qui neque petitus honeste ab his 2 neque probabiliter gestus est. Caesari lege, quam Pompeius

---

1 ut cupi⟨i⟩t *scripsi*: et cupit *PA*: ut cupit *Seebode*: ut coepit *Gelenius*   2 intenta *Wopkens*: interita *PA*   sanatus *A*   3 dignitate *A*   8 in senatu *PA*, *secl. Cuiacius*: in tribunatu *Heinsius*   10 quaestor⟨ius⟩ *Lipsius*   10–11 quaestore mitteretur *Gelenius*: -tor em- *PA*   12 Ptolomaeum *A*   15 ⟨haud⟩ laudari *Ruhnken*   17 per *secl. Burman*   18 iis *Aldus*   21 gereret *Stanger*   22 et *BA*: ac *P*   24 querens *A*   25 uictus pars *PA*, *obelis notaui*: inuictum par *Rhenanus*: uetus par *Ursinus, fort. recte*: inuidum p. *Ruperti*: inuisum p. *Acidalius*: alii alia   26 hiis *A*: iis *Orelli*   27 lege *Gelenius*: -ē *P*: -es *A*   quas *A*

ad populum tulit, prorogatae in idem spatium temporis
prouinciae, Crasso bellum Parthicum in animo molienti
Syria decreta; qui, uir cetera sanctissimus immunisque uoluptatibus, neque in pecunia neque in gloria concupiscenda
3 aut modum norat aut capiebat terminum. hunc pro- 5
ficiscentem in Syriam diris cum ominibus tribuni plebis
frustra retinere conati; quorum execrationes si in ipsum tantummodo ualuissent, utile imperatoris damnum saluo exer-
4 citu fuisset rei publicae. transgressum Euphraten Crassum
petentemque Seleuciam circumfusis immanibus copiis 10
equitum rex Orodes una cum parte maiore Romani exercitus interemit. reliquias legionum C. Cassius, atrocissimi
5 mox auctor facinoris, tum quaestor, conseruauit, Syriamque
adeo in populi Romani potestate retinuit ut transgressos in
eam Parthos felici rerum euentu fugaret ac funderet. 15
47 Per haec insequentiaque et quae praediximus tempora
amplius CCCC milia hostium a C. Caesare caesa sunt, plura
capta; pugnatum saepe derecta acie, saepe in agminibus,
saepe eruptionibus; bis penetrata Britannia; ⟨e⟩ nouem
denique aestatibus uix ulla non iustissimus triumphus emer- 20
itus, circa Alesiam uero tantae res gestae quantas audere uix
2 hominis, perficere paene nullius nisi dei fuerit. quinto ferme
anno Caesar morabatur in Galliis cum medium iam ex
inuidia po⟨te⟩ntiae ta⟨m⟩ male cohaerentis inter Cn. Pompeium et C. Caesarem concordiae pignus, Iulia, uxor 25
Magni, decessit; atque omnia inter destinatos tanto discrimini duces dirimente fortuna, filius quoque paruus
Pompeii, Iulia natus, intra breue spatium obiit.

---

2 prouinciae *om. A*   in *ante* animo *secl. Cludius*: iam *Heinsius*   5 ter-
minum *P*: terim *A*   6 cum *secl. Krause*   omnibus *P*   8 uile
Lipsius   10 circumfusis *Gelenius*: -os *PA*: -um *Vossius*: -us
Vascosanus   17 CCCC *PA*: DCCC *Lipsius*: CIƆC *Vossius*   18 directa
P: de recta *A*   in *secl. Lipsius*   19 ⟨e⟩ *Krause*   20 aestatum
Wopkens   21 gestae *BA*, *om. P*   22 quinto *Krause*: septimo *PA*:
quarto *Laurent*   23 Gallis *A*   24 po⟨te⟩ntiae *Lipsius*: ta⟨m⟩
Woodman: male *Rhenanus*: Ponti ac (et *A*) Camiliae *PA*: po⟨te⟩ntiae et
aemulatione *Laurent*: alii alia

3   Tum in gladios caedesque ciuium furente ambitu, cuius
neque finis reperiebatur nec modus, tertius consulatus soli
Cn. Pompeio etiam aduersantium antea dignitati eius
iudicio delatus est, cuius ille honoris gloria ueluti reconcil-
iatis sibi optimatibus maxime a C. Caesare alienatus est; sed 5
eius consulatus omnem uim in coercitionem ambitus exer-
4 cuit. quo tempore P. Clodius a Milone candidato consulatus
exemplo inutili[ter], facto salutari rei publicae circa
Bouillas contracta ex occursu rixa iugulatus est. Milonem
reum non magis inuidia facti quam Pompeii damnauit uol- 10
5 untas; quem quidem M. Cato palam lata absoluit sententia,
qui si maturius tulisset, non defuissent qui sequerentur
exemplum probarentque eum ciuem occisum quo nemo per-
niciosior rei publicae neque bonis inimicior uixerat.

48   Intra breue deinde spatium belli ciuilis exarserunt initia, 15
cum iustissimus quisque et a Caesare et a Pompeio uellet
dimitti exercitus. quippe Pompeius in secundo consulatu
Hispanias sibi decerni uoluerat easque per triennium absens
ipse ac praesidens urbi per Afranium et Petreium, consularem ac praetorium, legatos suos, administrabat, et iis 20
qui a Caesare dimittendos exercitus contendebant adsenta-
2 batur, iis qui ab ipso quoque aduersabatur. qui si ante biennium quam ad arma itum est, perfectis muneribus theatri et
aliorum operum quae ei circumdedit, grauissima temptatus
ualetudine decessisset in Campania (quo quidem tempore 25
uniuersa Italia uota pro salute eius primi omnium ciuium
suscepit), defuisset fortunae destruendi eius locus et, quam
apud superos habuerat magnitudinem, inlibatam detulisset
ad inferos.

---

4 uelut A   6 coercitionem B: coertionem PA   8 inutili[ter] Gelenius:
inutili sed Ursinus   12 quam si Gelenius   15 bellis P   19 Afran-
nium P: Africanium B: Africanum A   21–22 adsentabatur om.
A   22 is A   ab ipso quoque BA: dimittendos ab ipsoque P   24
tentatus P   26 primi Vascosanus: -o PA

3 Bello autem ciuili et tot, quae deinde per continuos XX
annos consecuta sunt, malis non alius maiorem fla-
grantioremque quam C. Curio tribunus plebis subiecit
facem, uir nobilis, eloquens, audax, suae alienaeque et fortunae et pudicitiae prodigus, homo ingeniosissime nequam 5
4 et facundus malo publico, cuius †animo uoluptatibus uel
libidinibus neque opes ullae neque cupiditates† sufficere
possent. hic primo pro Pompeii partibus (id est, ut tunc
habebatur, pro re publica), mox simulatione contra Pompeium et Caesarem sed animo pro Caesare stetit. (id gratis 10
an accepto centies HS fecerit, ut accepimus, in medio relin-
5 quemus.) ad ultimum saluberrimas [et] coalescentis condiciones pacis, quas et Caesar iustissimo animo postulabat et
Pompeius aequo recipiebat, discussit ac rupit, unice cauente
Cicerone concordiae publicae. 15

Harum praeteritarumque rerum ordo, cum iustis aliorum
uoluminibus promatur, tum (uti spero) nostris explicabitur;
6 nunc proposito operi sua forma reddatur si prius gratulatus
ero Q. Catulo, duobus Lucullis Metelloque et Hortensio,
qui, cum sine inuidia in re publica floruissent eminuiss- 20
entque sine periculo quieta aut certe non praecipitata, fatali
ante initium bellorum ciuilium morte functi sunt.

49 Lentulo et Marcello consulibus post urbem conditam
annis DCCIII ante annos LXXVIII quam tu, M. Vinici,
consulatum inires, bellum ciuile exarsit. alterius ducis causa 25
2 melior uidebatur, alterius erat firmior: hic omnia speciosa,

---

6 cuius *Gelenius*: huius *PA*   6–7 animo . . . cupiditates *PA*, *obelis notaui*:
animo *secl. Krause*: animi *Lipsius*: omnino *Acidalius*: a. ⟨immerso⟩ *Morgen-*
stern: fort. a. ⟨dedito⟩: uoluptatibus uel libidinibus *secl. Gruter*: c. omnino
cupiditatibus uel . . . neque uoluptates suff. p. *Wopkens*: *alii alia*   10
restitit *PA*, *corr. Gelenius*   11 S-H *P*: sextertio *A*   12 et *secl.*
Gelenius   16 praeteritarumque *BA*: praeteritumque *P*   iustis *Gel-*
enius: iustius *PA*   21 quieta ⟨ea⟩ *Lipsius*   praecipitata ⟨ciuitate⟩
Ruhnken   fatali *secl. Arnoldt*   24 DCCIII *Gelenius*: ACCIII *P*: A. (a.
A) cc. III *BA*   ante annos *Halm*: & annos *A*: 'leg. . . . & annos' *Burer*:
& *P*: et anno *Gelenius*: et ante *Lipsius*: et ⟨ante⟩ annos *Orelli*

illic ualentia; Pompeium senatus auctoritas, Caesarem
militum armauit fiducia. consules senatusque causae non
3 Pompeio summam imperii detulerunt. nihil relictum a
Caesare quod seruandae pacis causa temptari posset, nihil
receptum a Pompeianis, cum alter consul iusto esset ferocior, 5
Lentulus uero salua re publica saluus esse non posset, M.
autem Cato moriendum antequam ullam condicionem ciuis
accipiendam rei publicae contenderet. uir antiquus et grauis
Pompeii partes laudaret magis, prudens sequeretur Caesaris,
et illa gloriosa, haec terribiliora duceret.   10
4   Ut deinde spretis omnibus quae Caesar postulauerat, tantummodo contentus cum una legione titulum retinere
prouinciae †priuatusque in urbem uenire et se in petitione
consulatus suffragiis populi Romani committere decreueret†
ratus bellandum Caesar cum exercitu Rubiconem transiit. 15
Cn. Pompeius consulesque et maior pars senatus relicta urbe
50 ac deinde Italia transmisere Dyrrachium. at Caesar Domitio
legionibusque Corfinii, quae una cum eo fuerant, potitus,
duce aliisque, qui uoluerant abire ad Pompeium, sine dilatione dimissis, persecutus Brundusium ita ut appareret malle 20
integris rebus et condicionibus finire bellum quam
2 opprimere fugientes, cum transgressos reperisset consules, in
urbem reuertit redditaque ratione consiliorum suorum in
senatu et in contione ac miserrimae necessitudinis, cum
alienis armis ad arma compulsus esset, Hispanias petere de- 25
3 creuit. festinationem itineris eius aliquamdiu morata

---

5 alter consul *Gelenius*: altero COS. *PA*   7 ciuis *PA*: cuiusuis
Ruhnken   10 gloriosiora *Cuper*   haec *P*: illa *A*   12 legione ne
A   13-14 priuatusque ... decreuere *PA, obelis notaui*: 'ex. uet. sic
habet, ut legend. existimem, committere decreuerat' *Burer*: tantummodo
(11) ... decreuerat *parenthesin fecit Aldus, arbitratus* transiit (15) *ex* ut (11)
pendere: priuatus[que] ... ueniret ... committeret decreuere *Gelenius*:
priuatus ut ... -iret ... -eret decreuere *Mommsen*: *fort.* priuatus ut ...
ueniret ... committeret decreuerat ⟨senatus⟩: *alii alia*   18 quae *om.*
A   19 uoluerant *Gelenius*: uenerant *PA*   20 ita *PA*: iter
Ruhnken   21 et *secl. Nagel*   23 reuertitur *A*   24 cum *PA*: quod
Castiglioni

13

Massilia est, fide melior quam consilio prudentior, intempestiue principalium armorum arbitria captans, quibus hi se
debent interponere qui non parentem coercere possunt.
4 exercitus deinde, qui sub Afranio consulari ac Petreio praetorio fuerat, ipsius aduentus uigore ac fulgore occupatus se 5
Caesari tradidit; uterque legatorum et quisquis cuiusque
ordinis sequi eos uoluerat remissi ad Pompeium.

51 Proximo anno dum Dyrrachium ac uicina ei urbi regio
castris Pompeii retinetur, qui accitis ex omnibus transmarinis prouinciis legionibus, equitum ac peditum auxiliis, 10
regumque ⟨et⟩ tetrarcharum simulque dynastarum copiis
immanem exercitum confecerat et mare praesidiis classium
(ut rebatur) saepserat quominus Caesar legiones posset
2 transmittere, sua et celeritate et fortuna C. Caesar usus nihil
in mora habuit quominus et cum uellet ipse exercitusque 15
classibus perueniret et primo paene castris Pompeii sua
iungeret, mox etiam obsidione munimentisque eum com-
plecteretur. sed inopia obsidentibus quam obsessis erat
3 grauior. tum Balbus Cornelius excedente humanam fidem
temeritate ingressus castra hostium saepiusque cum Lentulo 20
conlocutus consulari dubitante quanti se uenderet, illis
incrementis fecit uiam quibus non Hispaniensis natus sed
Hispanus in triumphum et pontificatum adsurgeret
fieretque ex priuato consularis. uariatum deinde proeliis, sed

---

2 hisce *A*   4 Africanio (-ic- *del.*) *B*: Africano *PA*   Praeteio *A*   5
aduentus *Gelenius*: -tu *PA*   7 remissi *Gelenius*: remisit *PA*   8 dum
Ellis: cum *PA*   uicina *P*: -nia *BA*   9 Pompei *A*: 'Pompei, o literae
puncto deletili superscripto, sic ò' *Burer*: Pompeio *P*   retinetur *PBA*:
obtineretur *Heinsius*   11 ⟨et⟩ *Gelenius*   tetarcharum *A*   simulque
PB: simul *A*   12 praesidii dis *A*   13 ut rebatur *A* (*suprascr.*) *et Rhenanus*: uirebatur *PA*   15 et quo uellet *Acidalius*: eo cum uellet *Vossius*: et
cum ⟨uellet et quo⟩ uellet *Ruhnken*   18 obsessis erat *P*: obsesserat
A   21 consulari *Goodyear*: COS. *P*: consule *A*   22 Hispaniensis
Lipsius: Hispaniae Asiae *PA*: ⟨in⟩ Hispania a ciue *Laurent*: *alii alia*   24
consul *Ruhnken*   sed *PA*: est *Goodyear*

un⟨um e⟩o longe magis Pompeianis prosperum quo grauiter impulsi sunt Caesaris milites.

52   Tum Caesar cum exercitu fatalem uictoriae suae Thessa-
2 liam petiit. Pompeius, longe diuersa aliis suadentibus
(quorum plerique hortabantur ut in Italiam transmitteret – 5
neque, hercules, quicquam partibus illis salubrius fuit! – alii
ut bellum traheret, quod dignatione partium in dies ipsis
magis prosperum fieret), usus impetu suo hostem secutus est.
3 aciem Pharsalicam et illum cruentissimum Romano nomini
diem tantumque utriusque exercitus profusum sanguinis et 10
conlisa inter se duo rei publicae capita effossumque alterum
Romani imperii lumen, tot talesque Pompeianarum
partium caesos uiros non recipit enarranda hic scripturae
4 modus. illud notandum est: ut primum C. Caesar inclinatam uidit Pompeianorum aciem, neque prius neque anti- 15
quius quicquam habuit quam †in omnes partes ut militari et
5 uerbo et consuetudine utar dimitteret†. pro dii immortales,
quod huius uoluntatis erga Brutum suae posteā uir tam mitis
6 pretium tulit! nihil illa uictoria mirabilius, magnificentius,
clarius fuit, quando neminem nisi acie consumptum ciuem 20
patria desiderauit; sed munus misericordiae corrupit pertin-

---

1 un⟨um e⟩o ... prosperum *Woodman*: uno ... -o *PA*: unum ... prosperum *olim Kritz*   quo *secl. Fröhlich*   6 illius *Burman*   fuisset
Cludius   7 dignatione *Gelenius*: -i *PBA*: dignatione ... in dies
⟨crescente⟩ *Cludius*   partium *PA*: partem *B*   indies *PA*: indie *B*
ipsis *P*: ipsiis *B*: ipsis (*del.*) ipsiis *A*   8 foret *Cludius*   9 Romano
P: -i *BA*   10 profusi *Pluygers*   11 conlisa *Gelenius*: consilio *PA*   12
⟨et⟩ tot *Halm*   13 enarrandae *A*   16–17 in omnes ... et (*om. A*)
uerbo et consuetudine ... dimitteret *PA*, *obelis notaui*: quam ut (*iam
Gelenius*) omnes partes (ut m. [et] uerbo ex cons. utar) d. *Lipsius*: quam
incolumes p. ... d. *Heinsius*: quam ⟨ut⟩ in o. p. ⟨praecones clamantes
'parce ciuibus'⟩ ... d. *Ruhnken*: quam in o. p. ... dimittere ⟨praecones
'parce ciuibus' edicentes⟩ *Haase*: 'parce' *tantum post* partes *suppl. Scheffer,
Bothe*: alii alia   18 suae *om. A*: suum *Cludius*   post eam *PA*, *corr.
Rhenanus*   19–20 illa ... quando *PA*: ⟨in⟩ illa ... quam quod
Haase   21 corrupit *Rhenanus*: -umpit *PA*

acia, cum libentius uitam uictor[iam] daret quam uicti acciperent.

53 Pompeius profugiens cum duobus Lentulis consularibus
Sextoque filio et Fauonio praetorio, quos comites ei fortuna
adgregauerat, aliis ut Parthos, aliis ut Africam peteret, in 5
qua fidelissimum partium suarum haberet regem Iubam,
suadentibus, Aegyptum petere proposuit memor beneficiorum quae in patrem eius Ptolemaei, qui tum puero
2 quam iuueni propior regnabat Alexandriae, contulerat. sed
quis in aduersis beneficiorum seruat memoriam? aut quis 10
ullam calamitosis deberi putat gratiam? aut quando fortuna
non mutat fidem? missi itaque ab rege qui uenientem Cn.
Pompeium (is iam a Mytilenis Corneliam uxorem receptam
in nauem fugae comitem habere coeperat) consilio Theodoti
et Achillae exciperent hortarenturque ut ex oneraria in eam 15
nauem, quae obuiam processerat, transcenderet; quod cum
fecisset, princeps Romani nominis imperio arbitrioque
Aegyptii mancipii C. Caesare P. Seruilio consulibus iugulatus est.

3 Hic post tres consulatus et totidem triumphos domi- 20
tumque terrarum orbem sanctissimi ac praestantissimi uiri
in id euecti super quod ascendi non potest, duodesexagesi-
mum annum agentis, pridie natalem ipsius, uitae fuit exitus,
in tantum in illo uiro a se discordante fortuna ut, cui modo
4 ad uictoriam terra defuerat, deesset ad sepulturam. (quid 25
aliud quam nimium occupatos dixerim quos in aetate et
tanti et paene nostri saeculi uiri fefellit quinquennium, cum
a C. Atilio et Q. Seruilio consulibus tam facilis esset
annorum digestio? quod adieci non ut arguerem sed ne
arguerer.) 30

---

1 uictor daret *Gelenius*: uictoriam dare (darent *prius del. A*) *PA*: uictor iam
daret *Burer*: uictores darent *Rhenanus*   6 qua *Gelenius*: quo *PA*   8
Ptolomaei *PA*   9 prior (*suprascr.* pior) *A*   11 ullam (*del.*) in *A*   15
Achillae *P*: -ili *B*: Achi *A*   16 obuiam *om. A*   18 Publio *PA*   21
ac *P*: atque *A*   uiri *om. A*   24 in tantum *PA*: 'lege, intātum'
Burer   26 aetate *Rhenanus*: -em *PA*   28 et Qu. *P*: Quinto
A   facilis *Gelenius*: felix *PA*

16

54 Non fuit maior in Caesarem, quam in Pompeium fuerat, regis eorumque, quorum is auctoritate regebatur, fides. quippe cum uenientem eum temptassent insidiis ac deinde bello lacessere auderent, utrique summo imperatorum, alteri ⟨mortuo, alteri⟩ superstiti, meritas poenas luere sup- 5 pliciis.

2 Nusquam erat Pompeius corpore, adhuc ubique uiuebat nomine. quippe ingens partium eius fauor bellum excitauerat Africum, quod ciebat rex Iuba et Scipio (uir consularis, ante biennium quam exstingueretur Pompeius, 10 **3** lectus ab eo socer), eorumque copias auxerat M. Cato, ingenti cum difficultate itinerum locorumque inopia perductis ad eos legionibus; qui uir, cum summum ei a militibus **55** deferretur imperium, honoratiori parere maluit. admonet promissae breuitatis fides quanto omnia transcursu dicenda 15 sint. sequens fortunam suam Caesar peruectus in Africam, quam occiso Curione, Iulianarum duce partium, Pompeiani obtinebant exercitus. ibi primo uaria fortuna, mox pugnauit **2** sua, inclinataeque hostium copiae; nec dissimilis ibi aduersus uictos quam in priores clementia Caesaris fuit. 20

Victorem Africani belli C. Caesarem grauius excepit Hispaniense (nam uictus ab eo Pharnaces uix quicquam gloriae eius adstruxit), quod Cn. Pompeius, Magni filius, adulescens impetus ad bella maximi, ingens ac terribile conflauerat, undique ad eum adhuc paterni nominis magnitu- 25 dinem sequentium ex toto orbe terrarum auxiliis **3** confluentibus. sua Caesarem in Hispaniam comitata fortuna est, sed nullum umquam atrocius periculosiusque ab eo

---

1 N.f. non maior *BA*   4 summo⟨rum⟩ *Mommsen*: summo imperatori *Cludius*   5 ⟨alteri mortuo⟩ a. superstiti *Lipsius, cui simile scripsi*: ⟨sed⟩ alteri superstiti *Castiglioni*   7 uiuebat *Lipsius*: Iubae *P, secl. Gelenius*: Iubae (*suprascr.* uiuo) *A*   10 triennium *Lipsius*   11 socer *BA*: sacer *P*   13 a militibus *BA*: ambitus *P*   14 parere *Burer*: parare *P*: parari *A*   15 quando *A*   16 sunt *A*   in peru. in Africam et *A*   18-19 fortunam expugnauit uia *PA, corr. Acidalius, Lipsius*   20 quam *PA*: quae *Krause*   21 C. *om. A*

initum proelium, adeo ut plus quam dubio Marte descen-
deret equo consistensque ante recedentem suorum aciem,
increpita prius fortuna quod se in eum seruasset exitum,
denuntiaret militibus uestigio se non recessurum: proinde
uiderent quem et quo loco imperatorem deserturi forent. 5
4 uerecundia magis quam uirtute acies restituta, et a duce
quam a milite fortius. Cn. Pompeius grauis uulnere inuentus
inter solitudines auias interemptus est; Labienum
Varumque acies abstulit.

56 Caesar omnium uictor regressus in urbem, quod 10
humanam excedat fidem, omnibus, qui contra se arma
tulerant, ignouit; magnificentissimisque gladiatorii muneris,
naumachiae, et equitum peditumque simul elephantorum
certaminis spectaculis, epulique per multos dies dati cele-
2 bratione repleuit eam. quinque egit triumphos: Gallici 15
apparatus ex citro, Pontici ex acantho, Alexandrini testu-
dine, Africi ebore, Hispaniensis argento rasili constitit.
pecunia ex manubiis lata paulo amplius sexies milies HS.
3 Neque illi tanto uiro et tam clementer omnibus uictoriis
suis uso plus quinque mensium principalis quies contigit. 20
quippe cum mense Octobri in urbem reuertisset, idibus
Martiis, coniurationis auctoribus Bruto et Cassio (quorum
alterum promittendo consulatum non obligauerat, contra
differendo Cassium offenderat), adiectis etiam consiliariis
caedis familiarissimis omnium et fortuna partium eius in 25
summum euectis fastigium, D. Bruto et C. Trebonio aliisque
4 clari nominis uiris, interemptus est. cui magnam inuidiam
conciliarat M. Antonius, omnibus audendis paratissimus,
consulatus collega, imponendo capiti eius Lupercalibus

---

6 restitutae C.A. duce *B, corr. Orelli (iam* restituta ac a d. *Heinsius*: restitutae et a d. *Ruhnken*): -ae sunt a duce *PA*   7 graui *A^{mg}*   12 magnificentissimisque *A*: 'lege, magnificentissimisque' *Burer*: -imis *P*   17 Afri
A   18 sexiens miliens sextertium *A (ut uid.)*: sexagies m. HS *Hotoman*:
uicies m. HS *Laurent*   19 tanto uiro *om. A*   19–20 uictoribus suis
B, corr. Gelenius, om. PA   22 coniurationibus *A*   26 euectis *Gelenius*: reu- *PA*   Tribonio *PA*   28 paratissimos, *suprascr.* consulatos *A*

sedentis pro rostris insigne regium, quod ab eo ita repulsum
erat ut non offensus uideretur.

57   Laudandum experientia consilium est Pansae atque
Hirtii, qui semper praedixerant Caesari ut principatum
armis quaesitum armis teneret; ille dictitans mori se quam 5
timere malle dum clementiam, quam praestiterat, exspectat,
incautus ab ingratis occupatus est, cum quidem plurima ei
praesagia atque indicia dii immortales futuri obtulissent
2 periculi. nam et haruspices praemonuerant ut diligentissime
iduum Martiarum caueret diem, et uxor Calpurnia territa 10
nocturno uisu, ut ea die domi subsisteret, orabat, et libelli
coniurationem nuntiantes dati neque protinus ab eo lecti
3 erant. sed profecto ineluctabilis fatorum uis, cuiuscum⟨que⟩
fortunam mutare constituit, consilia corrumpit.

58   Quo anno id patrauere facinus, Brutus et C. Cassius prae- 15
2 tores erant, D. Brutus consul designatus. hi una cum coniurationis globo, stipati gladiatorum D. Bruti manu,
Capitolium occupauere. tum consul Antonius – quem cum
simul interimendum censuisset Cassius testamentumque
Caesaris abolendum, Brutus repugnauerat dictitans nihil 20
amplius ciuibus praeter tyranni (ita enim appellari Caesarem facto eius expediebat) petendum esse sanguinem –
3 conuocato senatu, cum iam Dolabella (quem substiturus
sibi Caesar designauerat consulem) fasces atque insignia
corripuisset consulis, uelut pacis auctor liberos suos obsides 25
in Capitolium misit fidemque descendendi tuto interfectoribus Caesaris dedit; et illud decreti Atheniensium celeberrimi exemplum, relatum a Cicerone, obliuionis
praeteritarum rerum decreto patrum comprobatum est.

1–2 ita … offensus *Rhenanus*: id … offensum *PA*   6 timere *Oudendorp*:
timere (*corr. in* timeri) *A*: timeri *P*   7 plurima ei *Orelli*: plurima *P et* (*sed
corr. in* plurimi) *A*: plurimi *B*   12 neque protinus ab eo *A*: ab eo n. p. *P*:
ab ⟨obu⟩io n. p. *Burman*: *alii alia*   13 cuiuscum⟨que⟩ *Gelenius*: cuius
cum (quom *P*) *PBA*   14 uoluit (*del.*) constituit *A*   18 tum *Haase*:
cum *PA*   20 ⟨M.⟩ Brutus *Ruhnken*   23 Dolobella *P*   quam substiturus *A*   24–5 consulem … consulis *A*: COS. … COS. *P*

59 Caesaris deinde testamentum apertum est, quo C.
Octauium, nepotem sororis suae Iuliae, adoptabat; de cuius
origine, etiamsi †praeuenit et†, pauca dicenda sunt.

2 Fuit C. Octauius ⟨pater⟩ ut non patricia ita admodum
speciosa equestri genitus familia, grauis, sanctus, innocens, 5
diues. hic praetor inter nobilissimos uiros creatus primo loco,
cum ei dignatio Iulia genitam Atiam conciliasset uxorem, ex
eo honore sortitus Macedoniam appellatusque in ea imperator, decedens ad petitionem consulatus obiit praetextato
3 relicto filio. quem C. Caesar, maior eius auunculus, educa- 10
tum apud Philippum uitricum dilexit ut suum, natumque
annos XVIII Hispaniensis militiae adsecutum se postea
comitem habuit, numquam aut alio usum hospitio quam
suo aut alio uectum uehiculo, pontificatusque sacerdotio
4 puerum honorauit; et patratis bellis ciuilibus ad erudien- 15
dam liberalibus disciplinis singularis indolem iuuenis Apolloniam eum in studia miserat, mox belli Getici ac deinde
Parthici habiturus commilitonem.

5 Cui ut est nuntiatum de caede auunculi, cum protinus ex
uicinis legionibus centuriones suam suorumque militum 20
operam ei pollicerentur neque eam spernendam Saluidienus
et Agrippa dicerent, ille festinans peruenire in urbem
omnem ordinem ac rationem et necis et testamenti Brundu-
6 sii comperit. cui aduentanti Romam immanis amicorum
occurrit frequentia, et cum intraret urbem, solis orbis super 25

---

3 praeuenit et *PA, obelis notaui*: per se nitet *Burman*: praenitet *Heinsius*:
praeminet *Cornelissen (1887)*: properanti hic *Acidalius*   4 ⟨pater⟩
Cludius   5 spetiose *A*   6 praeter *A*   7 Iulia g. Acciam *P*: iuliā Ati
(*del.*) g. Atiam *A*   8 ea *Gelenius*: eam *PA*   12 XVII *Oudendorp*   15
patratis *Aldus*: paratis *PA*: peractis *Gelenius*   erudiendam *A et coni.*
Ruhnken: -um *P*   16 indolis iuuenem *Vascosanus*   17 Gethici *P*   20
suam *Gelenius*: suas *PA*   21 pollicerentur *P*: -centur *BA*   23 ordinem
ac rationem *Munker*: ordinationem *PA*: ordinem *Gelenius*: ordine rationem
Heinsius   25 et cum intraret urbem *PA^{mg}*: et cum intraret, ⟨circa⟩
orbem s.o. *Haase*

caput eius curuatus aequaliter circumdatusque ⟨uers⟩icolor
arcus, uelut coronam tanti mox uiri capiti imponens, conspectus est.

60 Non placebat Atiae matri Philippoque uitrico adiri
nomen inuidiosae fortunae Caesaris, sed adserebant salutar- 5
ia rei publicae terrarumque orbis fata conditorem conserua-
2 toremque Romani nominis. spreuit itaque caelestis animus
humana consilia et cum periculo potius summa quam tuto
humilia proposuit sequi, maluitque auunculo et Caesari de
se quam uitrico credere, dictitans nefas esse,. quo nomine 10
Caesari dignus esset uisus, semet ipsum uideri indignum.
3 Hunc protinus Antonius consul superbe excepit (neque is
erat contemptus sed metus) uixque admisso in Pompeianos
hortos loquendi secum tempus dedit, mox etiam uelut insidiis eius petitus sceleste insimulare coepit, in quo turpiter 15
4 deprehensa eius uanitas est. aperte deinde Antonii ac Dolabellae consulum ad nefandam dominationem erupit furor.
HS septies milies, depositum a C. Caesare ad aedem Opis,
occupatum ab Antonio; actorum eiusdem insertis falsis
⟨immunitatibus⟩ ciuitatibusque corrupti commentarii 20
atque omnia pretio temperata, uendente rem publicam
5 consule. idem prouinciam D. Bruto designato consuli decretam Galliam occupare statuit, Dolabella transmarinas decreuit sibi; interque naturaliter dissimillimos ac diuersa
uolentes crescebat odium, eoque C. Caesar iuuenis coti- 25
dianis Antonii petebatur insidiis.

1 circumdatusque ⟨uers⟩icolor arcus *Woodman*: rotundatusque in colorem
arcus *PA*: in *secl. Orelli*: r. in morem a. *Bothe*: r. in circulum a. *Halm*: r.
cum colore a. *Laurent*: r. et colore uarius *Cornelissen* (*1887*): curuatum . . .
rotundatumque ⟨uers⟩icolorem arcum *Hottinger*: radiatusque in colorem
arcus *E. Wilhelm: alii alia*   4 Acciae *P*   6 orbi *Burman*   10 credere
Gelenius: ced- *PA*   11 sibimet *Ursinus*   12 excepit *Cludius*: excipit
PA   18 S-H septies *P*: sestertium septiens *A*   20 ⟨immunitatibus⟩
Perizonius   ciuitatibusque *PA*: uitiatique *Ruhnken*: uitiatisque
Cludius   corrupti commentarii *Ruhnken*: -is -is *PA*   23 occuparet *A*

61   Torpebat oppressa dominatione Antonii ciuitas. indignatio et dolor omnibus, uis ad resistendum nulli aderat cum C.
Caesar XVIIII annum egressus, mira ausus ac summa consecutus priuato consilio maiorem senatu pro re publica
2 animum habuit primumque a Calatia, mox a Casilino 5
ueteranos exciuit paternos; quorum exemplum secuti alii
breui in formam iusti coiere exercitus. mox, cum Antonius
occurrisset exercitui quem ex transmarinis prouinciis Brundusium uenire iusserat, legio Martia et quarta, cognita et
senatus uoluntate et tanti iuuenis indole, sublatis signis ad 10
3 Caesarem se contulerunt. eum senatus honoratum equestri
statua, quae hodieque in rostris posita aetatem eius scriptura
indicat (qui honor non alii per CCC annos quam L. Sullae
et Cn. Pompeio et C. Caesari contigerat), pro praetore una
cum consulibus designatis Hirtio et Pansa bellum cum 15
4 Antonio gerere iussit; ⟨id⟩ ab eo annum agente uicesimum
fortissime circa Mutinam administratum est, et D. Brutus
obsidione liberatus. Antonius turpi ac nuda fuga coactus
deserere Italiam; consulum autem alter in acie, alter post
paucos dies ex uulnere mortem obiit. 20

62   Omnia, antequam fugaretur Antonius, honorifice a
senatu in Caesarem exercitumque eius decreta sunt maxime
auctore Cicerone; sed ut recessit metus, erupit uoluntas pro-
2 tinusque Pompeianis partibus rediit animus. Bruto Cassioque prouinciae, quas iam ipsi sine ullo senatus consulto 25
occupauerant, decretae; laudati quicumque his se exercitus
tradidissent; omnia transmarina imperia eorum commissa
3 arbitrio: quippe M. Brutus et C. Cassius, nunc metuentes
arma Antonii, nunc ad augendam eius inuidiam simulantes
se metuere, testati edictis libenter se uel in perpetuo exilio 30
uicturos dum res publica constaret concordia, nec ullam

---

3 XVIIII ... egressus *Chishull*: XVIII ... ing- *PA*: XVIII ... eg- *Heinsius*: XVIII ... ing- *Gelenius*   5 Calatia *Gelenius*: G- *PA*   7 breui
BA: in b. *P*   forma ... coire *BA*   9 Martio *A*   10 senatum
A   12 in (*del.*) striptura *A*   14 Cn. P: C. *A*   pro praetore *Sigonius*:
pro P.R. *PA*   16 ⟨id⟩ *Gelenius*   17 est et *P*: esset *A*   26 his se *P*: se
secl. Gelenius: se hiis se *A*   28 arbitrio *P*: imperio *A*   31 rei publicae
Gelenius: res p. constaret ⟨et⟩ c. *Haase*

22

belli ciuilis praebituros materiam, plurimum sibi honoris
esse in conscientia facti sui, profecti urbe atque Italia intento
ac pari animo sine auctoritate publica prouincias exercitusque occupauerant et, ubicumque ipsi essent, praetexentes
esse rem publicam, pecunias etiam, quae ex transmarinis 5
prouinciis Romam ab quaestoribus deportabantur, a uolen-
4 tibus acceperant. quae omnia senatus decretis comprensa et
comprobata sunt, et D. Bruto, quod alieno beneficio uixerat,
decretus triumphus; Pansae atque Hirtii corpora publica
5 sepultura honorata; Caesaris adeo nulla habita mentio ut 10
legati, qui ad exercitum eius missi erant, iuberentur
summoto eo milites adloqui. non fuit tam ingratus exercitus
quam fuerat senatus: nam cum eam iniuriam dissimulando
Caesar ferret, negauere milites sine imperatore suo ulla se
6 audituros mandata. hoc est illud tempus quo Cicero insito 15
amore Pompeianarum partium Caesarem laudandum et
tollendum censebat, cum aliud diceret, aliud intellegi uellet.

63 Interim Antonius fuga transgressus Alpes, primo per con-
loquia repulsus a M. Lepido (qui pontifex maximus in C.
Caesaris locum furto creatus decreta sibi Hispania adhuc in 20
Gallia morabatur), mox saepius in conspectum ueniens
militum (cum et Lepido omnes imperatores forent meliores
et multis Antonius, dum erat sobrius) per auersa castrorum
proruto uallo militibus receptus est; qui titulo imperii
2 cedebat Lepido, cum summa uirium penes eum foret. sub 25
Antonii ingressum in castra Iuuentius Laterensis, uir uita ac
morte consentaneus, cum acerrime suasisset Lepido ne se
cum Antonio hoste iudicato iungeret, inritus consilii gladio
se ipse transfixit.
3 Plancus deinde dubia (id est sua) fide, diu quarum esset 30
partium secum luctatus ac sibi difficile consentiens, et nunc

---

6–7 auolantibus *A*   8 D. *P*: Decio *A*   quod *PA*: quom
Acidalius   uixerat *Woodman*: uiueret *PA*   14 Caesar *Gelenius*: -i *PA*:
C. i⟨pse⟩ *Halm*   19 qui … maximus *om. A*   23–4 auersa … proruto
Gelenius: -am … ta *PA*   24 ⟨a⟩ militibus *Heinsius*

adiutor D. Bruti designati consulis, collegae sui, senatuique
se litteris uenditans, mox eiusdem proditor, Asinius autem
Pollio firmus proposito et Iulianis partibus fidus, Pompeianis
64 aduersus, uterque exercitus tradidere Antonio. D. Brutus
desertus primo a Planco, post etiam insidiis eiusdem petitus, 5
paulatim relinquente eum exercitu fugiens, in hospitis cuiusdam nobilis uiri (nomine Camelii) domo ab iis, quos miserat
Antonius, iugulatus est iustissimasque optime de se merito
2 uiro C. Caesari poenas dedit, cuius cum primus omnium
amicorum fuisset, interfector fuit, et fortunae, ex qua 10
fructum tulerat, inuidiam in auctorem relegabat, censebatque aequum, quae acceperat a Caesare, retinere, Caesarem, qui illa dederat, perire.
3 Haec sunt tempora quibus M. Tullius continuis action-
ibus aeternas Antonii memoriae inussit notas, sed hic ful- 15
gentissimo et caelesti ore, at tribunus Cannutius canina
4 rabie lacerabat Antonium. utrique uindicta libertatis morte
stetit; sed tribuni sanguine commissa proscriptio, Ciceronis
uel satiato Antonio poena finita.
Lepidus deinde a senatu hostis iudicatus est, ut ante fuerat 20
65 Antonius. tum inter eum Caesaremque et Antonium commercia epistularum et condicionum iacta mentio, cum
Antonius subinde Caesarem admoneret et quam inimicae
ipsi Pompeianae partes forent et in quod iam emersissent
fastigium et quanto Ciceronis studio Brutus Cassiusque 25

---

3 propositi *Acidalius*   5 postea *A*   6 hospitiis *A*   7 Camelii
Vossius: -li *PA*: Capeni *Gelenius*: Camilli *Cludius*   iis *Cludius*: his *PA*
9 fuisset (*del.*) primus *A*: primis *P*   13 qui *Gelenius*: quia *PA*   perire
uel perisse *Rhenanus*: peris *P*: per isthaec *A*: perdidisse *Pluygers*   15 notas
(*del.*) in. notas *A*   16 coelestiore *P*: scelestiore *A*   canina *Ruhnken*:
                                                              B   a
continua *P*: continna *A*   18 Ciceronis prostriptio *A*   19 uel *PA*:
uelut *Lipsius*: ut *Halm*   poena *P*: pene *A*: paene *Heinsius*   21 Caesarem quae *A*   22 epistularum ⟨inita⟩ *Novák*   facta *Burer*   23 et,
quod post Antonius *habent PA, post* admoneret *transpos. ed. Bipont., obelo not.*
Ellis

attollerentur, denuntiaretque se cum Bruto Cassioque (qui
iam decem et septem legionum potentes erant) iuncturum
uires suas si Caesar eius aspernaretur concordiam, diceretque plus Caesarem patris quam se amici ultioni debere.
2 ⟨igi⟩tur inita potentiae societas, et hortantibus oran- 5
tibusque exercitibus inter Antonium etiam et Caesarem
facta adfinitas, cum esset priuigna Antonii desponsa
Caesari; consulatumque iniit Caesar, pridie quam uiginti
annos impleret X Kal. Octobres, cum collega Q. Pedio, post
urbem conditam [abhinc] annis DCCVIIII, ante LXXII 10
3 quam tu, M. Vinici, consulatum inires. uidit hic annus
Ventidium, per quam urbem inter captiuos Picentium in triumpho ductus erat, in ea consularem praetextam iungentem
praetoriae; idem hic postea triumphauit.

66 Furente deinde Antonio simulque Lepido, quorum 15
uterque (ut praediximus) hostes iudicati erant, cum ambo
mallent sibi nuntiari quid passi essent quam quid emeruiss-
ent, repugnante Caesare sed frustra aduersus duos, instaura-
2 tum Sullani exempli malum, proscriptio. nihil tam
indignum illo tempore fuit quam quod aut Caesar aliquem 20
proscribere coactus est aut ab ullo Cicero proscriptus est;
abscisaque scelere Antonii uox publica est, cum eius salutem
nemo defendisset qui per tot annos et publicam ciuitatis et
priuatam ciuium defenderat.

3 Nihil tamen egisti, M. Antoni – cogit enim excedere pro- 25
positi formam operis erumpens animo ac pectore indignatio
– nihil (inquam) egisti mercedem caelestissimi oris et clarissimi capitis abscisi numerando auctoramentoque funebri ad

2 iuncturam A   4 ultioni Gelenius: -ne PA   5 ⟨igi⟩tur Rhenanus: tur
P: tuc (suprascr. deberetur) A: tum uel tunc Burer   7 desponsata A   9
collegaq. Pedio A   10 abhinc secl. Gelenius   DCCVIIII Gelenius:
ACCVIIII P: a CC VIIII A   12 M. (del.) Ventidium A   14 praetoriae Gelenius: -ia PA   16 cum BA: quom P   17 meruissent
A   18 aduersus duos om. A   21 ab ullo Rhenanus: bullo P et (sed prius
bull del.) A   22 abscissaq. A   publica audita est A   27 sceles-
tissimi (del., suprascr. caelestissimi) A   28 abscisi A

conseruatoris quondam rei publicae tantique consulis inci-
4 tando necem. rapuisti tu M. Ciceroni lucem sollicitam et
aetatem senilem et uitam miseriorem te principe quam sub
te triumuiro mortem; famam uero gloriamque factorum
5 atque dictorum adeo non abstulisti ut auxeris. uiuit 5
uiuetque per omnem saeculorum memoriam, dumque hoc
uel forte uel prouidentia uel utcumque constitutum rerum
naturae corpus – quod ille paene solus Romanorum animo
uidit, ingenio complexus est, eloquentia inluminauit –
manebit incolume, comitem aeui sui laudem Ciceronis 10
trahet; omnisque posteritas illius in te scripta mirabitur,
tuum in eum factum execrabitur, citiusque [in] mundo
genus hominum quam ⟨M. Cicero⟩ cedet.

67   Huius totius temporis fortunam ne deflere quidem quisquam satis digne potuit, adeo nemo exprimere uerbis potest. 15
2 id tamen notandum est, fuisse in proscriptos uxorum fidem
summam, libertorum mediam, seruorum aliquam, filiorum
nullam. adeo difficilis est hominibus utcumque conceptae
3 spei mora. ne quid ulli sanctum relinqueretur, uelut documentum inuitamentumque sceleris, Antonius L. Caesarem 20
auunculum, Lepidus Paulum fratrem proscripserant; nec
Planco gratia defuit ad impetrandum ut frater eius Plancus
4 Plotius proscriberetur. eoque inter iocos militares, qui
currum Lepidi Planciqui secuti erant inter execrationem
ciuium, usurpabant hunc uersum: 'De germanis non de 25
Gallis duo triumphant consules.'

1–2 incitando *Woodman*: inritando *PA*: inuitando *Lipsius*   2 tu M. *Gel-*
enius: tum *PA*   4 tribuno (*del.*) triumuiro *A*   12 tum *A*   in *P, secl.*
Kritz: citius quem mundo *A*   13 ⟨M. Cicero⟩ *Kritz*: q. ⟨Cicero⟩ cadet
Gruter: q. ⟨M. Cicero⟩ occidet *Orelli*   14 ne *uel* nec *P*: nec *BA*   16 in
om. A   19 ulli *PA*: usquam *Cludius*   19–20 uelut documentum
Woodman: uel in dotem *PA*: uelut in dotem *Gelenius*: uelut in cotem
Bothe   23 interio c͞o͞s *A*   inter ... militares *secl. Bothe*   24 ⟨et⟩
inter *Heinsius*   24–5 inter ... ciuium *secl. Novák (1892)*

68   Suo praeteritum loco referatur: neque enim persona
umbram actae rei capit. dum in acie Pharsalica †Africaque
de summa rerum Caesar dimicat, M. Caelius, uir eloquio
animoque Curioni simillimus sed in utroque perfectior nec
minus ingeniose nequam, cum †in modica† quidem seruari 5
2 posset (quippe peior illi res familiaris quam mens erat), in
praetura nouarum tabularum auctor extitit nequiitque
senatus et consulis auctoritate deterreri. accito etiam
Milone, qui non impetrato reditu Iulianis partibus infestus
erat, in urbe seditionem aut in agris occulte bellicum tumul- 10
tum mouens, primo summotus a re publica, mox consularibus armis auctore senatu circa Thurios oppressus est.
3 ⟨in⟩ incepto pari similis fortuna Milonis fuit, qui Compsam
in Hirpinis oppugnans ictusque lapide tum P. Clodio tum
patriae, quam armis petebat, poenas dedit, uir inquies et 15
4 ultra fortem temerarius. quatenus autem aliquid ex omissis
peto, notetur immodica et intempestiua libertate usos
aduersus C. Caesarem Marullum Epidium Flauumque Caesetium tribunos plebis, dum arguunt in eo regni uoluntatem,
5 paene uim dominationis expertos. in hoc tamen saepe lacess- 20
iti principis ira excessit ut censoria potius contentus nota
quam animaduersione dictatoria summoueret eos a re
publica, testareturque esse sibi miserrimum quod aut natura
sua ei excedendum foret aut minuenda dignitas. sed ad
ordinem reuertendum est. 25

---

2 Africaque *PA, obelo notauit Ellis, secl. Krause*: circaque *Lipsius*: acriter
Haupt   5 in modica *P, obelis notaui*: īmodica *A*: ne mod. q. ⟨re⟩ *Aldus uel*
⟨pecunia⟩ *Novák (1892)*: ⟨ne⟩ immod. q. ⟨re⟩ *Halm*: ne modica q. soluere
Laurent: *alii alia*   8 consulis (*iam Lipsius*) auctoritate *Cludius*: auct.
COSS. (consulū *A*) *PA*: sen. auct. et COSS. *Gelenius*: sen. ⟨consulto⟩ et
auct. consulis *Orelli*: *alii alia*   9 imperator *A*   10 aut *Woodman*: haud
PA: et *Ruhnken*   in agris *Lipsius*: magis *PA*   in agris autem (aut. *iam
Burer*) occulte *Burman*: in agris haud occ. *Mommsen*   12 Turios
PA   13 ⟨in⟩ *Madvig*   14 Irpinis *PA*   cum P. *Orelli*   16 fortem
B: sortem *PA*   17 repeto *Heinsius*   18–19 Caesetium *B*: Caese etiam
PA   19 duum *A*   20 Domitianis *A*   21 contemptus *BA*

69 Iam et Dolabella in Asia C. Trebonium consularem, cui succedebat, fraude deceptum Smyrnae occiderat, uirum aduersus merita Caesaris ingratissimum participemque caedis eius a quo ipse in consulare prouectus fastigium
2 fuerat; et C. Cassius acceptis a Staio Murco et Crispo 5 Marcio, praetoriis uiris imperatoribusque, praeualidis in Syria legionibus, inclusum Dolabellam (qui praeoccupata Asia in Syriam peruenerat) Laodiceam expugnata ea urbe †fecerat ita tamen ut ad ictum serui sui Dolabella non segniter ceruicem daret, et decem legiones in eo tractu sui iuris 10
3 fecerat; et M. Brutus C. Antonio, fratri M. Antonii, in Macedonia Vatinioque circa Dyrrachium uolentes legiones extorserat (sed Antonium bello lacessierat, Vatinium dignatione obruerat), cum et Brutus cuilibet ducum praeferendus uideretur et Vatinius nulli hominum non esset postferendus, 15
4 in quo deformitas corporis cum turpitudine certabat ingenii adeo ut animus eius dignissimo domicilio inclusus uideretur,
5 eratque septem legionibus ualidus. at lege Pedia, quam consul Pedius collega Caesaris tulerat, omnibus, qui Caesarem patrem interfecerant, damnatis aqua ignique interdictum erat; quo tempore Capito, patruus meus, uir ordinis 20
6 senatorii, Agrippae subscripsit in C. Cassium. dumque ea in Italia geruntur, acri atque prosperrimo bello Cassius Rhodum (rem immanis operis) ceperat, Brutus Lycios deuicerat et inde in Macedoniam exercitus traiecerant, cum per 25

---

2 succensebat *Ruhnken*   Zmyrnae *A*   5 Caio Murco *A*   6 Martio *PA*   imperatoribusque *Bonhomme*: imp. qui *PA*   8 Laodiceam *P*: -ia *BA*: -eae *Vossius*   expugnat *BA*   8–9 urbe fecerat *PA*: *obelum inserui*: interfecerat *Rhenanus*: fecerat *secl. G. A. Koch*: urbe ⟨obire⟩ f. *Ellis*: urbe ⟨mori⟩ coegerat *Novák (1892)*: *alii alia*   9 ad ictum *Rhenanus*: adiectum *PA*   12 Atinioque *A*   uolentis *BA*: uoluentis *P*   13 Vatinium *Gelenius*: -ius *PA*   15 hominum *Woodman*: nomini *P*: noi *A*: homini *uel* nulli [nomini] non *Aldus*: n. in omnia non *Heinsius*: [nulli] nemini non *Fähse*   16 corporis *BA*, om. *P*   18 at *Lipsius*: et *PA*: sed *Kreyssig*   20 damnatis interdictum *PA*: damnatis *ante* aqua *transposuit Gruner, secl. Delbenius, obelo notauit Ellis*

omnia repugnans naturae suae Cassius etiam Bruti clementiam uinceret; neque reperias quos aut pronior fortuna
comitata sit aut ueluti fatigata maturius destituerit quam
Brutum et Cassium.

70 Tum Caesar et Antonius traiecerunt exercitus in Macedo- 5
niam et apud urbem Philippos cum M. Bruto Cassioque acie
concurrerunt. cornu, cui Brutus praeerat, impulsis hostibus
castra Caesaris cepit (nam ipse Caesar, etiamsi infirmissimus
ualetudine erat, obibat munia ducis, oratus etiam ab Arto-
rio medico ne in castris remaneret, manifesta denuntiatione 10
quietis territo); id autem, in quo Cassius fuerat, fugatum ac
2 male mulcatum in altiora ⟨se⟩ receperat loca. tum Cassius
ex sua fortuna euentum collegae aestimans, cum dimisisset
euocatum iussissetque nuntiare sibi quae esset multitudo ac
uis hominum quae ad se tenderet, tardius eo nuntiante, cum 15
in uicino esset agmen cursu ad eum tendentium neque
puluere facies aut signa dinotari possent, existimans hostes
esse qui irruerent, lacerna caput circumdedit extentamque
3 ceruicem interritus liberto praebuit. deciderat Cassii caput,
cum euocatus aduenit nuntians Brutum esse uictorem; qui 20
cum imperatorem prostratum uideret, 'sequar,' inquit,
'eum quem mea occidit tarditas'; et ita in gladium incu-
4 buit. post paucos deinde dies Brutus conflixit cum hostibus
et uictus acie, cum in tumulum nocte ex fuga se recepisset,
impetrauit a Stratone Aegeate, familiari suo, ut manum 25
5 morituro commodaret sibi; reiectoque laeuo super caput
bracchio, cum mucronem gladii eius dextera tenens sinistrae
admouisset mamillae ad eum ipsum locum qua cor emicat,

---

10 manifesta *Heinsius*: -te *PA*: -tae *Vascosanus*   12 mulcatum *Puteanus*
(*ut uid.*): mult- *P*: mulct- *A*   ⟨se⟩ *Gelenius*   14 nunciari *A*   17
dinotari *Woodman*: den- *PA*   22–3 occubuit *A*   24 tumulum *Gelenius*
(*ut uid.*): tumultum *PA*   25 imperauit Astratone Aegeatae *A*   26
sibique (que *del.*) *A*   28 mamillae *A*: māmillae *P*

impellens se in uulnus uno ictu transfixus exspirauit
prot⟨inus.

71   Coru⟩inus Messalla, fulgentissimus iuuenis, proximus in
illis castris Bruti Cassiique auctoritati (cum essent qui eum
ducem poscerent), seruari beneficio Caesaris maluit quam 5
dubiam spem armorum temptare amplius; nec aut Caesari
quicquam ex uictoriis suis fuit laetius quam seruasse Coruin-
um aut maius exemplum hominis grati ac pii quam
Coruinus in Caesarem fuit. non aliud bellum cruentius
2   caede clarissimorum uirorum fuit. tum Catonis filius cecidit; 10
eadem   Lucullum   Hortensiumque,   eminentissimorum
3   ciuium filios, fortuna abstulit; nam Varro ad ludibrium
moriturus Antonii digna illo ac uera de exitu eius magna
cum libertate ominatus est. Drusus Liuius, Iuliae Augustae
pater, et Varus Quintilius ne temptata quidem hostis miseri- 15
cordia alter se ipse in tabernaculo interemit; Varus autem
liberti (quem id facere coegerat) manu, cum se insignibus
honorum uelasset, iugulatus est.

72   Hunc exitum M. Bruti partium XXXXII annum agentis
fortuna esse uoluit, incorrupto animo eius in diem quae illi 20
2   omnes uirtutes unius temeritate facti abstulit. fuit autem
dux Cassius melior quanto uir Brutus, e quibus Brutum
amicum habere malles, inimicum magis timeres Cassium: in
altero maior uis, in altero uirtus; qui si uicissent, quantum
rei publicae interfuit Caesarem potius habere quam Anton- 25
ium principem, tantum retulisset habere Brutum quam
Cassium.

---

1 transfixit (it *del.*, *suprascr.* us) *A*   2–3 expirauit prot⟨inus. Coru⟩inus
Mess. *Halm*: expirauit. Protinus Messalla *P, quod retin. Scheffer aliique puncto
post* protinus *transposito*: exp. protenus Mesalla *A*: expirauit. Coruinus
Mess. *ed. Bipont.*   4 authoritate *A*   6 tentare *P* (*item* 15)   19
XXXXII *Paterson*: septimum & X̄X̄X̄ (& XXX^VII *A*) *PA*: III et XXXX
Cornelissen (*1887*)   20 fortunae *A*   corrupto *PA, em. Tollius*   aio
(*del.*, *suprascr.* aio) *A*   21 facti *Rhenanus*: fecit *PA*   26 relit (*del.*)
retulisset *A*

3   Cn. Domitius, pater L. Domitii nuper a nobis uisi, eminentissimae ac nobilissimae simplicitatis uiri, auus huius Cn.
Domitii, clarissimi iuuenis, occupatis nauibus cum magno
sequentium consilia sua comitatu fugae fortunaeque se com-
4 misit, semet ipso contentus duce partium. Staius Murcus, 5
qui classi et custodiae maris praefuerat, cum omni commissa
sibi parte exercitus nauiumque Sex. Pompeium, Cn. Magni
filium, qui ex Hispania reuertens Siciliam armis
5 occupauerat, petit; ad quem et e Brutianis castris et ex Italia
aliisque terrarum partibus, quos praesenti periculo fortuna 10
subduxerat, proscripti confluebant (quippe nullum habentibus statum quilibet dux erat idoneus, cum fortuna non
electionem daret, perfugium ostenderet, exitialemque tem-
pestatem fugientibus statio pro portu foret).

73   Hic adulescens erat studiis rudis, sermone barbarus, 15
impetu strenuus, manu promptus, cogitatione celer, fide
patri dissimillimus, libertorum suorum libertus seruo-
rumque seruus, speciosis inuidens ut pareret humillimis;
2 quem senatus paene totus adhuc e Pompeianis constans partibus post Antonii a Mutina fugam, eodem illo tempore quo 20
Bruto Cassioque transmarinas prouincias decreuerat,
reuocatum ex Hispania ubi aduersus eum clarissimum
bellum Pollio Asinius praetorius gesserat, in paterna bona
3 restituerat et orae maritimae praefecerat. is tum, ut praediximus, occupata Sicilia seruitia fugitiuosque in numerum 25
exercitus sui recipiens magnum modum legionum effecerat;
perque Menam et Menecraten, paternos libertos, praefectos
classium, latrociniis ac praedationibus infestato mari ad se

---

5 Status Murus (*del.*) Murcus *A*   6 preerat (*del.*) p̄fuerat *A*   7 exercitus *Gelenius*: -tu *PA*   9 petiit *Gelenius*   ad quem et e *P*: adque
(atque *A*) me T e *BA*   12 statim *Lipsius*   13 ⟨sed⟩ perfugium
Gelenius   15 rudis is serm. *A*   16 cogitatione *Rhenanus*: cogitator *uel*
(*teste Stegmann*) cogitatur *P*: cogitator *A*: cogitato *Heinsius*: cogitatu
Scheffer   20 Antonii a Mutinam fugam *B, corr. Burer*: Antonianam
fugam *PA*   24 is tum *Vascosanus*: istum *PA*   27 per quem *A*

exercitumque tuendum rapto utebatur, cum eum non depuderet uindicatum armis ac ductu patris sui mare infestare
piraticis sceleribus.

74 Fractis Brutianis Cassianisque partibus Antonius transmarinas obiturus prouincias substitit; Caesar in Italiam se 5
recepit eamque longe quam sperauerat tumultuosiorem
2 reperit. quippe L. Antonius consul, uitiorum fratris sui
consors sed uirtutum, quae interdum in illo erant, expers,
modo apud ueteranos criminatus Caesarem, modo eos, qui
instante diuisione praediorum nominatisque coloniis agros 10
amiserant, ad arma conciens magnum exercitum con-
3 flauerat. ex altera parte uxor Antonii Fuluia, nihil muliebre
praeter corpus gerens, omnia armis tumultuque miscebat.
haec belli sedem Praeneste ceperat; Antonius pulsus
undique uiribus Caesaris Perusiam se contulerat; Plancus, 15
Antonianarum adiutor partium, spem magis ostenderat
4 auxilii quam opem ferebat Antonio. usus Caesar uirtute et
fortuna sua Perusiam expugnauit. Antonium inuiolatum
dimisit; in Perusinos magis ira militum quam uoluntate
saeuitum ducis; urbs incensa, cuius initium incendii prin- 20
ceps eius loci fecit Macedonicus, qui subiecto rebus ac pen-
atibus suis igni transfixum se gladio flammae intulit.

75 Per eadem tempora exarserat in Campania bellum, quod
professus eorum, qui perdiderant agros, patrocinium ciebat
Ti. Claudius Nero praetorius et pontifex, Ti. Caesaris pater, 25
magni uir animi doctissimique ingenii. id quoque aduentu
2 Caesaris sepultum atque discussum est. quis fortunae muta-
tiones, quis dubios rerum humanarum casus satis mirari

---

1 depuderet *P*: puderet (de *suprascr.*) *A*: dispuderet *Kenney*   2 ductum
A   7 repperit *A*   10 instante *E. Thomas, Goodyear*: iuste *PA*: iusta
Vascosanus: iniuste (*uel* -ta) *Lipsius*: instituta *Ruhnken*: iussa *Heinsius*: *alii*
alia   coloniis *Ruhnken*: -nis *PA*   13 tumultūque *A*   14 bellis
sedem *PA, corr. Gelenius*   16 spem *P*: spe *B* et (*sed prius* spem, *del.*)
A   19 demisit *A*   25 T. *PA, corr. Gelenius* (*bis*)   26 uir *P*: uiri
BA   doctissimique *PA*: promptissimique *Ruhnken*: clarissimique *Bothe*:
alii alia

queat? quis non diuersa praesentibus contrariaque exspec-
3 tatis aut speret aut timeat? Liuia, nobilissimi et fortissimi
uiri Drusi Claudiani filia, genere probitate forma
Romanarum eminentissima, quam postea coniugem
Augusti uidimus, quam transgressi ad deos sacerdotem ac 5
filiam, tum fugiens mox futuri sui Caesaris arma, ⟨mi⟩nus
bimum hunc Tiberium Caesarem, uindicem Romani
imperii futurumque eiusdem Caesaris filium, gestans sinu,
per auia itinerum uitatis militum gladiis uno comitante, quo
facilius occultaretur fuga, peruenit ad mare et cum uiro 10
Nerone peruecta in Siciliam est.

76   Quod alieno testimonium redderem, [in] eo non fraudabo
auum meum. quippe C. Velleius, honoratissimo inter illos
CCCLX iudices loco a Cn. Pompeio lectus, eiusdem Mar-
cique Bruti ac Ti. Neronis praefectus fabrum, uir nulli 15
secundus in Campania, digressu Neronis a Neapoli, cuius ob
singularem cum eo amicitiam partium adiutor fuerat, grauis
iam aetate et corpore cum comes esse non posset, gladio se
ipse transfixit.

2   Inuiolatam excedere Italia Caesar passus Fuluiam Plan- 20
cumque, muliebris fugae comitem; nam Pollio Asinius cum
septem legionibus, diu retenta in potestate Antonii Venetia,
magnis speciosisque rebus circa Altinum aliasque eius
regionis urbes editis, Antonium petens, uagum adhuc Domi-
tium (quem digressum e Brutianis castris post caedem eius 25
praediximus et propriae classis factum ducem) consiliis suis
3 defectum [ac] fide data iunxit Antonio. quo facto quisquis

---

1 expectatis, *suprascr.* expectans *A*   3 Claudiani *Burer*: Calidiani
PBA   6 arma, ⟨mi⟩nus *Vossius*: arma nus *P*: arma (*sed* c *supra* r *scr.*) *A*:
arma ⟨ac ma⟩nus, *Gertz, Ellis*: [ar] manus, *Ruhnken*: alii alia   7
Tiberim *A*   8 futurum eiusdemque *Acidalius*   8–9 si nuper *A*   12
in eo *P*: meo *A*: in *secl. Gelenius*   14 lectos *Gruter*   15 Ti. Neronis
Aldus: Tyronis *P*: Tir- *A*   18 cum comes *Aldus*: cum *PA*: comes
B   26 proprae *B*   27 defectum *Woodman*: electum *PA*: eiectum
Damsté: illectum *Gelenius*   ac *PA*, *secl. Cludius*

aequum se praestiterit, sciat non minus a Pollione in Antonium quam ab Antonio in Pollionem esse conlatum.

Aduentus deinde in Italiam Antonii praeparatusque
contra eum Caesaris habuit belli metum, sed pax circa
4 Brundusium composita. per quae tempora Rufi Saluidieni 5
scelesta consilia patefacta sunt, qui natus obscurissimis initiis
parum habebat summa accepisse et proximus a Cn.
Pompeio ipsoque Caesare ex equestri ordine consul creatus
esse, nisi in id ascendisset e quo infra se et Caesarem uideret
et rem publicam.   10
77   Tum expostulante consensu populi, quem grauis urebat
infesto mari annona, cum Pompeio quoque circa Misenum
pax inita, qui haud absurde, cum in naui Caesaremque et
Antonium cena exciperet, dixit in Carinis suis se cenam
dare, referens hoc dictum ad loci nomen in quo paterna 15
2 domus ab Antonio possidebatur. in hoc pacis foedere placuit
Siciliam Achaiamque Pompeio concedere, in quo tamen
animus inquies manere non potuit; id unum tantummodo
salutare aduentu suo patriae attulit, quod omnibus proscrip-
tis aliisque, qui ad eum ex diuersis causis fugerant, reditum 20
3 salutemque pactus est. quae res et alios clarissimos uiros et
Neronem Claudium et M. Silanum Sentiumque Saturnin-
um et Arruntium ac Titium restituit rei publicae; Staium
autem Murcum, qui aduentu suo classisque celeberrimae
uires eius duplicauerat, insimulatum falsis criminationibus, 25

---

3 paratusque *Gelenius*: apparatusque *Sylburg*   4 contra eum Caesaris
BA: C. c. e. *uel* C. circa e. *P*   4–5 circa Brundusium *P*: contra Brundisium *BA*   5 perque *A*   Rufi *A*: Ruffi *P*   5–6 Saluidienis caelesta
A   7 summa *Acidalius*: -ā *P*: -am *A*   7–8 proximum ... consulem
creatum *Novák (1907)* (creatum *iam Ursinus*)   8 ex equestri ordine *Gelenius*: ex equestri (sequestri *A*: equestris *P*) ordinis *PBA*: equestris ordinis
Heinsius   9 nisi in id *Puteanus*: nisi in is *BA*: ni simul *P*   e quo *P*:
equo *BA*   11 urgebat *Cludius*   13 absurde *Rhenanus*: -o *PA*   19
aduentu suo *secl. Ruhnken*: conuentu s. *Halm*   tulit *A*   22 Silanum
BA: Syllanum *P*   Sentiumque *P*: Sentium Q. *B*: Sentium q. *A*   23
Aruntium *Gelenius*: Atruntium *P*: Atruncium *A*: Atruucium *B*

quia talem uirum collegam officii Mena et Menecrates
fastidierant, Pompeius in Sicilia interfecerat.

78 Hoc tractu temporum Octauiam, sororem Caesaris, M.
Antonius duxit uxorem. redierat Pompeius in Siciliam,
Antonius in transmarinas prouincias quas †magnis 5
momentis† Labienus ex Brutianis castris profectus ad
Parthos perducto eorum exercitu in Syriam interfectoque
legato Antonii concusserat; qui uirtute et ductu Ventidii
una cum Parthorum copiis celeberrimoque iuuenum
2 Pacoro, regis filio, exstinctus est. interim Caesar per haec 10
tempora, ne res disciplinae inimicissima, otium, corrumperet militem, crebris in Illyrico Dalmatiaque expeditionibus patientia periculorum bellique experientia durabat
3 exercitum. eadem tempestate Caluinus Domitius, cum ex
consulatu obtineret Hispaniam, grauissimi comparandique 15
antiquis exempli auctor fuit: quippe primi pili centurionem
(nomine Vibillium) ob turpem ex acie fugam fusti percussit.

79 Crescente in dies et classe et fama Pompeii Caesar molem
belli eius suscipere statuit. aedificandis nauibus contrahen-
doque militem ac remigem naualibusque adsuescendo certa- 20
minibus [atque exercitationibus] praefectus est M. Agrippa,
⟨uir⟩ uirtutis nobilissimae, labore uigilia periculo inuictus,
parendique (sed uni) scientissimus, aliis sane imperandi
cupidus, et per omnia extra dilationes positus consultisque
2 facta coniungens. hic in Auerno ac Lucrino lacu speciosis- 25
sima classe fabricata cotidianis exercitationibus militem

---

1 Menocres P, *corr. Rhenanus* (Mencrates): Menotrades B: Menocrates
A   4 redierat *om. A*   5-6 magnis momentis *PA, obelis notaui*:
mo⟨li⟩mentis *Ruhnken*   7 perducto *Arntzenius*: prod- PA   8-9
Ventidi una P: uenti diuina A   10-11 per haec tempora (*del.*) interim
C. per hec tempora A   16 primi pili *Kreyssig*: primipili PA   17
Vibillium BA: Iubillium P   opturpem A   fusti BA: fusti *uel* fuste
P   20 militem ... remigem *Ellis*: -e ... -e PA: -i ... -i *Gelenius*   21
adq. A   atque exercitationibus *secl. Bothe*   22 ⟨uir⟩ *Ruhnken*
uirtuti A   25 coniuges A

remigemque ad summam et militaris et maritimae rei perduxit scientiam. hac classi Caesar, cum prius despondente ei
Nerone (cui ante nupta fuerat) Liuiam auspicatis rei publicae ominibus duxisset eam uxorem, Pompeio Siciliaeque
3 bellum intulit; sed uirum humana ope inuictum grauiter eo 5
tempore fortuna concussit. quippe longe maiorem partem
classis circa Veliam Palinurique promontorium adorta uis
Africi lacerauit ac distulit. ea patrando bello mora fuit, quod
4 postea dubia et interdum ancipiti fortuna gestum est. nam et
classis eodem loco uexata est tempestate, et ut nauali primo 10
proelio apud Mylas ductu Agrippae pugnatum prospere, ita
inopinato 〈Pompeii〉 classis aduentu grauis sub ipsius Caesaris oculis circa Tauromenium accepta clades: neque ab
ipso periculum abfuit; legiones, quae cum Cornificio erant,
legato Caesaris, expositae in terra paene a Pompeio oppres- 15
5 sae sunt. sed ancipitis fortuna temporis matura uirtute correcta: explicatis quippe utriusque partis classibus paene
omnibus exutus nauibus Pompeius Asiam fuga petiuit, iussu-
que M. Antonii, cuius opem petierat, dum inter ducem et
supplicem tumultuatur et nunc dignitatem retinet, nunc 20
6 uitam precatur, a Titio iugulatus est; cui in tantum durauit
hoc facinore contractum odium ut mox ludos in theatro
Pompeii faciens execratione populi spectaculo, quod praebe-
bat, pelleretur.
80   Acciuerat gerens contra Pompeium bellum ex Africa 25
Caesar Lepidum cum XII semiplenis legionibus. hic uir
omnium uanissimus neque ulla uirtute tam longam fortunae
indulgentiam meritus exercitum Pompeii, quia propior
fuerat, sequentem non ipsius sed Caesaris auctoritatem et

2–3 & merone *del.*, *suprascr.* ei Nerone *A*   3 Liuia *A*   4 hominibus
A   eam *secl. Heinsius*   9 indubia sed *Bothe*   10 primum *A*   11
aput Milas *A*   12 〈Pompeii〉 *nescioquis*: 〈aduersae〉 aduentu
Heinsius   14 *fort.* abfuit 〈et〉 legiones   15 legatae *A*   in terram
Haase   pene paene *A*   16 mature *Ruhnken*   18 Asiā fugam
A   20 tumultuatur *PA*: fluctuatur *Cornelissen (1877)*: multum luctatur
Halm   23 quod *om. A*

36

2 fidem sibi iunxerat; inflatusque amplius XX legionum
numero in id furoris processerat ut inutilis alienae uictoriae
comes (quam diu moratus erat dissidendo in consiliis
Caesari et semper diuersa his, quae aliis placebant, dicendo)
totam uictoriam ut suam interpretaretur, audebatque 5
3 denuntiare Caesari, excederet Sicilia. non ab Scipionibus
aliisque ueteribus Romanorum ducum quidquam ausum
patratumque fortius quam tunc a Caesare. quippe cum
inermis ac lacernatus esset, praeter nomen nihil trahens
ingressus castra Lepidi, euitatis quae iussu hominis prauis- 10
simi tela in eum acta erant, cum lacerna eius perforata esset
4 lancea, aquilam legionis rapere ausus est. scires quid interesset inter duces: armati inermem secuti sunt, decimoque
anno quam [ad] in dissimillimam uitae suae potentiam
peruenerat, Lepidus et a militibus et a fortuna desertus pul- 15
loque uelatus amiculo inter ultimam confluentium ad Caesarem turbam latens genibus eius aduolutus est. uita
rerumque suarum dominium concessa ei sunt, spoliata,
quam tueri non poterat, dignitas.

81 Subita deinde exercitus seditio (qui plerumque contem- 20
platus frequentiam suam a disciplina desciscit et, quod
cogere se putat posse, rogare non sustinet) partim seueritate
2 partim liberalitate discussa principis; speciosumque per id
tempus adiectum supplementum Campanae coloniae, cuius
⟨agri⟩ relicti erant publici; pro his longe uberiores reditus 25
duodecies HS in Creta insula redditi et aqua promissa, quae

---

2 in alienae *BA*   3 quamdiu *A*   4 Caesari *Acidalius*: -is *PA*: d. consiliis Caesaris *olim Halm*   iis *Orelli*   hisq. *A*   5 totam *BA*: tutam
P   interpretaretur *Gelenius*: interpretabatur *PA*: interpretaretur
auderetque *Ruhnken*   10–11 euitatis ⟨telis⟩ ... [tela] *Orelli*   11 tela
P, om. A   iacta *Gelenius*   14 ad *secl. Bothe*   uitae suae *Vascosanus*:
-a -a *PA*: ad·indignissimam uita sua pot. *Ruhnken*   19 tueri *P*: int- *BA*:
ui tueri *Acidalius*   23 idem *A*   24–5 cuius ⟨agri⟩ rel. *Woodman*: eius
rel. *PA*: ⟨agri⟩ eius rel. *Ruhnken*: *alii maiorem ante* eius *lacunam
posuerunt*   26 duodec. S-H *P*: duodet. sestertii *A*

37

hodieque singulare et salubritatis instrumentum et amoe-
3 nitatis ornamentum est. insigne coronae classicae, quo nemo
umquam Romanorum donatus erat, hoc bello Agrippa singulari uirtute meruit. uictor deinde Caesar reuersus in
urbem contractas emptionibus complures domos per pro- 5
curatores, quo laxior fieret ipsius, publicis se usibus destinare
professus est templumque Apollinis et circa porticus facturum promisit, quod ab eo singulari exstructum munificentia
est.

82 Qua aestate Caesar tam prospere †Libium in Sicilia 10
bene† fortuna in Caesare et re publica titubauit ad orientem. quippe Antonius cum XIII legionibus ingressus Armeniam ac deinde Mediam et per eas regiones Parthos petens,
2 habuit regem eorum obuium; primoque duas legiones cum
omnibus impedimentis tormentisque et Statiano legato 15
amisit, mox saepius ipse cum summo totius exercitus discrimine ea adiit pericula ⟨a⟩ quibus seruari se posse desperaret; amissaque non minus quarta parte militum captiui
cuiusdam (sed Romani) consilio ac fide seruatus, qui clade
Crassiani exercitus captus, cum fortuna non animum 20
mutasset, accessit nocte ad stationem Romanam praedix-
itque ne destinatum iter peterent sed diuerso siluestrique
3 peruaderent. hoc M. Antonio ac tot illis legionibus saluti
fuit; de quibus tamen totoque exercitu haud minus pars
quarta (ut praediximus) militum, calonum seruitiique 25
desiderata tertia est; impedimentorum uix ulla superfuit.
hanc tamen Antonius fugam suam, quia uiuus exierat, uic-

1 instrumentum *Cludius*: instar *PA, obelo not. Ellis*   4 meruerit *A*   6
laxior, *suprascr.* laxius *A*   10–11 Libium ... bene (Bn̄ *A*) *PA, obelis
notaui*: ⟨in⟩ Lepidum in Sicilia, paene *Schegk*: ⟨rem⟩ ciuium in S. tenet,
Huth: ⟨sepe⟩liuit in S. bellum, *Ruhnken*: *alii alia*   11 et in re p.
A   titubauit *Goodyear*: militauit *PA*: inclinauit *Sauppe*: *alii alia*   12
XVI *Freinsheim*   ingressus *Gelenius*: egr- *PA*   17 ⟨a⟩ *Kreyssig*: ⟨e⟩
Heinsius   desperaret *Haupt*: desperauerat *PA*: -auerit *Bothe*   19
⟨est⟩ seruatus *Gelenius*   20 fortuna *BA*: -ā *P*   22 predestinatum
A   23 loco (*del.*) peruaderent loco (*del.*) *A*   ac tot illis *Heinsius*: acto
illis *PA*: atque illis *Gelenius*: ac tot leg. *Lipsius*   26 desiderat[ ] (*ult. litt.
del.*) *A*   27 uiuos *A*

toriam uocabat; qui tertia aestate reuersus in Armeniam
regem eius Artauasden fraude deceptum catenis (sed, ne
4 quid honori deesset, aureis) uinxit. crescente deinde et
amoris in Cleopatram incendio et uitiorum (quae semper
facultatibus licentiaque et adsentationibus aluntur) magni- 5
tudine bellum patriae inferre constituit, cum ante Nouum se
Liberum Patrem appellari iussisset, cum redimitus hederis
coronaque uelatus aurea et thyrsum tenens cothurnisque
succinctus curru uelut Liber Pater uectus esset Alexandriae.
83   Inter hunc apparatum belli Plancus, non iudicio recta 10
legendi neque amore rei publicae aut Caesaris (quippe haec
semper impugnabat) sed morbo proditor, cum fuisset humillimus adsentator reginae et infra seruos cliens, cum Antonii
librarius, cum obscenissimarum rerum et auctor et minister,
2 cum in omnia et [in] omnibus uenalis, cum caeruleatus et 15
nudus caputque redimitus arundine et caudam trahens
genibus innixus Glaucum saltasset in conuiuio, refrigeratus
ab Antonio ob manifestarum rapinarum indicia transfugit
ad Caesarem; et idem postea clementiam uictoris pro sua
uirtute interpretabatur, dictitans id probatum a Caesare cui 20
ille ignouerat. mox autem hunc auunculum Titius imitatus
3 est. haud absurde Coponius, uir e praetoriis grauissimus, P.
Silii socer, cum recens transfuga multa ac nefanda Plancus
absenti Antonio in senatu obiiceret, 'multa,' inquit,
'mehercules fecit Antonius pridie quam tu illum relin- 25
queres!'
84   Caesare deinde et Messalla Coruino consulibus debella-
tum apud Actium, ubi, longe antequam dimicaretur, exploratissima Iulianarum partium fuit uictoria. uigebat in hac
parte miles atque imperator, ⟨in⟩ illa marcebant omnia; 30

8–9 coth. subnixus *Ruhnken*   15 in *secl. Gelenius*   21 mox autem hunc
auunculum *uel* hunc mox auunculum *P*: mox autem (aut *A*) hunc mox
auunc. *BA*   22 ⟨C.⟩ Coponius *Kreyssig*   e praetoriis *Schegk*: E. praetorius *BA*: praetorius *P*   22–3 P. Silii *Gelenius*: pater, Silii *P*: patersilii
A: pater ∗ Sili *Ellis*   27 Messala *PA* (cf. 71.1)   29 uigebat, *suprascr.*
ur *A*   30 ⟨in⟩ *Vascosanus*   illam arcebant *BA*

hinc re⟨mi⟩ges firmissimi, illinc inopia adfectissimi; nauium
haec magnitudo modica nec celeritati aduersa, illa specie
[et] terribilior; hinc ad Antonium nemo, illinc ad Caesarem
cotidie aliquis transfugiebat. denique in ore atque oculis
Antonianae classis per M. Agrippam Leucas expugnata, 5
Patrae captae, Corinthus occupata. bis ante ultimum dis-
2 crimen classis hostium superata. rex Amyntas meliora et utiliora secutus; nam Dellius, exempli sui tenax, ut a Dolabella
*** ad Caesarem; uirque clarissimus Cn. Domitius, qui
solus Antonianarum partium numquam reginam nisi 10
nomine salutauit, maximo et praecipiti periculo transmisit
ad Caesarem.

85   Aduenit deinde maximi discriminis dies, quo Caesar
Antoniusque productis classibus pro salute alter, in ruinam
2 alter terrarum orbis dimicauere. dextrum nauium Iulia- 15
narum cornu M. Lurio commissum, laeuum Arruntio,
Agrippae omne classici certaminis arbitrium; Caesar, ei
parti destinatus in quam a fortuna uocaretur, ubique
aderat. classis Antonii regimen Publicolae Sosioque commissum. at in terra locatum exercitum Taurus Caesaris, Antonii 20
3 regebat Canidius. ubi initum certamen est, omnia in altera
parte fuere, dux, remiges, milites; in altera nihil praeter
milites. prima occupat fugam Cleopatra; Antonius fugientis
reginae quam pugnantis militis sui comes esse maluit, et
imperator, qui in desertores saeuire debuerat, desertor exer- 25

---

1 hic ... illic *Kritz*   re⟨mi⟩ges *Lipsius*   2 hac ... illac (illā *Ruhnken*)
Heinsius   modica nec celeritati *Heinsius*: modicane (m. ne *A*: modicaue
P) celeritate *BAP*   3 et *secl. Rhenanus*: *post* et *lacunam posuit Ellis*   huc
(*del.*) hinc *A*   4 aliquis *Heinsius*: aliquid *B*: aliquis (*ut uid., del.*) aliquid
A: aliqui *P*   transfugiebat *BA*: -bant *P*   adque *A*   6 Corinthiis,
suprascr. Corinthus *A*   7 rex ... (12) Caesarem *post* transfugiebat (4)
transposuit Haase   Amyntas *Gelenius*: Myntas *PA*   melior *A*   8
Dellius *Ruhnken*: de illius *PA*: Deillius *Lipsius*   exempli sui tenax ut a
Lipsius: exemplis uitae naxuta *PA*   *post* Dolabella *lacunam posuit*
Krause   11 pericula *A*   16 Lurio *Ursinus*: Lario *PA*   Arruntio
Gelenius: Adr- *PA*   19 Publicolae Sosioque *Rhenanus*: Publico Laeso-
sioque *PA*

4 citus sui factus est. illis etiam detracto capite in longum fortissime pugnandi durauit constantia et desperata uictoria in
mortem dimicabatur. Caesar, quos ferro poterat interimere,
uerbis mulcere cupiens clamitansque et ostendens fugisse
5 Antonium, quaerebat pro quo et cum quo pugnarent. at illi, 5
cum diu pro absente dimicassent duce, aegre summissis
armis cessere uictoriam citiusque uitam ueniamque Caesar
promisit quam illis, ut ea precarentur, persuasum est.
fuitque in confesso milites optimi imperatoris, imperatorem
6 fugacissimi militis functum officio, ut dubites suo an Cleo- 10
patrae arbitrio uictoriam temperaturus fuerit, qui ad eius
arbitrium derexerit fugam. idem locatus in terra fecit exercitus, cum se Canidius praecipiti fuga rapuisset ad Antonium.

86   Quid ille dies terrarum orbi praestiterit, ex quo in quem 15
statum peruenerit fortuna publica, quis in hoc transcursu
2 tam artati operis exprimere audeat? uictoria uero fuit clementissima nec quisquam interemptus est ⟨nisi⟩ paucissimi et
ii qui ⟨ne⟩ deprecari quidem pro se [non] sustinerent; ex
qua lenitate ducis colligi potuit qu⟨em fin⟩em aut initio 20
triumuiratus sui aut in campis Philippiis, si sic licuisset, uictoriae suae facturus fuerit. at Sosium L. Arruntii prisca
grauitate celeberrimi fides, mox diu ⟨cum⟩ clementia luc-
3 tatus sua Caesar, seruauit incolumem. non praetereatur

---

1 detracto *Vascosanus*: detrectato *PA*   6 aegressum missis *A*   7 uictoria *Heinsius*: uictori *Herel*   8 eam *Salmasius*   9 fuit qui in confessio
A   imperatore *A*   10 officio *om. A*   ut dubites suone (ne *om.*
Vossius) *Burer*: uidebit e suo *P*: uidebitis ne *A*: ne dubites suo an *Ellis*
11 fuerit *Rhenamus*: -at *PA*   11–12 ad eius fugam direxit arbitrium
fugam *A*   12 direxerit *Halm*: -xit *PA*   in terra, *suprascr.*
interea *A*   18 ⟨nisi⟩ *Heinsius*: int. nisi pauc. *Gelenius*   18–19 et ii
Gelenius: et hi *PA*: paucissimi ⟨summ⟩oti *Ellis*   19 ⟨ne⟩ ... [non]
Heinsius   20 qu⟨em fin⟩em *Goodyear*   21 Philippis *Aldus*: Philippicis
Gelenius   si *om. A*   22 fuerit ⟨modum⟩ *Rhenanus*   at *Puteanus*: ad
PA: C. *Madvig*   Sosium L. Arruntii *Puteanus*: solium (folium *P*) alarunt
in *PA*   23 ⟨cum⟩ *Lipsius*

Asinii Pollionis factum et dictum memorabile. namque cum
se post Brundisinam pacem continuisset in Italia neque aut
uidisset umquam reginam aut post eneruatum amore eius
Antonii animum partibus eius se miscuisset, rogante Caesare
ut secum ad bellum proficisceretur Actiacum, 'mea,' inquit, 5
'in Antonium maiora merita sunt, illius in me beneficia
notiora: itaque discrimini uestro me subtraham et ero
praeda uictoris.'

87 Proximo deinde anno persecutus reginam Antoniumque
Alexandriam, ultimam bellis ciuilibus imposuit manum. 10
Antonius se ipse non segniter interemit, adeo ut multa desidiae crimina morte redimeret; at Cleopatra frustratis custodibus inlata aspide, in morsu sane eius expers muliebris
2 metus, spiritum reddidit. fuitque et fortuna et clementia
Caesaris dignum quod nemo ex his, qui contra eum arma 15
tulerant, ab eo iussuue eius interemptus: D. Brutum Antonii
interemit crudelitas; Sextum Pompeium ab eo deuictum
idem Antonius, cum dignitatis quoque seruandae dedisset
3 fidem, etiam spiritu priuauit; Brutus et Cassius, antequam
uictorum experirentur animum, uoluntaria morte obierunt; 20
Antonii Cleopatraeque quis fuisset exitus narrauimus. Canidius timidius decessit quam professioni ei, qua semper usus
erat, congruebat; ultimus autem ex interfectoribus Caesaris
Parmensis Cassius morte poenas dedit, ut dederat ⟨primus⟩
Trebonius. 25

---

1 namque *BA*: nam *P*   2 Brundisinam *BA*: -usinam *P*   3 tum (*del.*,
suprascr. un) quam *A*   4 miscuisset *BA*: imm- *P*   5 Actia cum
A   7 discrimini *Acidalius*: -e *PA*   9 deinde *BA*, *om. P*   10 Alex-
andream *BA*   12 redemerit *Halm*   13 aspide in *B*: aspidem *A*:
aspide *P*   morsu (morsus *ult. litt. del. A*) sane eius *BPA*: m. eius sane
Acidalius: morsus sanie eius *Ellis*   mulieris *A*   16 iussusue *A*   17
ab eo deuictum *Acidalius*: ab (ob *P*) eodem uictum *BPA*: a Caesare deuictum *Purser*   18 seruandae *om. A*   21 Cleo. quae *A*   fuisset *P*:
fuerit (*quod in* fuisset *mutasse uid. A*) *Krause*   22 ei *Cludius*: eius *PA*   24
primus *suppl. hic Aldus, post* Trebonius *Halm*   25 Trebonius *P*: Trib- *BA*

88 Dum ultimam bello Actiaco Alexandrinoque Caesar imponit manum, M. Lepidus, iuuenis forma quam mente melior, Lepidi eius, qui triumuir fuerat rei publicae constituendae, filius, Iunia Bruti sorore natus, interficiendi, simul
2 in urbem reuertisset, Caesaris consilia inierat. ⟨erat⟩ tunc 5 urbis custodiis praepositus C. Maecenas, equestri sed splendido genere natus, uir, ubi res uigiliam exigeret, sane exsomnis, prouidens atque agendi sciens, simul uero aliquid ex negotio remitti posset, otio ac mollitiis paene ultra feminam fluens, non minus Agrippa Caesari carus, sed 10 minus honoratus (quippe uixit angusto clauo †pene contentus) nec minora consequi potuit sed non tam concu-
3 piuit. hic speculatus est per summam quietem ac dissimulationem praecipitis consilia iuuenis et mira celeritate nullaque cum perturbatione aut rerum aut hominum 15 oppresso Lepido immane noui ac resurrecturi belli ciuilis restinxit initium; et ille quidem male consultorum poenas exsoluit. aequetur praedictae iam Antistii Seruilia Lepidi uxor, quae uiro igni deuorato praematura morte immortalem nominis sui pensauit memoriam. 20

89 Caesar autem reuersus in Italiam atque urbem, ⟨qu⟩o concursu, quo fauore omnium hominum, aetatium, ordinum exceptus sit, quae magnificentia triumphorum eius, quae fuerit munerum, ne in operis quidem iusti materia, nedum huius tam recisi digne exprimi potest. 25

---

1 Actioq (q *del.*) *A*   5 ⟨erat⟩ *Madvig*: ini⟨t⟩. erat *Wistrand*   6 equestri sed *Vascosanus*: equestris et *PA*   7 exi exigeret *A*   8 exomnis *PA*   prudens *A*   11 angusto clauuo *Gelenius*: angusti (Augusti *A*) -i *PA*   pene *P, obelo notaui*: paene *A*: bene *uel* plane *Lipsius*: angusti claui fine *Heinsius*: *alii alia*   18 Antistii *Vossius*: -tiae *PA*   19 uiro *van Herwerden*: uiuo *PA*   19–20 'Exemp. uetustum sic habet, ut potius legendum existimem, praematura morte immortalem … memoriam' *Burer*: praematuram mortem immortali … memoria *P*: praematuram mortem immortalem … memoriam *A*   21–2 ⟨qu⟩o concursu, quo fau. *Damsté*: occursus quo fau. *PA*: ⟨quo⟩ occursu, quo fau. *Lipsius*: quo concursu, fau. *Vascosanus*   24 ne in operis quidem *Gelenius*: nedum in operis siquidem *PA*

2 Nihil deinde optare a diis homines, nihil dii hominibus praestare possunt, nihil uoto concipi, nihil felicitate consummari quod non Augustus post reditum in urbem rei publicae populoque Romano terrarumque orbi repraesentauerit. 3 finita uicesimo anno bella ciuilia, sepulta externa, reuocata 5 pax, sopitus ubique armorum furor; restituta uis legibus, iudiciis auctoritas, senatui maiestas; imperium magistratuum ad pristinum redactum modum: tantummodo octo 4 praetoribus adlecti duo; prisca illa et antiqua rei publicae forma reuocata. rediit cultus agris, sacris honos, securitas 10 hominibus, certa cuique rerum suarum possessio. leges emendatae utiliter, latae salubriter; senatus sine asperitate nec sine seueritate lectus; principes uiri triumphisque et amplissimis honoribus functi hortatu principis ad ornandam 5 urbem inlecti sunt. †consulatus tantummodo usque ad 15 undecimum quem continuaret Caesar cum saepe obnitens repugnasset impetrare potuit† nam dictaturam quam per- 6 tinaciter ei deferebat populus, tam constanter repulit. bella sub imperatore gesta pacatusque uictoriis terrarum orbis et tot extra Italiam domique opera omne aeui sui spatium 20 impensurum in id solum opus scriptorem fatigent; nos memores professionis uniuersam imaginem principatus eius oculis animisque subiecimus.

90 Sepultis (ut praediximus) bellis ciuilibus coalescentibusque rei publicae membris, †et coram aliero† quae tam 25 longa armorum series lacera31uerat. Dalmatia, XX et CC ⟨annos⟩ rebellis, ad certam confessionem parata est imperii;

---

1 dis A   dii P: de A ·   5 finito A   bellaci Iulia A   8 redactus A   9 Allectio (del.) allectio A   10 redit A   14 adhortatur A   15–17 consulatus … impetrare (prius imperare A) potuit PA, obelis notaui: fort. cons. tantummodo usque ad undecimum ut continuaret Caesar, cum saepe obnitens repugna⟨turus e⟩sset, impetrari potuit   21 fatigent Acidalius: -ant PA: -arent Vossius   25 et coram aliero PA, obelis notaui, secl. Gelenius: egit curam externorum ed. Bipont.: erat cura alienorum Purser: et coaluere Rhenanus: alii alia   27 annos suppl. hic Lipsius, ante XX Orelli   parata Bothe: pacata PA

Alpes feris incultisque nationibus celebres perdomitae; Hispaniae nunc ipsius praesentia, nunc Agrippae (quem usque in tertium consulatum et mox collegium tribuniciae potestatis amicitia principis euexerat) multo uarioque Marte pacatae.   5

2 In quas prouincias cum initio Scipione et Sempronio Longo consulibus, primo anno secundi ⟨belli⟩ Punici, abhinc annos CCL, Romani exercitus missi essent duce Cn. Scipione (Africani patruo), per annos CC in his multo mutuoque ita certatum est sanguine ut amissis populi 10 Romani imperatoribus exercitibusque saepe contumelia, etiam nonnumquam periculum Romano inferretur imperio.

3 illae enim prouinciae Scipiones consumpserunt; illae contumelioso XV annorum bello sub duce Viriatho maiores nostros exercuerunt; illae terrore Numantini belli populum 15 Romanum concusserunt; in illis turpe Q. Pompeii foedus turpiusque Mancini senatus cum ignominia dediti imperatoris rescidit; illa ** tot consulares, tot praetorios absumpsit duces, patrumque aetate in tantum Sertorium armis extulit ut per quinquennium diiudicari non potuerit, Hispanis 20 Romanisne in armis plus esset roboris et uter populus alteri

4 pariturus foret. has igitur prouincias tam diffusas, tam frequentes, tam feras ad eam pacem abhinc annos ferme L perduxit Caesar Augustus ut, quae maximis bellis numquam uacauerant, eae sub C. Antistio ac deinde P. Silio 25 legato ceterisque postea etiam latrociniis uacarent.

91 Dum pacatur occidens, ab oriente ac rege Parthorum

---

1 incultisque *Heinsius*: multisque *PA*   per do *A*   6 ⟨P.⟩ Scipione *Goodyear*   7 ⟨belli⟩ *Heinsius*   8 anno CCL *A*   misissent *A*   10–11 populi Romani *Gelenius*: Praetor *PA*   12 nonnumquam etiam *Gelenius*   14 XV *Vossius*: XX *PA*: X *Lipsius*   15 timore (*del.*), *supra-scr.* terrore *A*   17 dedit *A*   18 restindit *A*   *post* illa *lacunam posui* (*fort.* illa⟨arum acies⟩ *uel sim.*): illae ... absumpserunt ... (19) extulerunt *Cludius*: illa ⟨natio⟩ *Goodyear*   20 poterit *BA*   25 hae *A*   Antistio *Gelenius*: Aristio *PA*   27 pacatus *A*

45

signa Romana, quae Crasso presso Orodes, quae Antonio pulso filius eius Phraates ceperant, Augusto remissa sunt (quod cognomen illi uiro Planci sententia consensus uniuersi senatus populique Romani indidit).

2 Erant tamen qui hunc felicissimum statum odissent: 5 quippe L. Murena et Fannius Caepio, diuersis moribus (nam Murena sine hoc facinore potuit uideri bonus, Caepio et ante hoc erat pessimus), cum inissent occidendi Caesaris consilia, oppressi auctoritate publica, quod ui facere uol-

3 uerant, iure passi sunt. neque multo post Rufus Egnatius, 10 per omnia gladiatori quam senatori propior, collecto in aedilitate fauore populi, quem extinguendis priuata familia incendiis in dies auxerat, in tantum quidem ut ei praeturam continuaret, mox etiam consulatum petere ausus, cum esset omni flagitiorum scelerumque conscientia mersus nec melior 15 illi res familiaris quam mens foret, adgregatis simillimis sibi interimere Caesarem statuit, ut quo saluo saluus esse non

4 poterat, eo sublato moreretur. quippe ita se mores habent ⟨ut⟩ publica quisque ruina malit occidere quam sua proteri et idem passurus minus conspici. neque hic prioribus in 20 occultando felicior fuit, abditusque carcere cum consciis facinoris mortem dignissimam uita sua obiit.

92 Praeclarum excellentis uiri factum C. Sentii Saturnini

2 (circa ea tempora consulis) ne fraudetur memoria. aberat in ordinandis Asiae orientisque rebus Caesar, circumferens ter- 25 rarum orbi praesentia sua pacis suae bona. tum Sentius, forte et solus et absente Caesare consul, cum alia prisca seueritate summaque constantia, uetere consulum more ac †seueritate gessisset, protraxisset publicanorum fraudes,

---

1 oppresso *Gelenius*   2 Phraates *Krause*: Phrahates *P*: Prahates *A*   3 uiro *PA*: uino *Burman*: iure *Orelli*   8 hoc ante *PA*, *corr. Gelenius*   iniissent *A*   14 continuarent *A*   15 omnium *Burman*   ceu sentina *Heinsius*   19 ⟨ut⟩ *Burer*   20 et *om. A*   ⟨inter⟩ idem passuros *Stanger*   21 carceri *PA*, *corr. Krause*   24 in *secl. Heinsius*   26 sua *secl. Ruhnken*   28 ueterum *Ruhnken*   28-9 uetere ... seueritate *secl. Krause*   29 seueritate *PA, obelo notaui*: ac seu. *secl. Ruhnken*: ac sanctitate *Laurent*

punisset auaritiam, redegisset in aerarium pecunias publicas, tum in comitiis habendis praecipuum egit consulem:
3 nam et quaesturam petentes, quos indignos iudicauit, profiteri uetuit, et cum id facturos se perseuerarent, consularem,
4 si in campum descendissent, uindictam minatus est; et 5
Egnatium florentem fauore publico, sperantemque ut praeturam aedilitati ita consulatum praeturae se iuncturum,
profiteri uetuit, et cum id non obtinuisset, iurauit, etiam si
factus esset consul suffragiis populi, tamen se eum non
5 renuntiaturum. quod ego factum cuilibet ueterum consulum 10
gloriae comparandum reor – nisi quod naturaliter audita
uisis laudamus libentius et praesentia inuidia, praeterita
ueneratione prosequimur et his nos obrui, illis instrui cred-
imus.

93 Ante triennium fere quam Egnatianum scelus erumperet, 15
circa Murenae Caepionisque coniurationis tempus, abhinc
annos LII, M. Marcellus, sororis Augusti Octauiae filius –
quem homines ita (si quid accidisset Caesari) successorem
potentiae eius arbitrabantur futurum, ut tamen id per M.
Agrippam securo ei posse contingere non existimarent – 20
magnificentissimo   munere   aedilitatis   edito   decessit
admodum iuuenis, sane (ut aiunt) ingenuarum uirtutum
laetusque animi et ingenii fortunaeque, in quam alebatur,
2 capax. post cuius obitum Agrippa, qui sub specie minis-
teriorum principalium profectus in Asiam (ut fama 25
loquitur) ob tacitas cum Marcello offensiones praesenti se
subduxerat tempori, reuersus inde filiam Caesaris Iuliam,
quam in matrimonio Marcellus habuerat, duxit uxorem,
feminam neque sibi neque rei publicae felicis uteri.

1 redegisset *Stanger*: regessisset *PA*   3 quod *A*   3–4 profiteri *om.*
A   9 eum *P*: cum *A*   10 cuiuslibet *Herel*   13 illis ... his
Bothe   17 LII *Woodman*: L *PA*   20 securo *Gelenius*: securos *PA*:
secure *Rhenanus*   22 ut aiunt ing. *BA*: ing. ut aiunt *P*

COMMENTARY

.

41–43 CAESAR'S CHARACTER AND EARLY CAREER

By 59 B.C., when he became consul at the age of 40, Julius Caesar had earned distinction as a soldier, politician and orator. Remarkably, however, V. has now (41.1) reached that year without making any reference at all to Caesar except in passing in a literary excursus (36.2). There is thus a considerable body of material on which he has to catch up, and he does so in chh. 41–3 with a (somewhat idealised) sketch of Caesar's character and a survey of his career to date. This section, by explicitly suspending the main narrative (cf. 41.1 *morari*), turns the spotlight fully on Caesar and establishes him as the dominant personality of the next fifteen years (44–59.1 in V.'s text).[1]

41.1 consulatus C. Caesaris   For his consulship in 59 see *MRR* 2.187–8; for Caesar in general see Gelzer, *Caes.* and Weinstock *passim*. Bibliographical material will be found esp. in Gesche and Christ 205–18. On his early career see Strasburger, who provides (7–23) in schematic form a list of parallel sources for the events of Caesar's life up to 59 B.C. and attempts (72ff.) to establish the relationship between these various sources (V. and Plut. are said to derive from the same pro-Caesarian tradition).[2]

---

[1] Starr (1978), 55–68, has argued against there being any 'biographical divisions' in V.'s work on the grounds that they fall 'prey to the problem of overlap' (65) and that they are 'simplistic' and do not 'accurately reflect the complexities of the narrative' (134 n. 1). It is of course true that Pompey lives on until ch. 53, but the elaborate introduction of Caesar at 41.1 and the retrospective survey of his career in chh. 41–3 suggest to me that V. has gone out of his way to indicate that Pompey's moment has now passed and that until 59.1 we are to regard Caesar as the dominant figure. Caesar's death in ch. 56 means that no one overlaps with Augustus in 59.2–93; and Starr himself admits that the biographical division at ch. 94 'is correct, since Tiberius does dominate the history from that point on' (66 n. 2). I therefore see no reason to change the view I expressed in *TN* 41. [Starr prefers to divide Book 2 into three 'epochs' which are 'moral not political' (2.1–89 the age of immorality, 89–125 the restoration of the republic, 126–31 the reign of Tiberius) and within which other divisions (e.g. the civil wars at 49–89) may be subsumed.]

[2] 'Aus einer ursprünglichen Materialmasse (Biograph A) sind zwei verschiedene Überlieferungszweige herausgewachsen; ich nenne den Mittelsmann für Sueton und den Autor *de viris illustribus* Biograph B, den für Velleius und Plutarch Biograph C ... nötigen die Abweichungen, die zwischen Plutarch und Vell. bei gleichem Kern und gleicher Tendenz bestehen, zwischen einer älteren Tradition (Vell. = C₁) und ihrer Überarbeitung (Plut. = C₂) zu unterscheiden. Die C-Tradition ist einheitlich caesarfreundlich' (73–4).

51

qui scribenti manum iniicit et . . . morari cogit   The clause echoes Cic. *Rosc. Com.* 16 'ipsa mihi ueritas manum iniecit et paulisper consistere et commorari cogit', cf. also Val. Max. 4.1.15 'ad externa iam mihi exempla transire conanti M. Bibulus [cos. 59 B.C.] . . . manus inicit'. For the legal expr. *manum inicere* cf. 99.3n., adding D. Daube, *The Classical Tradition* (*Studies . . . Caplan*, ed. L. Wallach, 1966), 226ff.; *scribenti* may perhaps be regarded as a substantival present part., for which see J. N. Adams, *Glotta* 51 (1973), 132.

festinantem is an allusion to the summary form of V.'s work, which requires brief or 'speedy' writing: see 108.2n., Woodman (1975), 278–87, Starr (1981), 170. *morari* and the noun *mora* are natural words to use in the context of *festinatio*; but they seem also to be used technically of expansions of the narrative or digressions (see 117.1, Ov. *Met.* 3.225 'quosque referre mora est' [a joke: a 19-line expansion has just preceded]; Woodman (1975), 284 n. 1; Lausberg 1.220 top, 246, 367). Here in V. the digression consists of the retrospective survey of Caesar's early career which ends at 43.4 (cf. 44.1n.).

Lana remarks (213) that from the moment of Caesar's entry into V.'s narrative 'chiaro si delinea il piano dell'opera': henceforward through the Caesarian, Augustan and Tiberian sections of the work there is a 'moto ascensionale' which culminates in the principate of Tiberius himself.

nobilissima Iuliorum genitus familia   'The Julii were one of the original patrician families, but one that had so far left little mark upon history' (Gelzer, *Caes.* 19). Caesar's father was C. Iulius Caesar, praetor *c.* 92 and proconsul in Africa *c.* 91 (*MRR* 2.17, 22); the latter's brother Sextus was consul in 91 (*MRR* 2.20). Caesar himself preferred to emphasise his descent from Venus, grandmother of Iulus the legendary ancestor of the Iulii: she appears with Anchises on the coins of 47/46 (*RRC* 1.471 no. 458), and see in general Weinstock ch. 2 'The ancestral tradition'.

quod inter omnes antiquissimos constabat   Another echo of Cic.: *Orat.* 218 'ut inter omnes constat antiquos'. The echo makes Acidalius' *constat* look attractive but also suggests that there is nothing wrong with *antiquissimos*. For the equation antiquity = authority cf. e.g. Liv. 2.40.10 'Fabium, longe antiquissimum auctorem'.

uigore animi acerrimus   'animi uigore praestantissimum arbitror genitum Caesarem dictatorem' (Plin. *NH* 7.91). References to a man's *genus*, *forma* and *animus* are of course standard in character sketches (*TN* 41); so too are allusions to his age (below 2 *XVIII annos*, 3 *postea . . . iuuenis*), and the resumptive use of *hic* (44.1n.). For the importance of the *forma* of a ruler see 94.2n. *uigore animi*, also at Virg. *Aen.* 9.611, Ov. *Her.* 16.51 (F.), has a Livian tone (cf. 5.18.5, 9.16.12, 10.13.6, 28.6 [35.1.8, 38.17.18]).

munificentia effusissimus 'Caesar beneficiis ac munificentia magnus habebatur' (Sall. C. 54.2, but later [3] 'Caesar dando . . . gloriam adeptus est'). See in general Kloft 47 and n. 43; P. Kranz, *Beneficium im politischen Sprachgebrauch der ausgehenden Republik* (diss. Münster, 1964), 128–34; also 126.4n.

I have printed Gelenius' *munificentia* since *effusus* seems not to be found with the gen.; for the sense of the adj. cf. Cic. *Cael.* 13 'quis in largitione effusior?'. For *super . . . euectus*, below, cf. Plin. *NH* 34.38 'euecta supra humanam fidem ars', 56.1n., 130.1n.

magnitudine cogitationum The allusion is to political and military vision: cf. Tac. *D.* 21.5 'concedamus sane C. Caesari ut propter magnitudinem cogitationum et occupationes rerum minus in eloquentia effecerit quam diuinum eius ingenium postulabat'. For *magnitudo c.* elsewhere cf. Sen. *D.* 9.1.14.

celeritate bellandi A quality desired by all generals (cf. 129.3n.) but one for which Caesar was famous: 51.2 'sua . . . celeritate', *Bell. Afr.* 73.1 'Caesar . . . ex pristina bellandi consuetudine celeritateque excesserat', Cic. *Att.* 7.22.1, 8.9.4, 10.9.1 'Caesariana celeritas', *Marc.* 5, Plin. *NH* 7.91, App. *BC* 2.149. *patientia periculorum*, below, is another stock characteristic of the ideal general, cf. 79.1n., 105.1n., 114.1–3 intro. n.

Magno illi Alexandro . . . simillimus More or less explicit comparisons between Caesar and Alexander are at e.g. Suet. *Iul.* 7.1, App. *BC* 2.149, Dio 37.52.2, Strabo 13.1.27. That Caesar consciously modelled himself on Alex., as Strabo suggests, has been recently argued by Michel 67–107 but contradicted by Weippert 105–92 and P. Green, *AJAH* 3 (1978), 1–26 (with long bibliog.). On Alex. see further 82.4n.; for his drunkenness and anger cf. e.g. Liv. 9.18.4–6 ('. . . uini amor . . . acrior . . . trux ac praeferuida ira'); Hamilton on Plut. *Alex.* 23.1, 50.8; for Caesar's sobriety cf. Suet. *Iul.* 53.

41.2 qui . . . et somno et cibo in uitam non in uoluptatem uteretur The subjunctive expresses a characteristic: 'the kind of man who . . .' (so Rockwood). It was a topos that the ideal general keeps to a frugal diet (114.3n.). It was a tenet of Stoic philosophy that food is taken for nourishment rather than pleasure: Cic. *Off.* 1.106 'uictus cultusque corporis ad ualetudinem referatur et ad uires, non ad uoluptatem'. Thus Artemidorus, who 'nihil in cibo in potu uoluptatibus tribuat' (Plin. *Ep.* 3.11.6), was likely to appeal to his father-in-law, the Stoic Musonius Rufus, who held that προσήκει ἐσθίειν ἡμῖν ἵνα ζῶμεν οὐχ ἵνα ἡδώμεθα (fr. 18B, p. 102.7–8 Hense, referred to our passage by Ruhnken in his Addenda) and αἱρεῖσθαι σῖτον οὐχ ἵνα ἥδηται ἀλλ' ἵνα τρέφηται (p. 101.16–17 H). Such beliefs naturally became topoi of popular philosophy (see A. C. van Geytenbeek, *Musonius Rufus and Greek Diatribe* (1963), 106–8) and influenced the way in which the frugal diet of ideal generals was described: Liv. 21.4.6 'cibi potionisque desiderio naturali, non uoluptate modus finitus (of Hannibal, cf. Just. 32.4.10), Luc. 2.384 'huic epulae uicisse famem' (of the Stoic Cato). See too Sall. *J.* 89.8 'cibus illis aduorsum famem atque sitim, non lubidini neque luxuriae erat'; as Verhaak 57 notes, the opposite topos is at Sall. *C.* 13.3, where see Vretska; also below, 88.2n. (§ 3), on the morality of *somnus*.

somnus and *cibus* are commonly joined (*TLL* 3.1043.84–1044.4); for the order as found in P cf. Ov. *Met.* 14.424 'somnique cibique', Tac. *G.* 15.1 'somno ciboque' (Cic. *Sest.* 138 'somno et conuiuiis', Liv. 4.37.2 'somno epulisque', 23.18.12 'somnus et uinum et epulae', and cf. Ov. *Fast.* 4.332).

cum fuisset C. Mario . . . Cinnae gener The younger Marius (cos. 82) was Caesar's cousin, the latter's aunt Julia having married the elder Marius. Sulla allegedly said 'Caesari multos Marios inesse' (Suet. *Iul.* 1.3, Plut. *Caes.* 1.2). Caesar's wife was Cornelia, Cinna's daughter. These relationships with *both* of Sulla's principal opponents (this is the force of *atque idem*) put Caesar at risk in 82; hence *cum* with *fuisset* must be causal, although with *habuissetque* below it seems to be concessive (perhaps influenced by the intervening *cum . . . dimisisset*). For *Mario . . . coniunctissimus* cf. Lentul. in Cic. *Fam.* 12.14.7 'coniunctissimus sanguine Antoniis' (F.).

M. Piso consularis M. Pupius Piso Frugi Calpurnianus was not consul until 61 (*MRR* 2.178); *consularis* is thus anachronistic. For *in . . . gratiam*, below, cf. Liv. 28.21.4, 39.12, 35.2.6, 39.26.12, 40.17.2, 42.43.2, and then in Sen. *Contr.* 9.8.3, Curt. 6.11.15, 7.5.28, Plin. *Pan.* 7.4, Tac. *H.* 3.78.2, Suet. *Tib.* 49.1, Just. 38.5.8 (F.).

habuissetque fere XVIII annos eo tempore quo Sulla rerum potitus est Sulla became dictator late in 82 (*MRR* 2.66–7). It is generally accepted that Caesar was born in 100 B.C., probably on 13 July (see Gelzer, *Caes.* 1 n. 1, Gesche 11–13, cf. 236–7). But Mommsen's arguments in favour of 102 were supported by Rice Holmes, *Rep.* 1.436–42, and this date has recently been canvassed by Sumner, *Orators* 134–7.

rerum potiri 'belongs to the vocabulary of Roman politics' (Shackleton Bailey on Cic. *Fam.* 1.8(19).4, quoting *Acad.* 2.126, *Cat.* 2.19, Nep. *Att.* 9.6, Lucr. 2.13, *RG* 34.1; F. E. Adcock, *CQ* 1 (1951), 130).

magis ministris . . . quam ipso conquirentibus The opposite impression is given by Suet. *Iul.* 1.3, Plut. *Caes.* 1.2. For *conquirentibus* cf. 22.4 'cum ad mortem conquireretur'; for *minister + adiutor* cf. Plin. *Ep.* 6.9.2; for *adiutor partium* cf. 74.3, 76.1. For *indutus + accus.*, below, cf. *TLL* 7.1.1267.1ff.; for *dissimilis fortunae* cf. Ov. *Tr.* 1.5.16, though without V.'s *comparatio compendiaria* (viz. 'different from ⟨that of⟩ his station in life'); such brachylogy is common after *similis* and *dissimilis*, cf. K–S 2.566–7;

also W. B. Anderson on Liv. 9.10.3. For *elabi* + abl. cf. K–S 1.370. For *mutata ueste*, 'part of the stock-in-trade of escape stories', see T. E. V. Pearce, *CQ* 20 (1970), 319–20, who refers to Nisbet on Cic. *Pis.* 92.

41.3 spatium, quo ab his retentus est Cf. Suet. *Iul.* 4.1 'hibernis iam mensibus . . . mansitque apud eos . . . prope XL dies'; Plut. *Caes.* 2.2 specifies 38 days. The winter in question is that of 75/74, when Caesar was 25. See also 42.3n.

terrori uenerationique According to Plut. *Caes.* 2.1–2, Caesar treated the pirates with contempt, demanded that they keep quiet when he went to sleep, shared in their sport, read to them his poems and speeches, and was generally treated by them as if he were a royal guest. For *uenerationi . . . esset* cf. Plin. *NH* 34.45 (F.); for the combination of the two nouns cf. Plin. *Ep.* 8.24.6 'male terrore ueneratio adquiritur'.

si narrari uerbis speciosis non potest I.e. both *excalceare* and *discingere* are *uerba sordida*. The choice of words (*delectus uerborum*, ἐκλογὴ ὀνομάτων) and the avoidance of *uerba sordida* greatly exercised ancient writers both in theory and in practice: see esp. [Long.] *Subl.* 43, where Russell notes as follows. 'The principle that some words are low and to be avoided in formal writing is of the greatest importance in ancient . . . literature. It is the negative side of the doctrine that the use of certain words actually imparts dignity and distinction. Both notions rest on the concept of propriety . . . The qualities which blackball words from "good" literature are (i) obscenity, (ii) association with the common material things of life, (iii) technicality.' Now neither *excalceare* nor *discingere* appears to be intrinsically *sordidum* (see *TLL* s.vv.);[1] each must therefore belong to the second category mentioned by Russell, who illustrates the theory by quoting Arist. *Poet.* 1458a18ff. and exemplifies the Roman attitude to *uerba sordida* by comparing our passage of V. with that of Albucius Silus in Sen. *Contr.* 7 *praef.* 3, whose view is 'more catholic'. Yet if we compare Albucius in his turn with Vibius Rufus at *Contr.* 9.2.25 ('antiquo genere diceret: belle cessit illi sententia sordidioris notae "praetor . . . soleas poposcit"'), we see that 'the use of *uerba sordida* like *soleae* . . . was already being rejected by the modernists at the very beginning of the 'Silver' age of Latin prose' (J. Fairweather, *Seneca the Elder* (1981), 192, who has a helpful discussion of the whole subject). Now I have no doubt that V. was as sensitive as his contemporaries to *uerba sordida* and that he was as concerned as other historians to use in his work *uerba speciosa* which befitted the nobility of his theme (see Lana 263–4); on the other hand, his apologia here, while revealing his awareness of the stylistic convention, is perhaps caused less by his regard for verbal purity than by a desire for rhetorical effect. These are 'shock tactics'.

---

[1] There seems to be no evidence that *discingi* is a euphemism for *cacare*.

For general discussions of *delectus uerborum* see e.g. W. Kroll, *Studien zum Verständnis der röm. Literatur* (1924), 108ff. (refers to V.) and 247–8; L. R. Palmer, *The Latin Language*⁵ (1966), 95ff., 118ff.; Lausberg 2.90–1 § 592, 2.389–90 § 1074.2; Brink on Hor. *AP* 46/5–72 (intro. n.). I know of nothing on its detailed application in historiography, although Tac. notoriously refused to call a spade a spade (Syme, *Tac.* 344–5; see further Goodyear, *Comm. Tac.* 1.342–3); there are, however, some brief remarks in Avenarius 61–3 and Herkommer 112–15.

For V.'s expr. cf. Quint. 1.5.3 'uni uerbo uitium saepius quam uirtus inest. licet enim dicamus aliquod . . . speciosum', Hor. *Epist.* 2.2.116 'speciosa uocabula rerum' (Pluygers suggested *re* for *uel* in V.'s text).

in hoc scilicet ne, si quando . . . uariaret, suspectus his . . . foret I infer from the presence of *scilicet* that this is V.'s own explanation of Caesar's unusual behaviour; yet there are objections to it. First, it is difficult to see why the pirates should become suspicious if Caesar simply changed his clothes – unless, as Prof. Goodyear notes, they might have supposed that he was stripping off to escape by swimming. Secondly, Caesar's alleged desire not to vary his routine is hard to reconcile with *ita se . . . apud eos gessit ut pariter his terrori uenerationique esset* above and with *quid et quoties ausus sit* below (42.1). I can only think that Caesar was engaged in a war of nerves with his captors: by always doing the unexpected (i.e. by behaving arrogantly and energetically one moment, and by not changing his clothes the next) he hoped to retain a psychological advantage over them. Such behaviour would presumably mean that the pirates watched him all the more closely and thus made escape less likely; but Caesar had no wish to try and escape, for an unsuccessful attempt would jeopardise the revenge he intended to have on the pirates as soon as he was ransomed (cf. 42.2–3). For *ex solito* cf. Sen. *Ep.* 78.12 (Fletcher; *e coniect.* at Prop. 1.17.3).

oculis tantummodo 'haud animo' (Krause); 'he was not bound' (Rockwood). The former would very well suit the explanation of Caesar's behaviour which I have just put forward, but the latter is probably what V. intended. See further last n.

42.1 longum est narrare . . . euasuri uiri There are several difficulties in the paradosis of this passage, which Mommsen (in Haase x) found necessary to rewrite. They are: the precise reference of *longum . . . ausus sit*, the asyndeton and apparent change of subject at *quanto . . . destituerit*, the meaning of *eius* (= *Caesaris* or *magistratus?*), and *motu* (PA: *metu* Gelenius). I shall outline two main approaches.

(1) Ruhnken understood *longum . . . ausus sit* to refer to Caesar's activities at the start of the third Mithridatic war (74 B.C., cf. Suet. *Iul.* 4.2) and proposed a lacuna to fill out the sense. He also accepted Gelenius' *metu*.

Krause however objected to the insertion of an alien and later episode into the otherwise unified pirate story (41.3–42.3). Krause nevertheless wished to retain a lacuna (after *sit*, eliminating the asyndeton and perhaps easing the change of subject) and *metu*; he also considered deleting *eius* (= *Caesaris*) to avoid the awkward juxtaposition.

(2) Kritz agreed with Ruhnken's interpretation of *longum . . . ausus sit* but made it a complete sentence. He then made *quanto . . . euasuri uiri* a single new sentence in which *quanto . . . destituerit* depends on *documentum*, the subject of *destituerit* is Caesar, *motu* is retained, and *eius* agrees with *magistratūs*. This radical proposal eliminates the stylistic difficulties and is attractive precisely because of its simplicity; but there is a significant objection to Kritz's formulation. Kritz says that *documentum* must refer to what follows in 2–3; but while 2–3 is certainly an 'example of Caesar's greatness' (*documentum tanti . . . uiri*), it is not an 'example of how Caesar frustrated the governor of Asia': it simply *is* how Caesar frustrated him. Thus *quanto . . . destituerit* cannot depend on *documentum*.

It has however been pointed out to me by Mr DuQuesnay that this objection may be avoided if we regard *illud* as referring to *quanto . . . destituerit*, and *documentum . . . uiri* as being in apposition to *illud*. The passage will now run: 'It would take too long to describe all of Caesar's many bold initiatives; ⟨but⟩ as an illustration of his imminent greatness I may relate how far he, by a manoeuvre of his own, frustrated the designs of the magistrate of the Roman people who was in charge of Asia' (alternatively, *magistratus* may be regarded as nomin. in apposition to *qui*). On this interpretation, *conata* looks forward to *quod cum ille . . . dixisset*, and *motu suo* to *incredibili celeritate . . . suffixit cruci*, at 3 below; the two sentences form a chiasmus (*longum est narrare quid . . .*; *quanto opere . . ., illud referatur*); and for this sense of *motus* see *OLD* s.v. 5. However, I still feel, for the reasons given above under (1), that the first sentence *longum est . . . ausus sit* is unlikely to have any reference beyond the pirate story. The fact is that V.'s readers were brought up on a diet of pirate adventures in the schools of declamation (see Winterbottom, *Sen.*, General Index s.v. 'pirates'), and they no doubt anticipated a full treatment of an episode in Caesar's career which naturally 'lent itself to embellishment' (Gelzer, *Caes.* 24 n. 2); but such a treatment was of course outside the scope of V.'s summary work: therefore he characteristically refuses to deal fully with all aspects of this conventionally attractive topic (*longum est narrare quid . . . ausus sit*, cf. 96.3n.), promising instead to mention only one (further) part of the story to illustrate Caesar's greatness (*illud referatur*, cf. 67.1n.).

For the use of *destituo* cf. *TLL* 5.1.763.54ff., 65ff.; for *euasuri uiri* cf. 94.3n.; for *documentum . . . uiri* cf. Suet. *Galba* 14.1 'd. principis', Amm. 15.7.1 'iudicis d.' (both in plur.).

42.2 contracta classe et priuatus et tumultuaria ⟨manu⟩ Ellis retained the paradosis ('though he was himself in no public position, and the fleet was raised for an emergency': *Hermath.* 10 (1897–9), 11), but the hyperbaton, interrupted by *priuatus*, seems to me impossible.[1] Oudendorp emended to *priuata*, but given the surrounding abll., how could this have been 'corrupted' to *priuatus*? Scriner transposed *contracta classe* to follow *tumultuaria*, and F. Rühl (*Phil. Woch.* 18 (1898), 1598) suggested that *et* . . . *et* hid scribal indications that *priuatus* and *tumultuaria* should be transposed (this is accepted by Stegmann); yet, curiously, there seems to be no parallel for the phrase *tumultuaria classis*. We are thus left with Cludius' *et priuatim et tumultuarie* and Halm's ⟨*manu*⟩. The latter seems to me preferable: it is relatively simple and easily paralleled (Liv. 22.21.4, 31.2.6, Curt. 4.16.24, Tac. *A.* 15.3.2).

multosque mortales cepit Perhaps borrowed from Sall. *J.* 20.3 'multos mortales . . . cepit' (Ruhnken), though *multi mortales* is found elsewhere (Naev. Cato, Claud. Quadr. Plaut. Varr. Cic. Liv.); for discussion of the phrase see Gell. 13.29, Ogilvie on Liv. 1.9.8, Lebek 255, J. Marouzeau, *Traité de stylistique latine*[2] (1946), 199–202.

laetus at 3 below could in theory govern either *expeditionis* (Acidalius) or *triumpho* (Manutius); I think the latter is correct because *triumpho* used absol. normally refers to a real triumph (e.g. Liv. 30.45.2).

42.3 Iunium ⟨Iun⟩cum (idem enim Asiam eamque obtinebat) Almost everything here has been questioned, but thanks to C. Nipperdey and esp. A. M. Ward we can now see that the difficulties are not great. Ward has recently established ('Caesar and the pirates II', *AJAH* 2 (1977), 26–36) that the governor of Asia in 75/74 was M. Iunius Iuncus, as others (cf. *MRR* 2.98, 100 [n. 6]) had already supposed. Nipperdey, who first emended *Iunium cum* to *Iuncum* as if the error were dittography (*Philol.* 6 (1851), 377 = *Opuscula* (1877), 448–9), subsequently proposed *Iunium ⟨Iun⟩cum* as if the error were haplography (*RhM* 19 (1864), 378 = *Opusc.* 326). The latter, self-evidently correct, was rightly supported by Ward, whose detailed arguments (p. 28) should be consulted. Ward also suggests a timetable for Caesar's movements in 75/74 (p. 31).

For *eamque* cf. e.g. Liv. 4.57.6 'collegas eumque intuentibus'. For *mandatis custodiae*, above, cf. Cic. *Cat.* 4.10 'uinculisque mandare'.

sequebatur inuidia inertiam Though the sentiment and the manner of expression have a proverbial air (cf. e.g. Sall. *J.* 55.3 'post gloriam inuidiam sequi', Vell. 1.9.6 'eminentis fortunae comes inuidia'; Otto 176), both *inertiam* and *inuidia* have a precise reference. The former refers to *se facturum negasset* immediately above, and the latter to *uenditurumque*

---

[1] Such passages as Tac. *Agr.* 25.4 'diuiso et ipse in tres partes exercitu incessit' are no real support because such hyperbata seem restricted to the phrase *et ipse* (see Ogilvie ad loc.) and because we would still have to account for the second *et* in V.'s text.

captiuos dixisset: Iuncus, jealous of the fact that Caesar had pocketed the pirates' spoils for himself (Plut. *Caes*. 2.3–4 ἐποφθαλμιῶντος), hoped to make some money himself by selling the pirates as slaves.

redderetur epistula Kritz preferred this reading because of the singular *ulli*, I think rightly. For *incredibili celeritate*, above, cf. *TLL* 3.755.11ff. (Cic. Caes. [4 exs.] Liv. Sen. elder Plin. Suet. Amm.).

43.1 pontifex factus erat C. Aurelius Cotta, Caesar's uncle and the consul of 75, died in 73 and was replaced by Caesar at the instigation of his mother Aurelia: see Gelzer, *Caes*. 25 and Weinstock 30, both with further refs.

paene puer . . . flamen Dialis creatus Two problems are connected with this statement. (1) It is stated by Tac. *A*. 3.58.2 and Dio 54.36.1 that L. Cornelius Merula, who died in 87 B.C. (cf. 22.2), was the last *flamen Dialis* until 11 B.C. Now since entry to this priesthood involved the twin procedures of co-optation and inauguration, it follows that the boy Caesar was co-opted but not inaugurated; as a consequence it has been assumed (e.g. by L. R. Taylor, 'Caesar's early career', *CP* 36 (1941), 114–15) that Suet. has the truth of the matter with his statement *flamen Dialis destinatus* (*Iul*. 1.1) and that V. with *creatus* has not. Yet *creatus*, as Lipsius seems to have sensed, could be used as a synonym for *cooptatus* (cf. Liv. 27.36.5 'in locum M. Marcelli P. Ael. Paetus augur creatus inauguratusque', 29.38.6 'Ti. Vet. Philo flamen Martialis in locum M. Aem. Regilli . . . creatus inauguratusque'). *creatus* therefore does not conflict with Tac. and Dio; and *amisisset* below = 'lost ⟨the chance of⟩ the priesthood' (when Sulla became dictator in 82). (2) V.'s statement that Caesar was co-opted as *flamen* by Marius and Cinna suggests that the event took place early in 86 B.C., since the two men were joint consuls between 1 and 13 Jan., when Marius died. Caesar would then have been 13, assuming he was born in 100 (41.2n). Yet Suet. states that he was co-opted as *flamen* in the year after his father's death and that his father died when Caesar was 15 (*Iul*. 1.1 'annum agens sextum decimum');[1] that would place the priesthood in 85/84 B.C., since Suet. also believes that Caesar was born in 100 (cf. *Iul*. 88). I can see no way of reconciling these two statements; but since Merula died in 87 (above), V.'s date does seem far more likely (so too Gelzer, *Caes*. 20, Weinstock 30).

merito . . . infestis These words are also coupled at Liv. 8.39.10, Val. Max. 1.1.14 (*infensus* at Liv. 34.20.3, 36.14.9). For *effusissimum* below cf. Hor. *Epist*. 1.11.26, Mela 1.32, 3.1, to which F. adds Plin. *NH* 16.2, Val.

---

[1] Prof. Goodyear however notes that *sextum* may be a corruption of *quartum* (*XIV* > *XVI*).

Fl. 4.714; the word contrasts with the smallness of Caesar's craft (Krause).

43.2 alterutri se fortunae parans   Perhaps an heroic note, cf. Virg. *Aen.* 2.61 'in utrumque paratus' (Krause), itself echoed by Lact. *Mort. Pers.* 44.[1] For *frustratum . . . uisum* below cf. *oculos frustrari* at [Ov.] *Hal.* 22, Ap. *Met.* 2.22.3.

43.3 Reliqua eius acta in urbe   I.e. in addition to those already mentioned at 1 above and 41.2. The main verb comes at the very end of the paragraph.

Dolabellae accusatio   In 77 Caesar prosecuted Cn. Cornelius Dolabella for extortion in his province of Macedonia (*MRR* 2.89). His performance, of which Cicero was an auditor (*Brut.* 317), won him an outstanding oratorical reputation (*Brut.* 261, Suet. *Iul.* 55.1, Tac. *D.* 34.7, Plut. *Caes.* 3.2): hence *nobilissima . . . accusatio* (a Ciceronian phrase, cf. *Off.* 2.47). Dolabella was nevertheless acquitted: hence *maior . . . fauor quam . . . solet* (where *in ea* = 'in the case of' or 'during the course of' the prosecution).[2] For Dol. see further *RE* 4.1297 = Cornelius 134 (Münzer).

contentionesque ciuiles cum Q. Catulo . . .   'Not surprisingly, Caesar found himself at odds with some of Rome's more conservative senators, in particular with Q. Catulus, the most distinguished of aristocrats. When Caesar sought to revitalise the memory of Marius, Catulus raised strenuous objection, though in vain [Plut. *Caes.* 6.4]. Caesar's election as *pontifex maximus* in 63 came at the expense of Catulus, who did not forgive or forget [Plut. *Caes.* 7.1–3, Dio 37.37.2, Sall. *Cat.* 49.2]. The two men clashed again in senatorial debate on the fate of the Catilinarian plotters [Cic. *Att.* 12.21.1, Plut. *Caes.* 8.1, *Cic.* 21.3]. Catulus endeavored even to implicate Caesar in the conspiracy itself [Sall. *Cat.* 49.1–2, Plut. *Caes.* 7.3]. And the latter retaliated in 62 by charging Catulus with failure to carry out a public commission [Cic. *Att.* 2.24.3, Suet. *Iul.* 15, Dio 37.44.1]. The friction and bitterness between them proved implacable' (Gruen 77). In addition, the two men had found themselves on opposite sides over the Gabinian law in 67 (cf. 31.2–32.2, Plut. *Pomp.* 25.4–6; Seager, *Pomp.* 33–5).

Since two of the above mentioned clashes are mentioned specifically by V. in the phrases *et ante praeturam . . . senatus princeps* and *et restituta . . . monumenta C. Marii* below, I suspect that *contentionesque . . . celeberrimae* is meant to embrace all Caesar's battles with Catulus and that the two subsequent phrases are illustrative: 'his celebrated confrontations with

---

[1] I owe the latter ref. to Dr E. L. Harrison.
[2] For the former use of *in* cf. 100.5, where I believe Purser's emendation is almost guaranteed by Hor. *S.* 1.2.64–5 'Villius in Fausta . . . | . . . poenas dedit'.

Catulus . . . and in particular Catulus' defeat in the pontifical election and Caesar's restoration of Marius' monuments'. Krause however argues from the phrase '*ante* praeturam uictus . . . Q. Catulus' below that 'contentionesque . . . celeberrimae' refers to Caesar's confrontation with Catulus *during* his praetorship, viz. the accusation of maladministration which he levelled against Catulus in 62 concerning the latter's commission to rebuild the temple of Capitoline Jupiter.

uictus . . . Q. Catulus For his defeat by Caesar in 63 cf. Gelzer, *Caes.* 46–7, Weinstock 31, Rice Holmes, *Rep.* 2.241–2, 252–3, *MRR* 2.171–2 (n. 3).

senatus princeps So too Cic. *Pis.* 6 'Q. Catulus, princeps huius ordinis'. On the position itself see J. Suolahti, *Arctos* 7(1972), 207ff.

43.4 restituta . . . monumenta C. Marii In 65, cf. Gelzer, *Caes.* 38, *MRR* 2.158. *aduersante . . . nobilitate* is of course an allusion to Catulus (see above).

simulque reuocati . . . proscriptorum liberi The evidence on this matter is complicated. Several sources state that as dictator in 49 Caesar restored to the sons of the proscribed the right to stand for office (e.g. Suet. *Iul.* 41.2, Plut. *Caes.* 37.1, Dio 41.18.2). It is also stated (Dio 37.25.3–4) that the tribunes of 63 proposed such a restoration but were successfully thwarted by Cicero; and Cic. himself refers to his success at *Pis.* 4, *Att.* 2.1.3, *Leg. Agr.* 2.10, and cf. Quint. 11.1.85 for the contents of the speech.

How may we square with this evidence V.'s statement *simul reuocati . . . liberi*, where *simul* = 'at the same time as his aedileship' (65 B.C.)? Strasburger (117) suggests that V. has mistakenly transposed to 65 Caesar's successful action of 49 and that V.'s account is therefore 'falsch'. Yet an error of such magnitude seems to me unlikely. Strasburger curiously dismisses the more likely possibility that V. is alluding to the tribunes' motion of 63; yet *simul*, in an abbreviated and retrospective survey such as this, may not unreasonably be taken to include the year 63; and Strasburger himself concedes that Caesar would have sympathised with the tribunes' motion. We may, I think, reasonably infer that V. is alluding to the motion of 63 and that Caesar actively supported it.

reuocati, nevertheless, seems flatly contradicted by the evidence of Cicero himself. The obvious explanation is that V. has, whether intentionally or not, attributed to 63 Caesar's successful action of 49; yet perhaps the truth lies elsewhere. Dio's account of the tribunes' motion of 63 seems to suggest that it was temporarily successful: 37.25.4 ταῦτα μὲν πρός τε τοῦ Κικέρωνος . . . προκαταληφθέντα, πρὶν ἔργον τι ἀπ' αὐτῶν συμβῆναι, ἐπαύθη. Possibly, therefore, V. alludes to this temporary success but refrains from saying that it was short-lived and ineffectual.

praetura quaesturaque ... obita in Hispania Caesar served in Hispania Ulterior as quaestor in 69 and again, after his praetorship in 62, as proconsul in 61–60 (*MRR* 2.132, 184–5). His latter period of office saw victories over the Gallaeci and Lusitani: hence *mirabili uirtute atque industria*. The common combination of these two qualities (cf. e.g. *Rhet. Herenn.* 4.13, Cic. *Leg. Man.* 29, Liv. 38.23.11) marks out Caesar as the 'ideal republican leader', but does not mean that V.'s own attitude to *industria* was one of unqualified admiration: see 88.2n. esp. § 7.

Vetere Antistio Antistius Vetus was propraetor in Hisp. Ult. in 69 (*MRR* 2.132–3); for him see *RE* 1.2258 = Antistius 46 (Klebs). His son was C. Ant. Vetus, who became Caesar's quaestor and eventually cos. suff. in 30 B.C. (*RE* 1.2258 = Antistius 47 (Klebs), *PIR*² 1.146–7 no. 770); and his grandson, 'the present Vetus' (for this use of *huius* cf. 75.3n.), was C. Ant. Vetus, who was pontifex perhaps by 16 B.C. and consul in 6 B.C. (*RE* 1.2258–9 = Antistius 48 (v. Rohden), *PIR*² 1.147–8 no. 771, M. W. Hoffman Lewis, *The Official Priests of Rome under the Julio-Claudians* (1955), 30 no. 16). The latter's sons were Gaius, cos. A.D. 23, and Lucius, cos. suff. a few years later: see respectively *PIR*² 1.148–9 nos. 772 and 775, and Hoffman Lewis, op. cit. 62–3 no. 7 and 32 no. 27. There is a family tree in *RE* 1.2259–60; and see also Lana 152–3.

uiri ... intellegi potest, below, seems = 'a man whose excellence reaches our highest conception of human integrity' (Shipley). For the expr. cf. 1.9.3 'uirum in tantum laudandum in quantum intellegi uirtus potest'; and for *in tantum ... in quantum*, 114.5n.

quo notiora sunt, minus egent stilo Cf. Sulp. *Chron.* 1.45.3 'quae omnia notiora sunt quam ut stilo egeant', Solin. 7.9 'notiora sunt quam ut stilo egeant' (Ruhnken; cf. Klebs 298–9). Cf. also Ascon. p. 80.4C 'egere enarratione'.

44–48 PRELUDE TO CIVIL WAR
(59–50 B.C.)

44 CAESAR'S CONSULSHIP (59 B.C.)

44.1 Hoc igitur consule With this phrase V. resumes the narrative which he suspended at *consulatus C. Caesaris* (41.1) for the 'digression' on Caesar's character and early career (ring composition: see 99.4n.). It was, in addition, conventional to resume a narrative after a character sketch by some form of *hic* (109.5n.).

inita potentiae societas   V., who sees the triumvirate in identical terms at 65.2 (n.), correctly dates the present alliance to Caesar's consulship, when Crassus joined in. Those who assign the alliance to the previous year seem to have been misled by Horace's statement that Pollio began his history *ex Metello consule* (i.e. 60, cf. *C.* 2.1.1 with Nisbet–Hubbard ad loc.; also Gruen 88–9, Seager, *Pomp.* 84 n. 71).

urbi orbique terrarum . . . exitiabilis   The 'belief that the coalition of 59 made civil war inevitable was the standard view in antiquity and still is today' (Lintott 498, quoting Luc. 1.84–5, Plut. *Caes.* 13.3, App. *BC* 2.14, Flor. 2.13.8–11, Dio 37.56.1–2). For *urbi orbique* see below, p. 225 n. 1 (on 85.1).

Several emendations have been proposed for the paradosis *diuerso quoque tempore*, which, if we assume *quŏque* rather than *quōque*, makes little sense. Acidalius, believing that *-i-* had dropped out, wrote *quoique*; Laurent, presumably thinking that a dative had been assimilated into the same case as *diuerso . . . tempore*, wrote *cuique*; Heinsius, wishing to underline the concessive nature of the phrase, suggested *quamquam*; and Haase, believing the word in question to be *quōque*, transposed it to follow *ipsis*, where it makes good sense and produces an expr. comparable to that at 95.2 (*nec non derecta quoque acie*). Of these four suggestions, the first two seem to me simplest and best; and of these two, I prefer to believe that a scribe assimilated a dat. into an abl. rather than that V. produced the archaism *quoique*.

44.2 acta . . . quibus (ut praediximus) multi obtrectabant   Cf. 40.5, where the objections result from *inuidia*, the bane of Pompey's life (cf. 30.3, 31.4, 34.2). Caelius was later to say of the present alliance: 'sic . . . inuidiosa coniunctio non ad occultam recidit obtrectationem sed ad bellum erumpit' (Cic. *Fam.* 8.14(97).2: 50 B.C.). See too next n. and, for *obtrectatio* + *inuidia*, Hellegouarc'h, *VL* 199 n. 4.

For *causam habere ut*, above, cf. Cic. *Quinct.* 78; for *c. h. quod*, below, *Fam.* 12.14.5; *causa* + *quod* is common, cf. *TLL* 3.675.82–676.26.

inuidia . . . in illum relegata   With equal plausibility a similar motive is attributed to Pompey by Cicero and Seneca (respectively *Off.* 3.82 '. . . qui etiam socerum habere uoluit eum cuius ipse audacia potens esset? utile ei uidebatur plurimum posse alterius inuidia' and *Ben.* 5.16.4 'quasi potentiae suae detracturus inuidiam si, quod nulli licere debebat, pluribus licuisset', both passages quoted by Ruhnken). All three authors echo the language of the fifties (e.g. Caes. *BC* 1.7.1 'deprauatum Pompeium queritur (Caesar) inuidia atque obtrectatione laudis suae') but their disagreement over motive is perhaps influenced by the schools of declamation. See esp. Sen. *Contr.* 1.8.10 'inuidiosum esse unum hominem totiens optare omnes honores intercipere; quam periculosa res esset inuidia, quam magnos uiros oppressisset. Hic exempla': we have no record of what the

63

exempla were, but it is easy to imagine the declaimers debating the rival claims of Caesar and Pompey. Similarly the commonplace that Pompey could tolerate no equal (cf. 29.3, 33.3) is used by some authors of Caesar (see Lintott 494). For a more elaborate analysis of motive, with both similarities to and differences from V., cf. Dio 37.54.4–56.5; for *inuidia* as a topic see further Cic. *Part. Or.* 63, Sen. *Contr.* 7.6.20; in general Gudeman on Tac. *D.* 40.1, Otto 176. *inuidia* recurs at 5 and 47.2 below, and its successful avoidance by 'non-triumvirs' is appropriately recorded at the end of the section (48.6).

For *inuidia . . . relegata* cf. 64.2 (n.); for *cedere gloriae*, above, cf. Mart. Cap. 6.640; for *gloriam augere* cf. *Comm. Petit.* 14 'Cn. Pompei', *TLL* 6.2.2065.16–20 and Hellegouarc'h, *VL* 377 n. 8 (esp. Cic., also Nep. Liv. Tac. Suet. Plin.) and ibid. 375 n. 2 for the antithesis *inuidia ∼ gloria*; for *inuidia potentiae* cf. Cic. *Inu.* 1.22. For *animaduerto* (= *intellego, cognosco, cerno*) + acc. and inf. cf. *TLL* 2.76.24–53 (Ter. Varr. Cic. Caes. Sall. Nep. Liv. before V.); for *confirmare uires*, below, cf. Sen. *Ben.* 7.20.1, Sulp. *Chron.* 2.47.4, 49.1 (F. adds Tac. *A.* 3.60 'uim . . . firmans').

44.3 filiam . . . duxit uxorem Pompey had married Julia by early May (Cic. *Att.* 2.17(37).1 'repentina adfinitatis coniunctio').

44.4 legem tulit ut . . . diuideretur Caesar's second agrarian law of the year, which was passed in May (see *MRR* 2.187–8; Brunt, *IM* 312, 314–18; Gruen 398–401) and actively supported by Pompey (Cic. *Att.* 2.16(36).1–2, 17(37).1). As Mr Seager observes, V.'s ignoring of the first agrarian law is striking evidence of his preoccupation with Campania (see also next n. but one).

ius ab his restitutum Vossius said that *his* = Caesar and Pompey, but Krause, wrongly attributing this view to Popma, objected on the grounds that '*ius ciuitatis* . . . a populo solo dari, adimi et restitui possit, et ad latorem legis saltem . . . non ad suasorem tale beneficium referri queat'. I can see no force in this objection. It was Caesar's law and Pompey supported it, as V. says; besides, Pompey personally supervised the operation (as a member of the board mentioned at 45.2) on the spot, or so scholars seem to infer from Cic. *Att.* 2.19(39).3. But there is another objection to *his*: it must, says Kritz, hide a word like *ciuitatis*, since *ius* cannot by itself signify *ius ciuitatis*. Yet *ius* is used in this sense (cf. *TLL* 7.2.687.24ff.: Cic. Sall. Liv. *al.*) and so used at 1.14.1 and, in a passage not unlike the present case, Liv. 35.16.6 'bello superatas a maioribus et stipendiarias ac uectigales factas in antiquum ius repetit'. Nor can it further be objected that in these last two passages the meaning is made clear by the context, since here at 44.2 there is an explicit contrast with *in formam praefecturae redacta*. I therefore believe that *ius ab his* may stand and that *his* = Caesar and Pompey.

64

Popma referred *his* to the colonists; for *ciuitatis* and other suggested emendations see app. crit. For the figure *XX* ⟨*milia*⟩ *ciuium* cf. Suet. *Iul.* 20.3, App. *BC* 2.10. For the phrase *ius . . . restitutum* cf. Ov. *Fast.* 1.626.

post annos circiter CLII quam . . . redacta erat Capua was reduced in 211 B.C.; for its status and administration thereafter see Brunt, *IM* 528–35. V.'s dating discloses both his sense of history (49.1n.) and his interest in the area (see esp. 75–76.1 nn.): contrast Dio 38.7.3 διὰ τοῦτο καὶ ἄποικος τῶν ʿΡωμαίων ἡ Καπύη τότε πρῶτον ἐνομίσθη.

44.5 Bibulus . . . maiore parte anni domi se tenuit By remaining at home for either 11 (Seager, *Pomp.* 190 n. 1) or 8 months of the year (Shackleton Bailey's edn of Cic. *Att.*, vol. 1, Appendix) and by practising *obnuntiatio* (Shackleton Bailey on Cic. *Att.* 2.16(36).2), Bibulus rendered Caesar's actions technically invalid (see further *MRR* 2.187; Gelzer, *Caes.* 78–9). For Bibulus see *RE* 3.1368–70 = Calpurnius 28 (Münzer); *MRR* 2.173, 187–8, 242, 250, 261, 275. For *augere inuidiam* cf. 62.3n.; for *aug. potentiam* cf. Cic. *De Or.* 1.186, Tac. *H.* 3.45.1, *A.* 4.41.2.

decretae . . . Galliae Caesar was given Cisalpine Gaul by the *lex Vatinia* in May 59 and Transalpine Gaul shortly afterwards ʿper senatumʾ (Suet. *Caes.* 22.1): see in general *MRR* 2.190, Gelzer, *Caes.* 86–7.

45 CLODIUS VERSUS CICERO AND CATO (58–56 B.C.)

This section is an excellent illustration of V.'s use of literary allusion. When focussing on Clodius (1), he appropriately echoes Sallust's turbulent narrative; but when referring to Cicero's exile and return (2–3), he echoes Cicero's own speeches from the period in question.

V. has also compared and contrasted the episodes of Cicero and Cato (4n.). ʿIn each story the evil Clodius manages to get a good man sent away, but the good man returns gloriously . . . [Yet Cato's] haughty return is to be contrasted with Cicero's a few lines earlier . . . Both through parallelism and through contrast Vell. has enlivened the two accounts' (Starr (1978), 112 and n. 1).

45.1 nobilis, disertus, audax . . . The third epithet, with its revolutionary connotations (48.3n.), colours the other two in a Tacitean manner: though *nobilis*, Clodius curried favour with the *plebs*; though *disertus*, he turned his eloquence on Cicero and Cato. V.'s whole sketch of Clodius is adapted from that of the troublesome Q. Curius at Sall. *C.* 23.1–3 (see Woodman (1968), 795–6); see too next n. For P. Clodius Pulcher see *RE* 4.82–8 = Claudius 48 (Fröhlich); *MRR* 2.180, 184, 195–6, 208; T. P. Wiseman, *Clio's Cosmetics* (1979), 107–10, 121–4, 131–4 with further refs.

qui ⟨ne⟩que dicendi neque faciendi . . . nosset modum   Like
Burman before him, Löfstedt (*Vermischte Stud. z. lat. Sprachkunde und Syntax*
(1936), 3, and *Synt.* 1.269–70) tried to defend the paradosis as an ex. of
neque . . . neque from which the first element is omitted; but this takes no
account of *quique*, where *-que* is otiose. Are we to assume that V. committed two 'irregularities' in one clause, or that the text is corrupt? The
latter is simpler and more convincing: ⟨ne⟩*que* is, as Ruhnken noted, supported by the echo of Sall. *C.* 23.2 'neque dicere neque facere', and is
thoroughly Velleian (cf. 46.2 'qui . . . neque . . . neque . . . modum
norat'). Clodius' lack of *moderatio* would naturally disgust an admirer of
Tiberius: the emperor regarded *moderatio* as a virtue (122.1 n.).

infamis etiam sororis stupro   For the acts of incest with which
Clodius was frequently charged see e.g. Cic. *Mil.* 73, *Sest.* 16, *Fam.* 1.9.15,
Catull. 79.1 (with commentators ad loc.). Such charges were the common
stuff of Roman invective (Nisbet (1961), 194). For *infamis* + abl. cf. *TLL*
7.1.1341.55–60; with *stupro* at Prop. 3.19.20. *executor* (above) occurs first
here, then mostly in later Latin.

actus incesti reus ob initum . . . adulterium   '*initum* intelligendum
est de conatu adulterii committendi, non de perpetrato flagitio' (Kritz).
The attempt was made when Clodius disrupted the Bona Dea festival in
62, the object of his affections allegedly being the wife of Caesar, by whom
she was promptly divorced on the grounds that she should be above suspicion (Plut. *Caes.* 10.9). In 61 Clodius was charged with *incestum*, 'any
offence which defiled the sanctity of religious laws' (Ogilvie on Liv.
2.42.11), but bribed sufficient members of the jury to ensure his release
(Gelzer, *Caes.* 59–60, Rice Holmes, *Rep.* 1.291–8, *MRR* 2.173, 178, J. P.
V. D. Balsdon, *Historia* 15 (1966), 65ff.; in general Ph. Moreau, *Clodiana
Religio: un procès politique en 61 avant J.C.* (1982)). The case was naturally
popular with the prurient; an analogous one forms a leitmotiv of Petronius' novel (cf. *Sat.* 16–17).
    For *agere reum* (first in Liv.) + gen. cf. e.g. Ov. *Fast.* 4.308, Val. Max.
6.8.1 'incesti reus agebatur'.

cum graues inimicitias cum M. Cicerone exerceret   An echo of
Sall. *C.* 49.2 'uterque cum illo graues inimicitias exercebant', though
both *graues inimicitiae* and *inimicitias exercere* occur elsewhere (Woodman
(1968), 793).

quid enim inter tam dissimiles amicum esse poterat?   Another
Sallustian echo, this time a *contaminatio* of *C.* 51.17 'quid enim in tales
homines crudele fieri potest?' and *J.* 31.24 'potestne in tam diuorsis mentibus pax aut amicitia esse?' (ibid.). For Clodius' transferral to the *plebs* in
59 see *MRR* 2.195.

legem . . . tulit ⟨ut⟩ qui . . . interemisset, ei aqua et igni interdiceretur The *lex Clodia de capite ciuis* was passed early in Clodius' tribunate in 58 (*MRR* 2.196): hence *per idem tempus* at the beginning of the sentence is not to be understood too precisely.

I have accepted Gelenius' *ei*: the form *et aqua et igni* seems not to be found (*TLL* 7.1.2174.44ff.), and, while the dative is not strictly necessary, it perhaps reflects the over-elaborate language of legal documents.

etsi non nominabatur, Cicero tamen solus petebatur The same point is made, in almost the same words, by Dio 38.14.4. Laws against an individual (*priuilegia*) were forbidden in the XII Tables (Cic. *Leg.* 3.11), but shortly after Cicero left Rome to go into exile (probably in the third week in March: see Shackleton Bailey's edn of *Att.*, vol. 2, App. I), Clodius passed a second bill, the *lex Clodia de exilio Ciceronis*, in which Cicero was mentioned by name (*MRR* 2.196). Though privately Cicero naturally acknowledged that two laws had been passed (*Att.* 3.15(60).5), in his later speeches he 'telescoped the two measures and obfuscated the issue', alleging that he had been the unjustified victim of a *priuilegium* (Gruen 245–5, cf. *Pis.* 30, *Sest.* 65, *Dom.* 43ff.).

45.2 uir optime meritus de re publica So Cic. refers to himself at *Dom.* 9, 85 (cf. 87).

conseruatae patriae pretium calamitate⟨m⟩ exilii tulit *patriam conseruare* is found often in Cic. (*De Or.* 2.134, *Sull.* 40, *Dom.* 72, *Sest.* 129, *Pis.* 17, *Rep.* 6.13, *Leg. Agr.* 2.42, *Off.* 1.159), who also calls himself *conseruator* (e.g. *Pis.* 52, cf. 66.3n.). Similarly Cic. regularly refers to his exile by the word *calamitas*, though only once does he use the phrase *calamitas exilii* and then not of himself (*Fam.* 13.19.2; also Sen. *D.* 9.9.3).

I have adopted Gelenius' *calamitate⟨m⟩* because *pretium ferre* (for which cf. 125.1n.) seems not to be found with the abl.; *suspicione carere* (below) is found in Cic. *Rosc. Am.* 56, 144, *Sull.* 53, but also in Nep. *Paus.* 3.5, Quint. 4.2.96; for the accompanying gen. cf. e.g. Liv. 25.35.4 'suspicionem acceptae cladis'.

quod inter XX uiros . . . esse noluisset See Cic. *Att.* 2.19(39).4, 9.2a(169).1. For *contrahere sibi* = 'bring upon oneself involuntarily' (above) cf. *OLD* s.v. 8*b*.

45.3 intra biennium . . . dignitati patriaeque restitutus est Cic. left Dyrrachium on 4 Aug. 57, 'ipso illo die quo lex est lata de nobis' (*Att.* 4.1(73).4). A month later he delivered his speech *Post Red. Sen.* (ibid. 5). At *Dom.* 9 he refers to himself as 'in meam pristinam dignitatem restitutus', cf. *Sest.* 52; *restituo* is one of his favourite verbs.

sera Cn. Pompeii cura uerum (ut cupi⟨i⟩t) intenta Cf. Cic. *Sest.*
67 'hic aliquando, serius quam ipse uellet, Cn. Pompeius . . . excitauit
illam suam non sopitam sed . . . retardatam consuetudinem r.p. bene
gerendae' (Krause), *Dom.* 25 'sed excitatus aliquando Cn. Pompeii . . .
nimium diu reconditus et penitus abstrusus animi dolor subuenit subito
r.p. ciuitatemque . . . ad aliquam spem . . . pristinae dignitatis erexit'.
There seems no doubt that Wopkens' *inten'a* is correct: though not in
Cic., *i. cura* is found regularly elsewhere, esp. in Liv. (e.g. 25.22.4, 39.2.4;
TLL 4.1461.74–7). Ruhnken supported Gelenius' *ut coepit* with Liv.
21.10.7 'quo . . . segnius incipiunt, eo cum coeperint uereor ne per-
suerantius saeuiant', Sen. *Ira* 1.1.2 'in quod coepit pertinax et intenta';
but *cupi⟨i⟩t* takes the edge off V.'s 'malicious but hardly unfair' remark
(Seager, *Pomp.* 110 n. 48) and is in my opinion confirmed by the allusion
to *Sest.* 67 (above): 'as he wanted to do all along' (but had been prevent-
ed by Clodius).[1] It might be objected that we should expect the pluperf.,
but the perf. is often found instead, esp. in subordinate clauses as here (cf.
K–S 1.129–30). *uerum* is only here in V.

uotisque Italiae ac decretis senatus In July the senate had decreed
that anyone impeding Cicero's return should be deemed *hostis*, and they
then promulgated the law concerning his return which was passed by the
com. centuriata on 4 Aug. (last n. but one): see *Pis.* 35, *Sest.* 129. An earlier
attempt to achieve this in January had proved abortive. For *uotis* in
particular cf. *Planc.* 97 'uota de meo reditu exaudiens'; for the motif of
'all Italy' cf. *Red. Quir.* 10, *Dom.* 71, *Sest.* 72, *Pis.* 34, *Mil.* 39 'cunctae
Italiae cupienti'.

uirtute atque actione Annii Milonis For Milo's efforts see *MRR*
2.201; for him in general, *RE* 1.2271–6 = Annius 67 (Klebs). Cic. combines *uirtus* and *actio* at *Sest.* 72 (of Lentulus, cos. 57, also instrumental in
his recall) and *Fin.* 5.58.

neque post Numidici . . . quisquam . . . receptus est laetius See
Cic.'s own accounts at e.g. *Att.* 4.1.(73).4–5, *Pis.* 51–2, *Sest.* 131. For Q.
Caecilius Metellus Numidicus' exile in 100 and return in 98 see 2.15.4;
MRR 1.575–6, 2.5. The comparison was no doubt suggested by Cic., who
regularly compared himself to Numidicus: *Red. Sen.* 37, *Dom.* 87, *Red.
Quir.* 6, *Fam.* 1.9.16, *Sest.* 37 and Holden ad loc.

domus . . . a senatu restituta est Cf. *Att.* 4.2.4 'senatui placere mihi
domum restitui', *Har. Resp.* 16 'domus est . . . restituta'. For *domus . . .
disiecta* cf. Nep. *Hann.* 7.7.

---

[1] *ut cupit* was suggested by Seebode in Cludius's edn.

45.4 in senatu . . . a re publica relegauit   The first two words were deleted by Cuiacius and emended by others on the grounds that Clodius' tribunician bill would not concern the senate; yet at 38.6 V. again says that Cyprus became a province '*senatus consulto*, ministerio Catonis, regis morte' (where Cuiacius proposed *plebiscito*), and the probability is that V. is right. See esp. E. Badian, 'M. Porcius Cato and the annexation and early administration of Cyprus', *JRS* 55 (1965), 117: 'He [Vell.] is often disbelieved; but the details he gives on Cato show that he was fairly well informed. Cicero himself does not dare say that the Senate as a whole opposed the annexation, and it is clear that in fact it did not. Faced with the grain law [see *MRR* 2.196] and its consequences, the Fathers probably agreed that there was no good alternative.' V.'s phrase thus means: 'Clodius effected in the senate Cato's relegation from the state'.

relegare is also Cic.'s word for Clodius' treatment of Cato: *Sest.* 60 (Schegk), *Dom.* 65 'M. Cato inuisus quasi per beneficium Cyprum relegatur'. The fact that Cato was despatched to a distant island, as often happened in cases of genuine *relegatio*, gives point to the metaphor and draws a parallel between the circumstances of Cato and Cicero himself (cf. *Dom.* 65–6 'Cato fuerat proximus . . . eiciuntur duo, quos uidere improbi non poterant'). For *a re publica* cf. *Phil.* 10.6. For such exprr. as *sub titulo* cf. Liv. 2.56.3, 3.67.9; K–S 1.570–1.

quaestor cum iure praetorio   'It seems that when in the post-Sullan period a man who was a *priuatus* and not a magistrate was appointed at Rome to a special independent administrative commission in the provinces, he was given the acting rank of the highest magistracy which he had previously held . . . Cato, therefore, when he was given his special appointment to Cyprus in 58, ranked "pro quaestore" – he had been quaestor probably in 64 and tribune in 62 – and as, for the discharge of his commission, he required full imperium, he was appointed "pro quaestore pro praetore"; and both Vell. Pat. and the author of *De uiris illustribus* [80.2] are certainly wrong in suggesting that he was sent as "quaestor pro praetore"' (J. P. V. D. Balsdon, *JRS* 52 (1962), 134–5). There seems little doubt that Balsdon is right; either V. is using *quaestor = quaestorius* (for which there seems to be no parallel) or else he or his text is wrong (Lipsius wrote *quaestor⟨ius⟩*). For Cato cf. *RE* 22.168–213 = Porcius 16 (Miltner–Gross); for his commission see *MRR* 2.198, E. Badian, art. cit. (last n.) 110–21. For *spoliandum regno*, below, cf. Cic. *Leg. Man.* 21; for *contumeliam meritum* cf. Vitr. 1.1.6, Petron. 105.11.

Ptolemaeum . . . uitiis . . . meritum   V. here diverges from Cicero's interpretation of events: whereas the latter had represented Ptolemy as the unfortunate victim of a wicked Clodian law (*Dom.* 20 'cum lege nefaria Ptolemaeum . . . eodem iure regnantem . . . publicasses populumque Romanum scelere obligasses . . .', cf. *Sest.* 62₂), V. appears to echo Clodian propaganda to the effect that the king deserved what he got (cf. Strabo 14.6.6 ἔδοξε πλημμελής τε εἶναι καὶ ἀχάριστος εἰς τοὺς εὐεργέτας). *morum uitia* perhaps suggests that one of Clodius' allegations concerned incest: the charge was an obvious one for a Roman to bring against a Ptolemy, since their brother–sister marriages were notorious (Grant, *Cleo.* 53–5); but it was also the charge which was brought against Clodius himself (see above, 1n.)!

For Ptolemy see *RE* 23.1755–6 = Ptolemaios 34 (Volkmann).

45.5 cuius integritatem laudari nefas est *integritas* was regularly applied to Cato, cf. Cic. *Att.* 1.18.7, *Sest.* 60, Sall. *C.* 54.2, *Bell. Afr.* 88.5; Hellegouarc'h, *VL* 283. For V.'s conceit, which is presumably a form of the 'inexpressibility' topos (cf. 104.4n.), cf. Liv. fr. 45 'cuius gloriae neque profuit quisquam laudando nec uituperando quisquam nocuit', Tac. *Agr.* 9.4 'integritatem . . . in tanto uiro referre iniuria uirtutum fuerit', Plin. *Pan.* 42.4 'non uis in te ea laudari, nec fortasse laudanda sint', and perh. Claud. *Theod.* 216 'nulla potest laus esse tibi quae crimina purget'; Schegk compares also Arist. *Eth. Nic.* 1101b22. By using this conceit V. implicitly rebuffs the charge of malpractice which Clodius brought against Cato (Plut. *Cat. Min.* 45.1) and which was evidently notorious (Sen. *Contr.* 10.1.8 'quae maior indignitas illius saeculi esse potuit quam aut Pulcher accusator aut reus Cato!', quoted by Ruhnken). For *nefas* + acc. and inf. cf. *OLD* s.v. 2b. For *uitae suae uim intulit*, above, cf. Cic. *Rab. Post.* 22, Sen. *Ep.* 70.14, Quint. 5.14.22, Suet. *Otho* 12.2, *Vesp.* 6.2, Tac. *A.* 6.38.4, 12.59.2 (F.); for *insolentia . . . argui*, below, cf. Tac. *A.* 3.59.2.

effusa ciuitate obuiam cum per Tiberim subiret, nauibus non ante is egressus est quam . . . Rhenanus and subsequent edd. have taken *nauibus* with *subiret*; but since *nauibus* is strictly redundant alongside *per Tiberim*, I think Mr DuQuesnay is right to suggest that we take *nauibus* with *egressus est*. If we do, then Aldus' *iis*, for the paradosis *is*, cannot be correct; and while *is* is not essential to clarify the meaning of the sentence, the word is perhaps emphatic, suggesting that Cato acted in a way in which others would not. Burman reasonably deleted *per*, in which case *subiret* would unequivocally mean 'go upstream' (*OLD* s.v. 5b); but *per* can be retained if we understand the verb to mean 'approach' (*OLD* s.v. 6a, where V. is listed as the first to use the verb abs. in this sense), and for *per* used with the prefix *sub-* cf. Virg. *Aen.* 10.588 (diff. sense, however).

Cato was back from Cyprus by 56 (*RE* 22.182); for the story which V. tells cf. Plut. *Cat. Min.* 39.1–2.

46–47 THE YEARS 55–52 B.C.

46.1 immanes res uix multis uoluminibus explicandas C. Caesar . . . ageret To emphasise the importance of certain events V. regularly says that he cannot deal with them in the present work, or that he hopes to treat them in a later and larger work, or that he will scarcely be able to treat them in a larger work (the 'inexpressibility' and 'other work(s)' topoi: cf. 96.3nn., 103.4n., 104.4n.). Here he produces a variant which, as Mr DuQuesnay suggests, perhaps contains a panegyrical allusion to Caesar's own works, the *commentarii*. By their nature the *commentarii* were intended to provide the raw material for historians to elaborate (cf. Cic. *Brut.* 262 'dum uoluit alios habere parata, unde sumerent qui uellent scribere historiam'), but their excellence was such that they were more likely to put people off (ibid. 'sanos quidem homines a scribendo deterruit'; P. T. Eden, *Glotta* 40 (1962), 75–8).[1] For V.'s opinion of Caesar as a writer cf. 36.2 ('proximum Ciceroni'); for *explicare = tractare fusius* cf. 48.5, 96.3; *TLL* 5.2.1733.15ff. (76ff. for its being used of items too big to handle); for *multis uoluminibus* cf. 29.2 'uiri magnitudo multorum uoluminum instar exigit' (of Pompey). For *immanis* = 'very great' etc. cf. 105.3n., Ov. *Met.* 9.247 with Bömer's n.; for *res agere* cf. e.g. Sall. *J.* 7.6, Liv. 26.28.1, Val. Max. 2.7.15; *TLL* 1.1389.4ff.

alterum paene imperio nostro (ac suo) quaerens orbem   It was conventional to describe Alexander as having sought (an)other world(s) to conquer (Val. Max. 8.14 *ext.* 2, Sen. *Suas.* 1.1, 3, 4.3, *Contr.* 7.7.19, Curt. 7.8.12, 9.6.20, Sen. *Ep.* 119.8, Juv. 10.168–9 (and Mayor ad loc.), Quint. 3.8.16; Kohl 85–6). It was also conventional to compare Caesar with Alexander (41.1n.) and to describe Britain as a world separate from the Roman (Virg. *Ecl.* 1.66, Hor. *C.* 4.14.47–8, Tac. *Agr.* 12.3, Flor. 1.45.2; Pease on Cic. *ND* 2.88, Vogt 165–7, *TLL* 9.2.918.31ff.). It therefore became conventional to describe Caesar's exploits in Britain in terms similar to those used of Alexander (Flor. 1.45.16, Luc. 1.369, 10.456, *Pan. Lat.* 8.11.2, Hegesipp. 2.9.1);[2] and a globe became a feature of the coinage connected with Caesar in his later years (Weinstock 43). Two others of whom the topos is used are Germanicus (cf. Albinov. Pedo, *FPL* (ed. Morel) p. 115, line 19; *POxy* 25.2435; Goodyear on Tac. *A.* 2.59.1 (*Comm. Tac.* 2.374); Weippert 257) and Don Juan (in Molière's play, act 1, sc. 2: 'comme Alexandre je souhaiterais qu'il y eût d'autres mondes, pour y pouvoir étendre mes conquêtes amoureuses').

imperio . . . suo perhaps alludes to the title *Imperator* which, according to Dio 43.44.2 and Suet. *Iul.* 76.1, Caesar was to acquire in 45 (see Weinstock 103–11; *contra* Syme, *RP* 365–6). Cf. esp. Cic. *Lig.* 7 (46 B.C.) 'cum ipse [Caesar] imperator in toto imperio pop. Rom. unus esset'.

†uictus pars† consulum   Rhenanus' *par* has been well received; Heinsius in support quoted Liv. 27.34.10 'egregium par consulum'. The corrupt *uictus* has posed more problems. Some scholars have preferred *iunctum* or *uinctum*, both of which seem, however, redundant with *par*.

---

[1] For a similar point elsewhere cf. Cic. *Att.* 2.1.1–2.
[2] Verhaak (56) notes that Caesar is thus the logical successor of Pompey, 'cui . . . ad uictoriam terra defuerat' (53.3).

Others prefer *inuidum* (*uel sim.*), anticipating the points made in *qui neque
. . . gestus est* below; but it is hard to see how the ending became corrupted
to *-us*. Neither of these objections can be laid against Ursinus' *uetus*, which
suggests the additional point that while Caesar was searching for a whole
new world (*alterum . . . orbem*), the 'old firm' embarked on a mere second
consulship (*alterum . . . consulatum*). For this sense of *uetus* cf. *OLD* s.v. 6*a*.
Yet I am not quite convinced that *uetus par* is right and I have therefore,
perhaps too timorously, obelised the phrase.

alterum . . . consulatum   In 55, having previously been colleagues in
70. For the circumstances of their election and their conduct in office see
MRR 2.214–15. *probabiliter* = 'commendably', below, occurs first here
and in Val. Max. 2.8.2; cf. *OLD* s.v.1, to which F. adds Gell. 1.16.9.

**46.2 Caesari lege . . . prorogatae . . . prouinciae, Crasso . . . Syria
decreta**   Conventionally the first of these measures is attributed to the
lex Licinia Pompeia and the second to the *lex Trebonia*; but there is considerable evidence to suggest that the former was also known as a *lex Trebonia*
(see esp. Plut. *Pomp.* 52.4; Pocock's comm. on Cic. *Vat.*, pp. 163ff., esp.
164–5), which would explain why V. has come to use the singular *lege* to
refer to two separate *leges*.

   Cludius deleted *in* before *animo* (cf. Liv. 1.47.6 'moliri . . . animo'), but
the preposition precludes *molienti* being taken with *animo* (rather than
Crasso) by mistake; cf. Liv. 21.2.2 'agitare in animo bellum'. For *bellum
moliri* cf. *TLL* 2.1838.36–40 (Liv. Trog. Curt. Colum. Luc. Sil.).

qui, uir cetera sanctissimus . . . capiebat terminum   This clause,
with its emphatic pleonasm and chiasmus, pointedly sums up the essential
Crassus: he had a 'predilection for moderation' in all things except one,
ambition, for the realisation of which his vast wealth provided the means
(A. M. Ward, *M. Crassus and the Late Roman Republic* (1977), 292–4). For
uir used in apposition cf. 79.1n., 129.1n.; *cetera sanctissimus* perhaps echoes
Sall. *H.* 1.116 'sanctus alia'; for *cetera* in general see 119.4n. For
immunis + abl. cf. 35.2, 115.2 and n., *TLL* 7.1.506.22ff.; for *gloriam concupi-
scere* cf. 33.3, Cic. *Phil.* 1.29, Sen. *D.* 6.5.5; for *capere terminum* cf. Virg. *Aen.*
10.106 'capit finem', Liv. 5.51.6, Tac. *H.* 4.3.3 (F.).

   On Crassus see also *RE* 13.295–331 = Licinius 68 (Gelzer); B. A. Mar-
shall, *Crassus: a Political Biography* (1976).

46.3 hunc proficiscentem . . . diris cum ominibus   Crassus left
Rome in Nov. 55 (Cic. *Att.* 4.13(87).2). His levies had been unpopular
and his enterprise (for his intentions were well known: Plut. *Crass.* 16.3)
met strong opposition, esp. from Cato (see Ward, op. cit. 284–5): there
was thus no doubt a political motive behind the tribunician announce-
ment of bad omens which accompanied his departure (cf. Cic. *Diu.* 1.29,
App. *BC* 2.18, Dio 39.39.5–7, Plut. *Crass.* 16.3–6).

Krause suggested deleting *cum*: the simple abl. is indeed the norm (cf. 79.2) but see Liv. 40.56.9 'cum diris exsecrationibus'.

quorum execrationes si in ipsum . . . ualuissent, utile imperatoris damnum . . . fuisset r.p. This sentence clearly alludes to the curses which, according to Dio and Plut. (above), were uttered against Crassus, either by more than one tribune (so too Dio) or by C. Ateius Capito alone (so Plut.), on a separate occasion from the announcing of bad omens and perhaps in response to his ignoring of them.[1]

If we are to understand V.'s sentence properly, we must, I think, assume that the curses were intended to be directed at Crassus alone, the hope being that he would be forestalled, e.g. by shipwreck (and indeed this precise fate befell some of his ships: Plut. *Crass.* 17.1); in the event, however, Crassus' death was not encompassed without the loss of most of his army at Carrhae, something which the tribune(s) no doubt never intended but for which he/they were later called to account (Plut. *Crass.* 16.6, Cic. *Diu.* 1.29). This is therefore a classic case of a curse being fulfilled according to its letter rather than to the intention of the curser, precisely the distinction envisaged by V. in this sentence. A not dissimilar case is described by Cicero when he refers to the departure of Piso and Gabinius to Macedonia in 58 (*Sest.* 71 'exierunt malis ominibus atque execrationibus duo uulturii paludati. quibus utinam ipsis euenisset ea quae tum homines precabantur! neque nos prouinciam Macedoniam cum exercitu neque equitatum in Syria et cohortes optimas perdidissemus'). Given V.'s acquaintance with Cic., and esp. this speech (see 45.2–4nn.), he may well be recalling this passage here.[2]

The passage of Cic. also helps to show, I believe, that V. wrote *utile . . . damnum* and not, as Lipsius excellently suggested, *uile damnum* (a phrase easily paralleled: see Goodyear on Tac. *A.* 2.85.4): for if Gabinius and Piso had not reached Macedonia, the province and the armies would not

---

[1] Dio and Plut. also mention an intermediate action which V. omits: the attempted arrest of Crassus. The fact that the curses are not mentioned by the only contemporary of the events, Cicero (cf. *Diu.* 1.29), persuaded A. D. Simpson that they never took place. She argued that a common source of the later versions, perhaps an epitomator of Livy, mistakenly transferred to 55 the curses which the tribune Atinius Labeo uttered against Q. Metellus in 131 (*TAPA* 69 (1938), 532–41). Her arguments (unfortunately too detailed to repeat here) are certainly ingenious but have been contradicted by Ward (op. cit. 285 n. 50) and J. Bayet ('Les malédictions du tribun C. Ateius Capito', *Hommages à G. Dumézil* (1960), 31–45 = *Croyances et rites dans la Rome antique* (1971), 353–65). See too next fn.

[2] The similarity is used by A. D. Simpson (last fn.) to argue that V. transposed the Ciceronian sentiment to 55 B.C. and that Plut. then used V. for part of his account.

have been lost and this would have been *utile rei publicae*. That a similar interpretation holds good for V. is confirmed by Plut.'s account of the tribune's curses (*Crass.* 16.6): ἐμέμφοντο τὸν Ἀτήιον, εἰ δι' ἣν ἐχαλέπαινε τῷ Κράσσῳ πόλιν, εἰς αὐτὴν ἀρὰς ἀφῆκε (Dio appears to make a similar point but the text is uncertain).

46.4 rex Orodes ... interemit The battle of Carrhae took place in June 53 (Rice Holmes, *Rep.* 2.312–15). For King Orodes II see *RE* 18.1135–42 = Orodes 1 (Lenschau).

reliquias legionum C. Cassius ... conseruauit See *MRR* 2.229; for him see *RE* 3.1727–36 = Cassius 59 (Fröhlich); for his part in Caesar's murder cf. 56.3–58.2.

46.5 fugaret ac funderet The inverted word-order echoes Sall. *J.* 21.2 (Ruhnken); for this idiosyncrasy of Sall. cf. W. Kroll, *Glotta* 15 (1927), 299; for the usual order cf. 112.5n.

47.1 pugnatum saepe derecta acie, saepe in agminibus, saepe eruptionibus Despite the plural form *agminibus*, I think *in* is supported by Liv. 10.45.12 'saepe in acie, saepe in agmine, saepe circa ipsam urbem aduersus eruptiones hostium pugnatum'. Note how V. here returns to Caesar's Gallic successes, which he has already mentioned at 46.1, because he 'wants to frame Crassus' catastrophe with Caesar's victories, the better to highlight both' (Starr (1978), 113). For *derecta acie* cf. 95.2n.

⟨e⟩ nouem denique aestatibus uix ulla non ... ' In scarcely any of his nine campaigns did he not deserve a full triumph.' Several edd. and translators retain the paradosis, but the juxtaposition of two simple abll., *aestatibus* and *ulla*, seems to me meaningless. I think a partitive construction is required, and Krause's ⟨e⟩, improving on Burman's ⟨ex⟩, seems more plausible than Wopkens' *aestatum*, the corruption of which would be hard to explain. For the constr. cf. e.g. Cic. *Phil.* 13.12 'satis inconsiderati fuit ... rem ullam ex illis attingere', *Dom.* 108. Ruhnken preferred to read *ullus*, but that produces an extremely awkward form of expression, and again it is hard to see why *ullus* should have been corrupted to *ulla*. For *iustissimus triumphus* cf. Cic. *Pis.* 44, 57, 59, *Planc.* 89, *Fam.* 3.10.1, Hor. *C.* 1.12.54, Liv. 7.15.8, Suet. *Cal.* 48.2 (F.).

circa Alesiam See Caes. *BG* 7.68–89; Rice Holmes, *Rep.* 2.211–22 (52 B.C.). For the suggestion that Caesar's conquests made him divine see Weinstock 186–8.

47.2 cum medium ... pignus ... decessit The inverted *cum*-clause underlines the final severing of an alliance which, as the remarkable hyperbaton *medium . . . pignus* perhaps symbolises, was being kept together only with difficulty. For *medium pignus* cf. Sen. *Contr.* 1.1.3 (Ruhnken); for *concordiae p.* cf. Cic. *Phil.* 12.22 'pignus libertatis p. R., D. Brutum' (F.). *decessit* cannot properly go with its true subject *pignus* but is used on account of the appositional noun *Iulia* (zeugma).

Julia's death is referred to by Cic. in a letter of Sept. 54 (*QF* 3.1(21).17, cf. Sen. *Marc.* 14.3 'C. Caesar, cum Britanniam peragraret . . . , audiit decessisse filiam'), i.e. during Caesar's fifth year in Gaul. Yet the paradosis here reads *septimo ferme anno*. It seems unlikely that V. can have got this particular date wrong, in which case one must assume that *quinto* became somehow corrupted into *septimo* (perhaps *vo* [= *quinto*] was misread as *vii*). Laurent, with admittedly more plausibility, suggested that *IIII* was corrupted to *VII*; but *quarto* would of course produce a wrong date of 55 B.C. for Julia's death.

The view that Julia's death was instrumental in dissolving triumviral *concordia* is 'the favoured ancient explanation' (Gruen 450, with refs.): see esp. Sen. *Cons. Pol.* 15.1 'cuius morte optime cohaerentis Romanae pacis uincula resoluta sunt', Luc. 1.111ff.

iam ex inuidia po⟨te⟩ntiae ta⟨m⟩ male cohaerentis ... concordiae 'of the agreement which was already holding together so badly on account of political jealousy'. There is general agreement that *po⟨te⟩ntiae*, 'inter praecipuas Lipsii emendationes' (Boeclerus), is correct. Rhenanus' *male* has been less readily accepted, yet none of the alternatives (involving forms of *familia* or *aemulatio*) is at all plausible. *male (co)haerere* is easily paralleled (Cic. *Fam.* 6.7.3, Liv. 23.24.9, Sen. *NQ* 6.1.15, Quint. 10.6.6), *a* and *i* are regularly confused (Kritz lxxxvi), and cf. Luc. 1.87 'o male concordes'. For *Ca-* I suggest *ta⟨m⟩* (*c* and *t* are also often confused, e.g. 55.4, and for this use of *tam* = 'very' cf. *tanto discrimini* just below). For *inuidia* cf. 44.2n.; for *concordia*, 48.5n.

filius ... Pompeii So too Suet. *Iul.* 26.1; a daughter according to Dio 39.64. For *omnia . . . dirimente*, above, cf. Cic. *Leg.* 1.54 (F.). Note the impressive alliteration of the whole sentence.

47.3 tertius consulatus soli Cn. Pompeio 52 B.C. (*MRR* 2.233–4; Seager, *Pomp.* 144ff.). He had been proposed by Bibulus and seconded by Cato, two of his principal enemies (Plut. *Pomp.* 54.3–4): hence *aduersantium . . . iudicio*. For *iudicium* used of senatorial *decreta* etc. cf. TLL 7.2.609.47ff. *dignitas*, almost a byword in connection with Pompey (cf. 29.4, 33.3; Raaflaub 206 n. 456), is here presumably a generalised reference to his 'elevated position'; but it perhaps also contains an allusion to an earlier proposal, which Cato had opposed, that Pompey should be made dictator (Ascon. p. 35C, Dio 40.50.3, App. *BC* 2.84, Plut. *Pomp.* 54.2). For the last five months of his consulship Pompey had Scipio Nasica (54.2n.) as his colleague.

For *in gladios . . . furente*, above, cf. Luc. 2.439 'Caesar in arma furens', 7.295 'in tela furentes' (at 1.68 *in arma* is ἀπὸ κοινοῦ with *furentem* and *impulerit*); *ciuium*, from its position, is presumably object. genit. with *caedes* (so too Watson, H–W, Shipley). For the election violence of 53 see Seager, *Pomp.* 142–4.

a C. Caesare alienatus est This, the view of numerous modern scholars, has been queried by Gruen 153–4 (with refs.).

in coercitionem ambitus 'The *lex de ambitu* represents a solid achievement, recalled by writers of much later eras as a milestone in the war against electoral corruption' (Gruen 237, quoting Plin. *Pan.* 29.1, Cic. *Brut.* 245, Caes. *BC* 3.1.4, Tac. *D.* 38.2, Plut. *Pomp.* 55.4, Dio 40.52.3–4, besides V.). For *uim . . . exercere* cf. *TLL* 5.2. 1374.2–5.

47.4 quo tempore P. Clodius a Milone . . . iugulatus est Clodius' murder by Milo, his long-standing adversary and now a consular candidate, on 18 Jan. 52 was principally instrumental in Pompey's subsequent election as sole consul (*MRR* 2.234): hence *quo tempore* is not to be taken too specifically. For Cicero's account of the murder see *Mil.* 28–9.
 Gelenius emended *inutiliter* to *inutili* on the reasonable grounds that a scribe had expected an adverb before *facto*; Ruhnken supported him by quoting V.'s imitator Sulp. *Chron.* 2.30.2 'licet malo exemplo, bono tamen affectu r.p. ab improbis uindicandae . . . sumit imperium'. Others emend *-ter*, e.g. *uer⟨um⟩* Novák (1884). For V.'s contrast cf. also Tac. *A.* 1.38.1 'bono magis exemplo quam concesso iure', Sen. *Contr.* 10.6 *exc.* 'bono exemplo damnatus . . . malo inuentus' (such phraseology incorporating the abl. *exemplo* is common, cf. *TLL* 5.2.1334.25–53); for *salutaris rei p.* cf. Cic. *Phil.* 7.4. That Clodius' death was advantageous to the state was naturally argued by Cic. in his defence of Milo, e.g. 78. For *ex occursu* cf. Suet. *Tib.* 7.3, *Nero* 1.1, 23.2 (F.).

Pompeii damnauit uoluntas 'Although Pompey himself was officially neutral, it was common knowledge that he hoped for a conviction' (Gruen 338, with refs.). *inuidia facti* is a Sallustian phrase (*J.* 29.5, 35.8), used also by later 'Sallustians' (Pollio in Cic. *Fam.* 10.31.3, Tac. *A.* 1.44.3).

47.5 quem quidem *quem* = Milo; *quidem* is explanatory.

qui si maturius tulisset . . . Gelenius wrote *quam*, but 'uis sententiae inest in *personae* significatione; *Cato si prius tulisset sententiam . . .*' (Kritz).
 V.'s language in this final sentence is conspicuously and characteristically Ciceronian: for Clodius as *perniciosus ciuis* cf. *Phil.* 8.16 and (by implication) *Mil.* 82; for *perniciosus rei pub.* cf. *Dom.* 114, and for *bonis inimicus* cf. *Cat.* 1.33, 3.30, *Flacc.* 5, *Prou. Cons.* 11.

48.1–5 THE YEAR 50 B.C. AND THE ROLE OF CURIO

48.1 cum iustissimus quisque . . . uellet dimitti exercitus The proposal that both Pompey and Caesar should relinquish their armies was put forward in early 50 by Curio with Caesar's blessing (cf. Cic. *Fam.* 8.14(97).2, Hirt. *BG* 8.52.4–5, App. *BC* 2.27, Dio 40.62.3–4). The proposal was predictably rejected by Pompey, who had more to lose, but was generally popular (cf. App. loc. cit., Plut. *Caes.* 30.2) and was resoundingly supported on 1 Dec. 50 by the senate (370 votes to 22), which the consul Marcellus promptly dismissed (App. *BC* 2.30). Either through ignorance or accident or design, V. does not mention that the simultaneous abandonment of both armies was a proposal of Curio's; his language merely suggests that it was a possible solution which he himself would have favoured (cf. *iustissimus quisque*).

easque . . . per Afranium et Petreium . . . administrabat See *MRR* 2.220, 225–6, 230–2, 238–9, 243–5, 251–3. L. Afranius was consul in 60, M. Petreius praetor in perhaps 64; for them see further *RE* 1.710–12 = Afranius 6 (Klebs) and 19.1182–8 = Petreius 3 (Münzer) respectively.

For *a* + abl. with a gerundive, below, see J. G. Griffith, *CR* 10 (1960), 190–1, who finds that one of the regular occurrences of the constr. is in passages with marked legal associations, as here.

48.2 si . . . decessisset in Campania Pompey fell ill at Naples in mid-50 (Cic. *Fam.* 8.13(94).2, *Att.* 6.3(117).4, Plut. *Pomp.* 57.1, App. *BC* 2.28): *ante biennium . . . itum est* thus = 'two years before the fighting began', not 'before the civil war began' (the ref. is to the engagements of 48 which culminated in the battle of Pharsalus, as *defuisset* etc. (below) confirms).

perfectis muneribus theatri The theatre and its surrounding portico were dedicated, to the accompaniment of lavish games, in August 55: Cic. *Fam.* 7.1(24).2–3, *Pis.* 65 (with Nisbet (1961), 199ff.); Rice Holmes, *Rep.* 2.146–7.

uniuersa Italia uota pro salute eius . . . suscepit Cf. Cic. *Att.* 8.16(166).1, 9.5(171).3, Juv. 10.283ff. If by *primi omnium ciuium* V. means that no one had previously received such an honour, as the comparable phrasing at 24.3 suggests ('ad eum primum omnium Romanorum'), then he is in agreement with Dio 41.6.4 (see Ll. W. Daly, 'Vota publica pro salute alicuius', *TAPA* 81 (1950), 167–8); but according to *Vir. Ill.* 66.12 M. Livius Drusus had already been so honoured in 91 (see Weinstock 219). The discrepancy would be removed if we understood *primi omnium ciuium* to mean 'the leading citizen'; but perhaps V. has simply made a mistake.

defuisset fortunae destruendi eius locus et ... detulisset ad inferos For Pompey as an example *e contrario* of the topos *opportunitas mortis* see Cic. *TD* 1.86 'qui si mortem tum obisset, in amplissimis fortunis occidisset, is propagatione uitae quot quantas quam incredibiles hausit calamitates!' (the whole passage should be compared), Liv. 9.17.6, Prop. 3.11.37, Sen. *Marc.* 20.4 'cogita quantum boni opportuna mors habeat, quam multis diutius uixisse nocuerit. si Cn. Pompeium ... Neapoli ualetudo abstulisset, indubitatus p. R. princeps excesserat ...', Juv. 10.283–6, Plut. *Pomp.* 46.1–2 (Pompey's son is used by Flor. 2.18.7 'magnique famam ducis ad inferos secum tulisset si nihil temptasset ulterius'). Cf also Luc. 8.27–31. V., who produces a related topos when dealing with Pompey's death (53.2n.), emphasises his point here by the play on Pompey's name (Magnus: cf. also Sen. *D.* 10.13.7, Petron. 123.244) and by providing contrasting exs. of the same topos at 6 below (for Pompey himself as such an ex. see Luc. 7.706, where he is congratulated for having lost at Pharsalus). In general see 66.4n.

For *deesse fortunae* cf. Liv. 4.57.8 and (diff. sense) *Pan. Lat.* 12.15.6; for *fortuna destruit* cf. Sen. *NQ* 4 *praef.* 22 (also of Pompey); *destruere* + personal obj. is first here and in Val. Max. (Ungewitter 47); for *inlibatam* cf. Sen. *Suas.* 6.10 *i. dignitatis* (F.), Tac. *A.* 2.46.2 *i. gloriam*.

48.3 Bello autem ciuili et tot ... per continuos XX annos ... malis V. thus subscribes to the view that the civil wars of 49–29 were a unity, a view which he repeats at 89.3 and does not contradict at 59.4 (n.). The same view was held by Augustus himself and (with a slight discrepancy) by Livy (cf. 89.3n.); it is also found in Manil. (1.906–21), Sen. (*Ira* 2.11.3), Tac. (*A.* 3.28.1), *Octau.* (498–526), and probably Val. Max. (cf. 4.6.4) and Luc.: see in general R. T. Bruère, *CP* 45 (1950), 217–35, Jal 43ff., esp. 54.

non alius maiorem ... quam C. Curio ... subiecit facem V. does not mean that Curio put forward proposals which he knew Pompey would reject (so Seager, *Pomp.* 155 and n. 84), since he does not connect Curio with such proposals at 1 above (n.); he means that Curio caused disruption on a later occasion (see below, 5n.).

After the brief 'digression' on Pompey's fate in 2, *facem* resumes the fire metaphor which was introduced in 1 above (*exarserunt*; for this technique see 99.4n.); for *facem subicere* used metaphorically see *TLL* 6.1.402.47ff.

For C. Scribonius Curio see *RE* 2A.867–76 = Scribonius 11 (Münzer); *MRR* 2.224, 240, 249, 263–4, 266, 269.

uir nobilis, eloquens, audax Thus a second Clodius (cf. 45.1 'nobilis, disertus, audax' and n.), an *amicus* from whom Curio 'had learned much' (Gruen 474, cf. 482). Curio's eloquence and *audacia* are also combined at

Luc. 1.269 'audax uenali comitatur Curio lingua', and it has been argued that *audax* was a traditional epithet for Curio, constituting a derogatory allusion to his subversive activities (C. Wirszubski, *JRS* 54 (1964), 12–22, who defines an *audax* as 'is qui in re publica ausus est ea quae nemo auderet bonus', an adaptation of V.'s description of Cinna at 24.5). In addition to Clodius (cf. also Cic. *Sest.* 20, *Dom.* 130, *Mil.* 32, *Phil.* 8.16, Plut. *Pomp.* 48.8 *al.*) and Curio, others so described included C. Fimbria (Vell. 24.1, Cic. *Rosc. Am.* 33, Liv. *per.* 82, Dio fr. 104.1, Oros. 6.2.9), Antony (Vell. 56.4, Cic. *Phil.* 2.1, 19, 6.2, 8.21, 12.15) and Catiline (e.g. Cic. *Cat.* 1.1, 4, 2.1, *Mur.* 17 etc.). In V.'s opinion, Egnatius Rufus also qualified (cf. 91.3 and n.).

suae alienaeque et fortunae et pudicitiae prodigus 'Solemnis est haec formula . . . de libidinosis' (Krause): see Sall. *C.* 5.4, 12.2, 16.2, 54.32, Cic. *De Or.* 1.173, *Rab. Perd.* 8, *Cael.* 42, *Rhet. Herenn.* 4.52, Sen. *Contr.* 1 *praef.* 9, Sen. *Ben.* 4.11.1, Suet. *Gai.* 36.1, Tac. *D.* 29.2, *G.* 31.3, 46.5, *H.* 1.49.3. Some of these exs. are from Ruhnken, who remarks that V. 'respicit infamem Curionis in Antonium amorem', for which cf. Cic. *Att.* 1.14(14).5 and Shackleton Bailey ad loc., *Phil.* 2.44f.

homo ingeniosissime nequam So too Caelius is 'uir eloquio ani-moque Curioni simillimus . . . nec minus ingeniose nequam' at 68.1. *nequam* is a favourite term of Ciceronian abuse (Opelt 161–2). For such abl. phrases as *malo publico*, below, cf. *TLL* 8.235.78–236.7; normally the phrase is used with a verb or part. *uel sim.* (e.g. Cato, *Orat.* 171 'neque eos malo publico diuites feci', Sen. *Clem.* 1.18.3 'numerari inter publico malo natos'), but for its use with an adj. see e.g. Prop. 3.11.34 'totiens nostro Memphi cruenta malo'.

48.4 cuius †animo uoluptatibus uel libidinibus neque opes ullae neque cupiditates† sufficere possent This clause presents a number of difficulties. First, scholars have expressed considerable doubt over *animo*. If the word is correct, it can only be dative after *sufficere*; but this leaves *uoluptatibus uel libidinibus* as abl. and thus as tautologous with *opes* and *cupiditates*. (Gruter deleted *uol. uel lib.*, but the supposed interpolation would be odd and uncharacteristic of V.'s text.) Acidalius conjectured *omnino* for *animo*, but we should expect that word to follow *neque . . . neque*; Lipsius emended to *animi*, but *animi uoluptatibus . . . opes . . . sufficere* is curious Latin. Krause simply deleted *animo*, which is attractive since it could be argued that the word had intruded from the next sentence; but the deletion renders deficient the cross-reference at 68.1 to Curio's *animus* (see last n.). Although this objection is admittedly not decisive (for a similar case see 105.2 and n.), I believe, on balance, that *animo* is likely to be correct; in which case we need to supply a word to produce sense, e.g.

79

animo ⟨dedito⟩ . . . libidinibus (cf. Cic. *Cael.* 45 'animus libidini deditus') or *animo ⟨affecto⟩ . . . libidinibus*.

Secondly, whether or not *animo* is correct, *cupiditates* cannot be the subject of *sufficere* since 'desires' cannot 'satisfy' anything. We must therefore assume either that *cupiditates* hides a word meaning 'pleasures' or that *cupiditates* and *uoluptatibus* should be transposed and their cases interchanged. The latter suggestion, due to Wopkens, is attractive: given the number of synonymous nouns in the clause, it is quite possible that a scribe mixed them up.

Thus it may be that V. wrote something like: *cuius animo ⟨dedito⟩ cupiditatibus uel libidinibus neque opes ullae neque uoluptates sufficere possent* 'whose inclinations, addicted to desires and pleasures, neither riches nor delights were able to satisfy' (for *cupiditati deditus* cf. Cic. *Parad. Sto.* 37). But in view of the general uncertainty of the whole passage I have thought it wisest to obelise.

pro Pompeii partibus (id est, ut tunc habebatur, pro re publica) V. thus seeks to avoid the danger, of which Thuc. warned in a classic passage (3.82.4–8), that in times of civil unrest the meanings of words are liable to distortion. Cf. Flor. 2.13.15 'de successione Caesaris senatus (id est Pompeius) agitabat'; for further exs. of the idea see Vretska on Sall. *C.* 52.11, and for *id est* see Kritz on Sall. *J.* 31.20. Also next n.

simulatione contra Pompeium et Caesarem sed animo pro Caesare stetit Such contrasts between appearance and reality are a feature of Tacitus' style, as of Thuc.'s: see R. H. Martin, *Eranos* 49 (1951), 175. For *simulatione ∼ animo* cf. Cic. *ND* 2.168 'siue ex animo . . . siue simulate' (Ruhnken). For *stare pro* cf. 2.2.3; Krebs–Schmalz 2.602.

On Curio's changing sides see *MRR* 2.249.

in medio relinquemus V. is sceptical where others are certain: see Gruen 473 n. 87. For the expr. cf. *TLL* 8.591.65ff. (Claud. Quadr. Sall. Cic. Tac. Plin. *al.*).

48.5 saluberrimas [et] coalescentis condiciones pacis . . . discussit ac rupit According to Appian (*BC* 2.28) there was a moment during Pompey's illness when he wrote to the senate offering to relinquish his army, an offer which he repeated on his return to Rome. Appian's account is said by Rice Holmes (*Rep.* 2.250 n. 2) and Gruen (486 n. 124) to be unsupported and is thus treated by them with great scepticism; but it is accepted by Gelzer (*Caes.* 185) and Seager (*Pomp.* 157–8) and is, I believe, supported by V. here (*condiciones . . . quas . . . Pompeius . . . recipiebat*). Thus Pompey called Curio's bluff by agreeing to accept the proposals which the latter had laid down (see 1 above); Curio was therefore compelled to denounce Pompey's offer as insincere (App. loc. cit.), and hence it was Curio who *bello ciuili subiecit facem* (3).[1]

It is not easy to decide whether to follow Gelenius in deleting *et. coalescentes* (i.e. accus. pl.) could perhaps be defended as a very bold ex. of enallage (see 91.3n.), possibly resulting from a conflation of construction (*condiciones pacis discutere* with *coalescentem pacem discutere*); in addition Kritz points to the attractive antithesis *coalescentes . . . discussit ac rupit.* Yet *coalescentes condiciones* is a difficult phrase, whereas *coalescentis* (i.e. genit. sing.) . . . *pacis* is not (cf. Liv. 26.40.18); *coalescentis* does not eliminate the antithesis but merely makes it less explicit; and intrusive *et* is not uncommon in V.'s text (e.g. 107.2). I have therefore followed Gelenius; for the resulting interlaced word-order cf. 100.1n. For *condiciones . . . discussit* cf. *Vir. Ill.* 34.8 (Val. Max. 5.6 *ext.* 4).

unice cauente Cicerone concordiae publicae 'concordiae . . . auctor esse non destiti', said Cicero later (*Phil.* 2.24). His efforts were first revealed to Atticus on 9 Dec. 50 (*Att.* 7.3(126).5 'ipsum tamen Pompeium separatim ad concordiam hortabor') and they continued ceaselessly for over a month (see Seager, *Pomp.* 159–60, 161 (and n. 123), 162). I take V.'s phrase either to refer generally to Cicero's role throughout this period or, being an effective abl. abs. of the 'Tacitean' type (see 60.4n.), to act as a 'trailer' for his efforts in Jan. 49 ('Only Cicero was left to look after public concord'). In view of the elaborate dating at 49.1 below, the phrase cannot in my opinion be used to date the *whole* of the present sentence to Jan. 49 (see further below, n. 1).

As a theme, *concordia* 'was never so topical as during Caesar's rise to power' (Weinstock 261, q.v.; also Achard 38–9, 72–4). For *cauere* used with the dat. of a thing cf. Plin. *Ep.* 10.54.2, Suet. *Tit.* 6.2. Note V.'s emphatic alliteration at the end of an episode, as often (cf. 112.6n.).

48.5–6 OBITUARY NOTICES

V.'s narrative of the years 59–50 has now ended; that of the civil war is about to begin. To separate the two, V. interposes a brief section of obituary notices which covers roughly the whole of the decade with which he

---

[1] It might be inferred from the following reference to Cicero (*unice cauente* . . .) that V. has been alluding to the manoeuvres of early January 49 in which Cicero was prominent (so e.g. K. Raaflaub, *Chiron* 4 (1974), 318–19); but there are two objections to this. (a) It is clear from the elaborate dating at 49.1 below that V. has not yet reached the year 49. (b) V. would be contradicting himself (as indeed Raaflaub believes), since 49.3–4 clearly *does* refer to the moves of early Jan. 49 and the disruption is there attributed, not to Curio, but (correctly) to Lentulus and others. *ad ultimum* at 48.5 does not mean the final action before the civil war, but the climax of Curio's behaviour (cf. *primo . . . mox* at 48.4); and for the abl. abs. *unice cauente . . .* see above.

has been dealing. This method of separation is common in V. (below, p. 156), and the choice of obituaries reminds us of Tacitus, who often uses them to end his annalistic account of a year's events (Syme, *TST* 79–80).

nostris explicabitur   Sc. *iustis* as well as *uoluminibus* (cf. 96.3n.). For *ordo . . . explicabitur* cf. Cic. *Brut.* 15, Sen. *Ben.* 6.1.1, Quint. 4 *praef.* 6; for *proposito operi*, below, cf. 66.3n.

48.6 si prius gratulatus ero . . .   Having already remarked that Pompey was deprived of an *opportuna mors* (above, 2n.), V. now congratulates five individuals to whom the topos is applicable. They are arranged in chronological order of dying: Q. Catulus (43.3n.) died in late 61 or early 60 (Shackleton Bailey on Cic. *Att.* 1.13(13).2); L. Licinius Lucullus Ponticus (cos. 74) died between mid-Dec. 57 and 13 Jan. 56 (W. H. Bennett, *CR* 22 (1972), 314); M. Terentius Varro Lucullus (cos. 73), brother of the preceding, died shortly afterwards (*RE* 13.418; cf. Sen. *Cons. Pol.* 15.1); Q. Caecilius Metellus Creticus (cos. 69) is last heard of in 54 (*RE* 3.1211–12);[1] and Hortensius (cos. 69) died in 50 (*RE* 8.2478–9).

Ruhnken suggested that in Catulus' case V. recalled Cic. *Att.* 2.24(44).4 'nihil mi fortunatius est Catulo cum splendore uitae tum hoc tempore' (written 59), and Boeclerus that in Hortensius' case he recalled *Brut.* 329 'sed fortunatus illius exitus qui ea non uidit cum fierent quod prouidit futura. saepe enim inter nos impendentes casus defleuimus, cum belli ciuilis causas in priuatorum cupiditatibus inclusas, pacis spem a publico consilio esse exclusam uideremus' (cf. also 4–5). Tac. has similar obituaries of M. Lepidus at *A.* 4.20.2, of L. Piso at 6.10.3, and of L. Volusius at 13.30.2. Conversely Seneca regrets that Cato lived to see the crime of civil war (*Cons. Marc.* 20.6).

in re publica . . . quieta aut certe non praecipitata   Since *fatali . . . morte* below means a 'natural death' (cf. 2.4.6; Gell. 13.1; Gudeman on Tac. *D.* 13.6), it follows that *quieta . . . praecipitata* cannot qualify *morte* (tautology) but must agree with *re publica* (*fatali* was, however, deleted by J. Arnoldt, *NJb* 121 (1880), 248). To which clause does *quieta . . . praecipitata* belong? Krause believed that it referred to the main clause and punctuated after *periculo*; but the sentiment is redundant with *fatali ante . . . ciuilium morte*, and would probably require another word to clarify the sense (e.g. *quieta ⟨ea⟩* Lipsius; *praecipitata ⟨ciuitate⟩* Ruhnken; *praecipit⟨i ciuit⟩ate* Madvig 2.304–5). Kritz placed *quieta . . . praecipitata* in the *cum*-clause, I think rightly; the resulting word-order is perhaps odd, but can be explained as a combination of chiasmus and interlacing. For the exprr. cf. Cic. *Sull.* 1 and 87 'rei publicae praecipitanti', to which F. adds Liv.

---

[1] Hellegouarc'h believes V. means Q. Caecilius Metellus Celer, who died in 59; but this disrupts V.'s chronology, and Creticus and Hortensius (mentioned next) were consuls in the same year.

22.12.11 'ad rem publicam praecipitandam'; Cic. *Cat.* 2.19 'quieta re publica', Tac. *D.* 36.2. For *morte functi* cf. 131.2n., Pease on Virg. *Aen.* 4.696, Bömer on Ov. *Met.* 11.558–9.

49–54.1 CIVIL WAR (49–48 B.C.)

49–50 OUTBREAK (49 B.C.)

49.1 Lentulo ... post urbem conditam ... ante annos ... By this method of dating V. not only invests certain moments with an appropriate solemnity (cf. 103.3n.) but also ensures 'che il lettore sia involentariamente portato a riferire gli avvenimenti passati al presente, ed a confrontare le età passate e le morte stagioni con la presente e viva' (Lana 165). V., in other words, saw history as a 'seamless web' (F. W. Maitland's phrase), in this resembling Thucydides (cf. 1.2.1–21.1), Cicero (see E. Rawson, *JRS* 62 (1972), 34) and Livy (see Luce 230ff., esp. 248).[1]

For Vinicius see 100.2n. and 101.3n.; for *exarsit*, below, 75.1n.

alterius ... firmior So begins a *syncrisis* of Pompey and Caesar (in that order) to which the counterpart is found in the *syncrisis* between Octavian and Antony at 84.1–2 (see p. 219). *Syncrises* of Pompey and Caesar before Pharsalus are also in Luc. 1.129–57 and Dio 41.54.1ff., and it has been suggested that all three authors are dependent on Livy's lost 109th book (W. D. Lebek, *Lucans Pharsalia: Dichtungsstruktur und Zeitbezug* (1976), 64–5).

V.'s language echoes that of the period: see esp. Cael. ap. Cic. *Fam.* 8.14(97).3 (written mid-50) 'homines in dissensione domestica debeant, quam diu ciuiliter sine armis certetur, honestiorem sequi partem; ubi ad bellum et castra uentum sit, firmiorem, et id melius statuere quod tutius sit. in hac discordia uideo Cn. Pompeium senatum quique res iudicant secum habiturum, ad Caesarem omnis qui cum timore aut mala spe uiuant accessuros; exercitum conferendum non esse. omnino satis spati est ad considerandas utriusque copias et eligendam partem', Cic. *Lig.* 19 (written 46) 'causa tum dubia, quod erat aliquid in utraque parte quod probari posset; nunc melior ea iudicanda est quam etiam di adiuuerunt'. In addition, *causa melior (bona)* regularly describes the optimates (Hellegouarc'h, *VL* 419 n. 14), whose support Pompey now had (cf. L. R. Taylor, *Party Politics in the Age of Caesar* (1949), 148–61); and for *optima causa* used specifically of the *Pompeiani* see Raaflaub 195. *causa* was the jargon for referring to one side or the other in the struggle

---

[1] On the basis of Plb. 6.53, where the historian describes the funeral ceremonies, *imagines* and *tituli* of Roman aristocratic families, F. Klingner has suggested that this view of history is characteristically Roman. 'Die Vergangenheit erstreckt sich wirkend in die Gegenwart herein' (*Römische Geisteswelt* ([4]1961), 69).

(Hellegouarc'h, *VL* 419 n. 11; note esp. the pun at Cic. *Att.* 7.3.5 'causam solum illa causa non habet'), and for the expr. *causa firma* cf. e.g. Cic. *Clu.* 51, *Red. Sen.* 9, *Balb.* 19. Lucan too echoes this language at e.g. 4.259 'dux causae melioris eris' (of Caesar), and à propos of V.'s passage J. W. Duff remarked that 'one cannot help thinking of Lucan's famous antithesis concerning the same struggle, *uictrix causa deis placuit sed uicta Catoni*' (*A Lit. Hist. of Rome in the Silver Age* (1964 edn), 75). See also Sen. *Ep.* 14.13, esp. 'potest melior uincere, non potest non peior esse qui uicerit'.

For the contrast between *uideri* and *esse*, continued in *speciosa . . . ualentia* below, cf. Sall. *C.* 54.6 and Vretska ad loc. (the *syncrisis* of Cato and Caesar). Lucan again makes a similar point to V. at 1.135 'stat magni nominis umbra', cf. also 311ff.

49.2 Pompeium senatus auctoritas . . . armauit In Dec. 50 the then consul C. Marcellus had placed a sword in Pompey's hands and asked him to defend his country (Plut. *Pomp.* 59.1); and on 7 Jan. 49 a *senatus consultum ultimum* in effect charged Pompey with command against Caesar. But though Pompey at the time could thus be called *defensor r. p.* (Raaflaub 194), V. in his next sentence, as at 48.4 above (n.), is anxious to distinguish between the person and what he represented; so too Luc. 2.322–3, 5.14.

For *auctoritas . . . armauit* cf. Cic. *Mil.* 2, Sulp. *Dial.* 2.12.1; for *fiducia a.* cf. Liv. 37.45.17. For the forces available to both sides see Brunt, *IM* 473–5.

49.3 Lentulus uero salua re publica saluus esse non posset V. here and at 91.3 ironically inverts the language which Cic. had used to describe good citizens in 63 B.C. (*Cat.* 3.25 'qui salua urbe salui esse possent') and Caesar in 46 (*Marc.* 32 'nisi te, C. Caesar, saluo . . . salui esse non possumus'). For comparable ideas cf. Cic. *Phil.* 2.92, Tac. *H.* 3.55.2, Sen. *Ben.* 5.16.4 'ut (Pompeius) saluus esse non posset nisi beneficio seruitutis', Flor. 2.14.4 'aliter saluus esse non potuit (Antonius) nisi confugisset ad seruitutem'.

For L. Cornelius Lentulus Crus cf. *RE* 4.1381–4 = Cornelius 218 (Münzer); *MRR* 2.194, 256, 276. V.'s description alludes to his notorious debts (Caes. *BC* 1.4.2; I. Shatzman, *Senatorial Wealth and Roman Politics* (1975), 333–4). Lentulus' consular colleague was C. Claudius Marcellus, *RE* 3.2736–7 = Claudius 217 (Münzer); *MRR* 2.256, 276.

moriendum . . . contenderet 'argued that one should die rather than see the state forced to accept conditions from an individual citizen'. *ciuis* has been questioned but nothing more convincing has been proposed, and contrasts between *ciuis* and *res p.* are common, esp. in Cic.: an analogous case to ours is perhaps Cic. *Att.* 8.11D(161D).8, written to Pompey in Feb. 49: 'ego condicionibus . . . illi armis disceptari maluerunt; . . . perficiam profecto ut neque r.p. ciuis a me animum neque tu amici desideres'. For the attraction of the acc. + inf. into the subordinate clause cf. K–S 1.719 § 14.

uir antiquus et grauis . . .   This sentence illustrates the dilemma which faced men of V.'s temperament in the early empire. By instinct conservative and traditional (cf. 92.5n.), they tended naturally to sympathise with Pompey, the senate's man; yet they lived under a government made possible by Pompey's victorious opponent and the latter's adopted son. The dilemma was resolved, as in V.'s case, by glorifying Pompey himself, the 'soldier-citizen' whose death was a tragedy, but by criticising the *Pompeiani* in general and his son Sextus in particular. See P. Grenade, *REA* 52 (1950), esp. 57–61.

For *antiquus* see Plin. *Ep.* 2.9.4 'uir sanctus antiquus'; Landgraf on Cic. *Rosc.* 26.

49.4 ut deinde . . . decreuere†   An exceptionally difficult passage. PA read *decreuere* but Burer comments *ex. uet. sic habet, ut legend. existimem, committere decreuerat*, a characteristic ambiguity from which it is impossible to deduce the reading of (M) (see *TN* 9–10).

(a) Kritz assumed that *decreuere* was correct and that upon it depended everything from *tantummodo* to *committere*; this required his changing the nominatives to accusatives (*contentum . . . priuatumque*) and explaining as follows: 'quum Caesaris aduersarii . . . decernerent eum unice acquiescere in retento prouinciae titulo cum una legione, priuatumque in urbem uenire etc., Caesar Rubiconem transiit'. The objections to this, however, are (i) that the accus. + inf. cannot be used in the sense of *ut* + subjunc. after *decernere*; (ii) that in our other sources it is Caesar himself who suggested that he should retain a modified command (see next n.).

(b) Gelenius made *contentus* appositional to *quae Caesar postulauerat*, deleted -*que* after *priuatus*, changed the following infinitives to subjunctives (*ueniret . . . committeret*), and made them dependent on *decreuere*. This suggestion, which Mommsen improved by reading *ut* for -*que* (the hyperbaton of *priuatus* is attractive in the context), accords well with the realities of early Jan. 49: in response to Caesar's offer of a modified command (cf. *tantummodo . . . prouinciae*), the senate replied 'ueniret et peteret (consulatum) more maiorum' (Flor. 2.13.16, Eutrop. 6.19.2, but no other evidence). Yet there is an objection to this view also. What is the subject of *decreuere*? 'Scilicet Pompeio fauentes', says Krause, which indeed is the only possible explanation; yet I find it almost impossible to understand such a subject from the foregoing *syncrisis* of the two sides.

(c) Let us assume that *decreuerat* was in fact the reading of (M), as Burer perhaps suggests. Adopting this reading, Manutius repunctuated the whole sentence as follows: he made *tantummodo . . . decreuerat* a parenthesis, took *transiit* as the verb with *ut deinde*, and suggested *transmisere* as the main verb. The resulting sentence is characteristically Velleian, requires no emendation,[1] and corresponds suggestively to the realities of late Jan. 49

---

[1] Manutius in fact supplied *enim* before *contentus* and deleted -*que*, but neither change is essential to his interpretation.

when Caesar did indeed offer to come to Rome as a *priuatus* (Cic. *Fam.*
16.12(146).3 'ad consulatus petitionem se uenturum, neque se iam uelle
absente se rationem haberi suam'). There is only one snag. Manutius'
interpretation puts Caesar's offer before the crossing of the Rubicon on
c. 11 Jan., whereas the offer was not in fact made until 23 Jan. (Cic. *Att.*
7.14(138).1). It is true that, according to Plut. *Caes.* 30.1, Caesar had
already made a similar offer on an earlier occasion (the passage resembles
V.'s): ἠξίου γὰρ αὐτός τε καταθέσθαι τὰ ὅπλα, καὶ Πομπηίου ταὐτὸ
πράξαντος ἀμφοτέρους ἰδιώτας γενομένους εὑρίσκεσθαί τι παρὰ τῶν πολιτῶν
ἀγαθόν. It is, however, most improbable that Caesar offered to relinquish
the *ratio absentis* (which is, after all, what the argument was about) until
faced with the *s. c. u.* of 7 Jan.; but Plut. not only places his account of the
offer before the *s. c. u.* (cf. 31.2) but even before his account of Caesar's
other proposal of a modified command (31.1), which belongs to late Dec.
– early Jan. (see next n.). Sadly, therefore, Manutius' interpretation of
V.'s words must be abandoned.

(d) It is likely, then, that *ut deinde* . . . refers, not to Caesar's offer of late
Jan., but to the senate's ultimatum of earlier that month; and in order to
avoid the difficulty of *decreuere* (see (b) above), I suggest that V. might
have written as follows: 'ut deinde spretis omnibus quae Caesar postulauerat (tantummodo contentus cum una legione titulum retinere
prouinciae), priuatus ut in urbem ueniret et se in petitione consulatus
suffragiis populi Romani committeret decreuerat ⟨senatus⟩, ratus bellandum Caesar . . . transiit'. The insertion of *senatus* is not difficult, and the
passage now agrees with Flor. 2.13.16 (above); yet because the whole
issue is so uncertain, I have thought it wisest to place obeli in my text.

contentus cum una legione titulum retinere prouinciae In the
last weeks of December 50, Caesar had proposed that he should retain
onl Cisalpine Gaul and Illyricum with two legions. After various complicated negotiations, in which Cicero was prominent, it was suggested that
the *impasse* might be resolved if Caesar retained only Illyricum and one
legion (cf. Suet. *Iul.* 29.2 'cum aduersariis autem pepigit ut . . . etiam una
legio cum Illyrico concederetur'). This final proposal, to which V. here
alludes,[1] was allegedly acceptable to both Caesar and Pompey but was

---

[1] This is clear from the phrase *titulum retinere prouinciae*, 'to retain a
nominal province', which refers to the status of Illyricum at the time.
'In the late republic', as Seager remarks, 'Illyricum could be attached
to another province, Macedonia or Gallia Cisalpina, for no special
purpose other than administrative convenience' (*Pomp.* 89, referring to
RE 9.1087); and by the *lex Vatinia* of 59 it was so attached to Cisalpina
in the case of Caesar (Suet. *Iul.* 22.1 'Illyrico adiecto'). Thus when in
the present final proposal it was suggested that Caesar should relinquish
Cisalpina but retain Illyricum, an independent status was being
accorded to Illyricum which it strictly did not possess. See also Raaflaub
66 n. 269, who refers to E. Meyer, *Caesars Monarchie und das Principat des
Pompeius* (³1922), 286.

COMMENTARY 2.50.1

rejected by Lentulus and Cato (hence *nihil receptum a Pompeianis* [not *a Pompeio*], *cum . . . Lentulus . . . M. autem Cato . . .* at 3 above). Although these negotiations clearly lasted until the first week of Jan. 49, their precise chronology is controversial (see e.g. Rice Holmes, *Rep.* 2.331ff., Butler–Cary's edn of Suet. *Iul.*, pp. xxii–xxiv, Seager, *Pomp.* 161–2, all with further refs.).

Rubiconem transiit 'Caesar does not mention the Rubicon', but the 'decisive significance of the crossing' is mentioned by, in addition to V., Suet. *Iul.* 31.2, Plut. *Caes.* 32.5, App. *BC* 2.35 (Gelzer, *Caes.* 193 n. 3). Pompey left Rome on 17 Jan. (refs. in Seager, *Pomp.* 165 n. 5) and crossed to Dyrrachium on 17 March (Cic. *Att.* 9.15(184)).

50.1 Domitio . . . potitus L. Domitius Ahenobarbus, appointed by the senate to succeed Caesar as governor of Transalpine Gaul, was forced by Caesar to surrender on 21 Feb.; for the episode see Shackleton Bailey's edn of Cic. *Att.*, vol. 4, Appendix IV, who observes that 'the exact size and composition of Domitius' force is a matter of debate' (p. 448 n. 8; cf. Rice Holmes, *Rep.* 3.368ff.). For Domitius see *RE* 5.1334–43 = Domitius 27 (Münzer); *MRR* 2.153, 179, 194, 221, 237, 261–2, 277; also below, 3n.

No one seems to have been troubled by P's reading *legionibusque Corfini quae una cum eo fuerant* until it was discovered that A had omitted *quae*; whereupon Baiter (in Orelli's edn), on the false assumption that A = (M), suggested that *quae* had been inserted into P by Rhenanus but in the wrong place. Baiter therefore proposed *legionibusque ⟨quae⟩ Corfini una cum eo fuerant*. But of course A is *not* equivalent to (M) (see *TN* 16), and Burer's silence indicates that (M) and P are in agreement. I have therefore retained P's reading (though I have followed Stegmann in making the slight change to *Corfinii*); and for the expr. cf. Liv. 23.32.1 'exercitus Teani'. Gelenius' *uoluerant*, below, for the paradosis *uenerant*, is supported by *uoluerat* at 4 below.

sine dilatione dimissis 'clementiam Corfiniensem illam' (Cic. *Att.* 9.16(185).1). For Caesar's *clementia* in general see 4 below and 55.2n.

persecutus Brundusium Caesar arrived on 9 March (Cic. *Att.* 9.13A(181A).1 = Caesar's letter to Oppius and Cornelius) but was refused a meeting by Pompey. With *persecutus* we must understand either *eum* (which Krause suggested inserting after *Brundusium*) or *Pompeium* (which Friebel suggested reading for *per-*) or *eos*, or *iter* (which Ruhnken wrote instead of *ita*) or *uiam*.

integris rebus et condicionibus (1) Normally *integris rebus* is a set phrase = 'while matters were still undecided' (*OLD* s.v. *integer* 2a). If that is taken to be the meaning here, we must almost certainly assume that *integris* has a similar meaning when combined with *condicionibus* – unless, of

87

course, we assume that the adj. does not go with *condicionibus* at all but refers only to *rebus*. If we make the former assumption, then the whole phrase will mean something like 'while circumstances were still fluid and terms unprejudiced'. But if we make the latter assumption, then *condicionibus* will simply mean 'on terms', 'by means of a treaty' *uel sim.*; and in this case some readers may wish to follow Nagel in deleting *et*, the presence of which leaves it unclear that *integris* is not to be taken also with *condicionibus*. Yet without *et* we are left with two awkwardly juxtaposed abll.

(2) If the war is not yet ended (cf. *malle . . . finire bellum*), then surely 'matters' are *ipso facto* 'undecided' and the above interpretation of *integris rebus* results in tautology.[1] Let us try another approach. It appears from *appareret* that *integris . . . condicionibus* is a constituent element of the impression which Caesar wanted to create and which is presumably intended to redound to his credit. Perhaps, therefore, *integris rebus* = 'while things were still unaltered' (sc. by the onset of war).[2] What, then, of *condicionibus*? It is clear from Caesar himself and from other evidence that in the first two weeks of March he made several attempts to discuss terms with Pompey face to face (*BC* 1.24.5 'coram de omnibus condicionibus disceptetur', 26.3–4; Seager, *Pomp.* 174–5, Gelzer, *Caes.* 202–3). Now if V. believed that these were the same conciliatory terms which Caesar had put forward before (on 23 Jan.: see 49.4n. § (c)), then he might very reasonably have described them with the words *integris . . . condicionibus*, 'on unaltered terms'. Thus the whole phrase may well mean something like 'while everything, including his terms, still remained unaltered'.

It is perhaps not easy to decide between the two interpretations suggested above, and still other interpretations may be possible; but on the whole I favour (2).

50.2 ac miserrimae necessitudinis The noun = 'compulsion' or 'constraint' (*OLD* s.v. 3*a*), a standard method of defence in a law-court (cf. Cic. *Inu.* 2.98 'necessitudo . . . infertur cum ui quadam reus id, quod fecerit, fecisse defenditur'). No one seems to have considered deleting *ac*; but its deletion would produce a neat chiasmus in which both *consiliorum suorum* and *miserrimae necessitudinis* would apply equally to *in senatu* and *in contione*. (Caesar's speeches before the senate and assembly took place at the very beginning of April (Gelzer, *Caes.* 208–9); for what he said cf. *BC* 1.32.)

---

[1] Unless V.'s point is that the war, while not yet over, has hardly started: he might mean that neither side has had time to find itself in an entrenched position.

[2] Krause's 'antequam ad dimicationem ventum, et res in integro esset' and Kritz's 'certamine armorum nondum inito' are similar.

cum alienis armis ad arma compulsus esset On grounds of logic
this clause cannot be taken with *Hispanias petere decreuit* below. The most
obvious interpretation, since the notion of 'constraint' appears in both
places, is that the clause elaborates or explains *miserrimae necessitudinis*
above (thus Shipley: 'an account . . . of the deplorable necessity of his
position, in that he had been driven to arms . . .'); yet this usage of *cum* is
unusual and we might have expected (*quippe*) *qui* or conceivably *qua*. Now
it it certainly true that authors often write *cum* where they might have
written *qui* (see W. G. Hale, *The* Cum-*Constructions* (repr. 1965), 137ff.;
e.g. Juv. 1.61–2 'nam lora tenebat | ipse lacernatae cum se iactaret
amicae') and that *cum* can have as its antecedent a noun which describes a
situation (e.g. Cic. *Leg. Man.* 33 'quid ego . . . illam labem . . . querar
cum . . . classis ea . . . capta . . . est?'; *OLD* s.v. *cum* 10); but in the first of
these exs. *cum* expresses cause and in the second it expresses time, and I
have been unable to find a passage where *cum* both has a noun as its
antecedent and at the same time has a causal or explanatory sense. This
may be an argument for emending our *cum* to *qui*,[1] although I have ref-
rained from doing so.

A more remote possibility is that our clause refers, not to *necessitudinis*,
but to *ratione* further back. Now although I do not think that *ratio* can be
followed by *cum*, it can be followed by an indir. question (see *OLD* s.v.
ratio); it might therefore be tempting to write *cur* here, as at 1.3.2
'reddenda erit ei ratio cur . . .'. But *cur* makes no sense alongside *alienis
armis*; we would expect a word meaning 'how', a construction which *ratio*
seems not to take.

For V.'s expr. cf. Cic. *Marc.* 13 'ad illa arma [civil war] fato sumus . . .
compulsi'.

50.3 Massilia . . . armorum arbitria captans So too Luc. 3.390–2
'tenuit flagrantis in omnia belli | praecipitem cursum, raptisque a Caesare
cunctis | uincitur una mora'. Caesar's arrival at Massilia is usu. put at 19
Apr.: he was still *en route* on 16 Apr. (Cic. *Att.* 10.8B(199B) = Caesar to
Cic.) and the role played by the city is mentioned by Cic. on 6 May (*Att.*
10.12A(203).3). In fact the city was in a dilemma since previously Pompey
and Caesar had each conferred *beneficia* upon it and hence each could be
called its *patronus* (cf. Caes. *BC* 1.35.4 'patronos ciuitatis'); but the
balance was tipped against Caesar, not because (as Krause suggests)
Pompey had a prior claim, but more likely because of the presence in
Massilia of L. Domitius Ahenobarbus after his release from Corfinium (1
above). For Domitius, a long-standing opponent of Caesar's activities in
Gaul, was the grandson of Cn. Domitius Ahenobarbus, the consul of
122 B.C. who had done much to settle and begin the development of this

---

[1] At 112.3 (see n.) *cum* and *ut* are perhaps confused; but I do not think *ut* is
possible here: at Sall. *C.* 33.5 'neue nobis eam necessitudinem imponatis
ut quaeramus' *ut* is consecutive after *eam*.

area of Gaul (cf. 2.10.2) and whose family had many connections there (see C. Ebel, *Transalpine Gaul* (1976), 70–93, esp. 85f. [98–102 on the *beneficia* of Pompey and Caesar respectively]). L. Domitius used Massilia as a base to delay Caesar's progress to Spain (*MRR* 2.261–2; Gelzer, *Caes.* 212–13); and though after a few weeks Caesar entrusted the siege of Massilia to his legate C. Trebonius and himself proceeded on his way to Spain, the city succumbed to Caesar's forces in the following year. Hence *fide melior quam consilio prudentior*. For the military operations around Massilia see Rice Holmes, *Rep.* 3.78ff., 409ff.; for V.'s admiration of the family of the Domitii see 82.3n.

For *festinatio* + obj. gen., as here, cf. *TLL* 6.1.614.27–32 (V. not mentioned). For *consilio prudentior* cf. Sall. *J.* 7.5 ' bonus consilio ', Cic. *Clu.* 107 'ingenio prudentior', *Font.* 43 ' ad consilia prudentem ' (F.); for the comparative adj. after *quam* cf. 129.2n., *OLD* s.v. *quam* 8 (*fin.*); for *fides* ~ *consilium* cf. 82.2n. For *armorum arbitria* see Liv. 8.2.3, 32.37.5 ' arbitrium pacis ac belli ', 44.15.5, Just. 22.2.5; for *captans* cf. Flor. 2.13.61 ' captante fortuna hunc . . . regno exitum '; for this use of *principalis* cf. 124.3n.

quibus hi . . . coercere possunt   ' something [i.e. *principalia arma*] in which only those persons should intervene who are able to restrain the recalcitrant party '. For the idea Gruter quoted Liv. 9.14.5 ' uanissimam increpans gentem quae, suarum impotens rerum prae domesticis seditionibus discordiisque, aliis modum pacis ac belli facere aequum censeret '; but the notion that power is what counts in inter-state relations goes back to Greek thought (see G. E. M. De Ste Croix, *The Origins of the Peloponnesian War* (1972), 16ff.), though it was obviously a Roman assumption too (see Harris, *passim*).

For V.'s use of *interponere* cf. Liv. 35.48.9 ' bello se non interponant ', 35.49.13 ' non interponi uos bello '; for *parentem* cf. 108.2n.

50.4 ipsius aduentus uigore ac fulgore occupatus   It was a panegyrical motif that a general's mere arrival was effective (cf. 75.1n.): hence *ipsius* probably agrees with *aduentus* and does not mean ' of the general himself' (for which cf. 109.5n.). *aduentu occupatus* is found elsewhere (Liv. 9.12.5, Sen. *D.* 12.5.3, Just. 2.12.21) but V. has varied the expr. by adding *uigore ac fulgore*; the latter noun suggests that V. is thinking in metaphorical terms of lightning (so too Krause; Crusius emended to *fulgure*). *fulgor* is often used of lightning, Caesar can be described in terms of lightning (Luc. 1.151–7, 'die einzige Stelle, an der ein Held und seine kriegerische Tüchtigkeit mit dem wirklich detailliert ausgeführten Bild des Blitzes gezeichnet wird ', Lebek, op. cit. [above 49.1n.] 68),[1] and *occupare* is used of the actions of natural phenomena (e.g. Vitr. 3.3.9, Sen. *Ben.* 6.28.2). I can however find no ex. of *uigor* used of lightning *uel sim*.

---

[1] For the comparable metaphor *fulmina belli* see Virg. *Aen.* 6.842 with Norden's n.

V.'s ref. is to the battle of Ilerda (Rice Holmes, *Rep.* 3.51–77, 388ff.), which concluded with the surrender of Caesar's opponents on 2 Aug. 49 (*ILS* 8744). For Afranius and Petreius, above, see 48.1n.

51–54.1 DYRRACHIUM AND PHARSALUS (48 B.C.)

This section provides an excellent illustration of V.'s narrative technique. He says almost nothing about either campaign, even making an explicit allusion to his extremely abbreviated treatment of Pharsalus (52.3n.); instead he focusses on a colourful episode in each case (Balbus' *temeritas* at 51.3 and Caesar's *clementia* at 52.4–6). Far more time is spent on the aftermath of Pharsalus and Pompey's death, subjects which attracted considerable attention from rhetoricians, whose topoi V. deploys in abundance (see 53.1–4nn.).

51.1 dum Dyrrachium ... retinetur   Editors have objected to *retinere*, presumably on the grounds that it often means 'holding on to something which one is in danger of losing' (cf. 2.18.4 'ea urbs pertinacissime arma retinebat exercituque Romano obsidebatur') or 'retaining a certain element of something already lost' (cf. 40.3 'nihil praeter nomen imperatoris retinens'; also Krebs–Schmalz 2.513). Yet Vossius observed that *retinere = tenere* is found at Flor. 1.35.3 'prouinciam pop. Romanus non quidem bello nec armis sed ... iure retinebat', and such uses of compound verb for simple are found elsewhere, often involving the prefix *re-* (see S. Lilliedahl, *Florusstudien* (1928), 66, who refers to Munro on Lucr. 5.1141; L–H–S 300). I can thus see no real reason to change the verb here, and its use at 76.2 seems to me not dissimilar. Whether one should write the subjunctive here and retain *cum*, or retain *retinetur* and write *dum* (Ellis), is difficult to say; but the latter seems to me more economical.

51.2 sua et celeritate et fortuna ... usus   Caesar crossed with some of his troops on 4 Jan. 48 and landed the next day (*BC* 3.6); but the rest of his force was delayed by adverse conditions for several weeks (next n.), though their eventual crossing was put down to *Fortunae beneficium* (*BC* 3.26.4; Weinstock 116–17). For Caesar's famous speed and fortune in general see 41.4n. and 55.1n. respectively. There seems to be no parallel for *in mora habere*, below, though *esse in mora quominus* is common (e.g. Liv. 26.3.8, 30.44.3).

et cum uellet ipse ...   Scholars have been worried by the lack of a point of reference for *perueniret* and by the weakness and isolation of *cum uellet*; hence proposals such as Acidalius' *et quo uellet* and Ruhnken's *et cum ⟨uellet et quo⟩ uellet*. Yet the former difficulty seems to me insignificant since it is perfectly clear from the context what Caesar's destination is (cf. *castris Pompeii sua iungeret* etc. below). The latter difficulty would be solved if we were to assume that *et* here is co-ordinate with *-que* below. On this view V. would be drawing a distinction between Caesar and his army which tallies with the events which took place. For though Caesar crossed to Dyrrachium in a single day (i.e. *cum uellet*, see last n.), much of his army was, to his annoyance, delayed by adverse conditions for several weeks (Caes. *BC* 3.8.1, 25–6). But though *et . . . -que* is common (there is an ex. in the paradosis of Caesar's own account of this very episode, *BC* 3.26.3), it seems to be the rule that *et* is not separated from the part of speech (here *ipse*) corresponding to that to which *-que* is joined (e.g. Cic. *Fin.* 5.64 'et eos . . . nosque'; K–S 2.36). Thus, if V. intended *et . . . -que*, he ought to have written *et ipse, cum uellet, exercitusque . . . ueniret.* One could, I suppose, consider transposing *ipse* and *cum uellet*; but is the difficulty of *cum uellet* so great as to justify altering the paradosis at all? I do not think so. And if we retain the paradosis, we must therefore adopt Schoepfer's interpretation of it: viz. *et* is co-ordinate with *et* below, the latter being expanded by *primo . . . mox.*

paene castris Pompeii sua iungeret *paene*, which troubled Cludius, is presumably to be explained by the fact that the River Apsus separated the two camps (Caes. *BC* 3.19.1). No such precision at Luc. 5.461–3 'prima duces uidit iunctis consistere castris | tellus, quam uolucer Genusus, quam mollior Hapsus | circumeunt ripis'.

inopia obsidentibus quam obsessis erat grauior A topos of military narrative, e.g. Liv. 5.26.9 'copiaeque aliae . . . largius obsessis quam obsidentibus suppeterent', 9.23.7, 23.37.5, 25.11.12 'propiusque inopiam erant obsidentes quam obsessi', 34.34.2, 43.22.10 'cum inopiam prius obsidentes quam obsessi sensuri essent', Val. Max. 1.6.3, Tac. *H.* 3.73.1, Flor. 2.13.27, Dio 56.12.5. For the reality on this occasion see Caes. *BC* 3.47.4 'ipse autem consumptis omnibus longe lateque frumentis summis erat in angustiis . . .' etc.

51.3 excedente humanam fidem temeritate For such exprr. cf. 56.1n.; for their use in battle-narrative see 71.1n. Balbus later made his exploit the subject of a play which he put on in his native Cadiz (Pollio in Cic. *Fam.* 10.32(415).3 'praetextam de suo itinere ad L. Lentulum pro consule sollicitandum posuit et quidem, cum ageretur, fleuit memoria rerum gestarum commotus'). Piquancy was added to the exploit by the fact (if it is a fact) that Balbus' family acquired their citizenship through the good offices of Lentulus earlier in his career (see E. Badian, *Foreign Clientelae* (1958), 303, referring to Münzer in *RE* 4.1261 and 1382).

The above extract from Pollio's letter reminds us that at the time of the incident Lentulus was proconsul. Editors of V. tend to print *Lentulo . . . consule*, which is also the reading of A;[1] but our principal authority P reads *COS.*, and I have little doubt that Prof. Goodyear is right to suggest that

---

[1] It appears that Livy occasionally used *consul = pro consule* (see R. E. Smith, *Service in the Post-Marian Roman Army* (1958), 12 n. 1).

this should be interpreted as an abbreviation of *consulari* (for a similar abbreviation see 2.12.2, and for Lentulus as *consularis* see 53.1 below). Certainly the description of Lentulus as *consularis* here gives added point to the same word used of Balbus just below. For Lentulus' financial problems see 49.3n.

non Hispaniensis natus sed Hispanus   'not just born in Spain but an actual Spaniard'. It is tempting to say that if V. did not write *Hispaniensis*, which Lipsius conjectured for the nonsensical *Hispaniae Asiae*, then he ought to have done. Certainly no other conjecture is nearer the paradosis or is more convincing (though Kritz sets great store by Morgenstern's ⟨*in*⟩ *Hispania ex ciue natus*), and Lipsius' suggestion makes V.'s point with elegance and wit (he compared Mart. 12 *praef.* 'non Hispaniensem librum mittamus sed Hispanum'). For the use of *incrementum*, above, see 34.3; *OLD* s.v. 4*a*, adding Val. Max. 4.75, 5.7.2, 6.9.7; for *in . . . adsurgeret*, below, cf. Val. Max. 9.3. *ext.* 1 'obstitit quominus illuc adsurgeret' (F.).

fieretque ex priuato consularis   It is usually alleged that V. has here confused L. Cornelius Balbus (Minor), who rashly conversed with Lentulus, with his uncle L. Cornelius Balbus (Maior), who became cos. suff. in 40 without having held (it is said) any previous office. I think this is not the case. It is almost certain that Balbus Maior was an *eques* (see Nicolet 2.854 [no. 118]), in which case he would have been the next *eques* after Pompey and Octavian to rise straight to the consulship; yet at 76.4 V. says that Salvidienus Rufus, who became consul in the year *after* Balbus Maior, was 'the next of the equestrian order after Pompey and Octavian himself to become consul' (see n.). V.'s evidence on Salvidienus has never been questioned; thus, if it is true, he cannot here be referring to Balbus Maior. Against this it might be objected that there is some small evidence that Balbus Maior was propraetor in Spain in 41 (*RRC* 1.526–7 no. 518 and Crawford's n.) and thus not an *eques* when he became consul; yet this same evidence, if accepted, means that Balbus Maior was not a *priuatus* when he became consul and thus cannot qualify as the person with whom V. has confused his nephew.

The clue to V.'s meaning resides in the word *consularis*. (It is true that Ruhnken emended to *consul*, but there is no evidence that Balbus Minor ever became consul; the 'L. Cornelius' who was cos. suff. in 32 is generally assumed to have been L. Cornelius Cinna.) In his articles on Balbus Minor in *RE* (4.1268–71) and *PIR*² (2.310–12) E. Groag plausibly suggested that the man was adlected *inter consulares* by Augustus. Such an honour would have been most appropriate for someone whose triumph *ex Africa* in 19 was the last to be held by a senator and the first by a man who was not a Roman citizen at birth. And since Balbus Minor last held office as quaestor in 44 (unless it was he who was propraetor in 41), he would have been a *priuatus* when adlected. Nothing, finally, is known of his priesthood.

uariatum ... proeliis, sed un⟨um e⟩o longe magis ... prosperum quo grauiter impulsi ... Krause explained the paradosis *uno* *... prospero* as a kind of zeugma, understanding *pugnatum* (*est*) after *uariatum*; but this seems to me extremely difficult. Kritz proposed *unum ...* *prosperum*, and Fröhlich deleted *quo*; but neither of these is as attractive as writing *est* for *sed* and regarding *uno ... prospero* as an abl. abs., which Prof. Goodyear has suggested to me. My only reason for not adopting this suggestion is that it, like most others apart from Fröhlich's, leaves the clause *quo ... milites* rather lame after *uno ... prospero*. I therefore propose *un⟨um e⟩o ... prosperum quo*: 'but one was particularly favourable to the Pompeians, considering the severity with which Caesar's soldiers were repelled'. Once *eo* dropped out, and given the proximity of *quo*, the corruption to *prospero* was inevitable (and cf. how -*o* has been added to *alter* at 49.3 and *Pompei* at 1 above). For the lack of a comparative in the *quo*-clause see K–S 2.484–5.

For the battle in question, which is thought to have taken place at some point during the first two weeks of July (Rice Holmes, *Rep.* 3.480), see Caes. *BC* 3.62–72. For *impulsi* cf. 70.1.

52.1 Tum Caesar ... Thessaliam petiit Caesar began his long journey to Pharsalus almost immediately after the defeat mentioned in 51.3; for reconstructions of his timetable *en route* see Rice Holmes, *Rep.* 3.480.

fatalem = 'destined for'. Although I can find no parallel for this meaning with a simple dative of a thing, *fatalis* in this sense is found with *ad* + accus. (e.g. Cic. *Cat.* 3.9) and dat. gerundive (e.g. Tib. 2.5.57; both together at Liv. 5.19.2 'fatalis dux ad excidium illius urbis seruandaeque patriae'). *fatalis* + dat. normally = 'fatal to' (e.g. Liv. 5.33.1 'fatali urbi clade' [wrongly classified in *OLD* s.v. 2a] and of places etc. at Liv. 6.28.5, Flor. 2.17.6, Just. 12.13.3, [Vict.] *Orig.* 11.1); but if V. had intended the gen. here (= 'determining the fate of', cf. Gell. 14.1.18), he would have written *proelii* not *uictoriae*.

52.2 alii ut bellum traheret The view not only of Cic., as Krause notes (*Fam.* 7.3(183).2 'suadere institui ut bellum duceret'), but of Pompey himself, according to Plut. *Pomp.* 66.4–67.4, Caes. 40–41.1, App. *BC* 2.66. The various options open to Pompey are well set out and analysed in Seager, *Pomp.* 181.

For *hercules*, above, and similar forms in historical narrative cf. e.g. 110.5, *Bell. Afr.* 12.1, Liv. 7.11.1, Curt. 4.10.23, Tac. *A.* 1.3.5. In general see Neue–Wagener 2.992.[1] For *salubrius fuit*, where in Eng. we say 'would have been', see L–H–S 327–8, K–S 1.171*b*.

---

[1] I owe this ref. to Dr J. N. Adams.

quod dignatione partium . . . magis prosperum fieret The usual interpretation of this phrase is that of H–W: '. . . prolonger une guerre que l'éclat de leur parti leur rendrait de jour en jour plus favorable'. But though the Pompeians had just won a victory at Dyrrachium which they considered significant (*magis prosperum*, cf. Caes. *BC* 3.72.1 'uicisse iam sibi uiderentur', 4 'per orbem t. fama ac litteris uictoriam eius diei concelebrabant'), they could hardly attribute this to an *éclat* which Pompey had forfeited by his abandonment of Rome and Italy. It would be far more plausible if the Pompeians were to urge prolonging the war 'on the grounds that, because of the favour in which their side was *now* held [i.e. because of the recent victory at Dyrrachium], it would gradually turn out even more favourably for them'. But since such an interpretation would require *foret* (which Cludius actually proposed) for *fieret*, we must assume that the usual view of this passage is correct and that the Pompeians were simply deluding themselves.

For the genit. after *dignatio* see *TLL* 5.1.1132.28–32 (elder and younger Sen., elder Plin.).

usus impetu suo hostem secutus est Since the first part of this phrase contrasts with *longe diuersa aliis suadentibus* above, a concessive abl. abs. which is divided into *plerique . . . alii*, V. can only mean that Pompey himself wished for a third and hitherto unmentioned course, viz. pursuing Caesar with a view to a decisive battle. That this was not Pompey's wish, however, is shown by Plut. and App. (last n. but one). See also below, 53.1n.

52.3 aciem Pharsalicam For the various problems connected with the battle and its site see e.g. Rice Holmes, *Rep.* 3.166–70, 452ff., C. B. R. Pelling, *Historia* 22 (1973), 249–59, F. Paschoud, ibid. 30 (1981), 178–88. The date was 9 August. For *cruentus* + dat., below, cf. e.g. Tac. *A.* 2.18.1; for *c.* + *dies* cf. Ov. *Tr.* 4.10.14 (Luc. 7.427 'hac luce cruenta ').

conlisa . . . duo r.p. capita effossumque alterum . . . lumen For the mixed metaphor see 99.1n.; for *effossum lumen* see H. C. Nutting, *CP* 17 (1922), 313ff. For *profusum*, above, Pluygers wrote *profusi*; but V. perhaps wished to avoid a genit. after *exercitus*.

tot talesque . . . caesos uiros For a discussion of casualty statistics etc. see P. A. L. Greenhalgh, *Pompey the Republican Prince* (1981), 302–3 (Appendix II).

hic scripturae modus *modus* = 'limit' is almost technical among writers at transitional points in their works (e.g. at the end of a volume, cf. *Rhet. Herenn.* 2.50, Quint. 9.4.146), particularly when small-scale genres are in question (cf. e.g. Plin. *Ep.* 2.5.13, 9.13.26, Sen. *Ep.* 45.13, Front. p.

114.20 N = p. 136.16 VdH; Nep. *Epam.* 4.6 'modus adhibendus est quoniam uno hoc uolumine uitam ... uirorum ... concludere constituimus', *SHA Val.* 8.5 'ne modum uoluminis transeam'; Eutrop. 10.18.3 'operi modum dabimus', Sulp. *Chron.* 1.20.1 'suscepti operis modum custodientes solam historiam persequimur'). See further *TLL* 8.1259.58ff. V.'s work is of course a summary history, as he regularly reminds us by phraseology of this type (*modus* again at 29.2, cf. also 55.1, 66.3, 86.1, 89.1 etc.): see in general Woodman (1975), 277–87 (285 on Eutrop. and Sulp.); also Starr (1981).

For *recipere* (used by Hor. in a similar context at *Epist.* 2.1.258) + gerundive, common in Vitruv., cf. K–S 1.731; for such formulae as *illud notandum est*, below, cf. 67.1n.

52.4 quam †in omnes partes ut militari et uerbo et consuetudine utar dimitteret† Lipsius emended the second *et* to *ex* but this required his deleting the first *et*, a task which he tacitly performed without explaining how it came to be in the text. Almost all edd., especially those working after the discovery of A (in which the first *et* is omitted), have followed Lipsius; Ruhnken did not, but neither did he attempt to explain what *et* ... *et* would mean. I think it possible that we have here an example of hendiadys and that V. means: 'if I might resort to my military habit of using a military expression'.[1] *uerbo uti* and *consuetudine uti* are both common phrases,[2] but I admit that I can find no parallel for the form of words as a whole.

Whether or not Lipsius' [*et*] ... *ex* is accepted, we are faced with the problem of V.'s 'military expression'. Does *militare uerbum* mean an expression used *of* soldiers or *by* soldiers?[3] In the light of V.'s apologetic *ut*

---

[1] I see that hendiadys has also occurred to P. Santini (cited below), who however follows A's text and thus takes no account of the first *et*.

[2] Hence the whole phrase cannot exemplify zeugma, which would require the verb to combine naturally with only one of its two objects (cf. 47.2). Nor can it exemplify syllepsis, in which the same verb is used simultaneously in more than one of its normal meanings: here the required sense would have to be 'if I might use a military expression to describe a military custom', but *consuetudine uti* cannot = 'to describe a custom'.

[3] *militare uerbum* is used in the former sense by Porph. on Hor. *Epist.* 1.19.4 (*adscripsit*) and by Serv. *Aen.* 8.653 (*tenebat* allegedly technical = *defendebat*); and the comparable *militaria uocabula* is used in the latter sense by Gell. 10.9 to describe various terms ranging from *cuneus* and *alae* to *serra* and *forfices*. In certain contexts it is difficult to distinguish the two senses, partly because a word used by soldiers can by extension come to mean a word from a military context (this is true of those mentioned by Balsdon 119). For further exs. of the phrase *militare uerbum* (*uel sim.*) as used by ancient commentators see J. F. Mountford–J. T. Schultz, *Index Rerum et Nominum in Schol. Servii et Ael. Donati Tractatorum* (1930), 180, s.v. *verbum*.

... *utar*, it seems to me that he must mean the latter; we must therefore assume that the military expr. is unlikely to be *dimittere* (Popma, Vossius[1]), *partes* (Lipsius, following whom and Heinsius Ellis proposed *incolumes partes*), or *in omnes partes dimittere* (Burman, Kritz, the latter quoting numerous exs. from Caes. and Liv.). It follows that the *militare uerbum* does not appear in the paradosis and we must assume a lacuna.

To clarify the content of the lacuna we must first decide which incident V. is referring to. Ed. Bipont. and Orelli believed that he was referring to Caesar's well known efforts at saving Brutus, who is mentioned in the next sentence (cf. App. *BC* 2.112, Plut. *Caes.* 46.2, 62.2, *Brut.* 5.1); most others prefer Caesar's even better known efforts at more general salvation (Caes. *BC* 3.98.2, Flor. 2.13.50 '[sc. uox Caesaris] "parce ciuibus!"', Suet. *Iul.* 75.2 'acie Pharsalica proclamauit ut ciuibus parceretur', App. *BC* 2.80). The latter view was shared by W. Heraeus, who twice wrote on Roman 'Soldatensprache'. In *ALL* 12 (1901), 267n., he objected to Ruhnken's *partes* ⟨*praecones clamantes 'parce ciuibus'*⟩ *ut* and to Halm's *dimitteret* ⟨*tesseram 'parce ciuibus'*⟩ that neither was sufficiently significant to warrant V.'s apology. Instead he himself proposed *tesserarios* for *praecones*. Later, however, Heraeus changed his mind, evidently on the grounds that not all so-called *militaria uerba* are in fact specifically military (*Kleine Schriften* (1937), 153); warning that we should not hunt for a proper military expression here at all, Heraeus suggested *utar* ⟨*tesseram ut ciuibus parceretur*⟩ *dimitteret*. Yet despite the reservations I expressed about a similar apology from V. at 41.3 (n.), I nevertheless feel that *ut . . . utar* indicates that Heraeus' first instincts were correct. Whether *tesserarios* was the *militare uerbum*, however, it is of course impossible to say.

Finally, although I can find no ex. of *prius* combined with *antiquius*, *nihil antiquius habere quam* can be followed either by *ut*+subjunc. (K–S 2.213f.) or by the infin. (K–S 1.667), and at Liv. 2.48.1 *neque ullam aliam priorem curam agere quam* is followed by *ut*+subjunc. and at Liv. 39.47.4 *nihil prius . . . uisum est quam* is followed by the infin. Most scholars here insert *ut* after *quam*, some emend *in* to *ut*, Haase emended to *dimittere*; but in view of the general uncertainty surrounding the whole sentence, I have thought it best simply to obelise.

For *inclinatam . . . aciem*, above, see *TLL* 1.408.63ff., 7.1.946.50ff. (Enn. Sall. Liv. Tac. Suet. Sil.); for *pretium tulit*, below, 125.1n.

52.6 nihil illa uictoria . . . clarius fuit, quando . . . There is no justification for altering the text. For the expr. cf. 22.1 'nihil illa uictoria

---

[1] Also Hellegouarc'h (1976), 250–1, who like Lipsius before him writes *ut* for *in* (reproduced in his edn), and P. Santini (*Anazetesis* 1 (1978), 5–6), who inserts *eius* after *consuetudine* and makes the ingenious suggestion that *in omnes partes dimittere* is a Caesarian phrase to which V. is alluding in this Caesarian context ('per servirmi di una parola del gergo militare usata abitualmente da Cesare'). But, as Kritz points out, Caesar is not the only author to use that phrase.

fuisset crudelius' (noted by Scriner), and for *quando* = 'because' cf. 2.14.1; *OLD* s.v. 3). For *acie consumptum*, below, cf. Cic. *Font.* 42 'ducibus . . . ciuitatis discordiis ac r.p. calamitate consumptis', Quint. 12.10.13 'proscriptione consumptus', Just. 9.4.4, 27.3.1 'bello'. For V.'s point cf. also Cic. *Deiot.* 34 'solus, inquam, es, C. Caesar, cuius in uictoria ceciderit nemo nisi armatus', Suet. *Iul.* 75.3 'nec ulli perisse nisi in proelio reperientur' (Krause).

cum libentius uitam uictor[iam] daret quam uicti acciperent 'These proud adversaries did not always leap forward with alacrity to be exhibited as object-lessons of the *clementia* and *magnitudo animi* of Caesar' (Syme, *RR* 51). V. makes a similar point of Augustus at 86.2. As often (cf. 112.6n.), the strong alliteration *ui-* brings the episode to an effective conclusion, here preceded by further alliteration of *m-*.

uictoriam is clearly wrong. Burer suggested *uictor iam*, which has been widely accepted, but *iam* is without point. I prefer to assume (with Gelenius) that a scribe was expecting the word *uictoriam* in this context and wrote it by mistake.

For *munus . . . corrupit*, above, cf. Sen. *Contr.* 10.5.5, *Culex* 291, Plin. *Ep.* 4.13.6, Quint. *Decl.* 343 (p. 356.25).

53.1 Pompeius profugiens His route took him to Larisa, Amphipolis, Mytilene, Rhodes, Attalia and finally to Syhedra in Cilicia where he deliberated over his final destination (next n.). For his itinerary see e.g. Heinen 60–1.

According to Plut. *Pomp.* 74.1, App. *BC* 5.133 and Dio 42.2.3, Pompey linked up with his wife Cornelia and his son Sextus at Mytilene, where they had been throughout the Pharsalus campaign; but scholars have inferred from the present passage that V. believed (wrongly) that Sextus was with his father at Pharsalus and fled to Mytilene with him. The inference is not, as it happens, certain;[1] since V. merely implies that Sextus had joined his father by the time of the deliberations at Syhedra, the present passage is not contradicted by our other evidence. On the other hand, it may perhaps be inferred from the parenthesis at 2 below, from which all mention of Sextus is absent ('a Mytilenis Corneliam uxorem . . . fugae comitem habere coeperat'), that V. did indeed believe that Sextus was with his father from Pharsalus onwards. That V. did hold this belief, and was right to do so, has been argued by J. Rougé, *REL* 46 (1968), 180–93 (who also attempts to reconcile the conflicting passages at Luc. 6.827–8 and 8.204–5, the former suggesting that Sextus was at Pharsalus, the latter the opposite). Finally, note that the three other companions whom V. mentions are all said to have accompanied Pompey from the very start of his journey from Pharsalus (Plut. *Pomp.* 73.6).

---

[1] As Postgate (1917), xxix n.4, recognises.

COMMENTARY 2.53.2

For Pompey as exile see Westendorp Boerma on *Catal.* 3.7–8, adding *Anth. Lat.* 415.39; on Sextus see further 73.1nn. For *comites ei fortuna adgregauerat*, below, cf. Liv. 30.11.7 'aut uincentibus spes aut pulsis ira adgregat suos' (F.).

The two Lentuli were the consul of 49 (cf. 49.1, 3n.) and P. Cornelius Lentulus Spinther, cos. 57 (*RE* 3.1392–8 = Cornelius 238 (Münzer); *MRR* 2.183, 199–200, 210, 218, 224, 229, 242). For M. Favonius, pr. 49, see *RE* 6.2074–7 = Favonius 1 (Münzer); *MRR* 2.257, 277.

aliis . . . suadentibus For the deliberations at Syhedra see Plut. *Pomp.* 76.4ff., App. *BC* 2.83, Dio 42.2.4–6, from which it emerges that Pompey's own choice of destination was Parthia (denied by Dio; see in general Seager, *Pomp.* 182–3): he only chose Egypt on the advice of others and against his own better judgement. Thus V. once again, just as he did before Pharsalus (52.2n.), diverges from our other authorities and represents Pompey as ignoring the advice of others and following his own inclination – with disastrous results. Moreover, V. draws attention to the similarity between the two occasions by the similar way in which he has constructed his sentences in each place (52.2 *Pompeius . . . aliis suadentibus . . . ut . . . alii ut . . .*, 53.1 *Pompeius . . . aliis ut . . . aliis ut . . . suadentibus*: for a full analysis see further E. A. De Stefani, *SIFC* 18 (1910), 28). In the present case V.'s disagreement with our other sources may have been influenced by the fact that Pompey's deliberations after Pharsalus were a popular topic in suasorial declamation (cf. Quint. 3.8.33, Luc. 8.262ff.) and thus no doubt subject to considerable variation.

fidelissimum . . . Iubam Juba I of Numidia had as a young man been assaulted by Caesar (Suet. *Iul.* 71), to whom he was thereafter consistently antagonistic. In 49 there was a Pompeian proposal that the king should be declared 'socius atque amicus', but a tribune vetoed it (Caes. *BC* 1.6.3–4); and later the same year Juba defeated Caesar's supporter, Curio, in battle (cf. 55.1). See in general *RE* 9.2381–4 = Iuba 1 (Lenschau).

For the infin. after *propono*, below, cf. *OLD* s.v. 11a, adding Suet. *Aug.* 72.2, *Cal.* 49.2 (F.).

beneficiorum quae in patrem eius . . . contulerat Ptolemy Auletes had been restored to his throne in 55 by Gabinius, with Pompey's active support (Dio 39.55.2). His son, Ptolemy XIII, was now about 13 years old (App. *BC* 2.84); for him see *RE* 23.2756–9 (Volkmann); Heinen, *passim*.

53.2 sed quis . . . aut quis . . . aut quando . . . ? All three questions illustrate the topos *cum fortuna statque caditque fides* (Ov. *Ex P.* 2.3.10, cf. Sall. *J.* 24.4 'parum fidei miseris esse'), of which other exs. are collected by Otto 22, Häussler, *Nachträge* 131, 260, Nisbet–Hubbard on Hor. *C.*

1.35.26. For its application to Pompey cf. Caes. *BC* 3.104.1 'despecta eius fortuna, ut plerumque in calamitate ex amicis inimici exsistunt', Luc. 8.485ff. 'dat poenas laudata fides cum sustinet . . . | quos fortuna premit . . . | et cole felices, miseros fuge', 534–5 '. . . nulla fides umquam miseros elegit amicos', 9.246 'clausa fides miseris'. In laments (*conquestiones*), with which our passage has much in common (see below), it was conventional to move one's audience by using such topoi, of which Cic. *Inu.* 1.106–9 provides a list:[1] cf. esp. 108 'sextus (locus communis), per quem praeter spem in miseriis demonstratur esse et, cum aliquid exspectaret, non modo id non adeptus esse sed in summas miserias incidisse', 109 'tertius decimus, per quem . . . conquerimur quod ab eis a quibus minime conueniat male tractemur . . . amicis, quibus benigne fecerimus, quos adiutores fore putarimus'.[2] It may also be significant that Greek laments conventionally began with a series of questions (cf. M. Alexiou, *The Ritual Lament in Greek Tradition* (1974), 162–3), since V. here begins his lament-like passage with three questions. On the *conquestio* in general see further Lausberg 1.365–6 § 439.

For the expr. *seruat memoriam* cf. Cic. *Senec.* 81 'memoriam nostri . . . seruabitis', *Fam.* 4.13.7 'tuorum . . . meritorum erga me memoriam conseruabo', 12.17.1, Gell. 10.18.4 (F.); for *fortuna . . . mutat fidem* cf. Liv. 22.22.6.

princeps . . . imperio arbitrioque Aegyptii mancipii . . . iugulatus est 'The murder of Pompey earned . . . Ptolemy XIII a place in Dante's Inferno, in company with Judas and Cain' (Grant, *Cleo.* 97). Krause thought that *mancipii* referred to Pothinus, one of Ptolemy's advisers; but the young king's debt to Pompey made him a *cliens* (cf. Ov. *Ex P.* 4.3.41–2 'quid fuerat Magno maius? tamen ille rogauit | summissa fugiens uoce clientis opem', Sen. *Tranq. An.* 16.1 'Pompeius et Cicero clientibus suis praebere ceruicem', *Cons. Marc.* 20.4 'sacrosanctum uictoribus corpus satelliti praestitit' (ambiguous), Luc. 8.448–9), to which *mancipium* is an uncomplimentary equivalent (cf. Tac. *A.* 2.2.2; Opelt, index s.v.). Indeed it may be the case that on his father's death in 51 the young Ptolemy was made the ward of Pompey (cf. Liv. *per.* 112 'Cn. Pompeius . . . iussu Ptolemaei regis, pupilli sui, . . . occisus est', Sen. *Ep.* 4.7 (quoted below), Ampel. 35.6; Postgate xliii–xliv, Heinen 11ff.).

Pompey was often called *princeps* (Hellegouarc'h, *VL* 346–9); for the contrast with his insignificant murderer(s) cf. Sen. *Suas.* 6.6, Sen. *Ep.* 4.7 'de Pompeii capite pupillus et spado tulere sententiam', *Breu. Vit.* 13.7 'ultimo mancipio transfodiendum se praebuit', Flor. 2.13.52 'imperio

---

[1] I do not wish to imply that V. had *conquestiones* specifically in mind, merely that their techniques are equally relevant to historiography since each type of writing aimed equally at moving an audience.

[2] A similar topos, inverted, can be made to fit a *consolatio*, cf. Sen. *Cons. Marc.* 20.4 'quid enim erat turpius quam Pompeium uiuere beneficio regis?'.

uilissimi regis, consiliis spadonum', Luc. 8.536ff. The contrast was a manifestation of *commutatio fortunae*, one of those topoi (cf. Otto 142–3) which were appropriate to various rhetorical themes (Sen. *Contr.* 1 *praef.* 23); it was naturally applicable in the *conquestio* (cf. Cic. *Inu.* 1.107 'primus locus est misericordiae per quem quibus in bonis fuerint et nunc quibus in malis sint ostenditur') and particularly relevant in the case of Pompey (see 2–3nn., 48.2n.).

For the appropriately blunt *iugulatus est* cf. 79.5n.; for Ptolemy's advisers Theodotus and Achillas see Heinen 41ff.

53.3 post tres consulatus et totidem triumphos domitumque terrarum orbem These words in effect repeat the preceding topos in a varied manner; but such treatment is recommended by Cic. in his prescription for the *conquestio*, cf. *Inu.* 1.107 'quintus, per quem omnia ante oculos singillatim incommoda ponuntur'. V.'s words sadly recall what he said of Pompey at the height of his power (40.4); similar contrasts between Pompey's military and political achievements and his death are found both in historians (e.g. Dio 42.5, App. *BC* 2.86) and others (e.g. Cic. *Diu.* 2.22 'an Cn. Pompeium censes tribus suis consulatibus, tribus triumphis, maximarum rerum gloria laetaturum fuisse si sciret se in solitudine Aegyptiorum trucidatum iri?', Prop. 3.11.35 'tris ubi Pompeio detraxit harena triumphos', Manil. 4.50–6, Sen. *NQ* 4 *praef.* 22 'quam uelox foret ad imum lapsus ex summo, quamque diuersa uia magnam potentiam fortuna destrueret: uno enim tempore uidit Pompeium . . . ex maximo fastigio . . . ad extrema (deiectum)', Luc. 8.553ff. 'non domitor mundi nec ter Capitolia curru | inuectus . . . Romanus erat: quid uiscera nostra | scrutaris gladio?', 9.178).

Pompey's 3 consulships were in 70, 55 and 52; his three triumphs in 81 or 80 (79 has also been considered), 71 (cf. 30.2) and 61 (40.3). For Pompey as *domitor orbis* cf. Manil. 1.793 and prob. *Catal.* 3.3 'terrarum hic bello magnum concusserat orbem' (see Westendorp Boerma ad loc.); also Cic. *Pis.* 16 'omnium gentium uictore'. For *domare orbem* elsewhere cf. Ov. *AA* 1.177, 3.114, *Tr.* 3.7.52, *Fast.* 4.861, *Cons. Liu.* 381, *Vir. Ill.* 79.4.

uiri in id euecti super quod ascendi non potest Seager aptly sees this remark in the context of V.'s earlier statements that Pompey could not tolerate an equal (29.2, 33.3): V., he says, 'points the inevitability of the conflict between him and Caesar, who wanted to rise still higher, and perhaps implies a very discreet comment on Caesar's ambition' (*Pomp.* 187, comparing Luc. 2.562ff., where Pompey himself is made to speak in terms similar to V.'s). For other refs. to the pinnacle which Pompey reached cf. 40.2, 4, Sen. *Cons. Marc.* 20.4, Luc. 8.702, *Catal.* 3.2, Plut. *Pomp.* 73.1–2.

pridie natalem ipsius I.e. 28 Sept.; cf. Plin. *NH* 37.13 'pr. Kal. Octobres natali suo'. For the fascination of such coincidences see e.g. Tac.

A. 1.9.1; G. W. Trompf, *The Idea of Historical Recurrence in Western Thought* (1979), 112 and n. 209.

(Hic) uitae fuit exitus   For this formula, common amongst Roman historians, see 72.1n.; it is used by Virg. for the death of Priam (*Aen.* 2.554), thought by Serv. to allegorise that of Pompey (see Austin ad loc.), and its Greek equivalents are used by App. *BC* 2.86 (τόδε μὲν δὴ τοῦ βίου τέλος ἦν Πομπηίῳ) and Dio 42.5.1 (τοιοῦτον μὲν τὸ τέλος τῷ Π. . . . ἐγένετο) for Pompey's own death.

in illo uiro a se discordante fortuna   The same point is made about Pompey in more explicit terms by Plut. *Fort. Rom.* 324A ταῦτα πάντα κατώρθωσε δημοσίᾳ τύχῃ χρώμενος, εἶθ' ὑπὸ τῆς ἰδίας ἀνετράπη μοίρας. For the preposition *a* cf. Quint. 8.3.18, 11.3.45 (F.).

ut, cui modo ad uictoriam terra defuerat, deesset ad sepulturam   Cf. Cicero's eighth topos for the *conquestio*, 'per quem aliquid dicitur esse . . . non factum quod oportuerit, hoc modo . . . "inimicorum in manibus mortuus est, hostili in terra turpiter iacuit insepultus, . . . communi quoque honore in morte caruit"' (*Inu.* 1.108). The topos 'no land for burial' (Sen. *Oed.* 68, *Il. Lat.* 48) is of course extremely common (Pease and Austin on Virg. *Aen.* 4.620, Nisbet–Hubbard on Hor. *C.* 1.28.23), but Pompey was one of the most celebrated exs.: Virg. *Aen.* 2.557–8 (allegorical), Ov. *Ex P.* 4.3.43 'cuique uiro totus terrarum paruit orbis . . .' (a lacuna follows in which Ov. clearly made a point similar to V.'s), Val. Max. 5.1.10 'in suo *modo* terrarum orbe nusquam sepulturae locum habuit', Luc. 8.756f., *Anth. Lat.* 413–14, Lact. *Diu. Inst.* 6.6.17. Two interrelated topoi arose from the circumstances of Pompey's unburied corpse. The first was that this was a fitting fate since no one place could possibly hold such a great man: cf. esp. Luc. 8.796ff. 'cur obicis Magno tumulum manesque uagantes | includis? situs est qua terra extrema refuso | pendet in Oceano; Romanum nomen et omne | imperium Magno tumuli est modus'[1], 814ff. 'ter curribus actis | . . . quis capit haec tumulus . . . ?' (and cf. 54.2 below 'nusquam . . . nomine'). The second is that Pompey's sons carried on his cause and his cognomen until their own deaths in distant parts: cf. Mart. 5.74 'Pompeios iuuenes Asia atque Europa, sed ipsum | terra tegit Libyes, si tamen ulla tegit. | quid mirum toto si spargitur orbe? iacere | uno non poterat tanta ruina loco', Luc. 6.817–18, Sen. *Ep.* 71.9, *Anth. Lat.* 400–4, possibly 438, 454–6, Petron. 120.65–6 (with Stubbe ad loc.). The converse is at Sen. *Cons. Pol.* 15.1

---

[1] Postgate (1917) ad loc. compares Thuc. 2.43.3 ἀνδρῶν γὰρ ἐπιφανῶν πᾶσα γῆ τάφος (where Gomme quotes *Anth. Pal.* 7.45 = 1052–3 Page [*Further Greek Epigrams* (1981)]), *Anth. Pal.* 7.137, [Sen.] *Herc. Oet.* 1826–7 'quae tibi sepulchra, nate, quis tumulus sat est? | hic totus orbis; fama erit titulus tibi'.

'(Pompeiis) ne hoc quidem saeuiens reliquit fortuna ut una denique con-
ciderent ruina'. For *deesse* + *ad* cf. Caes. *BC* 2.6.1 'res nulla ad uirtutem
defuit', Sen. *Contr.* 1.7.5 (F.).

53.4 quos in aetate ... uiri fefellit quinquennium   Errors of this
type are in Val. Max. 5.9.2 and Tac. *A.* 13.6.3, both of whom imply a
birthday in 101. V.'s dating of Pompey's birth to 106 concurs with that of
App. (e.g. *BC* 2.86) and has been generally accepted (cf. J. van Ootegh-
em, *Pompée le Grand: bâtisseur d'empire* (1954), 31–2); but in a recent
attempt to date Pompey's first triumph to 80 rather than to 81, it has been
argued that he was born in 105 (B. L. Twyman, *Studies in Latin Literature
and Roman History* (ed. C. Deroux, 1979), 1.199–200, 205–8).[1] Yet either
triumphal date is compatible with a birthday in 106 (Seager, *Pomp.* 12).

V.'s criticism of other historians may seem inappropriate at this tragic
moment in the story; yet similar statements can be found in historians
from Hecataeus and Thucydides onwards and no doubt constituted a conventional element in historiographical *aemulatio*. Besides, as Mr DuQuesnay points out, this brief section defuses the emotional tone before V.
reverts to Caesar at 54.1.

Gelenius' *facilis* for the paradosis *felix* seems certain; as the older edd.
remark, the two words are often confused (e.g. twice at Flor. 1.22.38–9).

**54.1 utrique summo imperatorum, alteri ⟨mortuo, alteri⟩ super-
stiti, meritas poenas luere**   Caesar arrived in Egypt on 1 Oct. (cf.
Heinen 70–1) and there learned of Pompey's murder. After intrigue and
armed resistance from Ptolemy's advisers Pothinus and Achillas, Caesar
had the former executed, while the latter was assassinated by his own
forces. The *Bellum Alexandrinum*, as it is called, lasted until the following
year and finally ended on 27 March 47 with Ptolemy's death on the Nile
(cf. *CIL* 1² p. 212). For a full account of these events see Heinen 69–142;
also Rice Holmes, *Rep.* 3.182–202, 483–506, Gelzer, *Caes.* 246–52, Grant,
Cleo. 101–26. For the motif of vengeance (*meritas poenas*) cf. Luc. 10.515ff.
'non fatum meriti poenasque Pothini | distulit ulterior. sed non, qua
debuit, ira, | ... Magni morte perit', 523 'terribilem iusto transegit
Achillea ferro', Flor. 4.2.55 'ultionem clarissimi uiri manibus quaerente
fortuna'. The word-play *regis ... regebatur*, above, is contemptuous.

Lipsius supplied *alteri mortuo*, which I have adopted (slightly changed).
Some have attempted to make do with only one *alteri*, e.g. ⟨sed⟩ *alteri
superstiti* (Castiglioni); but this, while perhaps linguistically justifiable (cf.
OLD s.v. *alter²* 4a), provides the wrong emphasis. If it were a choice of
mentioning either Pompey or Caesar as the recipient of *meritas poenas*, V.
would surely have mentioned Pompey since the dues were paid too late

---

[1] Twyman suggests that V. interpreted too literally Cicero's statements
that Pompey was his *aequalis* (*Brut.* 161, 239; see Sumner, *Orators*
155–6).

for his deriving any consolation from them; hence we should expect V. to have written *alteri mortuo*, not *a. superstiti*. And since *a. superstiti* is already in the text, I assume that V., who is clearly anxious to compare the fortunes of both men (cf. *non fuit . . . quam . . .*, above), also wrote *alteri mortuo*. The mistake would of course be very easy (it happens again at 114.4). Kritz's improbable belief that *utrique* is nomin. (= Theodotus and Achillas, above) and subject of *luere*, with *summo imp. alteri superstiti* = Caesar, is demonstrably wrong: the whole point is that Ptolemy died too, and *utrique* cannot of course refer to three persons.

I have, on the other hand, retained the paradosis *summo* as an ex. of enallage (for which cf. 91.3n.); but it is admittedly an unusual case, and Mommsen's *summo⟨rum⟩* is undeniably attractive. For *fides* + *in* and accus., above, cf. 67.2n.

54.2–59.1   TRIUMPH AND TRAGEDY (47–44 B.C.)

This section of narrative is organised on dramatic lines into two halves (54.2–56.2 and 56.3–59.1), each of which is further sub-divided into three (see my headings, below). The key to the understanding of the first of these halves lies in the parenthesis at 55.2, where it emerges that V. has selected and arranged his material to illustrate Caesar's acquisition of *gloria* (see n.). There are three principal manifestations of this. First, V. omits to mention that Caesar returned to Rome in October 47 and July 46 since references to Caesar's domestic activities would detract from his military image. Secondly, V. elaborates the war in Spain (55.2–4) at the expense of that in Africa (54.2–55.2). This was a natural choice. Whereas Cato's suicide was one of the more memorable features of Thapsus, Munda showed Caesar at his best. It was one of his two most critical engagements (Suet. *Iul.* 36, cf. V.'s *grauius . . . atrocius periculosiusque*, 55.2–3) and was to be the last of his career; it contained a colourful episode on which to focus (55.3n.); and it involved a son of Pompey the Great, thereby giving a presentiment of things to come (55.2n.). Thirdly, and most drastically of all, V. reserves until October 45 the four triumphs which Caesar in fact celebrated in September 46 (56.1–2). It is of course theoretically possible that V. believed the four triumphs to have taken place at the same time as the Spanish triumph in 45, but that seems to me unlikely since the four triumphs of 46 had several unprecedented, and therefore memorable, features (Weinstock 60ff., 76–9). Rather, V. has placed all the triumphs together to form both a climax to the military narrative which has preceded, and an effective contrast with the tragedy which is to come.[1]

---

[1] In this way V. is also able to treat the fifth (Spanish) triumph, which aroused particular resentment since no foreign enemy had been defeated (Gelzer, *Caes.* 308–9), as if it were no different from the others.

Caesar's murder at 56.3 provides the περιπέτεια of the drama, and the second half of V.'s narrative is clearly intended to be viewed tragically in the light of the first half. Thus he suggests (misleadingly) that after his exertions abroad Caesar was entitled to expect a period of *quies*, an expectation that was cruelly terminated by his murder (56.3n.); we are given a poignant contrast between the man who forgave his enemies (56.3, 57.1, cf. 55.2, 56.1) and the man who was cut down by his friends (56.3, 57.1, 58.1, 3); and we are reminded that, had Caesar followed advice and remained the military man depicted in 54.2–56.2, his murder might not have occurred (57.1). Such hindsight is intensified by V.'s conventional concentration on neglected omens in ch. 57, and his language is elevated by allusions to Sallust and Virgil.

incautus ab ingratis occupatus est: V.'s epitaph for Caesar (57.1), with its repeated negative prefix reminding readers of what might have been, eloquently sums up the tragic nature of the Ides of March.

54.2–56.2 TRIUMPH (47–45 B.C.)

54.2–55.2 The war in Africa (47–46 B.C.)

54.2 Nusquam erat Pompeius corpore, adhuc ubique uiuebat nomine Either the paradosis *Iubae* is a scribal attempt to 'correct' another word, or it is simply interpolated from *Iuba* below. Gelenius and Scaliger thought the latter, and excised *Iubae*; but this leaves the sentence implausibly unbalanced. Lipsius thought the former, and wrote *uiuebat*, which is commonly accepted. For *corpore* ~ *nomine* cf. 124.3, Cic. *Arch.* 24 'idem tumulus qui corpus eius contexerat nomen etiam obruisset'. Pompey's reputation is one of Lucan's constant themes (e.g. 7.717, 8.320–1, 798–9, 858–9, 865–6).

ingens partium eius fauor Despite *TLL* 6.1.384.72, I think *partium* is objective gen.: 'a strong devotion to his cause' (Watson). The series of tenses *excitauerat . . . ciebat* means that Juba and Scipio kept alive a war which had already started (cf. Dio 42.56.2–3); cf. a similar series at 75.1. For Juba cf. 53.1n.; for Q. Caecilius Metellus Pius Scipio Nasica, cf. *RE* 3.1224–8 = Caecilius 99 (Münzer), *MRR* 2.189, 229, 234–5, 260–1, 275, 288, 297: consul in 52, he was at present proconsul in Africa, and committed suicide after his side's defeat.

For *bellum excitare* cf. 2.15.1 and regularly in Cic. and Liv. (*TLL* 5.2.1261.19–21); for *b. ciere* cf. 129.3n. (the word-play *excitare* ~ *ciere* is typically Velleian); *fauor ingens* is at Liv. 4.24.7, 28.38.6, 39.53.2, but in other authors too.

ante biennium . . . socer According to Plut. *Pomp.* 54.5–55.1, Scipio's daughter Cornelia married Pompey in 52 B.C., which, if correct, would be four, not two, years before Pharsalus. For *exstingui* cf. *TLL* 5.2.1918.56ff.

54.3 difficultate itinerum locorumque inopia   Both phrases have the flavour of a military despatch: cf. Cic. *Fam.* 15.2.1 (written from camp in Cappadocia), Liv. 38.40.6, 44.3.5, Tac. *A.* 13.53.2, Caes. *BC* 1.70.1 *uiarum d.*, Liv. 40.22.7 *uiae*, Veg. *Mil.* 3.10; Liv. 1.33.6, Sen. *D.* 11.12.3, Front. *Strat.* 1.5.28, Sall. *H.* 3.74 *l. egestate.* Cato was the last of the Pompeian protagonists to reach Africa, where, having landed at Berenice (Benghazi), he marched to join the others around Utica (Rice Holmes, *Rep.* 3.220–2, Nisbet–Hubbard on Hor. *C.* 1.22.5). It is curious that V., having described Cato so fulsomely in ch. 35, should refrain from alluding to his famous suicide; perhaps he felt constrained by brevity (cf. 55.1), more likely he was disinclined to divert attention from Caesar.

honoratiori   Viz. Scipio, a *consularis*, whereas Cato was only *praetorius*; for the incident cf. Liv. *per.* 113, App. *BC* 2.87, Dio 42.57.2–3.

55.1 promissae breuitatis fides   From the phraseology here and at 89.6 it may be inferred that in his lost preface V. had promised to write a brief or summary history: see Woodman (1975), 277–87, esp. 285. Here V. is certainly as good as his word: Caesar's return to Rome in October 47, and the political and economic measures he took while there (*MRR* 2.286), are omitted; and the African campaign of 28 Dec. 47–13 June 46 (below) is dismissed in ten words (*ibi . . . copiae*). For *transcursus* cf. 86.1n.; for *promissae . . . fides* cf. Cic. *Att.* 4.19.1 'promissi . . . fidem' (Krause).

sequens fortunam suam   The point is not that Caesar was an adventurer but that he was able to rely on the trusted supernatural *comes* which was his personal *fortuna* (3n.). It was to be inferred from this ability that he was a man of destiny. There is perhaps a similar idea at Liv. 22.27.4 '(Minucius dixit) secuturum se fortunam suam'.

peruectus in Africam   Caesar arrived at Hadrumetum (Sousse) on 28 Dec. 47; there are chronological tables of his movements throughout the African campaign (plus the relevant evidence) in Rice Holmes, *Rep.* 4.540 and A. Bouvet's edn of *Bell. Afr.* (1949), pp. 92–6.

occiso Curione   Having been appointed *legatus pro praetore* by Caesar, he was killed by Juba in 49 (*MRR* 2.263–4). For the *Pompeiani exercitus* in Africa see Brunt, *IM* 452, 473–4.

ibi . . . copiae   For details see Rice Holmes, *Rep.* 3.238–75 (map on p. 237), 516–40. The decisive battle was at Thapsus (Ras Dimas) on 6 Apr. 46 (*CIL* 1² p. 315). For *inclinatae* cf. 52.4n.

55.2 clementia Caesaris   References to Caesar's clemency conclude V.'s accounts of Ilerda (50.4), Pharsalus (52.4–6), Thapsus, and (in

effect) Munda (56.1); V. poignantly sees Caesar's murder in terms of the
clementia he had shown to others (57.1), and the episode of Marullus and
Flavus is a final demonstration of the virtue (68.4–5: see p. 157). Certainly Caesar's *clementia* after Thapsus is stressed elsewhere (e.g. *Bell. Afr.* 86.2
'suamque . . . clementiam commemorauit', 88.6 'Caesaris c.', 89.5 'pro
natura sua et pro instituto', 92.4), although not everyone escaped scot-
free (Gelzer, *Caes.* 269–70); but the reason for V.'s insistence on the virtue
lies in the emphasis which Caesar himself laid on *clementia*: he called it a
noua ratio uincendi, it became his 'principle' (*institutum*, cf. Cic. *Att.*
9.7c(174c).1–2), and a temple to Clementia Caesaris was scheduled (cf.
57.1n.). This emphasis is reflected in many other sources (e.g. Suet. *Iul.*
75.1 with Butler–Cary's n., Flor. 2.13.90) but esp. in Cic. *Marc.* and *Lig.*
From Caesar the virtue was 'inherited' by Augustus (see 100.4n., with
refs. to modern works, adding Gesche 138–41, 309).

For *dissimilis . . . quam*, for which Krause suggested *quae*, cf. Vitr. 6.5.2.
clementia + *in* and accus. is found elsewhere, but *aduersus* seems unparalleled (*TLL* 3.1335.36–42).

55.2–4   The war in Spain (46–45 B.C.)

Victorem Africani belli   Though V. does not say so, Caesar left Africa
on 13 June and returned to Rome on 25 July 46 (*Bell. Afr.* 98.1–2). There
in Sept. he celebrated four of the five triumphs which V. mentions at 56.2
(n.), and became involved in numerous other activities (cf. *MRR* 2.293–4,
Rice Holmes, *Rep.* 3.282–92) which V. also omits.

V. elsewhere uses the form *bellum Africum* (54.2, 129.4, cf. 56.2) and
Novák (1892) proposed to introduce it here; but *b. Africanum* is unexceptionable (Cic. *Deiot.* 25, Hirt. *BG* 8 *pr.* 8). For *excepit*, 'confronted', cf. Liv.
1.53.4, 6.42.9, Virg. *Aen.* 3.317–18 etc.

nam . . . uix quicquam gloriae eius adstruxit   *nam* explains why V.
has passed straight from the African to the Spanish campaign but has not
mentioned the encounter with Pharnaces which preceded both; the explanation is valuable in revealing that V. is here selecting his material
according as it illustrates Caesar's *gloria*. Caesar had defeated Pharnaces,
son of Mithridates VI and king of the Bosporus area, on 2 Aug. 47 at Zela
(Rice Homes, *Rep.* 3.210–15, 511–14); but the battle was notable mainly
for the speed with which it was over (*Bell. Alex.* 77.1, cf. Suet. *Iul.* 37.2 on
Caesar's slogan *ueni uidi uici*).

For *gloriae . . . adstruxit* cf. Front. p. 178 Naber = p. 169 Van den Hout
'tuae propriae gloriae addideris quantum dignitati . . . adstruxeris', Plin.
Ep. 3.2.5, 4.17.7.

Cn. Pompeius   *RE* 21.2211–13 = Pompeius 32 (Miltner), *MRR* 2.284,
291, 298, 309. V. ominously represents him in the same role as his brother
Sextus (*adulescens . . . confluentibus*, cf. 72.5–73.1). For the genit. *impetus* cf.

Sen. *Ep.* 24.3 'occurrent tibi ingenia . . . impetus magni'; for *impetus + ad* cf. *TLL* 7.1.609.17–19; for *bellum conflare* cf. Cic. *Ep.* 5.2.8, *Phil.* 2.23, 70, Hirt. *BG* 8.6.1, *Bell. Alex.* 1.1, Nep. *Chabr.* 2.3, Ascon. *Corn.* p. 73C, *Pan. Lat.* 2.23.2. The phrase *nominis magnitudo* (see below) occurs elsewhere (F. quotes Sall. *J.* 5.4, Liv. 33.21.3, Sen. *Ben.* 5.14.5), but the addition of *paterni* suggests a play on words similar to those at 2.1.4 'Pompeium magni nominis uirum', 27.6 'felicitatem diei . . . Sulla honorauit'.

55.3 sua Caesarem . . . comitata fortuna   Fortune is commonly represented as a companion (cf. 69.6n.), but here Caesar's own personal *fortuna* (97.4n., adding Gesche 188–9, 309) is in question, as Luc. 5.510 'sola placet fortuna comes'; see esp. Nock 670 = *JRS* 37 (1947), 112–13. Caesar set out for Spain in Nov. 46 (Rice Holmes, *Rep.* 3.541–2, Gelzer, *Caes.* 293–4).

nullum umquam atrocius . . .   The battle of Munda took place on 17 March 45 (*CIL* I² p. 212) and was uncharacteristically critical for Caesar (Flor. 2.13.75 'nusquam atrocius nec tam ancipiti Marte concursum est . . . [78] anceps et diu triste proelium', Suet. *Iul.* 36, Plut. *Caes.* 56.3, App. *BC* 2.104), who was alleged to have played a dangerously prominent role himself (next n.). His behaviour in the battle thus provided an excellent illustration of his *gloria*. Sources for the battle are cited by Rice Holmes, *Rep.* 3.548.

adeo ut . . .   Three ingredients heighten the drama of the crisis: Caesar dismounts (so too Flor. 2.13.82, Dio 43.37.4), he addresses *fortuna* (App. *BC* 2.104, cf. Flor. 2.13.78 'uideretur nescioquid deliberare fortuna'), and speaks to his men (Plut. *Caes.* 56.2, Flor. 2.13.82 'hortari, increpare', App. *BC* 2.104). 'The author of the *Bellum Hispaniense* makes no mention of such a crisis, but that is far from proving that it did not occur' (Butler–Cary on Suet. *Iul.* 36, who, like Flor. 2.13.83, adds that Caesar contemplated suicide). For *descendere* without *ex*, below, cf. Sall. *H.* 5.20, Val. Max. 2.2.4, 5.2.9, 8.5.6 (F.). *recedentem*, below, is effectively repeated at *non recessurum* later in the sentence.

increpita prius fortuna quod . . . exitum   For the exprr. cf. Vict. *Epit.* 20.12 'fortunae increpant' (Shackleton Bailey), Virg. *Aen.* 5.625 'cui te exitio fortuna reseruat?' (Ruhnken). For *increpare + quod* cf. *TLL* 7.1.1053.31ff., 1054.48 (Liv. Val. Max. Tac.).

55.4 uerecundia magis quam uirtute acies restituta   Flor. makes the same point (2.13.81): 'pudore magis quam uirtute resistere'; for the idea cf. Liv. 30.18.8 'pudore magis quam uiribus tenebat locum'. The textual corruption of this sentence arose through wrong word-division and the confusion of *t* and *c*, both common errors.

Labienum Varumque For the former cf. *RE* 12.260–70 = Labienus 6 (Münzer), *MRR* 2.167–8, 252–3, 268, 281, 291, 301, 311; for P. Attius Varus, *RE* 2.2256–7 = Attius 32 (Klebs), *MRR* 2.228, 237, 260, 275, 290, 300, 310–11. For *grauis uulnere*, above, cf. Liv. 21.48.4, 36.20.5, Stat. *Theb.* 9.44, Tac. *H.* 3.50.1; for *solitudines auias* cf. Ap. *Met.* 1.19.12, 4.27.2, 8.30.2 (F.).

56.1–2 The *triumphator* (46/45 B.C.)

56.1 Caesar omnium uictor regressus in urbem This is Caesar's final return to Rome, which (as we know from 3 below) took place in October 45. Many of the events which V. proceeds to mention in 1–2 below, however, belong to the autumn of 46 (see nn., and above, p. 104).

Earlier in 45 (May), after the news of the victory at Munda, a statue of Caesar had been set up with the legend *Deo Inuicto* (Dio 43.45.3, Cic. *Att.* 12.45(290).2, 13.28(299).3; Weinstock 186–8). For *omnium uictor* cf. Val. Max. 5.7.2 'Caesare omnium iam et externorum ⟨et⟩ domesticorum hostium uictore', and 79.3n., 107.3n.

quod humanam excedat fidem T. C. W. Stinton ('*Si credere dignum est*: some expressions of disbelief', *PCPS* 22 (1976), 60–89) has shown how such phraseology is used by a wide variety of authors to emphasise rhetorical climaxes, as here. At 130.1n. I collected exs. of such phraseology, to which F. adds Ov. *Met.* 7.166, Plin. *NH* 7.85, 28.52.

V. seems to be alluding to Caesar's demonstrations of *clementia* in 45/44 B.C., for which cf. Plut. *Caes.* 57.3–4, App. *BC* 2.107.

magnificentissimisque … spectaculis For the *gladiatorium munus* cf. Suet. *Iul.* 39.1 (a praetorian versus an ex-senator); for the *naumachia*, 39.4; V.'s *simul* indicates that the elephants participated in the joint cavalry and foot battle, cf. Suet. 39.3 'pugna diuisa in duas acies, quingenis peditibus, elephantis uicenis, tricenis equitibus hinc et inde commissis.' These celebrations, like 4 of the 5 triumphs mentioned below, belong to 46 rather than 45 B.C. (cf. e.g. App. *BC* 2.101–2, Dio 43.22ff.; other sources are listed by Butler–Cary on Suet. loc. cit., Rice Holmes, *Rep.* 3.282 n. 3, Degrassi 13.1.567).

epulique … celebratione repleuit eam Sc. *urbem. repleuit* is an ex. of virtual syllepsis, being used metaphorically with *spectaculis* (cf. 100.2, 103.1) but almost literally with *epuli celebratione*. For the event cf. again Suet. *Iul.* 38.2 'adiecit epulum ac uiscerationem et post Hispaniensem uictoriam duo prandia … quinto post die aliud largissimum praebuit' (and Butler–Cary ad loc.). Both the food and the games (above) were demonstrations of Caesar's *liberalitas* (Suet. loc. cit. 'pro liberalitate sua').

56.2 quinque egit triumphos   The first four triumphs were celebrated in September 46, the fifth in October 45: see Degrassi 13.1.567 (also above, p. 104). Further details of Caesar's financial acquisitions are in App. *BC* 2.102.

For the variation of construction after *constitit* cf. 126.2n.

56.3–59.1 TRAGEDY (44 B.C.)

56.3–4 Conspiracy

56.3 principalis quies   This is an unusual phrase (*principes* were normally supposed to demonstrate *uigilantia*). On the one hand it suggests that after his campaigns in foreign parts Caesar was entitled to expect a period of relaxation; yet V. knows that Caesar was planning to invade Parthia in 44 (cf. 59.4). On the other hand it suggests that after disposing of opposition Caesar was entitled to expect a secure tenure of power. It so happens, as Manutius points out, that in May 49 Cicero had predicted that Caesar's *regnum* would last no more than six months (*Att.* 10.8.7).

For *principalis* cf. 124.3n.; for *uictoriis . . . uso* cf. Sen. *Ira* 2.23.4 (of Caesar), Just. 25.5.2, Sulp. *Chron.* 2.23.5.

promittendo . . . differendo   Similarly Plut. *Caes.* 62.2. V. attributes no high-minded motives to the conspirators but sees them simply as *ingrati*.

D. Bruto et C. Trebonio   The former was designated consul for 42 (58.1) and was at present proconsul of Cisalpine Gaul through Caesar's influence (60.5). 'His part in the conspiracy against Caesar was noted especially because of Caesar's former favours and because he was named among the second heirs in Caesar's will' (*MRR* 2.328, with numerous refs.). For him see *RE* Suppl. 5.369–85 = Iunius 55a (Münzer), *MRR* 2.213, 239, 267, 281, 291, 301, 307, 347. Trebonius was named by Caesar as proconsul of Asia before his death (App. *BC* 3.2); for him see *RE* 6A.2274–82 = Trebonius 6 (Münzer), *MRR* 2.217, 226 (legate under Caesar in Gaul, 54–49 B.C.), 273–4, 289, 295, 305, 330, 349–50. The names of other conspirators are given by App. *BC* 2.113.

For *fortuna partium*, above, cf. Tac. *H.* 3.79.2; for *euectis*, 116.4n.

56.4 cui magnam inuidiam conciliarat M. Antonius . . .   'The colourful incident at the Lupercalia, 15 February 44, is one of the most discussed events in Caesar's life' (Weinstock 331). The various possible interpretations of the incident, of which Cicero provides a detailed and perhaps eye-witness account at *Phil.* 2.84ff., are set out succinctly by Denniston on that passage. 'Either it was stage-managed by Caesar, whose object may have been either to provide the people with an opportunity for a monarchist demonstration, or himself with one for repudiating monarchical ambitions once and for all. Or it was designed by Antony, who may have wished to press the monarchy upon Caesar, or to bring unpopularity upon him.' V. seems to me to accept the last of these possibilities, since he describes Antony as *omnibus audendis paratissimus*, a phrase which combines the pejorative notions of *audax* (48.3n.) and *omnia facere* (πανουργεῖν, cf. Kroll on Catull. 75.4).[1] *inuidiam conciliarat* thus represents a conscious action on Antony's part. This interpretation is not in my opinion inconsistent with V.'s later statement that Caesar did not seem to be offended by the incident (nor is that statement surprising in itself, since at 68.4 V. says that Caesar's position in early 44 was already one of *dominatio*).

Perhaps other views of V.'s sentence are possible (e.g. that Ant.'s *audacia* consists in a wish, not to bring *inuidia* on Caesar, but to impose a king on Rome), and of course the actual circumstances of the incident may have been different again. For a recent view, that the event was stage-managed by Caesar so that he could reject the *name* of king, see E. Rawson, *JRS* 65 (1975), 148–59.

For M. Antonius see *RE* 1.2595–2614 = Antonius 30 (Groebe); *MRR* 2.205, 220, 236, 242, 258, 260, 272, 280, 315–16, 332–3, 334, 337–8, 342–3, 357–8, 360, 371, 379, 386–7, 390–1, 396, 399–400, 406–7, 410, 411, 414–15, 417–18, 419–20; Huzar.

For *inuidiam conciliare* cf. Liv. 39.53.10; for 'daring all' cf. Liv. 22.39.20, 26.7.6, 35.31.12, Sen. *Med.* 267–8.

57 Neglected Advice

57.1 ut principatum armis quaesitum armis teneret For comparable exs. of idea and phraseology see Häussler, *Tac.* 340 (Thuc. Sall. Nep. Liv. Tac. Flor.); add Sall. *J.* 21.1 'regnum relinquendum esset aut armis retinendum', Vretska on Sall. *C.* 2.4 and Tarrant on Sen. *Ag.* 115 (to whose English parallels add Marvell's *Horatian Ode* 'The same arts that did gain | A power, must it maintain').[2] Ironically, Caesar famously passed judgement that 'Sullam nescisse litteras qui dictaturam deposuerit' (Suet. *Iul.* 77), and had himself set out 'praemia armorum armis defendere' (Flor. 2.13.17). For Hirtius' and Pansa's advice, given when Caesar decided to dismiss his bodyguard, cf. Plut. *Caes.* 57.4, though there they are not mentioned by name.

---

[1] The antithesis '*consulatus* collega ∼ insigne *regium*,' which is doubtless ironical, also supports this interpretation.

[2] Cf. too Sall. *J.* 85.1 'plerosque non isdem artibus imperium . . . petere et . . . gerere.' The motif is neatly reversed, apropos of Pompey, at Tac. *A.* 3.28.1 'quae armis tuebatur, armis amisit,' quoted by Häussler.

111

experientia, above, = 'in the light of experience,' but I cannot find a precise parallel for this absolute use. For *armis quaerere* cf. Column. 1 *pr.* 14, Curt. 4.4.20; *a. petere* is at 68.3; for *armis tenere* cf. Sall. *J.* 24.7 'regnum armis tenet,' Virg. *Aen.* 8.482, 9.166, Liv. 28.43.11.

mori se quam timere malle   Although P's *timeri* offers good sense (cf. the proverb in Otto 252 'quem metuunt, odere; quem quisque odit, periisse expetit', Tac. *A.* 6.2.4 'neque sibi uitam tanti, si armis tegenda foret'), Oudendorp's *timere* seems confirmed by remarks attributed to Caesar in Suet. *Iul.* 86.2 'insidias . . . subire semel quam cauere', Plut. *Caes.* 57.4 βέλτιον . . . ἅπαξ ἀποθανεῖν ἢ ἀεὶ προσδοκᾶν, App. *BC* 2.109 οὐδὲν ἀτυχέστερον . . . διηνεκοῦς φυλακῆς · ἔστι γὰρ αἰεὶ δεδίοτος. *timere* was at first written in A but 'corrected' to *timeri*; it is thus clear that both (R) and (M) read *timeri* and that A's true reading resulted from mistranscription, as elsewhere.

clementiam, quam praestiterat   An allusion to *clementia* was particularly apposite in 44 B.C. since a temple of Clementia Caesaris was planned (see Weinstock 241, 308–9 with refs.) and coins were issued reading *clementia Caesaris* (*RRC* 1.491 no. 480.21). In general see 55.2n. *exspectat*, below, = 'expected to receive in return'; for *clem. praestare* cf. Val. Max. 5.1 *pr.*, Sen. *Clem.* 2.5.1, Sulp. *Mart.* 22.4.

occupatus est   The verb combines the notions of *opprimere* and *praeuenire* (so, rightly, *TLL* 9.2.385.81–386.12). The pathos is further underlined by the prefix in *praedixerant, praesagia* and *praemonuerant*; cf. Manil. 4.59–60 'totiens praedicta cauere | uulnera non potuit' and Housman ad loc. For *ingratus* cf. 129.2n.

obtulissent   Ruhnken notes that the verb alludes to *auguria oblatiua*, cf. Serv. *Aen.* 6.190 'auguria aut oblatiua sunt, quae non poscuntur, aut impetratiua, quae optata ueniunt'. Orelli's *ei* seems the neatest way of accounting for the divergent readings of B and P.

57.2 haruspices   Principally Spurinna (Suet. *Iul.* 81.2, Val. Max. 8.11.2 'praedixerat C. Caesari ut proximos XXX dies quasi fatales caueret'; Weinstock 344–5).

territa . . . uisu   Other sources for Calpurnia's dream are listed by Butler–Cary on Suet. *Iul.* 81.3. For the expr. cf. Virg. *Aen.* 8.109, Liv. 7.26.5, 21.55.7; *exterritus* at Liv. 1.56.5.

dati neque protinus ab eo lecti   P offers *dati ab eo neque protinus lecti*, which was variously emended, e.g. *ab ⟨obu⟩io* (Burman, cf. Suet. *Iul.* 81.4); but there seems little doubt that A's reading, printed here, is correct. Either P, unlike A, wrongly transcribed their common parent (R) and Burer (as happens very occasionally) failed to note the discrepancy from (M); or P faithfully copied (R) and A either corrected it or, as at 1 above, mistranscribed it in such a way as to produce the truth. In general on such matters cf. *TN* 17 nn. 1, 4. It is interesting to note that no one before A's discovery had thought to emend P by transposition.

57.3 sed profecto ineluctabilis fatorum uis ... consilia corrumpit   Similar phraseology foreshadows the *Variana clades* at 118.4 (nn.). For *sed profecto* cf. Sall. *C.* 8.1 'sed profecto fortuna in omni re dominatur'; for *ineluctabilis* cf. Virg. *Aen.* 8.334 'i. fatum'; for *fatorum uis* cf. Liv. 8.7.8 'uis fati', to which F. adds Cic. *Fat.* 11, Flor. 2.13.94. Fortune is similarly invoked by Nic. Dam. 23 = F 130.83 Jacoby, App. *BC* 2.116. Note the effective alliteration and assonance with which V. concludes his *sententia*.

58–59.1 Aftermath

58.1 patrauere facinus   Both words are typically Sallustian (Syme, *Sall.* 261–2); but besides Sall. *C.* 18.8, the phrase recurs also in Liv. 23.8.11, Tac. *A.* 1.45.2, Amm. 16.11.9.

The distribution of abbreviated *praenomina* represents the most economical way of correctly distinguishing between the two Bruti and three Cassii who might otherwise have been confused.

58.2 Capitolium occupauere   The rush to the Capitol, immediately after the murder, is imaginatively described by Nic. Dam. 25 = F 130.94 Jacoby; cf. also App. *BC* 2.120, Dio 44.21.2ff., Plut. *Caes.* 67.2, Flor. 2.17.2. For *coniuratio = coniurati*, above, cf. Sall. *C.* 43.1 'multitudo coniurationis' before V.; for *globus* (originally a military term: Ogilvie on Liv. 2.47.6) + abstract noun cf. Sall. *J.* 85.10 'globo nobilitatis' (F.), Nep. *Att.* 8.4 'ille consensionis globus'.

censuisset Cassius   His plans are also mentioned by App. *BC* 2.114, 135, Plut. *Ant.* 13.2, *Brut.* 18.2, 20.1, but only in the last place is he named specifically; cf. also Nic. Dam. 25 = F 130.93 Jacoby.

Brutus repugnauerat   'Cicero in his orations and letters again and again returns to this ill-timed magnanimity' (Frisch 38 n. 56); cf. *Fam.* 10.28(364).1, 12.4(363).1 (to Cassius), *Ep. Brut.* 2.5(5).2, *Phil.* 2.34, 13.22, *Att.* 14.14(368).2, 15.2(379).2, 15.20(397).2.

113

ita enim . . . expediebat ' for it suited his action that Caesar should be so called'; Brutus refers to Caesar as *tyrannus* at *Ep. Brut.* 1.16(25).6, if the letter is genuine; for exs. elsewhere cf. J. Béranger, *REL* 13 (1935), 88; Hellegouarc'h, *VL* 561 n. 15. For *expedit* + acc. and inf. and non-personal dat. of advantage cf. Ascon. p. 70.20–1 C; with simple inf. and dat. at Cael. ap. Cic. *Fam.* 8.6.5, Liv. 25.7.12, Sen. *Contr.* 1.8.9, Sen. *D.* 7.27.2; with acc. and inf. without dat., cf. *TLL* 5.2.1615.62ff. For *petere sanguinem* cf. Cic. *Pis.* 99 'numquam sanguinem expetiui tuum' (F.), Luc. 7.511 'petitur cruor'. The hyperbaton *praeter . . . sanguinem* is both effective and characteristically Velleian.

conuocato senatu Not the meeting which Cicero suggested on 15 March (*Att.* 14.10(364).1) but, as is implied by Antony's being the subject of the sentence, that which the latter succeeded in calling two days later in the temple of Tellus (Cic. *Phil.* 1.1, App. *BC* 2.126).

58.3 cum iam Dolabella . . . insignia corripuisset consulis This action belongs to 15 March (App. *BC* 2.122, Dio 44.22.1): hence *iam*. For his choice as consul by Caesar see *MRR* 2.317. For *corripuisset* cf. Sall. *C.* 18.5 'fascibus correptis', *Vir. Ill.* 70.2 'correptis imperii insignibus'.

uelut pacis auctor liberos . . . misit Cicero explicitly says that on 17 March Antony sent only one son (*Phil.* 1.31 'tuus paruus filius . . . pacis obses', 2.90, cf. too Plut. *Ant.* 14.1, *Brut.* 19.2), to whom he refers by the rhetorical plural at *Phil.* 1.2 'pax . . . per liberos eius . . . confirmata est'. It is this latter which V. recalls, 'in offenbarer Nachahmung' (Landgraf on Cic. *Rosc.* 96, q.v.), although such use of the plur. is common (cf. 130.1n., adding Ogilvie on Liv. 3.44.3). For *fides* + gen. in relation to safety *TLL* quotes Liv. 43.18.10 (6.1.699.49).

58.4 relatum Probably not 'proposed' but 'recalled' or 'revived', cf. Cic. *Phil.* 1.1 'Atheniensiumque renouaui uetus exemplum' (the allusion is to the amnesty granted to the oligarchs in 403). For the expr. cf. Liv. 3.45.9 'neque tu istud umquam decretum sine caede nostra referres'. I think Krause was probably right to make *obliuionis* dependent on *decreto*: 'by a senatorial decree of amnesty for past actions' (*contra* Watson, Shipley). For *obliuio* = 'amnesty' cf. Val. Max. 4.1 *ext.* 4 'ne qua praeteritarum rerum mentio fieret. haec obliuio quam Athenienses amnestian uocant'; *OLD* s.v.3.

59.1 Caesaris deinde testamentum apertum est See esp. Suet. *Iul.* 83; the date (18 or 19 March) is disputed. In general on the will see Schmitthenner, *Test. passim*.

C. Octauium *RE* 10.275–381 = Iulius 132 (Fitzler–Seeck); *PIR*[2] 4.156–65, no. 215. A bibliography of work on Augustus (1900–72) is provided by B. Haller in *ANRW* (1975), 2.2.55–74; see also L. Wickert in *ANRW* (1974), 2.1.3–76 and Christ 218ff., esp. 313–21.

etiamsi †praeuenit et†   Did *et* arise through dittography? or mistaken word-division? or is there a lacuna to be placed after it? One or other of these has been assumed in the numerous emendations proposed for this clause. Heinsius suggested *praenitet*, a verb which V. uses at 35.1 and 39.2; but Cornelissen's *praeminet* (1887) seems to me almost equally plausible. Burman conjectured *per se nitet*, and Acidalius *properanti* (an allusion to V.'s *festinatio*). No conjecture, however, carries complete conviction, and I have decided to obelise.

59.2–64.4 THE YEARS 44–43 B.C.

There can be few periods in history more fascinating than that which followed the murder of Caesar. Not only does it provide the classic confrontation between Antony, the experienced consul, and Octavian, the eighteen-year-old upon whom greatness had suddenly been thrust; it is also unusually rich, for ancient history, in primary sources, enabling us to follow almost day by day the changing loyalties of individuals and the *temporum uarietates fortunaeque uicissitudines* which in Cicero's opinion constitute the true source of delight for the reader of history (*Fam.* 5.12.4).

There can be no doubt that V. was steeped in the primary sources. There are clear allusions to Cicero's correspondence (e.g. 62.n.), his *Philippics* (e.g. 60.4n., 64.3n.), and to the *Res Gestae*, which V. 'ripete talvolta quasi alla lettera' (Canfora 134, cf. 61.1–2nn.). What these sources have in common is not so much their enthusiasm for Octavian and his actions, subjects on which Cicero at least had decidedly mixed feelings, but their criticism of Antony; and in V.'s narrative this bias is naturally mingled with explicit admiration for Octavian himself.[1]

---

[1] There are two passages in V.'s Augustan narrative (59.6 in the present section, and 89.6) which invite comparison with passages in his Tiberian narrative, and on each occasion V. clearly shows less enthusiasm for Augustus than he does later for Tiberius (see nn. ad locc.). It is in theory possible to infer from this evidence that V. actually disapproved of Augustus; but, even if so, he could not be expected to express his disapproval openly since Tiberius' own devotion to Augustus is well attested (see *TN* 234, 238–9). It has even been argued that V. belongs to an anti-Augustan tradition of historiography and that he is ultimately dependent on the same hostile source as the elder Pliny, Tacitus and Dio (J. Wegner, *Vell. Pat., eine philologische Quellenuntersuchung zur Geschichte des Kaisers Augustus*, unpubl. diss. Berlin, 1922); but not only is this thesis inherently implausible but its methodology also is questionable. The very fact that V. apologises for Octavian's participation in the proscriptions, for ex., does not seem to me to prove that he belongs to the same tradition as these other authors, as Wegner appears to assume (pp. 52–3, cf. Vell. 66.1–2, 86.2). That V. was aware of the tradition is of course undeniable, but that is a different matter.

59.2–60.2 OCTAVIAN'S BACKGROUND AND ARRIVAL (APRIL/MAY 44 B.C.)

59.2 Fuit C. Octauius ⟨pater⟩ . . . It seems to me impossible that V., who has referred to Octavian as *C. Octauium* in the preceding sentence, should here refer to his father by the same name without further elucidation. Cludius proposed to insert *pater*; this usage is idiomatic in Latin to distinguish between a father and son of the same name (thus Suet. *Aug.* 3.1 ' C. Octauius pater a principio aetatis . . .'; cf. *OLD* s.v. 1*b*), and the word could easily have dropped out, esp. if it had been in an abbreviated form. The resulting paronomasia *pater . . . patricia* is characteristically Velleian.

For the elder Oct. cf. *RE* 17.2.1806–8 = Octavius 15 (Münzer); *MRR* 2.110, 162, 167, 179, 185, 482; Wiseman 246 no. 287; Nicolet 2.963 no. 249. His career is recorded: *CIL* 6.1311 = *ILS* 47.

speciosa equestri genitus familia . . . diues Cf. Suet. *Aug.* 2.3 'ipse Augustus nihil amplius quam equestri familia ortum se scribit uetere ac locuplete '. V. however uses the ' artificial ' *genitus* here instead of the more usual *natus* or *ortus*; so too below, *genitam*, and on numerous other occasions: see Adams (1973), 125, 140 n. 25, who observes that the word is avoided by Cic. and Caes. but is relatively common in Liv. For *genitus familia* cf. Tac. *A.* 2.85.2, 13.12.1 (F.).

cum ei dignatio . . . Atiam conciliasset uxorem *dignatio* cannot refer to Octavius' praetorship in 61 B.C., just mentioned, since he was already married to Atia in 63, the year of Octavian's birth. V. must mean either Octavius' general political standing or his reputation (cf. *OLD* s.v. 3, 2); and with *conciliasset* we must therefore understand *iam*. For V.'s expr. cf. Val. Max. 7.1.1 'uxorem . . . conciliauit'; *OLD* s.v. 1*b*.

For Atia cf. *RE* 2.2.2257–8 = Attius 34 (Klebs); for Julia cf. *RE* 10.1.894 = Iulius 546 (Münzer). See Syme, *RR* Table III for a convenient family tree.

decedens . . . obiit Having been proconsul of Macedonia in 60/59, where he was saluted ' imperator ' for conquering the Bessi (*MRR* 2.191), Octavius died in 59/58 B.C. V.'s language, as Mr Seager points out to me, suggests that he died in the summer of 59 before the consular elections, for which he had returned in the spring of that year. *decedens* is a technical term for leaving office and/or returning to Rome (*TLL* 5.1.121.68ff.); so too Suet. *Aug.* 4.1 ' decedens Macedonia, prius quam profiteri se candidatum consulatus posset, mortem obiit repentinam '. According to Cic. *Phil.* 3.15, Octavius would certainly have become consul if he had lived.

59.3 Philippum L. Marcius Philippus, cos. 56 B.C., *RE* 14.2.1568–71 = Marcius 76 (Münzer); *MRR* 2.180, 207, 350.

natumque annos XVIII Hispaniensis militiae adsecutum se postea comitem habuit In Nov. 46 Caesar had set out against the Pompeian forces in Spain (cf. 55.2–3), intending to take Octavian with him; but the young man was delayed by a serious illness and was compelled to follow on later by himself (Suet. *Aug.* 8.1 *subsecutus*, Nic. Dam. 10 = F 127.21–2 Jacoby). When Oct. eventually caught up, according to Nic. Dam. (loc. cit.), Caesar 'had already finished the war within 7 months' (διαπεπολεμηκότι ἤδη τὸν σύμπαντα πόλεμον ἐν μησὶν ἑπτά); and since Caesar had arrived in Spain in Dec. 46, having taken roughly a month over the journey from Rome (Suet. *Iul.* 56.5, App. *BC* 2.103), it seems to follow that uncle and nephew did not meet until July 45 B.C. Since we know that Caesar did not return to Rome until October of that year (cf. 56.3), the period during which he 'had Octavian as his companion' was July–October. It is of course true that Octavian, whose birthday was 23 Sept., was 'eighteen years old' for a mere month of this period; but that does not mean we should accept Oudendorp's emendation *XVII* here.

For *militiae . . . comitem* cf. 118.2n.

numquam . . . alio uectum uehiculo On their journey from S. Spain via Carthago Nova to Gallia Narbonensis, Caesar kept Octavian in his own quarters and took him on his own ship (Nic. Dam. 11 = 127.24–5 Jacoby); but as they journeyed through Italy later, it was Antony who, having travelled up to meet them, rode in Caesar's carriage, while Octavian came behind with D. Brutus Albinus (Plut. *Ant.* 11.1).

For such *figurae etymologicae* as *uectum uehiculo* cf. L–H–S 790ff.

pontificatusque sacerdotio puerum honorauit Oct. succeeded L. Domitius Ahenobarbus, who died in 47 B.C.: cf. Nic. Dam. 4 = F 127.9 Jacoby. See Weinstock 33.

59.4 patratis bellis ciuilibus . . . Apolloniam eum in studia miserat The abl. abs. refers to the end of the war in Spain (mentioned above) and, appropriately in the context, adopts Caesar's view that the civil wars had ended with Munda; V.'s own view is that they continued till 29 (48.3n.).

It is unclear whether Octavian left for Apollonia the same October, or waited till the turn of the year: App. *BC* 3.9 says that he had been there six months when he heard of Caesar's death, but Nic. Dam. says only three months (16 = F 130.37 Jacoby).

Aldus' correction *patratis* seems certain in view of the frequency with which V. uses the expr. elsewhere (114.4n.).

ad erudiendam . . . singularis indolem iuuenis P's reading is *erudiendum . . . indolem*, to 'normalise' which Vascosanus wrote *indolis iuuenem*, but Ruhnken *erudiendam*. The former produces a commonplace expr., the

117

latter a somewhat choicer idiom: cf. 61.2 'tanti iuuenis indole', Cic. *Rep.*
5.9 'summi uiri indolem', Liv. 35.15.3, Hor. *C.* 4.4.25–6 'indoles
nutrita', Flor. 1.6.1 'eximiam indolem uxor . . . educauerat', Amm.
15.8.10 'indolem bonis artibus institutam'; for the use of *erudire* cf. Sen.
Ep. 94.51 'animus . . . eruditur', Auson. *Grat. Act.* 31 'erudiisse indolem'
(F.). In 1835 it was discovered that A reads *erudiendam*, which I take to
confirm Ruhnken's conjecture, thus providing ammunition for anyone
who may still believe in the reliability of A. For *disciplinis erudire* cf. Nep.
Epam. 1.4, *Iph.* 2.4 (F.).

belli Getici ac deinde Parthici   For Caesar's planned wars against the
Getae and Parthians cf. Cic. *Att.* 13.27(298).1, App. *BC* 2.110.

59.5 ex uicinis legionibus   In Krause's view these are the Macedonian
troops who had already been in friendly contact with Oct. before Caesar's
death and with whom he was afterwards urged to take refuge in the interests of his own security (App. *BC* 3.10–11).

omnem ordinem ac rationem . . . comperit   It seems to me
extremely doubtful that the paradosis *ordinationem* can = 'account', 'the
whole story', which is the meaning required here. According to *TLL* the
noun is equivalent to *descriptio* at Front. *Aq.* 88.4 'deberi operi . . . eroga-
tionis ordinationem', but since the verb *ordinare* never seems to lack the
notion of ordering or listing, I think *ordinationem* must there = 'systematic
treatment'. Gelenius proposed *ordinem*, which has the right meaning (cf.
1.10.4, 119.1), but it is hard to see how the corruption might have arisen:
according to *TLL* (9.2.934.17–18) the two nouns are often confused, but
this presumably means that *ordo* was regularly written for *ordinatio*, not
vice versa. Heinsius suggested *ordine rationem*, which, if it meant 'by
degrees', would be attractive since it was only gradually that Oct., having
landed at Lupiae before proceeding to Brundisium, discovered the full
facts of the case from travellers and letters from his mother (Nic. Dam.
17–18 = F 130.48, 52 Jacoby, App. *BC* 3,10–11). But the more natural
meaning of *ordine* is 'in due order' (cf. 114.4, 117.4), which is inappropriate here. T. Munker (in Heinsius' edn) proposed *ordinem ac rationem*,
which has the right meaning and is unexceptionable apart from the slight
awkwardness of its being followed by two further nouns joined by *et . . . et*.
I have therefore adopted it.

For *festinare* + infin., above, often used with verbs of motion, cf. *TLL*
6.1.619.10ff. For Salvidienus Rufus cf. 76.4n.; for Agrippa, 79.1n.

59.6 immanis amicorum occurrit frequentia   'Velleio . . . descrive
il suo arrivo in Italia come un trionfo' (Canfora 132); more precisely, like
the *aduentus* of an emperor – although apart from *frequentia* (for which cf.
e.g. Cic. *Att.* 4.1.5, *Pis.* 31, Tac. *Agr.* 40.3, *Pan. Lat.* 7.8.7) and the solar
symbolism (p. 121) V. refrains from deploying many of the other panegyrical topoi at his disposal (for which cf. *TN* 130ff.). Similarly, whereas

he is happy to introduce Caesar (41.1ff.) and Tiberius (94.2) with conventional portraits, he has omitted to do so in the case of Octavian. The significance (if any) of these omissions is hard to estimate; but see below, pp. 26of. (and cf. Syme, *RR* 113).

For *immanis* used of large numbers etc. cf. *TLL* 7.1.441.1ff. (the usage is sometimes hard to distinguish from that illustrated at 105.3n.). For *aduentare* + simple accus. cf. *TLL* 1.836.51ff. (only Sall. *J.* 28.2 before V.).

cum intraret urbem We know from Cic. that he and Oct. were on adjacent estates at Puteoli on 22 April (*Att.* 14.11(356).2, 14.12(366).2) and that Oct. was in Rome by 11 May (14.20(274).5).

solis orbis super caput eius . . . conspectus est (1) Meteorology. The other sources for the phenomenon which V. describes are: Plin. *NH* 2.98 'cernuntur . . . plerumque et circa solis orbem ceu spiceae coronae et uersicolores circuli, qualiter Augusto Caesare in prima iuuenta urbem intrante', Sen. *NQ* 1.2.1 'quo die urbem diu. Aug. Apollonia reuersus intrauit, circa solem uisum coloris uarii circulum, qualis esse in arcu solet. hunc Graeci halo uocant, nos . . . coronam', Suet. *Aug.* 95 'repente liquido ac puro sereno circulus ad speciem caelestis arcus orbem solis ambiit' (repeated almost verbatim in Oros. 6.20.5), Obseq. 68 'cumque hora diei tertia ingenti circumfusa multitudine Romam intraret, sol puri ac sereni caeli orbe modico inclusus extremae lineae circulo, qualis tendi arcus in nubibus solet, eum circumscripsit', Lyd. *De Ostent.* 10b, Dio 45.4.4 ἐς γὰρ τὴν 'Ρώμην ἐσιόντος αὐτοῦ ἶρις πάντα τόν ἥλιον πολλὴ καὶ ποικίλη περιέσχεν.

That meteorological sense can be made of this evidence was demonstrated by H. Kleinstück (*Phil. Woch.* 52 (1932, nos. 35/38), 244), who argued that the phenomenon was, in modern terms, a halo.[1] Haloes encircle the sun at 22°, their colour (when visible) changes from red nearest the sun through to blue at the outer limit, and they are particularly common in spring. If Octavian arrived at Rome in late April (last n.), and if the time was 9 a.m. (Obseq., Oros.), the sun will have been at 35° above the SE horizon; and since it is likely that Oct. was arriving from the SE along the Appian Way, as Kleinstück suggested, the waiting crowds will have had the sun in their eyes and Octavian's appearance 'out of the sun' may well have produced the 'crowning' effect of which V. speaks.

---

[1] I assume that in Obseq. *puri . . . caeli* depends upon *orbe* rather than *sol*, thus indicating that sky was visible between the sun and its encircling ring, a characteristic which means that the phenomenon cannot have been a corona. If *puri . . . caeli* depended on *sol*, the meaning would be 'the sun of [i.e. in] a clear and cloudless sky'; but such a genit. seems to me unusual. It is true that haloes demand the presence of cirrus cloud, whereas it is stated by Suet. (and Oros.) that the sky was clear; but the fragmentation, dispersal and extreme height of cirrus would not invalidate Suet.'s description.

(2) Text. Although several scholars have argued that *solis orbis* here means 'ring round the sun', the normal meaning of the phrase is simply 'the sun' (*TLL* 9.2.913.49ff.). It seems to me highly unlikely that V., alone of our sources and in a meteorological context of such complexity, would give an unusual meaning to a standard phrase; to support the meaning 'ring round the sun' scholars quote Liv. 30.2.12 'arcus solem tenui linea amplexus est; circulum deinde ipsum maior solis orbis extrinsecus inclusit', but there, even if the text is correct, the meaning is clear from the context (H. B. Gottschalk, *LCM* 4 (1979), 165, deletes *solis*). I think *solis orbis super caput eius curuatus aequaliter* means that the sun was behind Octavian (*super* in this sense is not unusual, cf. 70.5) and that his head is represented as being in the centre of the sun's orb (*aequaliter* = equidistant from all points of the sun's circumference, cf. *TLL* 1.1001.62ff.).[1]

Far more difficulty resides in *rotundatusque in colorem arcus*. Some have interpreted *in colorem arcus* as 'like the colour of a rainbow', but *in* alone cannot express similarity: either it must govern a noun denoting similarity (hence Bothe suggested *in morem arcus*) or it must be used in conjunction with a word which helps out the sense (hence G. A. Koch suggested *rutilatusque in c. a.*, Bernays *coruscansque in c. a.*, and Halm *rotundatusque in circulum a.*). I am not at all certain, however, that *arcus* does mean 'rainbow' here. If I was right to restrict the meaning of *solis orbis* to 'sun' (above), we require a reference to the sun's halo – a reference which, unless we assume a lacuna, only *arcus* is capable of providing (for this sense cf. Liv. 30.2.12, quoted above). But if *arcus* = 'halo', we still need to express the facts that it was multicoloured (cf. Dio ποικίλη, Plin. *uersicolores*, Sen. *coloris uarii*) and that it encircled the sun (cf. Suet. Oros. *ambiit*, Dio περιέσχεν). Both these requirements would be met by reading *circumdatusque ⟨uers⟩icolor arcus*. The participle is not far from *rotundatus*: either one of the many abbreviations of *circum-* was simply misread, or a scribe, expecting a synonym after *curuatus*, wrote *rotundatus* (*o* and *i* are very often confused, cf. Kritz xc);[2] for the use of *circumdare* cf. Vitr. 9.8.8 'circuli sunt circumdati'. The omission of *uers-* can easily be explained by the proximity of *-que* (so Hottinger, on whose *curuatum aequaliter rotundatumque ⟨uers⟩icolorem arcum* I have based this part of my conjecture). The meaning of the whole sentence is: 'Behind his head, and outlining it equally on all sides, the sun was visible, and surrounding ⟨the sun⟩ a multicoloured halo, as if a crown were being placed on the future hero's head'.

---

[1] The latter detail, also in Obseq. (*eum circumscripsit*), is not mere fancy: provided the angles and distances were right, Oct. will have appeared thus to many in the crowd.

[2] Many scholars have assumed *rotundatus* as synonymous with *curuatus* and syntactically divorced from *in colorem*. Clearly *rotundatus* cannot govern *in colorem*, since the two items are different in sense (see above); but it is also very difficult to take it as a synonym, since *curuatus* refers to circular, but *rotundatus* usually to spherical, shapes.

(3) *Symbolism.* Dio interprets the meteorological phenomenon as a portent of the civil storms to come, but clearly this is not true of V. Throughout Greek and Roman antiquity great men were identified, compared, or said to have a special relationship, with the sun. Scipio Africanus, M. Brutus, Augustus himself and Tiberius were all called *Sol* (cf. Cic. *ND* 2.14 with Pease's n.; Hor. *S.* 1.7.24 and *C.* 4.2.46–7 with E. Doblhofer, *Die Augustuspanegyrik des Hor. in formalhistorischer Sicht* (1966), 86ff.; Manil. 4.765 with Housman's n.), and the practice became even commoner in later imperial panegyric, where the formula *Sol Inuictus Imperator* was often employed (cf. Menand. rhet. 3.378.10–12; J. A. Straub, *Vom Herrscherideal in der Spätantike* (1939, repr. 1964), 129–34; H. P. L'Orange, *SO* 14 (1935), 86ff.; Liebeschuetz 279ff.). Indeed it is particularly interesting to note, in the context of Octavian's *aduentus* in Rome here, that the identification of later emperors with *Sol* was a special feature of the *aduentus* (S. MacCormack, *Historia* 21 (1972), 729–33).

At Rome Sol himself was traditionally represented as wearing a radiate crown (e.g. *RRC* 1.474 no. 463, 4a–d); it was therefore natural that a similar crown should be worn by those with whom Sol was identified, e.g. Caesar (see Weinstock 382–3) and Augustus himself, who was seen wearing such a crown by his father in a dream (Suet. *Aug.* 94.6). There can be little doubt that V., who at 36.1 recorded Augustus' birth by saying that his brightness would eclipse that of everyone else, and who at 60.1 just below testifies to his *caelestis animus*, has presented the halo as a 'real-life' manifestation of Octavian's relationship with the sun (cf. *uelut coronam . . . imponens*; the phrase *tanti mox uiri* indicates that Oct. belongs to the same tradition as Caesar and Tiberius, cf. 94.3n.). The halo is thus analogous in function to the divine fire which appeared over the head of Servius Tullius (Liv. 1.39.1, with Ogilvie's n.) and over Augustus himself during the battle of Actium (Virg. *Aen.* 8.680–1); but it is at the same time a more significant manifestation because it foreshadows the special relationship which Augustus was later to develop with Apollo, the sun god, with whom on occasion he even seems to have identified himself (cf. Suet. *Aug.* 70.1, 94.4; see further Liebeschuetz 82f.).

The bibliography on solar symbolism is extremely extensive; much of it is listed in Pöschl s.v. *Sonne.* Cf. also 94.2n.

60.1 Non placebat . . . V.'s account in 1–2 here agrees closely with the more elaborate version of Nic. Dam. 18 = F 130.53–5 Jacoby. Nic. says that Atia and Philippus communicated with Oct. by post while he was still in S. Italy, whereas (in Jacoby's opinion) V. places their counselling in Rome after Oct.'s arrival there. It seems to me more likely that V. is speaking generally about the whole period from March (or April) to May 44, and that the tense of *placebat* = 'had not and still did not'. App. *BC* 3.11–13 realistically indicates that Atia and Philippus were in touch with Oct. throughout this time; and we know from Cic. that Philippus and Oct. were together in Puteoli on 21–2 April (*Att.* 14.11(365).2, 12(366).2).

nomen inuidiosae fortunae Caesaris   Though there are other possibilities, I think that *nomen* governs both *inu. fortunae* and *Caesaris*: 'a name whose fortune (had) attracted such hatred, ⟨viz.⟩ "Caesar"'. Names can be represented as having fortunes (e.g. Hor. *C.* 4.4.70–2 'occidit | . . . fortuna nostri | nominis', Ov. *Tr.* 4.12.5 'fortunaque nominis', Sen. *Ep.* 71.10 'Scipionem in Africa nominis sui fortuna destituat'), and *fortunae* is regularly used as a genitive of description; for the two dependent genitives cf. 124.2n., and for *inuidiosae fort.* cf. Sen. *Contr.* 10.2.12. V.'s point is admirably illustrated by letters of Cic. to Atticus in June and Nov. 44: 'in Octauiano . . . satis ingeni, satis animi . . . sed quid aetati credendum sit, quid nomini, . . . magni consili est' (15.12(390).2), 'plane hoc spectat [sc. Oct.] ut se duce bellum geratur cum Antonio . . . quem autem sequamur? uide nomen, uide aetatem' (16.8(418).1). At the time of which V. is speaking here, Oct.'s stepfather Philippus refused to call him Caesar (Cic. *Att.* 14.12(366).2; 22 April). On Oct.'s assumption of Caesar's name see further Schmitthenner, *Test.* 65ff.

adire (above) can of course be used with such nouns as *periculum, fortuna* and *inuidia* (*TLL* 1.627.16ff., 45ff.), but here the expr. is clearly analogous to the technical *adire hereditatem* (for which cf. 120.3n.).

conditorem conseruatoremque Romani nominis   'Augustus was no *conditor*' (Weinstock 184); 'Augustus had a real claim to be known and honoured as the Founder' (Syme, *RR* 520). The latter is surely correct. Aug. is actually called *conditor* also at Suet. *Aug.* 7.2 and *ILS* 6773, and cf. Virg. *Aen.* 6.792 'aurea condet saecula', Flor. 2.34.66 'quia condidisset imperium'; he was commonly called κτίστης in the East (*RE* 11.2.2086). In 27 B.C. Aug. is said to have desired the name Romulus (Dio 53.16.7), in 2 B.C. he allowed himself to be called *pater patriae* (*RG* 35.1 with Gagé's n.), and, above all, he issued at an unknown date an edict which Suet. has preserved (*Aug.* 28.2): 'edicto his uerbis testatus est: "ita mihi saluam ac sospitem rem p. sistere in sua sede liceat . . . ut optimi status auctor dicar et moriens ut feram mecum spem, mansura in uestigio suo fundamenta quae iecero". fecitque ipse se compotem uoti nisus omni modo ne quem noui status paeniteret'. The very name 'Augustus' was thought to be associated with founding (Suet. *Aug.* 7.2).

Although any founder will naturally be interested in conservation, *conditor* and *conseruator* do not seem to be coupled until Plin. *Pan.* 1.1, where they are used of Jupiter. But Augustus himself is called 'parenti conseruatori' on coins between 19 and 16 B.C. (*BMC Emp.* 1.cxi, 69–70 nos. 397–402). *conseruator* became a common, if semi-official, title (e.g. EJ 85, of Tiberius), and (cf. Cic. *Sest.* 53) is obviously analogous to *custos* (104.2n., cf. also *tutela* at 105.3n.). On 'founders' in general see Weinstock 175ff.

adserebant, above, apparently = 'claimed'; the verb's legal flavour (cf. *OLD* s.v.) is appropriate to the present context.

60.2 spreuit itaque caelestis animus humana consilia The significance of Oct.'s decision is emphasised both by the position of the main verb and by the fact that (with the exception of *festinans* at 59.5) this is the first time he is represented as taking any decisive action at all.[1] *caelestis animus*, normally = 'the mind of god' (*TLL* 3.71.19ff.), here confirms the relationship between Oct. and the divine which was suggested by the halo and the reference to fate. The contrast between this phrase and *humana consilia* is all the more effective because it was conventional to contrast *humana consilia* with the truly divine (F. quotes Liv. 1.42.2 'nec rupit tamen fati necessitatem humanis consiliis', 5.49.5, 9.9.10, 44.40.3, Cic. *I Verr.* 1, *Har. Resp.* 61, *Mil.* 85, *Lig.* 17, Val. Max. 1.7 *ext.* 5, Tac. *A.* 15.44.1); this contrast is also linked to the following contrast between *summa* and *humilia* because *humanus* was thought to derive from the same root as *humilis* ('ab humo humanus', Prisc. p. 79.8 K; cf. Quint. 1.6.34, Serv. *Geor.* 2.340, Hyg. *Fab.* 220.3, Isid. *Orig.* 1.29.3). As Rockwood notes, this link makes the double contrast all the more striking. See also 123.2n.

cum periculo potius summa quam tuto humilia proposuit sequi For similar and opposite contrasts cf. Dem. *De Cor.* 201 ἀσφάλειαν ἄδοξον μᾶλλον ἢ τὸν ὑπὲρ τῶν καλῶν κίνδυνον, Sall. *H.* 1.55.26 'potiorque uisa est periculosa libertas quieto seruitio', Tac. *H.* 4.76.2 'ut non idem pretium quietis quam periculi malit', *A.* 1.2.1 'tuta et praesentia quam uetera et periculosa mallent'. See also Vretska on Sall. *C.* 17.6. The most famous man to choose danger and glory rather than the safety of a quiet life was of course Achilles (*Il.* 9.410–16).

et Caesari 'who was after all Caesar'; *et = et quidem* (almost *idque*, καὶ τοῦτο), for which cf. *TLL* 5.2.873.81–4, 874.34ff.

60.3–61 OCTAVIAN AND ANTONY (APRIL/MAY 44–APRIL/MAY 43 B.C.)

60.3 Hunc protinus Antonius . . . Antony had left Rome between 22 and 28 April for Campania (Rice Holmes, *Arch.* 190–1), but in order to meet Octavian he returned in mid- or late May (as may be inferred from Cic. *Fam.* 11.2(329)). For *superbe excipit* cf. Tac. *A.* 2.37.1 'superbius accepisset' (F.).

---

[1] In 59.3–4 Julius Caesar is the subject of the main verbs, and Oct. their object. This technique certainly emphasises the relationship of the two men, but the emphasis should not be used (as it is by Starr (1978), 65) to argue that there is no break between V.'s narratives of Caesar and of Octavian. Cf. V.'s words at 59.1 'de cuius origine . . . pauca dicenda sunt'.

mox etiam ... sceleste insimulare coepit In a letter of early October 44, Cicero refers to an alleged attempt by Octavian on Antony's life (*Fam.* 12.23(347).2): 'de quo multitudini fictum ab Antonio crimen uidetur . . . prudentes autem et boni uiri et credunt factum et probant'. There is a similar divergence of opinion amongst the ancient authorities; in agreement with V. are Nic. Dam. 30 = F 130.123 Jacoby, App. *BC* 3.39, Plut. *Ant.* 16.7–8.

insimulare is used abs., as Cic. *Rosc. Com.* 25, Ov. *A.* 2.7.13.

60.4 aperte deinde ... erupit furor P. Cornelius Dolabella, whom Caesar himself had chosen as cos. suff., had 'seized the fasces and consular insignia' (58.3) on Caesar's death: cf. *MRR* 2.317. The *dominatio* to which V. refers is illustrated in his following sentences; but we know that in late April Dolabella also instigated a series of arrests and executions, for which cf. Cic. *Phil.* 1.5, 30, *Att.* 14.15(369).2(1). On Dol. see further *RE* 4.1.1300–8 = Cornelius 141 (Münzer). For *Antonii ... furor* see Achard 243.

HS septies milies ... occupatum ab Antonio The sum is confirmed by Cic. *Phil.* 2.93, 5.11, 12.12. 'It is sometimes stated . . . that Antony appropriated the whole sum at one sweep on the night after Caesar's murder. But the passages in the ancient authorities . . . show that what he really did was to perpetrate a series of embezzlements lasting over several weeks' (Denniston on Cic. *Phil.* 1.17). See esp. Nic. Dam. 28 = F 130.110 Jacoby, where it is stated that it took two months to empty the treasury – i.e. up to mid-May, roughly the time with which V. is here dealing.

actorum eiusdem insertis falsis ⟨immunitatibus⟩ ciuitatibusque corrupti commentarii 'The records of his decisions were falsified by the insertion of spurious immunities and grants of citizenship.' Perizonius' supplement (*ap.* Heinsius) seems confirmed by the number of times Cicero refers to Antony's grants of immunity: *Phil.* 1.3, 24 'ciuitas data non solum singulis sed nationibus . . . immunitatibus infinitis sublata uectigalia', 2.35, 91, 92 'neque solum singulis uenibant immunitates sed etiam populis uniuersis; ciuitas . . . prouinciis totis dabatur', 3.10 'quam hic immunitatem, quam ciuitatem . . . non . . . uendidit?', 5.11 'decreta falsa uendebat, regna, ciuitates, immunitates . . .', 12.12, *Fam.* 12.1.1. Ellis preferred the order *ciuitatibus ⟨immunitatibus⟩que*, Haase proposed ⟨*regnis*⟩ *ciuitatibusque* (a ref. to king Deiotarus, whom Antony recognised as ruler of Armenia, cf. Cic. *Att.* 14.12(366).1, *Phil.* 2.94ff.), while Krause simply indicated a lacuna thus: *insertis falsis, ciuitatibusque* *** *corrupti commentarii*. Hellegouarc'h (1976), 251–2, while admiring Perizonius' supplement, prefers to retain the (to me meaningless) paradosis.[1]

---

[1] In his edn Hellegouarc'h translates the paradosis: 'par l'insertion de faux et de concessions du droit de cité'.

An alternative way of tackling the text was suggested by Ruhnken, to whom we already owe the restoration of *corruptis commentariis* to the nom. case. He emended *ciuitatibusque* to *uitiatique*. It is true that *uitiare* and *corrumpere* are coupled at Cic. *Sest.* 115, but his suggestion introduces into V.'s text another example of the relatively rare *-que et* (cf. 77.1n.); and although a variation on Ruhnken's proposal would avoid this difficulty (e.g. *insertis falsis ciuitatibus ⟨uitiati⟩ corruptique comm.*), the evidence seems to me heavily in favour of Perizonius' solution.

The only grant of citizenship of which we know was that to the Sicilians, to which Cicero was already referring indignantly on 22 April, alleging that there were hundreds of similar cases (*Att.* 14.12(366).1 'sescenta similia'). Four days later he is taking for granted the falsification of Caesar's *commentarii* (*Att.* 14.13(367).6). Likewise, the only grant of immunity seems to have been that given to Crete (Cic. *Phil.* 2.97). Clearly V. is exaggerating, but not as much as Cicero himself.

uendente rem publicam consule   This trick of ending a sentence with an abl. abs. is frequent in Tacitus (cf. R. Enghofer, *Der Ablat. Absol. bei Tac.* (1961), 127–38), who often employs it for a sinister or cynical effect not unlike that of V. here (the deferring of *consule* is particularly good). Antony's venality was proverbial, esp. in Cic. *Phil.* (see last n.); cf. also Virg. *Aen.* 6.620–1 'uendidit hic auro patriam dominumque potentem | imposuit, fixit leges pretio atque refixit', generally taken to refer to Ant. (see Norden ad loc., who compares *dominatione Antonii* at 61.1 below).

60.5 idem . . . consuli decretam Galliam occupare statuit, Dolabella transmarinas decreuit sibi   At some time before 18 April 44, as may be inferred from Cic. *Att.* 14.9(363).3, Antony and Dolabella received the provinces of Macedonia and Syria respectively. Dio (45.9.3, 20.3) says that Antony obtained his province by lot, and most modern scholars assume that Dolabella did too; but App. *BC* 3.7 says that Dol. was persuaded by Ant. to appeal to the people, a procedure which V.'s *decreuit sibi* may well describe. The impropriety of Dol.'s action, as Mr Seager points out to me, is neatly underlined by the repetition *consuli decretam ~ decreuit sibi* (for the latter expr. F. compares Cic. *Prou. Cons.* 15).

In early April D. Brutus had departed for Cisalpine Gaul, the province to which he had been appointed by Caesar (cf. *MRR* 2.328). But it soon emerged that Antony was dissatisfied with Macedonia and, as Cicero learned from Atticus in late April, he intended on 1 June to bring forward proposals on the provinces and to assign Gallia Cisalpina and Gallia Comata to himself (*Att.* 14.14(368).4), relinquishing Macedonia but keeping control of its army. Not surprisingly Antony's intention was unwelcome in many quarters, and the senatorial meeting on 1 June was inadequately attended; undaunted, Antony appealed to the people, and on the same or the following day[1] there was passed the *lex de permutatione*

---

[1] More probably the latter (see Ehrenwirth 6ff.).

prouinciarum, by which Antony's intentions were realised. The *lex* placed him in direct confrontation with D. Brutus, who was naturally unwilling to give up his province and claimed the backing of the senate. The dispute resulted in Brutus' being besieged by Antony at Mutina at the turn of the year (cf. 61.3–4nn.).

On the issues outlined here the standard article is W. Sternkopf, *Hermes* 47 (1912), 349ff., 357ff.; see also Rice Holmes, *Arch.* 188–90, 192–6; *MRR* 2.315–6, 317.

C. Caesar . . . Antonii petebatur insidiis   Though repetitions are a common feature of V.'s style (cf. 100.5n.), the verbal echo of 3 above is here ironical: the alleged victim has turned *de facto* aggressor. For *diuersa uolentes*, above, cf. Sil. 11.602(F.).

61.1 Torpebat oppressa dominatione Antonii ciuitas   Although V.'s language derives ultimately from that of late republican politics (cf. Cic. *Att.* 2.21.1 'uidebatur . . . dominatio ciuitatem oppressisse', *TD* 5.57, Sall. *C.* 51.31 'ciuitas seruitute oppressa', Caes. *BC* 1.22.5 'p. R. factione paucorum oppressum', *Bell. Afr.* 22.2 'r. p. . . . oppressam'; Weber 137*–8* n. 557, with many parallels), he must, in view of the context and the allusions elsewhere in this section, be alluding principally to *RG* 1.1 'rem publicam a dominatione factionis oppressam'.

This correspondence between V. and *RG* has been used by Wirszubski (104–5) to support his argument that Augustus' phrase *dominatione factionis*, though rendered by τῆς τῶν συνομοσαμένων δουλήας in the Greek version, cannot refer to the tyrannicides: *factio* 'was a very handy substitute for Antony, and it misled no one'. Yet Canfora (134) has argued in the light of the Greek version that this interpretation, while possible, is not the only one; and Hellegouarc'h–Jodry (815) have said that V.'s concentration on Antony is significantly different from *RG*, where *factio* = 'l'opposition à César'. But Wirszubski is right to say (105 n. 2) that the correctness of the Greek version is precluded by other passages in *RG* and particularly by *eo nomine* at 1.2; I therefore conclude that V. and *RG* are here in harmony with each other, which is no more than we would expect.

For *oppressa . . . ciuitas* cf. also August. *Ciu. Dei* 3.30; for *torpebat oppressa* Ruhnken quoted Sall. *H.* 1.77.19 'torpedo animos oppressit' (VG: *obrepsit* F, Nonius); for *dominatione Antonii* cf. 60.4, Cic. *Phil.* 3.34, 8.12, *Ep. Brut.* 1.16(25).4, 17(17).2, Virg. *Aen.* 6.620 (above, 60.4n.).

uis ad resistendum nulli aderat cum C. Caesar . . .   The contrast between the general lethargy (*torpebat oppressa, uis . . . nulli aderat*) and Octavian's initiative (*ausus, consecutus, primumque . . . mox . . . breui*) is effectively rendered by an inverted *cum*-clause.[1] For *uis ad resistendum* cf. Liv.

---

[1] For this particular type of *cum*-clause, introducing 'un personnage . . . qui, par son intervention, va agir directement sur l'événement', see Chausserie-Laprée 570–1, who finds no exs. in Caes. or Sall. but several in Liv. Curt. Tac.

2.56.4, 5.9.7, 30.16.3, 44.20.3 (also 4.26.3, Vell. 109.1); for *indignatio et dolor*, above, cf. *TLL* 7.1.1180.82ff.; for 'lacking a leader' cf. 72.5, 125.2n.

XVIIII annum egressus   The paradosis reads *XVIIII annum ingressus*, which means 'having entered upon his 19th year', i.e. when Octavian had just turned 18. If the text is correct, V. cannot be referring to events which took place on or after 23 Sept. 44 B.C., which was Oct.'s 19th birthday and the day when he entered upon his 20th year; *XVIIII annum ingressus* cannot therefore be taken with *primumque . . . ueteranos exciuit paternos* below, since Octavian did not start to recruit his army until October 44 B.C. (see n. ad loc.).

However, there are in the present sentence two other expressions to which *XVIIII annum ingressus* might in theory apply, viz. *mira ausus ac summa consecutus* and *maiorem senatu pro r. p. animum habuit*; and since the former appears at first sight to refer back to *summa . . . proposuit sequi* at 60.2 above, it could perhaps be argued that *XVIIII annum ingressus* is a further (correct) reference to the earlier months of 44 B.C. when Octavian decided to enter the city and his inheritance.[1] There are, however, strong indications that this cannot be so.

First, *ingressus* ought to refer to the beginning of Oct.'s 19th year (cf. *TLL* 7.1.1571.30) and is thus hardly suitable to the events of May 44 B.C. when more than half his 19th year had already passed. Secondly, and more important, V. clearly has in mind Cic. *Phil.* 3.3 ('*C. Caesar adulescens*, paene potius *puer*, incredibili ac diuina quadam *mente* atque uirtute, cum maxime furor arderet Antoni cumque eius a Brundisio crudelis et pestifer reditus timeretur, . . . *ne optantibus quidem nobis*, quia non posse fieri uidebatur, firmissimum *exercitum* ex inuicto genere *ueteranorum* militum *comparauit* patrimoniumque suum . . . in *salute rei publicae* conlocauit . . . [5] qua peste *priuato consilio* rem p. . . . Caesar liberauit') and *RG* 1.1 ('*Annos undeuiginti natus exercitum priuato consilio* et priuata impensa *comparaui*'); and since both of these passages associate Octavian's bold stroke of collecting an army in 44 B.C. with the notion of patriotism, it would appear that in V.'s text *mira ausus . . . ueteranos exciuit paternos* all refers to the same event and cannot be split up into phrases of different dates. This of course means that *ausus* and *consecutus* are not true past participles but express actions which are simultaneous with *habuit* and *exciuit*; yet such participles are paralleled readily elsewhere (see below) and particularly at 29.1: 'Cn. Pompeius . . . XXIII *annos natus . . . priuatis* ut opibus ita *consiliis* magna *ausus* magnificeque conata *exsecutus* ad *uindicandam restituendamque dignitatem patriae* firmum ex agro Piceno, qui totus *paternis* eius clientelis refertus erat, *contraxit exercitum*.' Indeed the general similarity between this and the present passage is so striking that it is difficult to believe that the one

---

[1] This is assumed to be the case, without argument, by R. Waltz, *REA* 51 (1949), 44; cf. also A. Ernout–F. Thomas, *Syntaxe Latine* (²1953), 178, who say that V. here writes 'très exactement'.

should be interpreted differently from the other.[1] Octavian was at this time 'the new Pompeius' (Syme, *RR* 125, cf. 316), and V. no doubt intended to draw the parallel between the two men (cf. Weber 139–41, 136*–7*).

It would thus appear that *XVIIII annum ingressus* cannot be divorced from *ueteranos exciuit paternos*, i.e. from the events of October 44 B.C.; that being so, the date is incorrect since Octavian had then entered his 20th year. It is inconceivable that V. himself made a mistake over such an important date. Not only does he refer at 61.3 to an inscription recording Octavian's age at the time and is correct at 61.4 about Oct.'s age during the battle of Mutina in the following year (see n., also 94.3n.), but Augustus' birthday was a public festival and thus widely celebrated (cf. Gagé 181–2; Weinstock 196, 209–10). I therefore think that the text is corrupt; but what form should emendation take?

While it is of course quite possible that *XX* was corrupted to *XIX*, an equivalent form of which is found in the paradosis, a change to *XX* would obscure the allusion to the canonical opening words of *RG*. I therefore prefer, with E. Chishull, to retain the numeral and emend *ingressus* to *egressus*.[2] The two words are very often confused (cf. *TLL* 7.1.1567.44), and indeed *egressus* is wrongly written for *ingressus* in the paradosis at 82.1 below; for *annum egredi*, a more common expr. than *a. ingredi*, cf. *TLL* 5.2.286.23ff. *XVIIII annum egressus* means 'shortly after his 19th birthday': a more precise reference to Octavian's age in October 44 B.C. would be hard to imagine.

mira ausus ac summa consecutus I have already argued (last n.) that these are not true past participles but describe actions which are simultaneous with the main verbs; cf. also 29.1 (quoted above), 37.3 *persecutus*; K–S 1.759, with many other exs.

For *ausus . . . consecutus* cf. also 24.1 'quae pessime ausus erat, fortiter exsecutus' (80.3 'ausum patratumque'); for *mira* (subst.) cf. *TLL* 8.1076.52ff.; for *summa* cf. 60.2, 76.3, Liv. 6.35.2, Just. 2.6.2 etc.

priuato consilio See last n. but one; also Weber 135* n. 550 for numerous other exs.

maiorem senatu pro re publica animum habuit 'showed . . . a greater courage than ⟨that of⟩ the senate on behalf of the state,' a *comparatio compendiaria* (cf. 41.2n.). For somewhat similar phrases cf. Cic. *Verr.* 2.113, *Phil.* 11.26, *Fam.* 1.9.16.

---

[1] At 29.1 there can be no doubt that the participles express simultaneous action with *contraxit* since there is nothing earlier either in V.'s text or in Pompey's career to which they can refer.

[2] *Antiquitates Asiaticae . . . Accedit Monum. Latinum Ancyr.* (London, 1728), 177–8. Heinsius had already proposed *egressus* but strangely he also altered the numeral to *XVIII*. Hellegouarc'h (xci–xcii and ad loc.) assumes that V. has confused the ordinal with the cardinal numeral.

61.2 primumque a Calatia, mox a Casilino ueteranos exciuit paternos Since by his own account Octavian was already 19 when he recruited this army (*RG* 1.1), he must have done so after 23 Sept. 44 B.C., which was his 19th birthday. Such a date is supported both by those sources which state that Oct. began to recruit in response to a similar move by Antony (Nic. Dam. 30–1 = F 130.129–33 Jacoby, App. *BC* 3.40, Dio 45.12.1; cf. Rice Holmes, *Arch.* 28), who had already left for Brundisium on this mission on 9 October (Cic. *Fam.* 12.23(347).2), and also by Cic. *Att.* 16.8(418).1, where Cicero writes that he heard on 1 Nov. from Octavian himself of the latter's activity at Calatia and Casilinum. The former colony provided legio VII, the latter legio VIII; for Oct.'s and Ant.'s legions at this time cf. Brunt, *IM* 480–1.

alii breui in formam iusti coiere exercitus In addition to the defectors from Antony (see below), Oct. recruited one new legion and filled up the veteran legions, already mentioned, with new recruits (App. *BC* 3.47 οὐκ ἐντελῆ μὲν ταῦτα τοῖς ἀριθμοῖς . . . ὑπὸ δὲ νεοσυλλόγων καὶ ταῦτα ἀναπληρούμενα).

For V.'s expr. cf. Liv. 7.39.8 'iusti exercitus formam' (25.6.14 'speciem iusti exercitus').

legio Martia et quarta . . . ad Caesarem se contulerunt Antony evidently heard of the former's defection on 24 November and of the latter's on 28 Nov. (Frisch 152–3, with refs.), though there is some dispute over the details (cf. Rice Holmes, *Arch.* 32–3 and 199–200). *sublatis signis* = 'having decamped', cf. Caes. *BC* 2.20.4, Liv. 32.30.7, 39.30.9 etc. The phrase *cum A. occurrisset exercitui* of course refers to the journey which Antony had begun on 9 October (last n. but one).

cognita et senatus uoluntate et tanti iuuenis indole It is true that on 20 Dec. 44 Cicero publicly argued that Antony's two legions, by defecting, had followed the *auctoritas* of the senate (*Phil.* 3.8, quoted by Krause); and a few days earlier he had written to D. Brutus arguing that a private initiative against Antony would accord with *uoluntas senatus* (*Fam.* 11.7(354).2). It is also true that Oct. was far more generous than Ant. in his donatives to the troops (Dio 45.12, Cic. *Att.* 16.8(418).1, App. *BC* 3.40, 43), something to which the former naturally drew attention in the leaflets which his agents distributed amongst Antony's followers (App. *BC* 3.44). On the other hand Oct. had failed to gain senatorial support for his attempted coup on 10 November, and a large number of senators expressed their allegiance to Antony in an oath around 29 November (see e.g. Syme, *RR* 125–6). The troops too had melted away on 10 Nov., when they realised that Antony was to be their target (App. *BC* 3.42). Here V. has interpreted events strongly in Octavian's favour (*uoluntas senatus* is an almost official phrase: Cic. *Verr.* 2.95, *Phil.* 5.41, Liv. 28.39.18, 39.47.8 etc.).

For V.'s expr. cf. also Tac. *A.* 13.15.1 'indolem . . . cognitam'; F. quotes Sen. *Tro.* 504 'agnosco indolem'.

61.3 statua, quae hodieque ... scriptura indicat For similar evidence of autopsy in V.'s earlier narrative compare 25.4 'memoriam et inscriptio templi adfixa posti hodieque ⟨et⟩ tabula testatur aerea intra aedem'; the Tiberian narrative naturally has many more exs. (e.g. 104.3n., 118.1n.).

The statue was golden (App. *BC* 3.51), placed *in rostris* (Cic. *Phil.* 9.4), and depicted on coins (*RRC* 1.499–500 no. 490, 2.740). It was voted at the 4-day meeting of the senate which began on 1 Jan. 43 B.C. (for the timing cf. Frisch 178–80; Rice Holmes, *Arch.* 39), having been proposed by Octavian's stepfather Philippus (Cic. *Ep. Brut.* 1.15(23).7). A similar proposal, 'qui honos ... mihi maximus uidetur' (*Phil.* 5.41), was made on behalf of M. Aemilius Lepidus at the same time by Cicero; and since we learn from a later speech that Cicero's proposal was also carried (*Phil.* 13.8 'honores ei decreui ... in quibus mihi uos estis adsensi'), it is rather disingenuous of V. to allege here that no man, apart from the three stated exceptions, had been so honoured during the previous 300 years. V.'s statement is true, but it is not the whole truth.

For Julius Caesar's equestrian statue cf. Weinstock 86–7; for Pompey's cf. e.g. Dio 43.49.1, Suet. *Iul.* 75.4; for Sulla's cf. Cic. *Phil.* 9.13, App. *BC* 1.97. The last person before Sulla to be so honoured, as Krause notes, was Q. Marcius Tremulus, the consul of 306 B.C. (cf. Liv. 9.43.22, Plin. *NH* 34.23); V.'s *per trecentos annos* is thus a (legitimate) round number.

For *hodieque* cf. 98.1n.; for *scriptura* cf. Val. Max. 1.1.12 'duabus arcis lapideis ... quarum in altera scriptura indicabat corpus Numae Pompili fuisse' (F.).

pro praetore una cum consulibus designatis ... bellum cum Antonio gerere iussit A paraphrase of *RG* 1.3 'res p. ne quid detrimenti caperet me pro praetore simul cum consulibus prouidere iussit', where see Gagé's n. *designatis*, as Ruhnken observed, is curious, since Hirtius and Pansa were by now in office. Either V. has made a mistake; or he has dated the measure of 1 Jan. 43 as if it belonged to 20 Dec. 44 when Cic. began discussing the whole subject (Mr Seager's suggestion, cf. *Fam.* 11.6a(356).2, *Phil.* 3.39); or V. has drawn attention to the fact that 'non comitiis creati sed ... a Caesare ... designati erant' (Krause).

After the 'arms race' of October/November 44 B.C. and the show of loyalty by certain elements of the senate and others (see above), Antony had left in December to take possession of Cisalpine Gaul, the province which he disputed with D. Brutus (60.5n.). At the turn of the year he was besieging Brutus in Mutina, a confrontation which led to his defeat at Forum Gallorum and Mutina itself (next n.). For the events of this period cf. *MRR* 2.328, 342–3, 347; Huzar 101–9.

61.4 ⟨id⟩ ab eo annum agente uicesimum ... circa Mutinam administratum est On 14 April 43 B.C. (cf. Cic. *Fam.* 10.30(378).1, Ov. *Fast.* 4.627–8, *ILS* 108), when Octavian was indeed 'in his 20th year' (for the expr. cf. 94.3n.), he and the consul Hirtius defeated Antony at Forum Gallorum, less than ten miles from Mutina; in a letter to Cicero (*Fam.*, as above) Ser. Sulpicius Galba, a legate of Hirtius in command of the legio Martia, provides an eyewitness account of the battle, but does not tell us that the other consul, Pansa, was badly wounded in an earlier phase of the engagement (cf. App. *BC* 3.69, Cic. *Phil.* 14.26). Several days later – usually assumed on the basis of Cic. *Ep. Brut.* 1.5(9).1 to be 21 April, although the precise date is in fact uncertain (cf. *RE* 16.1.944) – a second and more decisive battle between the same protagonists took place at Mutina itself; as V. proceeds to say, Antony was compelled to raise the siege which he had been conducting against D. Brutus, but Hirtius was killed in the battle and Pansa died within a couple of days from the wounds he had received earlier (cf. Cic. *Fam.* 11.13(388).2). See in general Frisch 267ff., *MRR* 2.335–6.

For *bellum . . . administratum* cf. 33.1, 97.4; *TLL* 2.1834.32ff.

D. Brutus obsidione liberatus   Though the last two words are commonly coupled (*TLL* 9.2.224.79–81), V. is no doubt thinking of Cic. *Phil.* 5.51 'qui [i.e. Oct.] ad D. Brutum obsidione liberandum profectus sit', phraseology which Antony picks up in the letter quoted with such sarcasm by Cic. later at *Phil.* 13.25.

Antonius turpi ac nuda fuga coactus deserere Italiam   Though *turpis fuga* is a conventional expression (cf. 78.3, Sall. *J.* 106.3, Liv. 2.59.2, Tac. *H.* 3.9.2 etc.), V. may be alluding to the fact that Antony was evidently in a position to continue fighting but instead chose to withdraw (cf. Frisch 288, Huzar 109, Rice Holmes, *Arch.* 56). Once on the road, Antony's followers were apparently few and poorly armed (cf. Cic. *Fam.* 10.11(382).2 'si nudus huc se Ant. confert', 11.10(385).3 'Ant. qui ex fuga cum paruulam manum peditum haberet inermium', 11.12(394).1–2 'ita enim Romam nuntiatum, ita persuasum omnibus, cum paucis inermis, perterritis metu, fracto animo fugisse Antonium. qui si ita se habet ut . . . confligi cum eo sine periculo non possit, non ille mihi fugisse a Mut. uidetur sed locum belli gerendi mutasse'): hence *nuda fuga* (cf. Sil. 9.83). On 26 April Antony was declared a public enemy (cf. Cic. *Ep. Brut.* 1.3a(8), *Fam.* 10.21(391).4); at about the same time, or perhaps in early May, the proconsul of Transalpine Gaul, L. Munatius Plancus, wrote to Cicero rightly forecasting that Antony would be compelled to cross the Alps (Cic. *Fam.* 10.11(382).2), which is where we rejoin him at 63.1 below.

62   BRUTUS AND CASSIUS (APRIL–MAY 43 B.C.)

In ch. 61 V. had created the impression that Octavian had defeated Antony at Mutina almost single-handed (e.g. 1 *priuato consilio*, 4 *ab eo . . . fortissime . . . administratum est*). The present section is intended above all to contrast the warmth of feeling which was shown towards Octavian before that defeat with the later resurgence of courage among the Pompeians, whose duplicity and ingratitude are highlighted throughout (2 *sine ullo s.c.*, 3 *simulantes* [contrast 5 *iniuriam dissimulando Caesar*], *sine auctoritate publica, praetexentes*, 5 *ingratus . . . senatus*). In particular note how D. Brutus is rewarded for merely staying alive and the dead consuls Hirtius and Pansa are honoured (4), but the victorious Octavian is spurned by all except his troops (5) – a significant fact which the senate overlooked but which V. rightly points out. The section begins and ends with references to Cicero (1 *omnia . . . maxime auctore Cicerone* ~ 6 *Cicero . . . amore P. partium*) and with allusions to his words (1 *honorifice . . . decreta*, for which F. quotes *Sest.* 32, *Fam.* 3.9.4, 15.13.3, ~ 6 *Caesarem laudandum et tollendum*, cf. *Fam.* 11.20.1). The very fact that V. at the end of the section draws attention to the famous ambiguity of this last statement (*cum . . . uellet*) suggests that he sees it as typifying the hypocrisy with which the *Pompeiani* had been acting and at which his 'scorching attack' in this section has been directed.[1]

62.2 Bruto Cassioque prouinciae ... decretae Modern scholars agree that Cassius's Syrian command, for whose ratification Cicero had campaigned in *Phil.* 11 in Feb./Mar. 43, was not in fact ratified until after Mutina on 27 April (cf. Cic. *Ep. Brut.* 1.5(9).1 'A. d. V Kal. Mai . . . dixit Seruilius . . . ut Cassius persequeretur Dolabellam'); but scholars are equally unanimous in stating that Brutus' Macedonian command, for whose ratification Cicero had campaigned in *Phil.* 10 in early Feb., had *already* been ratified at the same meeting of the senate at which Cicero had spoken. Yet V. repeats his version of events both at 62.4 ('quae omnia senatus decretis comprensa et comprobata sunt') and, with greater emphasis and precision, at 73.2 ('quem [sc. Sex. Pompeium] senatus paene totus adhuc e Pompeianis constans partibus post Antonii a Mutina fugam *eodem illo tempore quo* Bruto Cassioque transmarinas prouincias decreuerat, . . . in paterna bona restituerat et orae maritimae praefecerat'); and his assertion, made here at 62.2 and repeated at 73.2, that both commands were ratified as a result of increased republican feeling after Mutina, makes convincing historical sense. Moreover, V.'s version is supported by Dio 46.40.3 (τῷ τε γὰρ Πομπηίῳ τῷ Σέξτῳ τὸ ναυτικὸν καὶ τῷ Βρούτῳ τῷ Μάρκῳ τὴν Μακεδονίαν τῷ τε Κασσίῳ τήν τε Συρίαν . . . ἐνεχείρισαν)[2] and perhaps also by App. *BC* 4.58 (χαλεπαίνουσα ἡ βουλὴ [on account of Mutina] . . . Βροῦτον δὲ καὶ Κάσσιον ἐς τὰς προτέρας ἡγεμονίας ἐπανήγαγον).[3]

---

[1] I owe this phrase, as well as several of the other points I have made here, to Mr DuQuesnay.

[2] Manuwald (57) thinks that Dio has simply made a mistake, which, comparing our passage of V., he suggests is 'traditionsbedingt'.

[3] The words προτέρας and ἐπανήγαγον are due to Appian's mistaken belief that Caesar had assigned Syria to Cassius and Macedonia to Brutus in 44 (see *MRR* 2.321); they do not affect the issue here.

The fact is that there is very little concrete evidence for the earlier ratification of Brutus' command apart from App. *BC* 3.63 and Dio 47.22.1–2. The former can be dismissed, not only because it is contradicted by *BC* 4.58 (just quoted) but also because it places the ratification of Cassius' command at the same early date as that of Brutus', something with which no one would agree. The latter must also be regarded with suspicion, because it in turn is contradicted by 46.40.3 (just quoted); but it is admittedly an important passage because of its unequivocal statement that the senate accepted the proposal which Cicero made in early Feb. that Brutus' command be legalised.

As it happens, modern scholars (rightly) place more reliance on the evidence of Cicero's own writings than on that of Dio's history; yet, of the passages which they quote to support their thesis (*Phil.* 11.25–7, 36, 13.30, 32, *Ep. Brut.* 2.4(4).4, 2.5(5).2, *Fam.* 12.5(365).2–3: cf. *MRR* 2.346, Rice Holmes, *Arch.* 45 n. 5, *RE* 10.1.1002, Frisch 222), only one seems to me to have any real bearing on the issue. That is *Phil.* 11.27, where Cicero, arguing in late Feb./early Mar. that Cassius' Syrian command be legalised, asks: 'num igitur Brutus exspectauit decreta nostra, cum studia nosset?' From this passage, which alone refers to any senatorial vote (*decreta nostra*),[1] scholars seem to have inferred that Cicero's proposal in *Phil.* 10 was carried. Yet Cicero's point in this section of his speech is the defence of Cassius' unilateral action in Syria, which he supports by appealing to the precedent of Brutus; Cicero is referring to a period in Brutus' career before the senate was even aware of what he had done, and thus before any question of a decree could arise. And lest it be objected that *decreta nostra* nevertheless implies the subsequent ratification of Brutus' command, I think it is significant that nowhere in the whole of *Phil.* 11 does Cicero use the senate's alleged ratification of Brutus' Macedonian command as a precedent for Cassius' in Syria. It would have been the most natural and most cogent argument of all, yet Cicero never mentions it; the clear inference, it seems to me, is that Brutus did not constitute a precedent precisely because his command had not been ratified. This indeed seems to be the implication of the phrase *pro decreto*, which occurs in the sentence preceding the key *decreta nostra*.

If I am right to argue that Cicero contains no evidence for the earlier ratification of Brutus' command, from where did Dio derive his information in the troublesome passage at 47.22.1–2? The obvious explanation is that he mistook Cicero's proposal in *Phil.* 10 for the *decretum* itself, an error into which he fell earlier at 46.29.2, where on the basis of Cicero's proposal in *Phil.* 5 he wrongly states that Octavian was allowed to sit among the *quaestorii* (cf. Frisch 180, not mentioned by Manuwald 268–9).

---

[1] It cannot be inferred from *imperium legitimum* at 11.26 that Brutus' command had been legalised since the phrase is explicitly applicable also to Cassius, whose Syrian command was *a priori* illegal. Cicero is pulling a fast one: the phrase refers to their legitimate commands in Crete and Cyrene respectively.

We are thus left with the explicit, repeated and emphatic evidence of V. that Brutus' and Cassius' overseas commands were ratified simultaneously as a result of pro-republican feeling after the battle of Mutina. That is, 27 April 43. On the synchronisation with Sex. Pompeius' appointment as *praefectus classis* cf. 73.2n.

laudati quicumque his se exercitus tradidissent Gelenius deleted *se* (dittography), but cf. Cic. *Phil.* 10.13 'legio quam L. Piso ducebat . . . Ciceroni se filio meo tradidit. equitatus qui in Syriam ducebatur bipertito alter eum quaestorem . . . reliquit . . . seseque ad Brutum contulit'. Rockwood explains *tradidissent* as 'the subjunctive of cases frequently occurring', but I prefer to regard it as virtual or. obl. after *laudati*: V. is repeating the grounds on which praise was given. For the armies that transferred allegiance cf. Rice Holmes, *Arch.* 76, *MRR* 2.343.

For *commissa arbitrio*, below, cf. Sen. *Ep.* 90.4, Suet. *Aug.* 28.1.

62.3 quippe From here to *quae omnia* (4) V. summarises the movements of Brutus and Cassius between mid-April 44 and late April 43 B.C.

testati edictis Having left Rome through fear of Antony (cf. *metuentes*) in April 44, Brutus and Cassius in late July issued a joint edict to which Cicero refers at *Phil.* 1.8 and *Att.* 16.7(415).1 and to which Antony responded with a counter-edict (cf. Cic. *Att.* 16.7.7) and a letter (Cic. *Fam.* 11.3(336).1). Brutus and Cassius in their turn replied with a second edict and the letter written on 4 August which we now know as *Fam.* 11.3(336); cf. *RE* 10.1.998, Ehrenwirth 66 and 72. Scholars have debated whether V. here refers to their first or their second edict; but the plural *edictis* may mean that he has simply amalgamated the two. At any rate his language in this passage clearly echoes the war of words between the parties: cf. Cic. *Phil.* 1.9 'erectus enim [sc. Brutus] maximi ac pulcherrimi *facti sui conscientia*', *Fam.* 11.3(336).3 'non licere praetoribus *concordiae* ac libertatis causa per edictum de suo iure decedere quin consul *arma minetur* . . . nos si alia hortarentur ut *bellum ciuile* suscitare uellemus . . .'

Shortly after 17 August (so Ehrenwirth 77–8) Brutus and Cassius left Italy altogether. For *inuidiam augere*, above, cf. 31.4, 44.5; *TLL* 2.1350.62ff.

dum res publica constaret concordia 'provided the state survived in harmony', cf. Sen. *D.* 3.5.3 'beneficiis enim humana uita constat et concordia' (also Liv. 45.19.10 'regnum . . . fraterna stare concordia').

intento ac pari animo 'both equally determined in their intention'; for *intentus an.* cf. *TLL* 7.1.2118.20ff.; for various combinations of *par* and *animus* cf. Liv. 1.25.13, 3.43.4, 60.7, 33.18.14, 36.16.1.

praetexentes esse rem publicam This was evidently Livy's view also, cf. *per.* 118 'sub praetexto rei p.'. For the constr. cf. Tac. *H.* 1.72.2 and *A.* 4.4.2.

pecunias etiam . . . a uolentibus acceperant Krause notes that V. means C. Antistius Vetus, quaestor pro praetore in Syria, and M. Appuleius, proquaestor of Asia, both of whom handed over public funds to Brutus (*MRR* 2.327; App. *BC* 3.63, 4.75 adds troops); and P. Cornelius Lentulus Spinther, proquaestor pro praetore in Asia, who handed over money and troops to Cassius (see his letter to Cic., *Fam.* 12.14(405).6).
   For the 'Grecism' *uolentibus* cf. 69.3, 123.1n.; the point of the word here is that the transfers of troops and cash were made before 27 Apr. 43 and so before Brutus' and Cassius' commands were legitimised. Antistius and Appuleius were acting of their own accord and wrongly.

62.4 comprensa et comprobata 'were covered and ratified by . . .'; for *comprensa* cf. *OLD* s.v. *comprehendo* 9*b*.

quod alieno beneficio uixerat The paradosis *quod . . . uiueret* naturally cannot express the grounds on which the triumph was granted unless we assume an 'illogical' use of the subjunc. as at 45.2 *noluisset* and 117.3 *haberent*; yet in neither case is the subjunc. positively misleading, as it is here, and at 117.3 the mood is easily explained by attraction. It is just possible that *quod* here = 'although', a meaning which is supposed by some to be found at e.g. Ov. *AA* 1.261, *Met.* 7.705, Vitr. 9.1.7, though these passages have been disputed (by A. Szantyr, *Gymn.* 79 (1972), 499ff.).[1] I therefore prefer to restore the indic. *uixerat* on the analogy of 82.3 'hanc tamen Antonius fugam suam, quia uiuus exierat, uictoriam uocabat'. Acidalius retained *uiueret* but wrote *quom* for *quod*.

corpora publica sepultura honorata Cicero's proposal, cf. *Ep. Brut.* 1.15(23).8; for the expr. cf. 119.5n., 124.3.

62.5 Caesaris adeo nulla habita mentio ut . . . So too App. *BC* 3.74 περὶ δὲ Καίσαρος οὐδὲν ἦν ἐν τοῖς γραφομένοις, οὐδὲ τοὔνομα ὅλως, but not Liv. *per.* 119 'senatus . . . Caesaris militumque eius mentionem non satis gratam habuit'. The slight discrepancy would perhaps be explained if, as is usually thought, Cicero's proposal of an *ouatio* for Octavian (*Ep. Brut.* 1.15(23).9) was rejected. For accounts of the insulting embassy to Octavian's army, below, cf. Dio 46.40–1, App. *BC* 3.86.
   For *mentionem habere* cf. *OLD* s.v. *mentio* 1*b*; for *adeo nulla* (*non* etc.) . . . *ut* cf. 66.4; K–S 2.239.

---

[1] The passage of Vitr. is entirely deleted by the latest ed., J. Soubiran (Budé, 1969).

135

62.6 Caesarem laudandum et tollendum The full form was evidently 'laudandum adulescentem, ornandum, tollendum' (cf. Cic. *Fam.* 11.20(401).1, written 24 May; on the multivocal nature of *tollere* cf. Bell 246ff., esp. 249); cf. also Suet. *Aug.* 12.

V. here attributes to Cicero *amor Pompeianarum partium*; on Cicero's own use of political *amor* cf. Hellegouarc'h, *VL* 146–7, who notes that 'l'emploi fréquent du mot à l'égard de Pompée atteste le prix qu'attache Cicéron à maintenir aussi étroites que possible ses relations avec le grand homme'. For *amor partium* cf. Sen. *Ira* 2.31.7.

For *aliud . . . uellet*, below, Ruhnken compared Sall. *C.* 10.5, where see Vretska's n.

63–64.2 INTRIGUE BY ANTONY (MAY–JUNE AND LATER 43 B.C.)

63.1 Interim Antonius fuga transgressus Alpes 'Antonius Id. Mai. [15 May 43] ad Forum Iuli cum primis copiis uenit' (Munatius Plancus to Cic., *Fam.* 10.17(398).1). 'Cum audissem M. Antonium cum copiis suis . . . in prouinciam meam uenire, . . . castra moui ac contra eos uenire institui. itaque . . . ad Forum Voconium ueni et ultra castra ad flumen Argenteum contra Antonios feci' (Lepidus himself (next n.) writing to Cic. around 19 May, *Fam.* 10.34(396).1, where Shackleton Bailey has a n. on the location of Forum Voconii).

repulsus a M. Lepido (qui . . . in Gallia morabatur) M. Aemilius Lepidus had been appointed by Julius Caesar to be proconsul of Gallia Narbonensis and Hispania Citerior (*MRR* 2.326, 341), and was made pont. max. after Caesar's death (*MRR* 2.333). In early May 43 he was evidently determined to resist Antony (cf. Plancus to Cicero, *Fam.* 10.15(390).2), and wrote to Cicero himself around 19 May saying 'nec senatui nec rei publicae deerimus' (*Fam.* 10.34(396).2). Communications between him and Antony were initially conducted by messengers (cf. App. *BC* 3.83). For him cf. also *RE* 1.1.556–61 = Aemilius 73 (v. Rohden).

cum et Lepido . . . V. naturally sees things from a soldier's point of view, cf. also 69.3; for Antony's reputation as a drinker cf. 82.4n.

per auersa castrorum proruto uallo 'at the rear of the camp after they had dismantled the fortifications'; so too Plut. *Ant.* 18.2 τὸν χάρακα διασπῶντας, though App. has them opening the gates (*BC* 3.84).

If we were to retain *auersam*, Aldus' ⟨*partem*⟩ would be the likely insertion (cf. Liv. 34.47.1); but Gelenius' *auersa* is simpler, for which cf. *TLL* 2.1324.39ff. For *proruto uallo* cf. Liv. 4.29.3, 9.37.9, Curt. 4.13.26.

militibus receptus est   And also, despite his earlier protestations, by Lepidus himself, who on 30 May wrote in grovelling terms to the senate, assuring them of his continued loyalty and blaming fate and his men for what had happened (Cic. *Fam.* 10.35(408)). The reconciliation between him and Antony had taken place on the previous day (cf. Plancus to Cic., *Fam.* 10.23(414).2, written on 6 June from Grenoble).

Heinsius wrote ⟨*a*⟩ *militibus*, but the dat. of agent seems supported by 39.1; cf. also K–S 1.324–5, L–H–S 96–7.

titulo imperii . . . summa uirium   The same point is made by Plut. *Ant.* 18.3, App. *BC* 3.84.

63.2 Iuuentius Laterensis, uir uita ac morte consentaneus
Lepidus' legate is described by Plancus as 'uir sanctissimus' (Cic. *Fam.* 10.21(391).3), possessing 'et fidem et animum singularem in rem publicam' (10.23(414).4). For him see *RE* 10.2.1365–7 = Iuventius 16 (Münzer); *MRR* 2.353.

For 'he died according as he lived' cf. 91.4n.; for *consentaneus* used in such contexts cf. Cic. *Phil.* 9.15 'mors consentanea uitae fuerit', Val. Max. 7.1.1.

gladio se ipse transfixit   Plancus wrote to Cicero on 6 June that Laterensis was still alive (*Fam.* 10.23(414).4): 'cum in fraudem se deductum uideret, manus, quas iustius in Lepidi perniciem armasset, sibi adferre conatus est; in quo casu tamen interpellatus, et adhuc uiuit et dicitur uicturus'. For *acerrime suadere*, above, cf. Liv. *per.* 49 (Ruhnken; also Cic. *Amic.* 44 'monendum . . . acriter' (F.), Suet. *Dom.* 9 'acrius monuit'); for *irritus* + gen. cf. K–S 1.444 (first in V. and Val. Max.).

For the declaration of Antony as a public enemy cf. 61.4n.

63.3 Plancus deinde dubia . . . fide   This is V.'s first reference to Plancus, whom he invariably treats, as here, with ironical contempt (see nn. at 74.3, 83.1 (*morbo proditor*), 95.3). Plancus' letters are a contemporary source for the events of this period.

secum luctatus ac sibi difficile consentiens   For *luctatus* cf. 86.2 and compare also Cic. *Phil.* 2.18 'tecum ipse pugnares', Ov. *Met.* 15.27 'pugnatque diu sententia secum' (Krause); I can find no parallel for *luctari* + indir. question; for *sibi consentire* of persons cf. Cic. *Off.* 1.5, Sen. *Ep.* 89.14.

D. Bruti . . . collegae sui   On 6 June Plancus, the proconsul of Transalpine Gaul, wrote to Cicero that he expected to join forces with his *collega* D. Brutus, the proconsul of Cisalpine Gaul, within three days (*Fam.* 10.23(414).3). They issued a joint despatch to the senate a few days later (*Fam.* 11.13a(418)).

senatuique se litteris uenditans   The tone of these letters, and the enthusiasm with which they were received, may be gathered from the correspondence of Cicero and Plancus: *Fam.* 10.16(404), 22(423), 24(428); cf. also 11.13a(418). For the expr. cf. Liv. 3.35.5 'se plebi uenditare' (Krause), to which F. adds Cic. *Verr.* 3.132, *Att.* 8.16.1, Nep. *Att.* 11.4; the frequentative form is here sarcastic.

firmus proposito et Iulianis partibus fidus   This phrase – with its pleonasm, chiasmus and chiastic alliteration – is intended above all to highlight Pollio's loyalty at the expense of Plancus (*dubia . . .fide, proditor*). 'Plancus ist das Gegenteil von Pollio' (Haller 45, believing V.'s portrait of the former to derive from Aug.'s autobiography). For Pollio see further 73.2n., 76.2n., 76.3n., 78.2n., 86.3nn., 128.3n., and the works of André, Bosworth and Haller.
   proposito, though taken as dat. in *TLL* 6.1.817.37–8, is presumably abl.: cf. 2.2.2 'proposito sanctissimus'; *firmus* is found with the abl. at e.g. Cic. *Phil.* 10.16, *Fam.* 15.1.6, *Bell. Afr.* 23.1, Ov. *M.* 7.457. Tac. *Agr.* 35.4 *firmus aduersis*, taken in *TLL* as a parallel for the dat., is either abl. (Ogilvie ad loc.) or abl. abs. (Goodyear on Tac. *A.* 2.14.3). *firmus* is more normally coupled with *fidelis* (F. quotes Cic. *Cael.* 14, *Scaur.* 31, Ov. *Tr.* 1.5.63, Liv. 31.9.4, Sen. *Ep.* 98.1, Amm. 31.14.2), but for *fidus* cf. Amm. 14.11.15. For *partibus fidus* cf. Tac. *H.* 1.87.1; for the chiastic alliteration cf. 115.5n.

64.1 D. Brutus desertus primo . . . post etiam . . .   From here to *perire* (2 below) V. anticipates slightly, since D. Brutus' flight and death must have taken place after the outlawing of Lepidus on 30 June 43 B.C., which is the moment at which the main narrative resumes after the 'coda' at 3–4 below (see nn.). Yet the anticipation causes no significant chronological problems and is readily explicable: V. wishes to spend time relishing the murder of someone who in his turn had assisted in the murder of his own benefactor Julius Caesar.
   primo . . . post occurs in Cic. among other authors (cf. K–S 2.69, *OLD* s.v. *primo* 1*b*), and I can see no reason to deviate from P's reading here.

nomine Camelii   Elsewhere he is called Capenus (Liv. *per.* 120) and Κάμιλος (App. *BC* 3.98). Camel(l)ius is certainly found in Gaul (*CIL* 13.1215, 5358), and I have retained the paradosis (with the ending -*ii* as emended by Vossius). Brutus' plan had been to escape to M. Brutus in Macedonia (cf. *MRR* 2.347).

iustissimasque. . . poenas   A Ciceronian phrase, cf. *Mil.* 11, 85, *Lael.* 37. For Caesar's services to Brutus cf. 56.3(n.), 58.1–2; V. character-istically underlines the irony of the situation by a series of contrasts and correspondences (*iustissimas ~ aequum, primus amicorum ~ interfector, fructum ~ inuidiam* etc.). For *iugulatus est* cf. 79.5n.

64.2 fortunae . . . inuidiam in auctorem relegabat, censebatque aequum . . . Caesarem . . . perire Brutus' treatment of Caesar, not unlike Caesar's own treatment of Pompey (cf. 44.2 'Caesar . . . animaduertebat se . . . inuidia communis potentiae in illum [sc. Pompeium] relegata confirmaturum uires suas'), is referred to in general terms at Cic. *Fam.* 11.28(349).3 'cum praesertim idem homines illi et inuidiae et exitio fuerint'. For the expr. cf. Liv. 2.43.4 'inuidia . . . uersa in auctorem', to which F. adds Quint. 7.4.13 'culpa in hominem relegatur'; for *fortunae fructus* cf. Cic. *Fam.* 4.6.2, Rut. Lup. 1.13 (also Liv. 45.25.9); for *fructum ferre ex* cf. *TLL* 6.1.1396.39ff.; for *fortunae . . . inuidiam* cf. 1.9.6; Otto 176. *aequum censere*, being an almost official phrase (*TLL* 1.1039.25ff.), adds to the general irony.

Persuaded by Kritz's argument that V. 'Bruti *consilium interficiendi* Caesaris respicit', I have printed *perire* rather than *perisse* (both are Rhenanus').

64.3-4 CICERO'S *PHILIPPICS*

Cicero's *Philippics*, with which this brief section deals, were delivered between 2 Sept. 44 and 20 Mar. 43 B.C., whereas the fortunes of D. Brutus, which V. has just described in 63.3–64.2, belong to June 43 and later. Yet the present section is not misplaced. As is clear from the plural forms *Haec sunt tempora quibus* (with which contrast *hoc est illud tempus quo* at 62.6), V. is not speaking specifically about the immediate aftermath of Brutus' death but generally about the period as a whole. The present brief section forms a coda to chh. 59–64, separating them from the new section of narrative which begins at *Lepidus deinde* below (see n.). The technique is characteristically Velleian (see below, p. 156) but is particularly effective in the present instance because it dramatically anticipates the *epitaphion* for Cicero with which so much of the following section is concerned (cf. esp. 4 *utrique . . . finita*).

64.3 aeternas Antonii memoriae inussit notas V. uses Ciceronian language to commemorate Cicero's achievement: *inurere notas* is a favourite phrase, but cf. esp. *Phil.* 1.32 'haec inusta est a te . . . nota ad ignominiam sempiternam', 13.40 'quem ego inustum . . . notis tradam hominum memoriae sempiternae', 14.7, *Pis.* 43 and, for *aeternas . . . notas*, *Pis.* 41 'sempiternas . . . notas'.

fulgentissimo et caelesti ore 'Metaphora egregie respondet praecedenti', says Krause laconically, without explaining that V. refers to the burns of flashing lightning. *fulgere*, which like *fulgor* was etymologically associated with *fulgur* (cf. Non. p. 28, Paul.–Fest. p. 92), is the *mot juste* for lightning (cf. *TLL* 6.1.1508.72ff.); and lightning flashes and/or thunderbolts are a conventional metaphor to describe oratory or orators: cf. e.g.

139

Cic. *Or.* 29 '(Pericles) fulgere tonare . . . dictus' (repeated at Quint. 2.16.19, Plin. *Ep.* 1.20.19), 234, *Att.* 15.1a.2, Plin. *NH praef.* 5 'fulgurat . . . uis eloquentiae . . . quanto tu ore patris laudes tonas'; the metaphor was applied to Cicero himself by his friend L. Papirius Paetus (cf. *Fam.* 9.21(188).1, believed by some scholars to be a ref. to *Phil.* 1 or 2) and Colum. 1 *praef.* 30. *caelesti* helps to sustain the image (cf. e.g. Front. p. 122.15–17 Naber = p. 116.14–15 Van den Hout 'fragoribus nubium et sonoribus procellarum, uelut quibusdam caelestibus uocibus').[1]

canina rabie lacerabat Antonium There is no linguistic objection to the paradosis *continua* (cf. Ov. *Tr.* 2.150 'continuus . . . furor'), nor is the repetition after *continuis* unusual (cf. 100.5n.); indeed Krause reasonably thought it expressed a strong contrast. The main objection is that Ti. Cannutius' invective evidently lasted only one day, 2 October 44 (cf. *MRR* 2.323–4). I therefore accept Ruhnken's imaginative *canina*; he compared Sall. *H.* 4.54 'canina . . . facundia', cf. also Otto 69. Certainly the phrase *rabie lacerabat* and the resulting word-play *Can- can-* make Ruhnken's suggestion highly plausible.

For Ti. Cannutius, trib. pleb. in 44, cf. also *RE* 3.2.1485–6 = Cannutius 3 (Münzer).

64.4 utrique uindicta libertatis morte stetit 'Their defence of liberty cost both of them their lives' (Watson). For *uindicta libertatis* cf. Liv. 24.37.10, 34.49.3; for *morte stetit* cf. Caes. *BG* 7.19.4 'morte . . . constare uictoriam', Liv. 23.30.2 'multo sanguine . . . Poenis uictoria stetit', Sil. 17.82; *OLD* s.v. *sto* 23.

tribuni sanguine commissa proscriptio The proscription was not begun by the death of Ti. Cannutius (above), who is said by Dio to have died in 41 B.C. after the fall of Perusia (48.14.4; the MSS read Τῖτος, emended by Fabricius to Τιβέριος). Krause thinks V. has confused Ti. Cannutius with Salvius, the tribune of 43 (cf. *MRR* 2.340), who is said by App. to have been the first to die (*BC* 4.17); alternatively he may have confused him with one of the other Cannutii (on whom cf. *RE* 3.2.1485–6), one of whom perhaps died early in the terror.

Ciceronis uel satiato Antonio poena finita Puteanus interpreted 'was ended with the revenge on Cicero which even satisfied Antony'; Ruhnken 'was ended ⟨by the death⟩ of Cicero, a revenge which even satisfied A.' (understanding *sanguine* from the previous colon). Something along the former lines seems to me less unnatural; but the word-order perhaps supports Ruhnken, who also compared Liv. 29.9.10 'nec satiatus uiuorum poena insepultos proiecit'.

---

[1] It must however be noted that V. regularly uses both *fulgentissimus* (e.g. 39.1, 71.1) and *caelestis* (e.g. 66.3, 104.3) without any such precise metaphorical significance, as Sauppe (70–1) among others has pointed out.

Bentley (according to Ellis), Heinsius and Burman all changed *poena* to *paene*, which, in the form *pene*, turned out to be the reading of A on its discovery in 1835. Attributing to this MS an authority which it does not possess, all subsequent edd. have printed *paene*, principally on the grounds that Cicero's death on 7 Dec. 43 did not end the proscriptions. But this argument takes no account of the rhetorical material which was no doubt in V.'s mind: see esp. Sen. *Suas.* 6.19 'Quibus uisis laetus Antonius, cum *peractam proscriptionem suam* dixisset esse, quippe non *satiatus* modo caedendis ciuibus sed differtus quoque, super rostra exponit', to which add Plut. *Cic.* 49. ὡς νῦν αἱ προγραφαὶ τέλος ἔχοιεν, quoted by Krause. For the usage of *poena* cf. 119.2 and Livy (as above). I have no doubt that *poena* is correct.

For *uel* Lipsius proposed *uelut*, accepted by Puteanus in his interpretation. But once again *Antonius satiatus* is clearly a stock element in the rhetorical accounts of Cicero's death (see Sen. loc. cit., Plut. *Ant.* 20.2) and does not need dilution; it is true that *uel* might more precisely precede *Antonio* rather than *satiato*, but V. perhaps regarded the word as qualifying the whole phrase.

64.4–67
TRIUMVIRATE AND PROSCRIPTIONS
(JUNE–DECEMBER 43 B.C.)

64.4–65 THE TRIUMVIRATE
(JUNE–NOVEMBER 43 B.C.)

64.4 Lepidus deinde . . . hostis iudicatus est Since Lepidus was outlawed on 30 June 43 B.C. (cf. Cic. *Fam.* 12.10(425).1), *deinde* naturally does not refer back to the 'extra-chronological' coda at 3–4 above but to the events which precede the coda at 63.3–64.2 (see 64.1n.); and *ut ante . . . Antonius* explicitly refers back to 63.2 *Antonio hoste iudicato*. For Antony cf. 61.4n.

65.1 iacta mentio Burer suggested *facta*. It is true that *mentionem facere* is an extremely common phrase (cf. *TLL* 8.775.36ff.), but *iacere* is commonly used with *sermonem*, *uocem* etc. (cf. *OLD* s.v. 8) and I think *iacta mentio* is just defended by Sisenn. fr. 95 'facti mentionem proiecit'; Krause compared Hor. *S.* 1.4.93–4 'mentio . . . iniecta', and Burman Liv. 38.25.5 'iactae sunt pacis condiciones'. For *commercia epistularum*, above, cf. Sen. *Ep.* 38.1.

cum Antonius subinde Caesarem admoneret et quam . . . *et* was transposed by ed. Bipont. from its position after *Antonius* in the paradosis to its present position after *admoneret*. The suggestion is attractive since *et* could easily have been omitted after *admoneret*, then noted in the margin and then later inserted into the text in the wrong place.

Kritz, understanding *et . . . quam* to be parallel with *et in quod* and *et quanto* below, defended the paradosis as a type of hyperbaton and Baehrens 379ff. quoted several other exs. of hyperbaton in support. Now it is certainly true that *et* is very commonly transposed by Latin authors (cf. H. Sjögren, *Commentationes Tullianae* (1910), 135ff.; *TLL* 5.2.886.55ff.), but the transposition usually involves an adjacent word (e.g. *et ut* for *ut et* at Cic. *Att.* 3.6 and 5.18.4) or is otherwise clarified by the structure of the sentence. Neither of these conditions is met here. Another way of defending the paradosis would be to assume that *et* goes with *admoneret* and is parallel to *denuntiaretque* and *diceretque* below; but the few other exs. of *et . . . -que . . . -que* seem restricted to the co-ordination of nouns (e.g. Stat. *Theb.* 12.232–3, Gratt. *Cyn.* 415ff.).

Finally, an alternative method of emendation may be mentioned. It is possible that a scribe was expecting a reference to the three persons mentioned at the beginning of the sentence and so wrote *et* but forgot to cancel his mistake. The error is all the more plausible if he took *subinde* as 'subsequently' rather than 'often', which is the right meaning here; but I do not consider the deletion of *et* preferable to the transposition of ed. Bipont.

For *in quod . . . emersissent*, below, cf. Lucr. 2.13 = 3.63 'ad summas emergere opes' (F.).

decem et septem legionum potentes erant   Brunt (*IM* 487 and n. 2) seems to imply that these are the 17 legions with which Brutus and Cassius fought at Philippi in 42; rather, I believe, V. has added together the legionary totals which at 69.2 and 4 (see nn.) he attributes to the tyrannicides in mid-43. For *attollere* = 'praise', 'honour', used first here, cf. Heubner on Tac. *H.* 1.90.2; for *studio* cf. *H.* 4.4.3 'studiis senatus attollebatur' (F.); for *iuncturum uires*, *H.* 2.54.1.

65.2 ⟨igi⟩tur inita potentiae societas   The triumvirate, which V. sees in the same terms as the alliance between Caesar, Pompey and Crassus in 60 (cf. 44.1), was agreed in the autumn and confirmed by the *lex Titia* of 27 Nov. 43 (*MRR* 2.337–8). For Oct.'s motives in joining it, see Rice Holmes, *Arch.* 214–15. For *potentiae societas* cf. also Tac. *A.* 13.2.3.

Instead of Rhenanus' ⟨igi⟩tur Burer proposed *tum* or *tunc*, which Kreyssig preferred on the grounds that *igitur* is never first word in V. Kritz however argued that the logic of this and the preceding sentence supports Rhenanus, and on the whole I agree with him. V. does occasionally place *itaque* (which he use more often than *igitur*) in second position: see statistics in *TLL* s.v. *ergo*.

hortantibus . . . exercitibus   Confirmed by Suet. *Aug.* 62.1, Dio 46.56.3, Plut. *Ant.* 20.1.

priuigna Antonii   Antony's stepdaughter was Claudia, the daughter of Fulvia (74.3n.) and P. Clodius (45.1n.): see *RE* 3.2.2886–7 = Claudius 390 (Stein). The marriage was shortlived (Suet. loc. cit.).

COMMENTARY 2.65.3

consulatumque iniit Caesar, pridie quam uiginti annos impleret X Kal. Oct. 'Caesar's heir marched on Rome and seized the consulate (August 19, 43). Velleius suppresses a damaging fact, changes the date to September 22, and further puts the consulship subsequent to the formation of the Triumvirate' (Syme, *Tac.* 367 n. 8). The most serious of these charges is in my opinion the precise date of the consulship, since both here and elsewhere (cf. 49.1n., 103.3n.) V. seems anxious to give accurate dates. Oct.'s first consulship is fixed by Dio 56.30.5 and Tac. *A.* 1.9.1 as 19 August 43 B.C. and no amount of juggling with Augustus' real or supposed birthday(s) (for which see A. Kaplan, 'The birthday of Aug.', *Classical Studies for A. D. Fraser* (Tuscaloosa, Alabama [n.d.]), 93–102; W. Suerbaum, *Chiron* 10 (1980), 334–5) will reconcile that date with the date which appears in V.'s text. Krause explained the discrepancy by suggesting that Dio and Tac. refer to the day of Oct.'s inauguration, while V. refers to his first acts as consul in Rome; but this seems to me implausible. An alternative suggestion is that *pridie quam* here = *priusquam* and that *X* should be changed to *IX*, in which case V. would mean 'became consul before his 20th birthday on 23 September'; but this interpretation of course depends upon the precise meaning of *pridie*. According to *OLD* s.v. *b*, the word can mean 'in the time preceding' and indeed one of the supposed exs. of the meaning is Vell. 83.3; but it will be seen from my n. ad loc. that none of the other alleged exs. of *pridie quam* = *priusquam* is at all definite or even likely, and that 83.3 itself can be interpreted without this meaning being given to the word. I am therefore compelled to dismiss this explanation too, albeit reluctantly. The only remaining alternative is to emend the text more radically.

Whether such a course is justified depends, I think, on the extent to which we believe V. is aiming deliberately to distort his account of events in this passage. His suppression of Oct.'s march on Rome is undeniable and is perhaps influenced by the similar suppression in *RG* (for the facts see *MRR* 2.336 and Syme, *RR* 185–6); on the other hand it is not as clear to me as it is to Syme that the order triumvirate–consulship is intended to be significant, and I am very tempted to suggest *pri⟨ore⟩ die quam . . . impleret ⟨I⟩X Kal. Oct.* ('became consul on an ⟨even⟩ earlier day than his 20th birthday on 23 September'). Yet perhaps this is too extensive a change in a passage which already involves considerable difficulty elsewhere; and in view of these circumstances I have decided to retain the paradosis.

For M. Vinicius, V.'s addressee and the consul of A.D. 30, cf. 101.3n.

65.3 Ventidium P. Ventidius Bassus, praetor in 43, recruited legions for Antony in his native Picenum (Brunt, *IM* 481) and on the formation of the triumvirate was appointed cos. suff. in succession to Octavian (*MRR* 2.337, 339). In the Social War in 89 B.C. he and his mother had been led in triumph by Pompeius Strabo; in 38 B.C. he was himself to celebrate a Parthian triumph (cf. 78.1n.). He therefore provided ideal material for

143

Val. Max.'s ch. *de mutatione morum aut fortunae* (6.9.9): 'qui captiuus car-
cerem exhorruerat, uictor Capitolium felicitate celebrauit; in eodem
etiam illud eximium quod eodem anno praetor ⟨et consul⟩ est factus'; cf.
also Dio 43.51.4. His career, summarised by Gell. 15.4, was clearly standard issue in the rhetorical schools. For him see also *RE* 8a.1.795–
816 = Ventidius 5 (Gundel); Syme, *RP* 393ff.

For such exprr. as *uidit hic annus* cf. Fletcher (1964), 62. I have adopted
Gelenius' *praetoriae* on account of 92.4 'ut praeturam aedilitati, ita con-
sulatum praeturae se iuncturum'. For such combinations as *idem hic* cf.
TLL 7.1.200.32ff.

66–67 PROSCRIPTIONS AND THE MURDER
OF CICERO (NOVEMBER–DECEMBER 43 B.C.)

The highlight of this section is the outburst on Cicero's murder, for which
V. feels obliged to exceed the limits usually imposed by the summary
nature of his work (cf. 66.3 *cogit enim excedere propositi formam operis erumpens
. . . indignatio*). Scholars have often compared his treatment with Sen.
Suas. 6 'Deliberat Cicero an Antonium deprecetur' and 7 'Deliberat
Cicero an scripta sua conburat promittente Antonio incolumitatem si
fecisset', and it is indeed true that V.'s language and motifs may be paralleled throughout the two *suasoriae*; but these similarities perhaps tend to
obscure rather than illuminate the precise area in which the comparison is
most valid.

Seneca's assembled material comprises three elements: the accounts of
Cicero's actual murder as written by various historians including Livy
and Cremutius Cordus (6.14–21); the *epitaphia* or obituary notices as
written for Cicero by various historians including Livy and Asinius Pollio,
and also by the poet Cornelius Severus (6.21–7);[1] and, finally, the suasorial speeches as made by various rhetoricians at the debates in question
(*passim*). Now V. has omitted the first two elements, i.e. those which are
more strictly 'historical', almost entirely: there is no description of
Cicero's murder, apart from the allusion *capitis abscisi* at 66.3, and there is
no direct praise of Cicero, apart from *quod . . . inluminauit* at 66.5. Instead,
V. has produced what is essentially a suasorial speech; but it is cast in a
historical mould by the initial verbs' being placed in the past tense
(66.3–4 *egisti . . . egisti . . . rapuisti*), and its generally eulogistic tone means

---

[1] The extant accounts of Cicero's death, including those of Plut. App. and
Dio, have been studied by H. Homeyer, *Die antiken Berichte über den Tod
Ciceros und ihre Quellen* (Deutsche Beiträge zur Altertumswiss. 18, 1964);
but her remarks on V. are cursory (pp. 37–8). The language of Livy's
account has been studied by H. Tränkle, *WS* 81 (1968), 142–9, and that
of Pollio's by Lebek 143ff. Cornelius Severus' verses are discussed by H.
Homeyer, *Ann. univ. Saraviensis (phil. Fak.)* 10 (1961), 327–34 and also
(in great detail) by Dahlmann 74–119.

that it functions as an *epitaphion* without actually being one.[1] The resulting composition may seem curious to some readers, but it is no more so than Livy's debate on Alexander at 9.17–19 or Tacitus' on chance and providence at *A.* 6.22. All three passages illustrate excellently the rhetorical nature of Roman historiography – just as Seneca's two *suasoriae* illustrate the often historical character of rhetoric. If more Roman historiography had survived, and if we understood more clearly the true nature of that which has survived, such passages as these would seem far less exceptional.

Within his chosen framework V. has striven in various ways to dramatise the pathos of Cicero's death and to pay tribute to the great man's accomplishments as statesman and orator. V. achieves dramatisation by availing himself of the motifs of consolatory literature (e.g. 66.4n.), as he does also in his account of Augustus' death at ch. 123,[2] and by resorting to several recognised oratorical devices, most notably *indignatio* which strikes the keynote of the passage (66.2n., 3n.). He pays tribute to Cicero by raising the stylistic level and producing sentences which are even more balanced than usual (e.g. the three sets of doublets at 66.4 *famam . . . auxeris* and the two sets of tricola at 66.5 *uel forte . . . eloquentia inluminauit*),[3] and by subtle allusions to Cicero's own political, rhetorical and philosophical works in turn (e.g. 66.3n., 4n., 5n.).

The general effect is not to everyone's taste. ' I know no better example of the abominable Asianistic deviations of the New Style in its most corrupt form ', writes A. D. Leeman in a book devoted to the stylistic appreciation of Latin prose literature.[4] H. Frisch, however, more generously, chooses to quote from V.'s passage at the very end of his book *Cicero's Fight for the Republic*. It is a gesture which V. would have appreciated.

66.1 ut praediximus   At 64.4; cf. also 61.4n.

repugnante Caesare sed frustra aduersus duos   So too Flor. 2.16.1 ' Quid contra duos consules, duos exercitus? necesse fuit uenire in cruentissimi foederis societatem. diuersa omnium uota, ut ingenia [cf. *diuersa uolentes* at 60.5 above] . . . (3) nullo bono more triumuiratus inuaditur, oppressaque armis re p. redit Sullana proscriptio'. The exculpation no doubt goes back to Aug. himself (cf. Sen. *Clem.* 1.10.11 'in adulescentia caluit, arsit ira, multa fecit ad quae inuitus oculos retorquebat'). See also Scott 19–20.

quid passi essent, above, presumably refers to the fact that Antonius and Lepidus had been pronounced public enemies (63.2, 64.4).

---

[1] For *epitaphia* in V. cf. *TN* 43.

[2] See *TN* 215ff., and remarks there.

[3] The structure of 66.2–5 has been fully analysed by E. A. De Stefani, *SIFC* 18 (1910), 23–4.

[4] *Orationis Ratio* (1964), 250.

instauratum Sullani exempli malum, proscriptio Cf. Cic. *Rosc.* 153 'ne noua et multo crudelior . . . proscriptio instaurata esse uideatur'. For the use of *exempli* cf. 2.6.2 'eiusdem exempli tribunatum', Liv. 8.7.22, 28.26.2 'tam foedi exempli defectio'.

66.2 indignum This word strikes the keynote for what follows; cf. 3 *indignatio* (and n.), 67.1 *digne*.

uox publica So too Corn. Sev. fr. 13.15 'publica uox saeuis aeternum obmutuit armis', on which Dahlmann (103) quotes Cic. *Cat.* 4.19 'ut mea uox . . . officio functa consulari uideretur'. For the metaphor cf. also Luc. 1.270 'uox quondam populi' (of Curio), Tac. *Agr.* 2.2 'illo igne uocem populi Romani . . . aboleri'; see also 131.1n. *abscisa . . . uox* is here used on the analogy of *abscidere linguam*.

cum eius salutem nemo defendisset qui . . . defenderat The distinction between Cicero's private and public speeches is also found in Corn. Sev. fr. 13.12–15 (Dahlmann 99ff.); the contrast between Cicero's fate (*abscisa . . . uox*) and his former defence of others is also found in Crem. Cord. *ap.* Sen. *Suas.* 6.19. Ironically, as V. perhaps recalled, Cicero had himself used these same contrasts when describing the fate of Mark Antony's grandfather, the famous orator (*De Or.* 3.10): 'iam M. Antoni in eis ipsis rostris, in quibus ille r. p. constantissime consul defenderat . . ., positum caput illud fuit, a quo erant multorum ciuium capita seruata'.

For public service as a theme of consolatory literature cf. 123.1n.; also below, 3n.

66.3 Nihil . . . egisti Rhetorical theorists recognised the emotional power of *indignatio* in oratory (see below), and recommended various ways in which it could be communicated. One such was apostrophe (cf. *Rhet. Herenn.* 4.22 'exclamatio est quae conficit significationem . . . indignationis'; Lausberg 2.223–4 § 809), which V. uses here; another was *descriptio*, the vivid portrayal of the consequences of an action to deter someone from embarking upon it (*Rhet. Herenn.* 4.51), a device which V. here neatly adapts: unable to dissuade Antony from his action, which is over and done with, he bluntly tells him that its consequences have been the opposite to those which were intended. The point is reinforced by V.'s language. Although combinations of *nihil* (*nil*) and *agere* are common (see e.g. *OLD* s.v. *nihil* 1*f*; Mayor on Juv. 10.155), the second-person forms seem colloquial (e.g. Hor. *S.* 1.9.15, Prop. 2.32.19): when addressing Antony directly, V. momentarily drops the high style in favour of plain speaking (so too with *auctoramento* below). Cf. *Anth. Lat.* 1.2.603 'nil agis, Antoni, scripta diserta manent'.

excedere propositi formam operis V.'s work is a summary history (see Woodman (1975), 277–87; Starr (1981)), but he occasionally gives more scope to important items, the reason here being *indignatio* (next n.). For the expr. cf. 1.16.1, Just. 43.1.2; F. adds Amm. 22.15.32 'opusculi nostri propositum excedentia' (Sen. *Ben.* 3.21.2 'officii formulam excedit').

erumpens animo ac pectore indignatio *indignatio* was a powerful weapon in the orator's armoury, and rousing the *indignatio* of one's audience was a standard device: cf. Cic. *Inu.* 1.98, 100 'i. est oratio per quam conficitur ut in aliquem hominem magnum odium aut in rem grauis offensio concitetur', Quint. 6.2.26, 11.3.61 'ueri (adfectus) naturaliter *erumpunt*, ut . . . *indignantium*'; Lausberg 1.362 § 433, 1.365 § 438; W. S. Anderson, *YCS* 17 (1961), 30–4 (on the background to Juv. 1.79 'facit indignatio uersum'). To achieve this arousal an orator was expected, like V. here (last n.), to exceed his terms of reference: cf. Quint. 4.3.5 'si expositio circa finem atrox fuerit, prosequamur eam uelut *erumpente* protinus *indignatione*', 15–16; Lausberg 1.294–6 §§ 341, 345. Naturally *indignatio* was also a feature of *consolationes*: the gods are unjust to have allowed the victim to die (cf. Esteve-Forriol 138–9).

For *erumpens . . . indignatio* cf. also Liv. 4.50.5, Val. Max. 6.3.1b; for *erumpere* + abl. cf. K–S 1.362; the pleonasm of *animo ac pectore* heightens the emotional tone.

nihil (inquam) egisti Such repetition, technically called *geminatio* or *anadiplosis* (among other names), is often used to express emotion and regularly involves *inquam*: see Lausberg 2.110–1 § 617; also *TLL* 7.1.1782.45ff.

mercedem ... numerando auctoramentoque funebri ... incitando 'by paying out a cash prize . . . for his severed head and by encouraging ⟨people⟩, by means of a murder contract, to kill him' (evidently an ex. of *hysteron proteron*). Accounts of Cicero's death customarily dwelt on the gruesome sight of his head being exhibited on the rostra (see Dahlmann 106–7), but V. concentrates rather on the bonus paid by Antony to Cicero's murderer, Popilius Laenas, in addition to the advertised reward (cf. App. *BC* 4.20). Crem. Cord. in Sen. *Suas.* 6.19 has both motifs (cf. 'pretium interfectoris sui').

abscisi is used literally with *capitis* and metaphorically with *oris*, but the syllepsis is slight since V. perhaps recalled the story that Fulvia pulled out the tongue from Cicero's severed head (Dio 47.8.4). *auctoramentum*, used also of the Sullan proscription at 28.3, is literally a contract or fee for gladiators (cf. *TLL* s.v.) and is doubly effective: its bluntness reflects the brutality of the murder, and V. no doubt remembered that Cic. had regularly abused Antony with the term *gladiator* (cf. Denniston on *Phil.* 2.7; Opelt 136). For *funebris* = 'fatal', 'deadly', cf. *OLD* s.v. 2.

The paradosis *ad conseruatoris . . .* [sc. *aliquem*] *inritando necem* has been questioned because *inritare* thus used has the wrong meaning (neatly illustrated by Sen. *Suas.* 7.1 'inritare inimicum in mortem tuam'). Lipsius wrote *inuitando*, but I consider *incitando* preferable. Like *inuitare* it can be used with *praemiis* (cf. Caes. *BC* 1.56.2, Cic. *or. fr.* 30 M); for V.'s *ad necem* compare Cic. *Cael.* 78 'ad caedem . . . incitauit', *Sest.* 34 'ad caedem . . . incitarentur' (*Sull.* 76 'ad perficiendum scelus'), and for its use without an expressed object cf. Ov. *AA* 3.601, Flor. 1.19.2. At *Phil.* 4.3 Cic. says of Antony himself: 'furorem crudelissimis consiliis incitatum'.

conseruatoris quondam rei publicae   Cicero had referred to himself by this 'title', cf. *Phil.* 2.51, *Vat.* 7. The contrast between his past services and his fate was commonly made in accounts of his death: see above, 2n., also *Anth. Lat.* 1.2.605 'seruator patriae'. *consulis* below refers to his political honours, a common theme in consolatory literature (cf. Esteve-Forriol 134): cf. Corn. Sev. fr. 13.4 'ingentia consulis acta' (Dahlmann 83), *Anth. Lat.* 1.2.609 'qui consul patriam caedibus eripuit'. For the pathetic *quondam* cf. Corn. Sev. fr. 13.12; similarly, e.g., Virg. *Ecl.* 1.74, Tib. 1.1.19.

66.4 rapuisti tu M. Ciceroni . . .   To pillory the dead Cicero's enemy, V. uses the topos *opportunitas mortis*, normally used in consolatory literature to comfort a dead man's friends. The topos occurs in a passage of Sall. which V. seems to echo elsewhere in this section (*J.* 14.15 'morte grauiorem uitam', 22 'quamquam tibi . . . uita erepta est, tamen laetandum magis quam dolendum puto casum tuum'), in Cic. himself (*Brut.* 4, *Phil.* 2.12, *De Or.* 3.8, but esp. *TD* 1.83–4 to which V.'s *uitam miseriorem* may also allude, although the phrase is admittedly common, e.g. Pollio in Cic. *Fam.* 10.31.3 'misera sub dominatione uita'; cf. also *TD* 1.96), and in Sen. *Suas.* on Cicero's death (e.g. 6.4, 6, 8 'uilis illi uita futura est et morte grauior detracta libertate', 7.1; cf. also 48.2n., Sen. *Cons. Marc.* 20.4–5). For bibliog. and exs. in other authors cf. C. v. Morawski, *Philol.* 54 (1895), 143–4; R. Kassel, *Untersuchungen zur gr. u. röm. Konsolationsliteratur* (1958), 82–3; T. Stork, *Nil igitur mors est ad nos* (1970), 150–1; Esteve-Forriol 152; Ogilvie on Tac. *Agr.* 45.1 and 3 (also Ogilvie on Liv. 2.40.5 for the related topos 'Was it for this that I was allowed to grow old?').

For *lucem sollicitam* cf. Ov. *Tr.* 4.10.116 (*uita s.* at Hor. *S.* 2.6.62); for *rapio*, normally used of Death itself, cf. Dahlmann 82. For the postponed pronoun *tu*, which Gelenius' excellent emendation demands, cf. e.g. Cic. *Fam.* 10.24.5; the usage perhaps returns to the colloquial tone of *nihil . . . egisti* above (see *OLD* s.v. *tu* 1*b*).

famam uero gloriamque . . . adeo non abstulisti ut auxeris   Cf. Cic. *Senec.* 77 and esp. 82 'anne censes . . . me tantos labores diurnos nocturnosque domi militiaeque suscepturum fuisse si isdem finibus gloriam meam quibus uitam essem terminaturus?' etc. For *adeo non . . . ut* cf. 62.5n.; for the common use of *auferre* in such contexts cf. Dahlmann 94–5; for *gloriam auferre* cf. Plin. *NH* 14.147 'hanc gloriam auferre Cicero uoluit interfectori patris sui M. Antonio' (F.), though the context there is quite different.

66.5 uiuit uiuetque per omnem saeculorum memoriam   It was a topos of consolatory literature to say that a dead man will live on in the fame of his deeds or in the honour paid to him by survivors (Esteve-Forriol 142–3, 149–50); and it was of course conventional to say that literary men will live on in their writings or that the writings themselves will live on (e.g. Nisbet–Hubbard on Hor. *C.* 1.32.3). Cicero's distinction as both statesman and orator means that each of these ideas is applicable to him. Cf. also Sen. *Suas.* 6.4 'si ad memoriam operum tuorum (respicis), semper uicturus es'.

   Here again V.'s language may echo that of Cic. himself, cf. *Marc.* 28 'illa . . . inquam, illa uita est tua quae uigebit memoria saeculorum omnium', and *(omnium) saeculorum memoria* is also at *Phil.* 4.3, but in other (later) authors too: F. quotes Val. Max. 3.2.22, Quint. 10.1.104 'uir saeculorum memoria dignus', Just. 12.16.3, and cf. Auson. 192.19 (p. 50 Peiper) 'uiuent per omnem posterorum memoriam'. For *uiuit uiuetque* cf. esp. Cic. *Amic.* 102 'Scipio quamquam est subito ereptus, uiuit tamen semperque uiuet' but also Plin. *Ep.* 2.1.11 'uiuit enim uiuetque semper atque etiam latius in memoria hominum et sermone uersabitur postquam ab oculis recessit', Tac. *Agr.* 46.4 'manet mansurumque est in animis hominum, in aeternitate temporum, fama rerum'; for the comparable *uiuit uigetque* cf. Wölfflin 280.

dumque hoc . . . rerum naturae corpus . . . manebit incolume   Cf. esp. Sen. *Suas.* 7.8 'quoad humanum genus incolume manserit, quamdiu suus litteris honor, suum eloquentiae pretium erit, quamdiu r.p. nostrae aut fortuna steterit aut memoria durauerit, admirabile posteris uigebit ingenium tuum, et uno proscriptus saeculo proscribes Antonium omnibus'; also Sen. *Cons. Pol.* 2.6 'quamdiu fuerit ullus litteris honor . . . uigebit cum maximis uiris'. The combination of *manere* and *incolumis* also occurs in the passage of Sall. to which ref. was made above at 4n. (*J.* 14.16); but its appearance in scientific authors too (e.g. Lucr. 1.246 'incolumi remanent res corpore', 457 'manet incolumis natura', 2.71, Manil. 1.518 'manet incolumis mundus'), coupled with V.'s use of *corpus* here (cf. Cic. *Tim.* 14 'uniuersi corpus', 15 'mundi c.', Manil. 1.133–4 'mundi . . . corpus', 148 etc.), perhaps gives the passage an appropriately philosophical tone. See also next n.

uel forte uel prouidentia uel utcumque constitutum   The question whether or not the world was governed by providence was a familiar topic in declamatory oratory (e.g. Sen. *Suas.* 4.4, Quint. 3.5.6, 5.7.35, 7.2.2, 12.2.21, Theon 2.126.3ff.) but was particularly at home in the *consolatio*: see e.g. Tac. *Agr.* 46.1 and Ogilvie ad loc., also Esteve-Forriol 139, 148. Once again V.'s language echoes that of Cicero himself: *Tim.* 10 'mundum . . . diuina prouidentia constitutum', *ND* 2.75 'prouidentia deorum mundum et omnes mundi partes . . . constitutas', 98 'quas (res) diuina prouidentia dicimus constitutas' (cf. 99 'animis . . . uidere'). See too next n.

rerum naturae corpus – quod ille paene solus . . . animo uidit Cf. Cic. *TD* 1.35 'si, quorum aut ingenio aut uirtute animus excellit, eos arbitramur, quia natura optima sint, cernere naturae uim maxime . . .' (the whole passage, 32–5, is worth comparison). *solus* is of course an allusion to the familiar '*primus*-motif' (for which cf. Nisbet–Hubbard on Hor. *C.* 1.26.10), a eulogistic device (Quint. 3.7.16 'gratiora esse audientibus quae solus quis . . . fecisse dicitur') which was naturally at home in posthumous panegyric (id. 3.7.18 'inter quae numerauerim ingeniorum monumenta quae saeculis probarentur . . . adferunt laudem . . . artes inuentoribus'): Mr DuQuesnay reminds me esp. of Lucr. 1.66ff. 'primum Graius homo mortalis tendere contra | est oculos ausus . . . [72] uiuida uis animi peruicit . . . [74] omne immensum peragrauit mente animoque', a similarly philosophical context. For *eloquentia inluminauit*, below, cf. 1.18.3, Quint. 2.16.10 'pulchritudinem rerum claritas orationis inluminet' (F.) [Note also Catull. 1.5 'unus Italorum'.].

comitem aeui sui laudem For the idea cf. Quint. 11.1.10 'aeuum saeculorum omnium consecutus' (of Socrates); for the expr., Ov. *Ex P.* 4.10.74 'comitem temporis . . . fidem', to which F. adds Mart. 10.78.3 'comitem trahit pudorem' (Hor. *C.* 4.12.1 'ueris comites . . . animae').

citiusque [in] mundo genus hominum quam ⟨M. Cicero⟩ cedet *in* arose through dittography before *m*-; for *cedere* + abl. cf. K–S 1.364–5. Gruter proposed *quam ⟨Cicero⟩ cadet*, Orelli *quam ⟨M. Cicero⟩ occidet*; but Kritz's simple suggestion that the abbreviation *M.C.* was omitted between *-m* and *c-* seems to me the most likely. For the idea that the person himself will live on see *Quality and Pleasure in Latin Poetry* (ed. Woodman and West, 1974), 121.

67.1 fortunam ne deflere quidem quisquam satis digne potuit . . . The 'inexpressibility topos' is a conventional method of inflating the importance of one's material. Often used for panegyrical purposes (cf. e.g. 104.4n., 126.1n.), it is here used to imply unspeakable horror: so too Virg. *Aen.* 6.624–7 'ausi omnes immane nefas [cf. V.'s *ne quid . . . sanctum* at 3 below] ausoque potiti. | non, mihi si linguae centum sint oraque centum, | ferrea uox, omnis scelerum comprendere formas, | . . . percurrere . . . possim' (see Austin and Norden on this passage, which also has similarities with 60.4 above: see n.), Val. Max. 5.3.4 'qui talem Ciceronis casum satis digne deplorare possit, alius Cicero non exstat', and esp. Flor. 2.16.4 'quis pro indignitate rei ingemescat, cum Antonius L. Caesarem auunculum suum, Lepidus L. Paulum fratrem suum proscripserint?'.

For *deflere* note Sextilius Ena in Sen. *Suas.* 6.27 'deflendus Cicero est Latiaeque silentia linguae'; Krause compares Thuc. 7.75.4 μείζω ἢ κατὰ δάκρυα. For *temporis fortunam* cf. 79.5, Cic. *Fam.* 9.8.2, Liv. 30.30.21; for *ne . . . quidem . . . adeo nemo* cf. K–S 2.57, and on the text of *ne . . . quidem* see below; for *exprimere uerbis* cf. 21.3, Cic. *Verr.* 2.154, *Rhet. Herenn.* 3.27 (F.); for *id tamen notandum est*, below, and similar formulae cf. 42.1, 52.4, 99.4, 103.4, 124.1; for the following accus. + inf. cf. 68.4 (n.).

The paradosis of 67.1 is of considerable interest since it is one of those places where different copies of the *ed. pr.* exhibit different readings. In the following table I list five places where my copy (which I have called simply P) differs from the only other copy I have seen (which I have called P^B after J. Broukhusius to whom it once belonged).[1] For further comparison I list the readings reported by Orelli (xii–xiii) in the four copies of which he had knowledge: P^{T1} and P^{T2} (two copies in Turin), P^G (Gelenius' copy in Basel) and P^O (Orelli's own copy). Page-references to the *ed. pr.* are given in square brackets; A = Amerbach's apograph, B^1 = Burer's readings of the lost archetype (M), and B^2 = Burer's lemmata (i.e. his readings of the copy of the *ed. pr.* from which he worked).

42.1 [30] al's destituerit, nisi paulo ante uelis legere obtinebant *in marg.* P^B P^{T1} P^{T2} P^O: *desunt marg.* P P^G

67.1 [40] ne P^B P^{T1} P^{T2} P^O: nec P P^G: nec B^1 A: ne B^2

78.3 [45] fuste P^B P^{T1} P^{T2} P^O: fusti P P^G: fusti B^1 A: fuste B^2

129.1 [68] Tacitus Rhescuporim *in marg.* P P^{T1} P^{T2} P^O: Tacitus Rescuporim *in marg.* P^B P^G

[sig. G1^a = intro. to Burer's appendix] erratulum P^B P^{T2} P^G: erratululum P P^{T1} P^O

The consistent nature of the evidence in the first three cases breaks down in the last two, warning us that it will be difficult to obtain a clear and systematic picture of Rhenanus' editorial practice. It is however a likely hypothesis that the more correct a copy of the *ed. pr.* is, the later it came in the print-run. But 'correct' means, not necessarily what we may think V. wrote, but what Rhenanus thought V. wrote; and divining Rhenanus' thoughts, except in his marginal notes, is not easy.

Here at 67.1, for ex., I believe *ne* to be correct on the grounds that *nec . . . quidem = ne . . . quidem* is extremely rare and quite possibly unparalleled:[2] the few alleged parallels in K–S 2.45 seem unconvincing to me and some at least are corrupt, but of course they may have been regarded as genuine by Rhenanus, assuming he was aware of them. Thus, while I think it likely that Rhenanus corrected *nec*, the reading of (M), to *ne*, we cannot dismiss the possibility that his practice was the opposite of this and that he at first normalised certain readings and then later restored them to their original and less normal form. If the latter was the case, then *nec* would of course be the later reading.

At 78.3 it is difficult to know whether V. wrote *fusti* or *fuste*. The distribution of *-i/-e* in other authors, being almost equally divided between the two endings (cf. *TLL* 6.1.1657.9–15), is unhelpful; but Rhenanus,

---

[1] There may be other differences which I have not come across.
[2] Not to be confused with the relatively common *nec . . . quidem = et ne . . . quidem.*

without *TLL* at his disposal, might have interpreted quite differently whatever evidence on the endings he had. Again, V. prefers the Ciceronian clausula $- \cup - - -$ (see Woodman, *EA* 24 n. 64; H. Aili, *The Prose Rhythm of Sallust and Livy* (1979), 127, 142),[1] but he does admit a double spondee (cf. 102.2n.); but whether Rhenanus was aware of this evidence and (if so) what he made of it, it is hard to say. On balance, given that the former clausula was a favourite also of Cicero, I think it likely that Rhenanus changed *fusti* to *fuste*;[2] but we cannot be sure.

I do not think any conclusions at all can be drawn from the variants at 129.1; but those copies of the *ed. pr.* which have the marginal note at 42.1 are presumably more correct, and therefore later, than those which do not.[3] And since it is the same copies of the *ed. pr.* which contain the marginal note at 42.1 and which also read *ne* at 67.1 and *fuste* at 78.3, I think it likely that these two readings do indeed represent Rhenanus' corrections (as the above evidence has already suggested) and that it is these copies of the *ed. pr.* which are more correct – and therefore later – than those which lack the marginal note at 42.1 and which read *nec* at 67.1 and *fusti* at 78.3. Thus, on this hypothesis, my own copy of the *ed. pr.* is, like Gelenius', an early one.

There are, however, two further pieces of evidence which complicate and perhaps cast doubt on this conclusion; and they both concern Burer's appendix. First: in my copy Burer's lemma reads *ne* at 67.1 and *fuste* at 78.3 *despite* the fact that in the main body of the text the readings are *nec* and *fusti* respectively. This inconsistency could be explained if we returned to the hypothesis, earlier rejected, that Rhenanus at first normalised and then later restored the less normal reading; but I still think, in the light of all the evidence, that he did not do this. We must therefore adopt the only other explanation for the inconsistency in my copy, namely that Burer's notes were based on a later and more correct copy of the *ed. pr.* than mine but were attached also to earlier and less correct copies. Secondly: while Gelenius' copy of the *ed. pr.* is in most respects apparently identical to mine, and is therefore *ex hypothesi* an early copy, it exhibits the undeniably correct *erratulum* in the introductory note to Burer's appendix, whereas my copy has the incorrect *erratululum*. The converse divergence may be observed in the above table, where P^{T1} and P^{O}, which otherwise

---

[1] Aili (pp. 126–7, 142, 146) discusses and analyses thoroughly V.'s clausulae, concluding that 'The prose of Vell. shows evidence of a very strong preference for certain metrical clausulae, but these do not belong to the "historical" system: Vell. is, in fact, a Ciceronian in his choice of clausulae, and one of a very personal kind' (p. 126).

[2] If he did, he may well have been right; but the available evidence does not justify my printing *fuste* since *fusti* is unobjectionable and was the reading of (M).

[3] I express myself cautiously because Rhenanus, whose note is itself cautious (*nisi* . . .), could always have changed his mind about the correction.

appear to be late copies, exhibit *erratululum*. I can only think that, while Burer's notes were based on a late copy but were attached to earlier copies irrespectively, those notes were themselves corrected in respect of the error *erratululum*[1] and it was possible for a late copy of the notes to be bound along with an early copy of the *ed. pr.* such as Gelenius'. Similarly it was possible for an early copy of Burer's notes to be bound along with a late copy of the *ed. pr.* such as Orelli's.

It is thus possible to obtain a fairly clear picture of the relationship between the six copies of the *ed. pr.* from which evidence has been taken. But it must be stressed that the relationship is conjectural and that the picture might need to be redrawn quite radically in the light of further evidence (see esp. 83.2n.). Such evidence certainly exists (or existed), but is unfortunately not available to me. Orelli's four copies, for ex., further diverged at 1.4.1 *Chalcide Erethryam/Chalcida Erethriam*, the latter being the reading of the only two copies I have seen; Haase (iv–v) knew the variants *non* (instead of *homo*) at 35.2 and *Mox autem hunc auunculum* (instead of *Hunc mox auunculum*) at 83.2;[2] and Stegmann knew the variants *cogitatur* (instead of *cogitator*) at 73.1 and *circa eum* (instead of *contra eum*) at 76.3. If more copies of the *ed. pr.*, containing these and perhaps still further variants, were readily accessible, one would be able to perform for V.'s text a service similar to that which C. Hinman performed for Shakespeare's (*The Printing and Proof-reading of the First Folio of Shakespeare* (1963), 2 vols). But even the few variants which I have been able to consider here are a tribute to Rhenanus' editorial enthusiasm and his desire for a correct text, virtues which he was able to practise on the printed text owing to the length of time it was in production[3] and which he continued to practise in his own hand in the margins of his personal copy long after the book had been published.[4]

Finally, if I have been right to suggest that Burer's appendix was based on a relatively late copy of the *ed. pr.*, variants in copies of the *ed. pr.* will not much affect the relationship between Burer's appendix and the *ed. pr.* proper which I put forward earlier (*TN* 16). And even if it transpires that I am wrong about the timing of Burer's appendix, the seemingly restricted number of variants is not in my opinion sufficient to outweigh my other arguments concerning the relationship between the *ed. pr.* and Amerbach's apograph (*TN* 12–25).

---

[1] *erratululum/erratulum* is the only variant which has been observed in Burer's appendix; there may of course be others, but I suspect not.

[2] See further my n. on 83.2.

[3] Though the latest date in the *ed. pr.* is 13 Dec. 1520, von der Gönna has shown (238) that the book was still not published by 13 Jan. 1521 and that the earliest reference to its being published is 11 Mar. 1521. But presumably the whole print-run need not have been completed by this last date, in which case Rhenanus' corrections might have continued beyond it.

[4] See von der Gönna 238ff.

67.2 fuisse in proscriptos . . . filiorum nullam No doubt family loyalty and treachery reflected the reality of the situation (see Jal 269–70, 401, 412ff.), but proscriptions and parricide provided stock material for the rhetorical schools (see Winterbottom, *Sen.*, General Index s.vv.), and cf. esp. Sen. *Suas.* 6.7 'alter fratrem proscribi, alter auunculum patitur; quid habes spei? ut Cicero periret, tot parricidia facta sunt', App. *BC* 4.12ff. (a detailed list of topoi), Tac. *H.* 1.3.1 (the eye-catching 'blurb' to the rest of the work) 'secutae maritos in exilia coniuges; propinqui audentes, constantes generi, contumax etiam aduersus tormenta seruorum fides'. For *fides + in* cf. 54.1, Cic. *Rab. Post.* 13, Liv. 21.52.6, *El. Maec.* 1.12 (F.).

adeo difficilis . . . spei mora 'So intolerable to men is the delay of hope, on whatever grounds it be conceived' (Watson): 'sententia haec . . . pertinet ad filios mortem patrum et hereditatem bonorum aegre expectantes' (Krause). For *spem concipere* cf. 103.4n.; *difficilis . . . mora* is also at 1.17.6.

67.3 ne quid ulli sanctum relinqueretur Such exprr. are extremely common: e.g. 26.2 'ne quid usquam malis publicis deesset', Cic. *Verr.* 3.87, Liv. 6.16.5, Sen. *Contr.* 1.7.6, 1.2.2, Val. Max. 9.2.2, Plin. *NH* 7.2, Tac. *Agr.* 2.2, Flor. 2.9.1 'hoc deerat unum pop. Romani malis', 2.13.52; also C. v. Morawski, *Eos* 2 (1895), 2, to whom some of these exs. are due.

†uel in dotem† inuitamentumque sceleris I think the obelised words hide an accus. in apposition to the sentence, parallel to *inuitamentum* and similar to *rem immanis operis* at 69.6; *uel in* is probably a corruption of *uelut*, which is sometimes used to introduce such phrases (e.g. Suet. *Cal.* 16.4 'decretum autem ut dies . . . Parilia uocaretur, uelut argumentum rursus conditae urbis'), and for *dotem* I suggest *documentum*: for the word used in apposition cf. 42.1, and for *documentum sceleris* cf. Cic. *Dom.* 50, 126. The error perhaps arose through abbreviation.

For L. Iulius Caesar, below, cf. *RE* 10.1.468–71 = Iulius 143 (Münzer); for L. Plotius Plancus, who before being adopted was called C. Munatius Plancus, cf. *RE* 16.1.541–4 = Munatius 26 (Münzer); *MRR* 2.339.

67.4 eoque . . . uersum I think this difficult and confusing sentence means: 'And for that reason amongst their ⟨customary⟩ military jokes ⟨the soldiers⟩ who followed Lepidus' and Plancus' chariot amidst the abuse of the citizens took up this refrain.' The principal difficulties lie in the phrases *inter iocos militares* and *inter execrationem ciuium*: not only is the repetition itself awkward (scholars have suggested deleting one phrase or the other) but the subject of the sentence (*milites*) has to be understood from the adjective *militares*. I think the repetition is less offensive if *inter . . . ciuium* is placed within the relative clause and *inter* taken to mean 'amidst' (cf. *OLD* s.v. 8); and understanding *milites* from *militares* is a type of synesis readily paralleled elsewhere (see L–H–S 441 top). The only remaining awkwardness (and it is very slight) is that in the rel. clause V. seems to have used the pluperf. instead of the imperfect tense.

For the custom of ribald and impromptu singing by soldiers in triumphal processions see esp. Suet. *Iul.* 49.4, where the wording is similar to V.'s here, and Ogilvie on Liv. 3.29.5.

'De germanis ... triumphant consules' Plancus, proconsul of Gallia Transalpina in 43, triumphed *ex Gallia* or *ex Raetis* on 29 Dec.; Lepidus, proconsul of Gallia Narbonensis and Hispania Citerior, triumphed *ex Hispania* on 31 Dec. (Degrassi 13.1. 567; *MRR* 2.348, 341–2). As neither man was consul till 42, they should strictly have been termed *consules designati*. For a brief discussion of V.'s story see Williams 83–5, who argues that much of it is a 'fabrication designed to blacken Plancus'.

The pun is comparable with that at Cic. *Phil.* 11.14 'iure Germanum Cimber occidit', which was evidently celebrated (Quint. 8.3.29). The verse is a trochaic septenarius, as were those sung at Caesar's Gallic triumph in 46 B.C. (cf. Suet. *Iul.* 49.4, 51); see E. Fraenkel, *Hermes* 62 (1927), 364.

68 DIGRESSION ON CAELIUS RUFUS (48 B.C.) AND CAESAR'S *CLEMENTIA* (44 B.C.)

Narrative historians wishing to recount the disintegration of the Roman republic are faced with considerable problems of organisation by the speed and multiplicity of events and by the unusually large number of extant contemporary writings which provide source material. Modern historians can of course resort to various typographical devices (such as footnotes and appendices) which were unknown to their ancient counterparts, but difficulties inevitably remain: for ex., Rice Holmes' narrative of domestic affairs reaches the year 42 B.C. before he feels obliged to break off and describe the foreign affairs of the previous year (*Arch.* 75 'It is time to describe the movements of Brutus and Cassius . . . '). Dio divided his history of the Ides to Philippi into two principal sections: 'He concentrates on the story of political events in Italy . . . and leaves his account of the movements of Brutus and Cassius until he has brought the narrative down to the formation of the Triumvirate and the proscriptions of the winter 43/42 B.C.'[1] Faced with exactly the same problem, V. reacted in a not dissimilar manner: in chh. 57–67 he concentrates on domestic affairs from March 44 to the proscriptions in late 43, while in chh. 69–72.2 he

---

[1] Millar, *CD* 56, adding 'This scheme is, as far as can be seen, his own.'

brings us up to date on the tyrannicides in the East and describes the battle of Philippi.[1]

Now it has already been observed that V., like other ancient historians, uses digressions to separate one section of his work from another (*TN* 154); in the Augustan narrative this happens at 64.3–4 (p. 139), 75–76.1 (p. 182), 78 (p. 179) and 88–89.1 (p. 237). Ch. 68, which is clearly signalled as a digression at its beginning and end and which in the past has wrongly been used as evidence of V.'s careless or hasty composition,[2] performs exactly the same function in separating the two sections of narrative mentioned above. The ch. shares features with two other discursive sections in particular: it is a 'double' digression (1–3 and 4–5), in this resembling the successive digressions (1.14–15 and 16–18) with which V. separates Book 1 of his history from Book 2; and it provides an effective interlude after the climactic treatment of Cicero's murder, in this resembling 88–89.1 which follows the battle of Actium and the ending of the civil wars.

The literary motivation for ch. 68 is therefore clear; but how did V. decide what material to include in it? In the case of Caelius Rufus (1–3) he says that he was struck by the man's *persona* (1). Personalities play a large part in V.'s history (see *TN* 40ff.) and he is always ready to dwell on the characters of individuals (e.g. 41.1 Caesar, 108.2 Maroboduus, 117.1 Varus 'et causa ⟨et⟩ persona moram exigit'). Caelius' personality was particularly engaging,[3] and he had the extra advantage of illustrating the kind of political violence which V., the product of a later generation, abhorred (cf. 88.2n.). Milo, similarly violent in character (3 *inquies*) and engaged in the same enterprise as Caelius at the time of his death, is mentioned merely to complete the episode.

For various reasons it is much less easy to understand why V. chose the story of the tribunes Caesetius Flavus and Epidius Marullus for the second part of his digression (4–5). First, although there are numerous and detailed sources for the incidents in which they were involved, their story is extremely confusing and the roles and intentions of the various parties are not at all clear. The tribunes appeared to be acting in Caesar's interests, yet they became the object of his accusations. Secondly, V.'s account of the episode is itself unclear. Readers who wish to discover his meaning will need to consider whether the emphasis of the first sentence is upon the tribunes' behaviour (*libertate usos*) or Caesar's reaction (*paene uim . . . expertos*), i.e. whether *usos* or *expertos* is the infinitive; also to be considered is the logic of *tamen* at the beginning of the second sentence. My own view is that, while the tribunes' allegedly prevaricating behaviour forms a thematic link with Caelius' activity in 1–3, V.'s main purpose was to provide

---

[1] The division between the two sections is clear but not absolute: Brutus' and Cassius' honours and departure are mentioned at 62.2–3 and their legionary strength at 65.1; and domestic affairs are noted briefly at 69.5.

[2] E.g. Schanz–Hosius, *Gesch. d. röm. Lit.* 2.585.

[3] See, e.g., R. G. Austin's edn. of Cic. *Cael.* (1960³), xv.

a further example of Caesar's *clementia* and perhaps to demonstrate that the actions of a dictator or *princeps* need be no different from those of the consuls and senate (5 *summoueret . . . a re publica* ~ 2 *summotus a re publica*). The example was all the more effective if, as seems possible (cf. 5n.), Caesar himself had claimed that his reaction to the tribunes' behaviour was uncharacteristically harsh.

68.1 Suo praeteritum loco referatur 'Reference should now be made to an episode which was passed over in its proper place.' For the expr. cf. *Bell. Hisp.* 10.2 'suo loco praeteritum est', though in V. *prae-teritum* is almost substantival (as Cic. *Acad.* 2.45 'nihil in praeteritis relinquamus').

neque enim persona umbram actae rei capit 'For the character in question does not admit of (only) an outline of his actions': i.e. had V. mentioned Caelius in his proper chronological position (51–2), he could have given him only a line or two (otherwise he would have distorted his narrative of Dyrrachium and Pharsalus, which, given his summary terms of reference (cf. 52.3), was compelled to be brief). But since in V.'s opinion such a mention of Caelius would have been inadequate, he deals with him at more length as soon as he has the opportunity here. No doubt the apologia is (at least partly) disingenuous, since V. clearly intended to insert the present digression for the reasons given above (p. 156).

Though the matter is by no means certain, I have assumed that *umbra* = 'outline', for which meaning see Pease on Cic. *ND* 1.75.[1] Watson imaginatively rendered 'the character of the agent does not allow a screen to be cast over his act'; but the sustained image breaks down because *umbra*, unlike *persona* and *rem agere*, is not a theatrical term. For the meaning of *capio* cf. *OLD* s.v. 28 (esp. Cic. *Pis.* 24 there quoted), adding Quint. 5.7.1 'si reprehensionem non capit ipsa persona'; for the expr. *actae rei* cf. Liv. 21.28.5 (Vossius); for the omission of a word meaning 'only' see below, 3n.

dum in acie Pharsalica †Africaque . . . Caesar dimicat Since the battle of Pharsalus took place in August 48 (52.3n.) and Caelius' activities began in Jan. of that year (Cael. ap. Cic. *Fam.* 8.17(156).2), *dum* is not to be taken literally; V. merely wishes 'contraporre . . . due avvenimenti di così diversa grandezza' (Volponi (cited below) 274).

Since no action was conducted in Africa that year either by Caesar or a representative (Curio's expedition belongs to 49, cf. 55.1), *Africaque* is clearly corrupt and was deleted by Krause as an ignorant gloss and by

---

[1] According to J. Nováková, *Umbra: ein Beitrag zur dichterischen Semantik*, *DAWB* 36 (1964), 83, this is the first occurrence in Latin prose of *umbra* = 'forgetfulness'; but no evidence is produced, nor can I find any elsewhere.

Orelli as dittography after -*alica*. Others have toyed with forms of *acer*, e.g. *acri eaque* (Jeep) or *acriter* (Haupt 1.272), and it may be that something like *acriter atque de summa* . . . is what V. wrote (for *acriter dimicare* cf. e.g. Liv. 3.5.7). But certainty is far off, and I have followed the example of Ellis in his edn. For the rest of the expr. cf. Nep. *Eum.* 10.3 'de summis rebus erat dimicandum', *Hann.* 8.3 'de summa imperii dim.'

M. Caelius, uir . . . Curioni simillimus For Caelius Rufus, a lover of Clodia at one time, cf. *RE* 3.1266–72 = Caelius 35 (Münzer), *MRR* 2.235, 248, 273; M. Volponi, *M. Celio Rufo 'Ingeniose Nequam'*, *Mem. dell'Ist. Lomb. Acc. di Scienze e Lettere* 31.3 (1971). Curio's eloquence and *animus* are described at 48.3–4, where also he is 'ingeniosissime nequam' (see n.).

cum †in modica† quidem seruari posset Some (e.g. Rosenheyn with *cum immota quiete s.* ⟨*non*⟩ *p.*) have attempted conjectures based on the epigram *cum* . . . *Lentulus* . . . *salua r.p. saluus esse non posset* at 49.3; yet the crucial word *saluus* does not occur in our passage. Proposals such as Novák's *ne modica quidem* ⟨*pecunia*⟩ *seruari p.* seem to me to fail through lack of logic: in such a sentence *modica* and *ne* . . . *quidem* are almost mutually exclusive, as Halm appears to have realised when proposing *ne immodica quidem* ⟨*re*⟩ *s.p.* On the other hand, V. might have written *cum ne a modica* ⟨*inopia*⟩ *quidem seruari posset* ('could not be saved even from modest debts', cf. 82.2 'pericula ⟨a⟩ quibus seruari se posse desperaret'), or something along those lines; yet the recurrence of *immodica* at 4 below perhaps suggests that that adj. should be found here also (on such repetitions see 100.5n., *TN* 200). In the light of the general uncertainty, I can see no alternative to obelising.

peior illi res familiaris quam mens erat Cf. the judgements of Cic. (*Brut.* 273 'nec uero M. Caelium praetereundum arbitror, quaecumque eius in exitu uel fortuna uel mens fuit') and Quint. (10.1.115 'dignusque uir cui et mens melior et uita longior contigisset') on the same man. For the phraseology see also 91.3.

68.2 extitit 'presented himself as'. *exsistere* is commonly found with a predicative noun (e.g. 1.8.2; cf. *TLL* 5.2.1870.75ff.), esp. *auctor* (e.g. Cic. *Ep. Brut.* 1.10.3, 17.2, *Sull.* 34 [text uncertain], Liv. 2.48.2, Val. Max. 4.7.4, Tac. *A.* 13.23.1). Less commonly *exstare* is also so used (e.g. *Bell. Hisp.* 42.7 'in quo uos uictores exstabatis'), and it too is coupled with *auctor* (e.g. Cic. *Planc.* 57, Liv. 44.22.6, cf. 1.18.2). I assume the former verb here. For Caelius' attitude cf. Cic. *Fam.* 8.17(156).2.

senatus et consulis auctoritate deterreri The paradosis reads *sen. et auctoritate COSS.*; the word order is impossible and *COSS.* is an error, one of the consuls (Caesar himself) being away at the time. Assuming that

COSS. is a scribal error (V. knew that Caesar was one of the consuls in 48, cf. 53.2), Lipsius' *consulis*, when transposed with *auctoritate* (so Cludius), solves both problems very neatly. Orelli suggested *sen.* ⟨*consulto*⟩ *et auct. consulis*; but it is not obvious why *consulto*, thus placed, should have been omitted, and the separation of *senatus* from *auctoritate* destroys the no doubt intentional echo in *auctore senatu* at the end of the next sentence: having ignored their *auctoritas*, Caelius was killed by an army acting precisely *senatu auctore*. Besides, *sen. auctoritas* is a set phrase (*TLL* 2.1225.82ff.) which V. uses elsewhere (2.15.4, 20.3, 49.2). For *auctoritate deterreri* cf. Cic. *I Verr.* 28, Liv. 37.51.6 ' patres auctoritate sua deterruerunt ', 38.47.5.

non impetrato reditu . . . infestus erat   In 49 Caesar had allowed all exiles except Milo to return (Dio 41.36.2, 42.24.2); on Milo cf. 45.3n., 47.4–5. On the comparative frequency of *infestus* over *infensus* cf. Adams (1974), 59; *TLL* 7.1.1406.30ff. V. does not use *infensus*.

aut in agris occulte bellicum tumultum mouens   The paradosis reads *haud magis occulte*; granted that Lipsius' change *in agris* is likely to be correct (for Caelius' rural activities cf. e.g. Caes. *BC* 3.21–2; for the antithesis *urbs ~ agri* cf. *OLD* s.v. *ager* 6), the only question concerns *haud* which Ruhnken emended (*at*) and which Mommsen transposed (*in agris haud occ.*). *haud occulte* can be justified only if it provides a significant contrast with the preceding *in urbe seditionem*; but, while *seditio* is no doubt often secret, Caelius' urban *seditio* was nothing if not blatant, as Dio makes abundantly clear (42.22.3–24.1). On the other hand, as Krause observed, secrecy is a keynote of Dio's narrative once Caelius had decided to retire to the countryside (42.24.3–25.3, cf. Caes. *BC* 3.21.4 *clam*). On these grounds Mommsen's transposition seems unlikely; V. appears to refer to Caelius' secret initiatives after leaving Rome. Here, however, a stylistic objection becomes relevant. While one can say *occulte coquere bellum* (Liv. 8.3.2) or talk of *occultum bellum* (Liv. 2.22.3), can one equally say ' *occulte bellicum tumultum* mouens'? I think the expr. can be defended on the grounds that *occulte mouens* refers to secret initiatives before the *bellicus tumultus* ever had the chance to take place; and indeed our sources stress precisely the abortive nature of Caelius' efforts (Caes. *BC* 3.22.4 ' ita magnarum initia rerum . . . celerem et facilem exitum habuerunt', Dio 42.25.3 ἂν ἔπραξέ τι ταραχῶδες . . . πρὶν ποιῆσαί τι λόγου ἄξιον). I therefore believe that *haud* requires emendation; and I prefer *aut* (= *et*, cf. L–H–S 500) to Ruhnken's *at*. For *tumultum mouere* cf. *TLL* 8.1545.79ff., for *seditionem m.*, 74ff.

summotus a re publica   ' senatusque Caelium ab re publica remouendum censuit ' (Caes. *BC* 3.21.3).

68.3 tum P. Clodio . . . poenas dedit   Cf. 47.4–5. For *tum . . . tum* cf. L–H–S 519. For *armis petebat* cf. Liv. 26.31.3, Sen. *HF* 1172, Mela 1.64, Tac. *A.* 2.88.2; *armis quaerere* is at 57.1.

COMMENTARY 2.68.4

68.4 quatenus . . . aliquid ex omissis peto   A similar technique is
used to link the two digressions which end Book 1, cf. 1.16.1 'cum haec
particula operis uelut formam propositi excesserit'. *quatenus* = 'seeing
that' is absent from Cic. Caes. Sall. Virg., cf. K–S 2.384 Anm. 1, E.
Wölfflin, *ALL* 5 (1888), 399–414, *OLD* s.v. B8. For *peto* cf. Tac. *H.* 3.51.2
'haec . . . ex uetere memoria petita' (Krause).

notetur . . . libertate usos . . . tribunos plebis   The tribunes L.
Caesetius Flavus and C. Epidius Marullus (on whom see *RE* 3.1310–
11 = Caesetius 4 (Münzer), *MRR* 2.323–4) removed, at some point in
Jan. 44, diadems which had been placed on Caesar's statue on the rostra
and they arrested the person responsible. On 26 Jan., when Caesar
entered Rome after celebrating the Feriae Latinae and was acclaimed as
king, he rejected the appellation and the tribunes arrested the first person
who had shouted it out. Evidently Caesar objected to the tribunes' behaviour (the grounds are unclear and disputed), whereupon they issued an
edict complaining that he was interfering with their freedom of speech. In
response Caesar delivered a speech against them in the senate (on which
see G. Dobesch, *Antidosis (Festschrift W. Kraus)*, *WS Beiheft* 5 (1972),
78–92) and had their powers removed from them. Such is the outline of
events which may be deduced from the evidence, although almost every
stage of the story has been questioned: thus Weinstock (319–20) mentions
the possibility that the first two events are the result of duplication in our
sources, and Münzer (loc. cit.) has doubted the existence of the tribunes'
edict, which is mentioned only by Dio (44.10.2 σφῶν προγραφὴν ἐκθέντων
ὡς οὔτε ἐλευθέραν οὔτ' ἀσφαλῆ τὴν ὑπὲρ τοῦ κοινοῦ παρρησίαν ἐχόντων).
Dobesch has however argued that V.'s present statement refers to, and
thus confirms the historicity of, the tribunes' edict (op. cit. 82 n. 13): 'Wir
haben keinerlei Grund, an dem vorzüglichen Bericht Dios zu zweifeln . . .
ferner klingt die "libertas" bei Velleius an die ἐλευθέρα παρρησία an; vor
allem hätte Velleius die bloße Verhaftung des Proklamierenden wohl
nicht als *immodica et intempestiva libertas* bezeichnet. In demselben Sinn
ist auch *saepe lacessiti principis* zu deuten: sie drängten sich schon bei der
Statuenkrönung und der ovatio hervor, jetzt erst beim dritten Male
schlug Caesar los. Da das Edikt ja inhaltlich eben nichts anderes als den
Vorwurf des Königsstrebens enthielt . . . ' Although the point about *saepe*
is well made, it is of no help in narrowing down the precise reference of
libertate. Again, it could perhaps be argued that *immodica et intempestiua
libertate* is a deliberate perversion on V.'s part of ἐλευθέρα καὶ ἀσφαλὴς
παρρησία which *ex hypothesi* was a phrase in the original edict; on the other
hand, V.'s sentence also suggests that the tribunes' *libertas* consisted in
their charging Caesar with monarchic ambitions (*dum arguunt in eo regni
uoluntatem*), and no such charge is mentioned by Dio in connection with
the edict (Dobesch is compelled to infer it). This last point is admittedly
not decisive, since the edict might have contained a reference to Caesar's
ambition as well as complaining of a lack of free speech; yet other sources

strongly suggest that it was the tribunes' behaviour, not their edict, which implied the charge of monarchy and therefore angered Caesar (next n.). On balance, I think that V.'s present sentence refers to the tribunes' general activities (not necessarily excluding the edict, if it ever existed). This conclusion may seem unsatisfactory, yet I cannot see that V. intended anything more precise.

For *notare* + acc. and infin. cf. 67.2 and *OLD* s.v. 11 (Sen. *Ep.* 108.31, Quint. 6.2.23, 9.4.15); for the expr. cf. Gell. 1.22.4 'immodice et intempestiue', Curt. 8.2.2 'immodice libertate abusum'.

dum arguunt in eo regni·uoluntatem Our most detailed sources, including Dio, testify that it was the tribunes' behaviour which, though suggesting otherwise, drew attention to the question of Caesar's alleged monarchic ambitions: App. *BC* 2.108 ὁ Καῖσαρ . . . κατηγόρησεν ἐπὶ τῆς βουλῆς τῶν περὶ τὸν Μάρυλλον ὡς ἐπιβουλευόντων οἱ μετὰ τέχνης ἐς τυραννίδος διαβολήν, Nic. Dam. 20 = F 130.69 Jacoby μείζονός τε γνώμης καὶ ἐπιβουλῆς εἶναι αὐτοῖς τὸ δρασθέν, εἴ πως δύναιντο εἰς τὸ πλῆθος αὐτὸν διαβαλόντες ὡς ἂν δυναστείας παρανόμου ἐρῶντα, cf. Dio 44.10.1 ὡς καὶ ὑπ᾿ αὐτῶν ἐκείνων προσστασιαζόμενος ὑπερηγανάκτησε [sc. ὁ Καῖσαρ]. Our other sources all associate the tribunes with the charge of *regni uoluntas* but, like V. (last n.), leave the circumstances vague (Suet. *Iul.* 79.2 'neque ex eo [sc. tempore] infamiam affectati etiam regii nominis discutere ualuit', Val. Max. 5.7.2. 'inuidiam ei [sc. Caesari] tamquam regnum adfectanti fecerat' to which similar wording is found in Liv. *per.* 116).

paene uim dominationis expertos There are two main reasons why I think we should understand *esse* here rather than with *usos* above. (1) I believe that V.'s purpose in mentioning the episode of the tribunes was to illustrate Caesar's *clementia* (see above, p. 157); and this illustration resides in the contrast between Caesar's allegation that the tribunes deserved to die (App. *BC* 2.108, cf. Dio 44.10.3), to which *paene uim . . . expertos* alludes, and his sparing of them, to which the next sentence refers. This contrast, pointed by *tamen* below (next n.), would be considerably obscured if *usos*, not *expertos*, represented the infinitive. (2) The word-order is entirely natural if *usos* is a genuine participle preceding the twin subjects of the indirect statement, which in turn are followed by the infinitive; whereas, if *expertos* were the participle, the order would be more typical of Tacitus than V.

dominatio (sc. *Caesaris*) reflects the language of the 40s: see Cic. *Att.* 7.22(146).1 (49 B.C.), Pollio in Cic. *Fam.* 10.31(368).3 (43 B.C.), Brut. in *Ep. Brut.* 1.16(25).1 (also 43 if the letter is genuine: it is considered spurious by Shackleton Bailey). For *uim experiri*, a common expr., cf. *TLL* 5.2.1678.7ff., adding Liv. 21.34.3, 28.3.5, 31.45.4, 44.9.1; for *uim dominationis* cf. Cic. *Rep.* 2.15, Tac. *A.* 6.48.2, 15.69.1.

68.5 in hoc tamen ... excessit ut ... summoueret eos a re publica The expr. is restrictive: 'only went so far as to ... remove them from politics', i.e. in contrast (*tamen*) to killing them, which was the alternative (last n.). Latin regularly omits *tantum* (*uel sim.*) where in English we say 'only' (see e.g. 1 above, 83.2, 84.1; Mayer on Luc. 8.51–2 with further refs.). Kritz emended *tamen* to *tantum*, but this ruins V.'s logic.

Caesar's anger is well attested (App. *BC* 2.108, Dio 44.10.2, Plut. *Caes.* 61.5), but whether he was responding to the tribunes' behaviour or to their edict depends upon the existence or otherwise of the edict (4n.). V.'s sentence is too generalised to help decide the question.

For the expr. cf. Liv. 8.33.19 'quo ultra iram uiolentiamque eius excessuram fuisse quam ut uerberaret necaretque?' (9.26.3 'eoque ira processit ut ...') (Ruhnken); for *excedere* see also *TLL* 5.2.1208.7ff.

censoria ... dictatoria Early in 44 Caesar had been appointed both censor (Dio 44.5.3) and *dictator perpetuus* (*MRR* 2.305, 317–18). *censoria nota* is a technical expr. (*RE* 17.1055–8), but *cens. animaduersio* is also found (*OLD* s.v. 3a): V. is here evidently contrasting roles rather than punishments.

testareturque esse sibi miserrimum quod ... aut minuenda dignitas 'and declared he greatly regretted that he had to choose between acting against his nature and having his dignity impaired'. The sentence sounds like authentic Caesar and may go back to his speech on this occasion (see Dobesch, op. cit. 84–5). For Caesar's famous *clementia* cf. 52.4n.; for his equally famous concern for *dignitas*, Caes. *BC* 1.9.2 'sibi semper primam fuisse dignitatem uitaque potiorem'; for the comparison between the two, C. Koch, *Religio* (1960), 106–7. According to V., Caesar alluded to his *clementia* by saying that his present behaviour was uncharacteristic: for this notion cf. 69.6n. For *minuenda dignitas* cf. Quint. 8.3.48.

sed ad ordinem reuertendum est Such formulae are commonly used to signal the end of a digression: for exs. see Fraenkel 98, Heubner on Tac. *H.* 2.38.2, T. Wiedemann, *LCM* 4 (1979), 14, A. Emmett, *Mus. Philol. Lond.* 5 (1981), 21–33.

69–73 THE YEARS 43–42 B.C.

After an initial ch. (69) in which he brings us up to date on various events, V. in the remainder of this section focusses on the battle of Philippi (70–72.2) and on Sextus Pompeius (72.3–73: see below, p. 174). His view of the battle is unromantic: it represents not the downfall of an idealised republic but the workings of *fortuna* (69.6n.) and the deplorable deaths of many distinguished men (71). It is true that V. delivers an *epitaphion* for the tyrannicides (72.1–2),[1] but his judgement on Cassius is unsympathetic (cf. also 69.6) and in the case of Brutus he chooses to dwell on his *temeritas* and his *corruptus animus* since the Ides of March (72.1).

69 PRELUDE TO PHILIPPI (43 B.C.)

69.1 Iam et Dolabella ... C. Trebonium ... occiderat The last event of the main narrative took place in Rome and belonged to late December 43 (67.4n.); capitalising on the digression in ch. 68, V. now turns to events abroad at the beginning of that year: hence *Iam et* ... [2] *et* ... [3] *et* ... and the sequence of verbs in the pluperfect tense, a compositional device which has the extra advantage of preparing the reader for some important action still to come,[2] in this case Philippi.

For fuller versions of Trebonius' murder cf. App. *BC* 3.26 and Cic. *Phil.* 11.5, 7–9; *MRR* 2.344. The event evidently belongs to mid-January 43 (Cic. *Phil.* 13.22; *MRR* 2.349–50). For Trebonius himself cf. 56.3n.; for Dolabella, 60.4n.

cui succedebat 'whom he was attempting to succeed'. Ruhnken had objected to *succedebat* on the grounds that Dolabella was proconsul of Syria, not Asia; he proposed *succensebat*, which has the advantage of supplying an explicit motive for Dolabella's treachery. Yet according to Kritz 'successisse Trebonio dicitur Dolabella, quia vi eius provinciam ingressus est, ac neglecta illius potestate imperio depellere eum studuit, et ut rectorem Asiae se gessit': V., in other words, is stating no more than the truth (cf. *praeoccupata Asia* at 2 below, Cic. *Phil.* 11.4, 6, *Fam.* 12.12(387).1 etc.). On the whole I agree with Kritz, especially since the impf. tense can have the conative force suggested by my translation.

For *ingratus + aduersus*, below, cf. *TLL* 7.1.1563.58–60, 77–80; for *ingratus* as a political term cf. 129.2n.

69.2 et C. Cassius acceptis ... legionibus On 7 March 43 Cassius wrote to Cicero with the news of his take-over (*Fam.* 12.11(366).1, cf. *Ep. Brut.* 2.3(2).3 of 1 April). For L. Staius Murcus, praetor in perhaps 45, cf. *RE* 3A.2136–9 = Staius 2 (Münzer), *MRR* 2.307, 330, 349, 363, 374–5, 383; for Q. Marcius Crispus, praetor *c.* 46, cf. *RE* 14.1555–6 = Marcius 52 (Münzer), *MRR* 2.295–6, 309, 329, 347. Both men are called *imperatores* in Cic. *Fam.* 12.11(366).1, 12.12(387).3.

---

[1] The *epitaphion* embodies a *syncrisis*: for both in V. cf. *TN* 42–3.
[2] For 'le *iam* d'ouverture et de préparation' cf. Chausserie-Laprée 498ff.; here in V. the main action is introduced at 70.1 by *tum* (cf. ibid. 520ff., 642), an equivalent of the more common '*iam* débouchant sur un *cum inuersum*' (513ff., with statistics from various historians).

inclusum Dolabellam . . . Laodiceam Since *includere* seems not to be found in prose with a place name in the abl., the reading of BA is unlikely to be correct. Rhenanus wrote *Laodiceam*, which I have accepted (cf. Liv. 36.16.5 'Heracleam sese incluserunt'), but Vossius' *Laodiceae* is also possible. On 13 June Cassius Parmensis wrote to Cicero that Dolabella was inside Laodicea and that Cassius Longinus was encamped 20 miles away (*Fam.* 12.13(419).4).

expugnata ea urbe †fecerat Rhenanus' *expugnata ea interfecerat* is the most attractive of the proposals which have been made for this passage: the structure is Velleian (cf. 94.4 'ingressus Armeniam, redacta ea . . .') and corruption explicable (*urbe* might have been a marginal gloss on *ea* which found its way into the text, dislodging *inter-*). My only reason for not printing it is that, while *interficere* can be used of suicide (cf. Tac. *A.* 1.2.1 'interfecto Antonio'), its use in this sense here, before the explicit *ita tamen ut . . . ceruicem daret*, seems rather obtuse.[1] Novák's *urbe ⟨mori⟩ coegerat* is also attractive (cf. Liv. *per.* 121) but too uncertain to print; and Ellis' *u. ⟨obire⟩ fecerat* is unlikely because that use of *facere* is extremely rare (cf. P. Thielmann, *ALL* 3 (1884), 177ff., K–S 1.694). On the whole I agree with those who think that *fecerat* is an intrusion from *sui iuris fecerat* below (for a comparable case cf. 79.1n.), and I have therefore obelised it; but in so doing I do not wish to imply that corruption is necessarily restricted to that word.

decem legiones Although Cassius ended the year 43 with more than 10 legions under his command (Brunt, *IM* 486), the words *in eo tractu sui iuris fecerat* suggest that V. is referring only to those legions which he acquired as a result of the activities mentioned in the foregoing sentence, i.e. those which took place in the small tract of land between Apamea, where Murcus and Crispus had been besieging Caecilius Bassus (App. *BC* 4.58–9), and Laodicea, where Cassius himself besieged Dolabella. On this hypothesis the legions in question were as follows: 3 each from Murcus and Crispus (App. *BC* 4.58); 2 from Caecilius Bassus when the Apamean siege was over (1 of these was locally recruited and not mentioned in Cassius' reports to Rome: Cic. *Fam.* 12.11(366).1, 12.12(387).3); and 1 from Dolabella when the Laodicean siege was over (App. *BC* 4.62; Dol.'s other, native, legion had already dispersed, cf. Cic. *Fam.* 12.15(406).7). Yet these figures total only 9 legions. Textual corruption is, I think, unlikely since 10 here plus 7 at 4 below produces the total of 17 to which V. refers at 65.1. Botermann (210 n. 5) suggests that V. is referring to some

---

[1] Rhenanus' alternative suggestion *confecerat* perhaps avoids this objection, but *con-* is less likely to have been dislodged by *urbe*. (Most edd. do not seem to have realised that Rhenanus wished to substitute *inter-* or *con-* for *urbe*. Thus Krause credits him with *ex. ea urbe ⟨con⟩fecerat* and notes that an abbreviation of *con-* might easily have dropped out after *-e*, which is doubtless true.)

earlier period, but that is also unlikely since we know from Cic. *Fam.* 12.13(419).4 that Cassius began the siege of Dolabella with 10 legions[1] and it would have been natural for V. to infer that he acquired Dol.'s 1 legion after the latter's defeat, making 11 in all. Perhaps, then, Murcus' 3 legions excluded (rather than included, as seems implied by Brunt, *IM* 480) the 1 legion with which Antistius Vetus had begun the siege of Bassus in Apamea before Murcus' and Crispus' arrival and that after the siege Cassius thus acquired 9 legions, not 8. There is admittedly no explicit evidence for this view, though App. *BC* 4.58 implies that Murcus already had 3 legions on arrival; yet the alternative view that Vetus' legion was included in Murcus' total is also based on silence (see esp. Brunt, *IM* 476 n. 3). For *tractus* cf. 94.1n.; for *sui iuris*, 108.2n.

69.3 Antonium bello lacessierat   C. Antonius had been appointed proconsul in Macedonia for 43, but the appointment was revoked late in 44. Having failed in his attempt to win over Vatinius' forces (below), he was besieged with the help of those same forces by Brutus in Apollonia, surrendering in mid-March 43. Brutus ordered his death early in 42. In general see *RE* 1.2582–4 = Antonius 20 (Klebs), *MRR* 2.266, 296, 319, 342; but note that Gaius Antonius is not to be identified with the Antonius whose death is mentioned at 71.2 below and who is presumably Gaius' more famous brother Marcus; V. simply omits to mention Gaius' death. For Gaius' soldiers see below.

Vatinium dignatione obruerat   As Vatinius was proconsul in Illyricum, he cannot have been 'out-ranked' by Brutus; *dignatio* must therefore be non-technical, as at 59.2 (n.). Vatinius had successfully resisted C. Antonius' efforts to win over his 3 depleted legions, but was soon compelled to hand them over to Brutus who used them against Antonius (above). In general see *RE* 8A.495–520 = Vatinius 3 (Gundel), *MRR* 2.168, 177, 190, 199, 216, 245, 286, 310, 330–1, 363. For the expr. cf. Curt. 7.1.27 'dignatione uincentem'.

cum et Brutus ... et Vatinius ...   It is clear from 'praeferendus *uideretur*' that *cum* explains *uolentes*, not *lacessierat ... obruerat*; the description of Brutus explains why Ant.'s troops changed sides, that of Vatinius why his troops acted likewise. As Botermann observes (91), V.'s account here agrees closely with that of Dio 47.21.6–7, especially his reference to Vatinius (οἱ γὰρ στρατιῶται ἀχθόμενοί τε αὐτῷ καὶ προσκαταφρονήσαντες αὐτοῦ διὰ νόσον μετέστησαν); Cicero however says that Vatinius himself handed over his troops (*Phil.* 10.13). See also Frisch 213–15.

---

[1] These 10 were drawn from the legions of Murcus, Crispus and Bassus, together with 4 extra legions en route from Egypt which Cassius had also acquired (App. *BC* 4.59; Brunt, *IM* 480) but which I have hitherto not mentioned because they seemed excluded by the words *in eo ... fecerat*.

nulli hominum non esset postferendus   Various emendations have been proposed for the paradosis *nulli nomini non*, of which the simplest is perhaps Aldus' *nulli homini non*; Krause rightly objected that this 'admodum languet', but I do not think the same can be said of the modification *hominum*, cf. Plin. *NH* 3.31 'nulli prouinciarum postferenda', to which F. adds Curt. 7.4.34 'nulli iuuenum postferendus': we now have a parallel to *ducum* above, and this use of the gen. plur. after *nullus* is of course common, e.g. Liv. 1.28.11 'nulli gentium', 6.18.8 'nulli uestrum', 22.49.14 'nulli fugientium', 32.35.12 'nulli omnium' (which is indeed what Acidalius proposed to read here in V.), 37.53.20, Val. Max. 2.6.9 'eorum nulli', 17 'nulli mortalium', Tac. *A.* 1.6.2; also below, 76.1n. Aldus alternatively suggested the deletion of *nomini* on the grounds that it was a corruption of *nemini* which in turn was an intrusive gloss on *nulli*; G. Fähse made the converse proposal of deleting *nulli* and emending *nomini* to *nemini*:[1] of the two I prefer Aldus', since *nulli* is in V.'s manner (cf. 2.11.1, 76.1), but I do not think it is superior to *hominum*.

69.4 deformitas corporis . . . inclusus uideretur   Two related conventions seem to lie behind V.'s repetitious statement. (1) The ancients believed that there was a relationship between a person's character and his physical appearance: see my n. on 94.2 (the 'ideal emperor' must have an appropriate countenance), Seel's edn of Trogus (1956), pp. 12–13, Nisbet on Cic. *Pis.* 1 (with T. E. V. Pearce, *CQ* 20 (1970), 309), Tarrant on Sen. *Ag.* 128, J. André's edn (Paris, 1981) of Anon., *De Physiogn. Liber*, Otto 147, Häussler, *Nachträge* 40–1, 57, 214, 237, 272, and the writings of E. C. Evans, *HSCP* 46 (1935), 43–84 (an excellent investigation of the practices of Roman historians and biographers), *TAPA* 72 (1941), 96–108 (on the second cent. A.D.), and *Trans. Am. Philos. Soc.* 59.5 (1969), 'Physiognomics in the ancient world' (a general account). Two interesting exs. occur in *Pan. Lat.* 6.17.3 'doctissimi uiri dicunt naturam ipsam magnis mentibus domicilia corporum digna metari, et ex uultu hominis ac decore membrorum colligi posse quantus illos caelestis spiritus intrarit habitator' (Vossius), 2.6.3 'siue enim diuinus ille animus uenturus in corpus dignum prius metatur hospitium, siue cum uenerit pro habitu suo fingit habitaculum' (Ruhnken). Thus the belief, which was elevated into a philosophical theory in the pseudo-Aristotelian *Physiognomonica* (but also elsewhere), was extremely common and doubtless lay behind the convention of Roman invective whereby a person's appearance was regarded as an appropriate target for attack (see Opelt 153, Nisbet (1961), 194), a convention which is in fact as old as Homer (*Il.* 2.212–20: Thersites' appearance is as disagreeable as his role). Cicero himself exploited the convention in the case of Vatinius' *struma* (*Vat.* 4 with Pocock's n., 39, cf. *Att.* 2.9.2, Catull. 52, Sen. *D.* 2.17.3; also Achard 227 and n. 64), no doubt the motivation behind V.'s remarks here (but note that Dio agrees closely with V.: above, 3n.).

---

[1] 'Observationes criticae in Vell. Pat.' in *Sylloge Lectionum* (1813).

(2) A *struma* is symptomatic of the disease goitre (see Cels. 5.28.7 etc.), and it was another convention that disease indicates moral deficiency: cf. esp. Lucil. 638 M = 662 K 'animo qui aegrotat, uidemus corpore hunc signum dare' (with Krenkel's refs. ad loc.); also Bramble 35. Once again the notion is extremely old: see F. Kudlien, 'Early Greek primitive medicine', *Clio Medica* 3 (1968), 310ff.[1]

septem legionibus ualidus The figure is correct for mid-43, the period with which V. is here dealing, but by the time Brutus had crossed to Asia to subdue the Lycians (below, 6) he had somehow acquired an eighth legion; cf. App. *BC* 3.79, 4.75, 88; Botermann 206–7, Brunt, *IM* 485–6.

69.5 omnibus ... damnatis aqua ignique interdictum erat For *damnatis ... interdictum* ('condemned and outlawed') cf. Cic. *Dom.* 82 'quibus damnatis interdictum est'; without Gruner's transposition of *damnatis* the interlaced word-order seems indefensibly perverse.

Q. Pedius, newly elected consul as Octavian's colleague on 19 August 43 (cf. 65.2), proposed his bill at Oct.'s instigation immediately upon election: *MRR* 2.336–7.

Capito A son of C. Velleius (76.1); cf. *RE* 8A.637 = Velleius 4 (Dihle), Nicolet 2.1066 no. 378, Wiseman 271 no. 472. 'Capito is designated as a man of senatorial rank, but it is not wholly clear whether he had already attained that status before his *subscriptio*. The rôle of *subscriptor* seems more appropriate for a young man at the threshold of politics than for an established senator' (Sumner 264 and n. 4). For the dat. after *subscribere* cf. Suet. *Rhet.* 27.1 (F.).

69.6 Cassius Rhodum ... ceperat, Brutus Lycios deuicerat These events are generally assigned to the first half of 42 B.C. (cf. e.g. *MRR* 2.360–1), but if *dumque ... geruntur* above is to be understood literally they presumably began in late 43.

For the combination of simple and superlative adjj. in *acri atque prosperrimo* above cf. 106.1n., adding K–S 1.478–9; for the appositional accus. *rem* cf. 67.3n.; for this sense of *immanis* cf. 105.3n.

repugnans naturae suae Since the ancients believed that a generally good person contained within him elements of evil, and an evil person elements of good (cf. 119.4n., adding Hor. *S.* 1.6.65–6), it was to be expected that these 'minor' elements would occasionally manifest themselves. Thus at 68.5 above Julius Caesar's harshness ('natura sua ei excedendum') is as uncharacteristic as Cassius' alleged clemency here.

---

[1] I owe this reference to Mr J. Longrigg.

On these and related ideas see Häussler, *Tac.* 351, A. R. Hands, *CQ* 24 (1974), 312–17. For the expr. cf. Sen. *Const. Sap.* 16.1 'dicas hoc naturae repugnare' (cf. 19.4).[1] For *per omnia* cf. 100.3n.

Cassius etiam Bruti clementiam uinceret Writing to Brutus in April 43, Cicero complained of his *lenitas* and *clementia* (2.5(5).5); but the punishments which both tyrannicides exacted from the people of Rhodes and Lycia (fully catalogued in Rice Holmes, *Arch.* 78–9) can hardly be described as clemency: rather they were 'the last expiring act of Republican brutality' (*CAH* 10.23). For *clementiam uincere* cf. Ov. *Ex P.* 2.121, *Tr.* 4.8.39, Flor. 2.13.92.

pronior fortuna comitata sit aut ueluti fatigata maturius destituerit The idea seems to be that of Fortune as a travelling companion (presumably on the journey through life): cf. 55.3 (slightly different: see n.), Enn. *Ann.* 289 'haudquaquam quemquam semper fortuna secuta est', Cic. *Rep.* 2.44, *Leg.* 2.28, *Fam.* 10.3.2; *pronus* is used of favourable deities, e.g. Luc. 5.501–2, Sen. *Phaedr.* 943, 1243, Stat. *Silu.* 4.8.61–2. For various exs. of *fortuna fatigata* the commentators quote Eur. fr. 1073N[2], Sen. *Contr.* 7.3.10, Curt. 8.3.1, Plin. *NH* 7.40, Plin. *Pan.* 61.10, Just. 12.8.15; its commonest context is that of Fortune being exhausted by human prayers (cf. Nisbet–Hubbard on Hor. *C.* 1.2.26), which is clearly not relevant here. Fortune is commonly a deserter (e.g. Sen. *D.* 9.8.3, Tac. *H.* 4.58.2, Curt. 4.1.29, Suet. *Aug.* 65.1); for tiredness and desertion combined cf. Luc. 2.727–8 'lassata triumphis | destituit fortuna tuis' (Ruhnken).

For *reperias* cf. 85.6n.

70 THE BATTLE OF PHILIPPI

70.1 apud urbem Philippos . . . acie concurrerunt There were two engagements, of which the second (4–5 below) took place on 23 October 42 (EJ p. 54 'Augustus uicit Philippis posteriore proelio Bruto occiso'); we do not know the precise date of the first battle, nor of Octavian's and Antony's journey to Macedonia. For various accounts of the fighting cf. Dio 47.42ff., App. *BC* 4.110ff., Plut. *Brut.* 41ff.; Rice Holmes (*Arch.* 81) has a map. For *acie concurrere* cf. e.g. Liv. 35.1.6, 40.46.10, 44.41.9; for *impulsis* = 'forced back', below, cf. e.g. 51.3, Liv. 9.27.9.

nam ipse Caesar . . . obibat munia ducis The effect of the dream (below) was that Oct., despite his illness, forsook the camp for the battle-line (Dio 47.41.4, 45.2, Val. Max. 1.7.1), a story which evidently goes

---

[1] I owe this reference to Miss Beatrice Smith.

back to his own memoirs (cf. App. *BC* 4.110, Plut. *Brut.* 41.4). *nam* nicely suggests that if Oct. had been in camp, Brutus would have failed to capture it. For the expr. cf. e.g. Sen. *D.* 6.14.3 'imperatoria ob. munia', Tac. *A.* 6.8.2 'militiae munia ob.', *H.* 1.77.1 'munia imperii ob.'.

manifesta denuntiatione quietis territo As *quies* is not strictly 'dream' (*pace* Goodyear on Tac. *A.* 1.65.2, q.v.) but 'the state in which dreams occur' (*OLD* s.v. 1*b*), I have written *manifesta* (Heinsius) rather than *manifestae* (Vascosanus); cf. Tac. *H.* 1.3.2 'praesagia . . . manifesta'. *denuntiatio* is almost technical in contexts of prediction etc. (*TLL* 5.1.551.71ff.); for its use with *terrere* cf. Cic. *Planc.* 87, *Flacc.* 14 (*conterritus* at Liv. 38.14.13, Curt. 6.5.19 *al.*). Dreams were the common stuff of epic (e.g. A. Grillone, *Il sogno nell'epica lat.* (1967)), declamation (they were a regular *color*, cf. Sen. *Contr.* 2.1.33, 7.7.15, *Suas.* 4.4), and historiography (e.g. Tac. *A.* 1.65.2; in general Val. Max. 1.7); this particular dream features in all accounts of Philippi, though App. attributes it to Oct. himself (*BC* 4.110).

male mulcatum 'badly mauled', a colloq. expr. which found its way into more elevated writing (*TLL* 8.1564.39ff., J. B. Hofmann, *Lat. Umgangssprache* (1951³), 74, 192). I have printed Gelenius' ⟨se⟩ *receperat* here. The paradosis is retained by K–S 1.92 and E. Wölfflin, *ALL* 10 (1898), 2–3, but cf. 4 below and 74.1; the intrans. use of the verb is not found in Cic. or Liv.

70.2 ex sua fortuna euentum collegae aestimans The phrase has a Livian ring: 21.43.2 'in aestimanda fortuna uestra', 8.10.1 'audito euentu collegae'. *euocatus* (below) = a veteran, often re-enlisted (*TLL* 5.2.1058.26ff.).

neque puluere facies ... dinotari possent According to *TLL* 5.1.536.75–7, *denotare* = 'make out, distinguish' is found only in the paradosis here and at Sen. *Ep.* 121.5 'artifex instrumenta sua tractat ex facili; rector nauis scit gubernaculum flectere; pictor colores . . . celerrime denotat et inter ceram opusque facili . . . manu commeat'; but the context of the latter strongly suggests that the verb should there mean 'lays on, applies'. *OLD* (s.v. 1*b*) gets the Senecan ex. right but (s.v. 3) wrongly classifies the Velleian ex. as meaning 'mark down, observe', paralleling Colum. 7.9.11, 9.8.12, *Ann. Epig.* 1947, no. 118 '⟨si quis mouer⟩it denotatus prouocabit ⟨seuerit⟩atem nostram' ('pointed out' or 'noted down'). In fact none of the basic meanings of *denotare* (which according to *TLL* are *notare, signare, uituperare*) makes it likely that the verb can mean 'distinguish', and I can find no parallel for that meaning here in V. *dinotare*, on the other hand, means 'distinguish' at Cic. *Acad.* 2.57 'ipsum sapientem . . . cum ei res similes occurrant quas non habeat dinotatas, retenturum adsensum' (*OLD* s.v. translates as 'mark with a distinctive label', but Cic. uses the verb as an alternative to *internoscere* and *distinguere* which occur elsewhere in the passage). Hitherto *dinotare* has been regarded as *hapax legomenon* (*TLL* s.v., Reid ad loc.), but I suspect that another ex. is to be found in the present passage of V.[1]

Cassius' fatal inability to see is attributed by Plut. to his bad eyesight (*Brut.* 43.3) but by App. to the dust of the battlefield (*BC* 4.113); V.'s choice of the latter tradition (assuming he had such a choice) is perhaps influenced by the fact that battlefields were conventionally dusty (Nisbet–Hubbard on Hor. *C.* 2.1.22).

lacerna caput circumdedit   Other exs. of this ritual are collected by R. Waltz, *REL* 17 (1939), 292–308 apropos of Sen. *NQ* 4 *praef.* 17. *interritus*, below, occurs first here and at Sen. *Suas.* 2.2 in extant Latin prose.

70.3 'sequar', inquit, 'eum . . .'   So too Val. Max. 9.9.2 ' "etsi imprudens", inquit, "imperator, causa tibi mortis fui, tamen, ne id ipsum impunitum sit, accipe me fati tui comitem" '; the same story occurs, but without the direct speech, at Plut. *Brut.* 43.7.

70.5 reiectoque laeuo   If such an action originally had a practical purpose (cf. Virg. *Aen.* 2.552–3 'implicuitque comam laeua, dextraque coruscum | extulit ac lateri capulo tenus abdidit ensem', where Austin quotes *Comm. Petit.* 10 'uiuo stanti collum gladio sua dextra secuerit, cum sinistra capillum eius a uertice teneret'), V. does not mention it, even though he describes Brutus' wounding (below) in almost Homeric detail. No doubt Brutus' suicide became stylised in literature (and art), and the parallels with Val. Max. (3n. above, 72.1n. below) perhaps suggest that V. had a specific literary representation of Brutus' (and Cassius') final days in mind.

reicere is the appropriate verb for throwing back arms (*OLD* s.v. 3*c*); for *super* cf. 59.6; for *emicare*, below, where *micare* would perhaps be more usual (*TLL* 8.929.37–9), cf. Plaut. *Aul.* 627 ' cor coepit . . . emicare' (similarly, in a different context, at 125.4 (n.)).

exspirauit prot⟨inus   So too 2.7.2 'protinusque . . . exspirauit', 120.6 'ut protinus . . . exspiraret'; for the text see next n. For *in uulnus*, above, cf. e.g. Lucr. 4.1049, Virg. *Aen.* 10.488, Liv. 1.58.12.

71–72.2 AFTERMATH AND EPITAPH

71.1 Coru⟩inus Messalla   Since this man is called Corvinus *tout court* immediately below and was similarly called Corvinus on his first (and hitherto only) appearance at 36.2, it is unlikely that V. confusingly called

---

[1] Ruhnken had already compared Cic. *Acad.* 2.57, but he read *denotatas*, found in one MS and in older editions.

him simply Messalla here. Ed. Bipont. emended *protinus* at 70.5, but the word is clearly needed there (see n.) and Halm's suggestion of parablepsy seems greatly preferable. The man's full name was M. Valerius Messalla Corvinus; he was consul in 31 B.C., an office that had been intended for Antony, and father of the two men mentioned at 112.1 (where he is again called simply Corvinus): see 112.1n.; *MRR* 2.367, 403, 406, 420, 422; Syme, *RR* 566 (index), *HO* 131–3, 240 (index); Lana 126–7. He was the half-brother of the Antonian L. Gellius Publicola (cf. 85.2n.) and patron of Tibullus.

For *fulgens* of people cf. Liv. 26.22.13 (Milkau), *Anth. Lat.* 837.5 (= Bücheler–Riese 1.2 p. 303). The superl. occurs first in V. (also 39.1, 64.3) and Val. Max. 1.1.10, 3.5.1. For *proximus* cf. 114.5.

seruari beneficio Caesaris maluit 'No writer of memoirs could touch Vell. Pat.', writes Syme, 'It was in fact to Antonius that Corvinus applied' (*HO* 132). True (cf. App. *BC* 4.136); but he subsequently left Antony for Octavian and became celebrated both for the *clementia* which Oct. displayed to him and the devotion which he displayed to Oct. (cf. App. *BC* 5.113): hence *hominis grati ac pii* below (on which see Weinstock 258). For Oct.'s *clementia* in general see 86.2n., 100.4n.

. . . maluit quam dubiam spem armorum temptare amplius Livy uses both *dubia spes* (3.2.3, 8.2.5, 36.8 etc.) and *spem temptare* (4.10.4 'exiguam spem in armis cum tentassent', 21.12.3, 26.3.10), but V.'s is an altogether striking phrase and it is echoed, I suspect, by Tacitus at *A.* 12.46.1, where I would suggest reading 'ne dubi⟨am spem ten⟩tare armis quam incruentas condiciones mallet' (*dubitare armis . . . malle* M: *dubiam rem armis . . . mallet* L: *dubia tentare armis . . . mallet* Sirker). For *exemplum*, below, cf. Sen. *Contr.* 10.2.16 'insignium uirorum exempla'.

non aliud bellum cruentius caede . . . fuit Such superlative expressions are especially common in Thuc. (e.g. 2.77.4, 7.29.5; cf. L. Pearson, *TAPA* 78 (1947), 47–8, J. H. Finley, *Three Essays on Thuc.* (1967), 126–40, J. R. Grant, *Phoenix* 28 (1974), 83–5) and Livy (cf. P. G. Walsh, *Livy* (1961), 200–1). For *bellum cruentum* cf. Flor. 2.30.36, Tac. *A.* 4.46.3, Sil. 11.131, Sen. *HF* 402; for *cruentus* + abl. cf. Sall. *C.* 47.2, Drac. *Laud. Dei* 3.104.

For the son of the younger Cato cf. *RE* 22.166–7 = Porcius 13 (Miltner), *MRR* 2.368; for M. Licinius Lucullus, son of the famous L. Licinius Lucullus Ponticus (cos. 74 B.C.), cf. *RE* 13.418–19 = Licinius 110 (Münzer): according to Val. Max. 4.7.4 'eum M. Antonius, quia Bruti et Cassii partes secutus fuerat, interemisset'; for Q. Hortensius, son of the famous orator, cf. *RE* 8.2468–9 = Hortensius 8 (Münzer), *MRR* 2.328, 361. For *fortuna . . . abstulit* cf. Catull. 101.5, Sen. *Ep.* 63.7, 10 *al.*, Sil. 13.383; the verb is of course commonly used in contexts of death (e.g. 55.4, 66.4 and n.).

71.3 nam Varro ad ludibrium moriturus Antonii   The interlaced word-order (cf. 100.1n.) and the use of *morior* (rather than an expr. denoting suicide)[1] suggest to me that *Antonii* is subjective (so H–W, *TLL* 7.2.1757.63–4) rather than objective genitive (so Shipley and others): Varro's death was a source of enjoyment to Antony. The reason for Antony's enjoyment presumably lies in the story told by Dio 47.11.3–4 about Varro, viz. that in 43 B.C. he had issued a public statement saying that he was different from the man of the same name who was on the list of the proscribed; ὁ μὲν διατριβὴν καὶ γέλωτα ἐπὶ τούτῳ ὠφλίσκανεν, says Dio. No doubt the joke looked even better when Varro was at last killed (? by Antony: see Lucullus, last n.) at Philippi, but perhaps he had the last laught after all (*uera*). For M. Terentius Varro Gibba cf. *RE* 5A.1.704– = Terentius 89 (Münzer): *MRR* 2.340. For *ludibrium* + subj. gen. cf. *TLL* 7.2.1757.57ff. (1756.62ff. for *ad l.*).[2]

As at 76.2 and 84.2 (see n.) *nam* explains the difference between listed items which are apparently similar: unlike the others, Varro was able to prophesy before he died (so Kritz).

ne temptata quidem hostis misericordia   No doubt an echo of *RG* 3.1, as at 86.2 (see n.). For *temptare mis.* cf. Liv. 38.28.9, Sen. *Ep.* 37.2.

For Livius Drusus cf. 94.1n.; for Iulia Augusta, as Livia was called after Augustus' death, cf. 75.3n.; for Sex. Quinctilius Varus (the identification was first made by S. V. Pighi, *Annales Romanorum* (1599–1615), 3.144) cf. R. Syme, *CP* 50 (1955), 135, *RE* 24.905–6 = Quinctilius 17 (Gundel): he was the father of Augustus' ill-fated general, and from the plural *honorum* it may be inferred that he had progressed beyond his quaestorship of 49 (*MRR* 2 Suppl. p. 52). For *cum se . . . uelasset* cf. Liv. 5.41.8, Flor. 2.21.11; Mommsen, *Staatsr.* 1³.441 and n. 2.

72.1 Hunc exitum . . .   Such expressions are almost formulaic among Roman historians when describing scenes of death (cf. 1.12.6, 2.7.1, 14.3, 53.3; Liv. 6.20.14; Austin on Virg. *Aen.* 2.554, Heubner on Tac. *H.*

---

[1] *morior* can of course be used of suicide but usually, I think, in contexts where the meaning is clear (e.g. Virg. *Aen.* 4.475 'decreuitque mori').

[2] Mr DuQuesnay nicely suggests that V.'s story of Varro is a Caesarian retort to the Antonian story told at Suet. *Aug.* 13.2 'in his [Oct.'s prisoners after Philippi] Fauonius, ille Catonis aemulus, cum catenati producerentur, imperatore Antonio honorifice salutato, hunc [sc. Caesarem] foedissimo conuicio coram prosciderunt'. On this interpretation *Antonii* will be obj. gen., and the interlaced word-order of no significance. The same idea had also occurred to Scott 22–3.

I should add that it is not certain that V. is referring to Varro Gibba. Hellegouarc'h (2.217) mentions the possibility of M. Terentius Varro Lucullus, an otherwise unattested brother of M. Licinius Lucullus; G. V. Sumner (*HSCP* 82 (1978), 191 n. 15) suggests A. Varro Murena, the curule aedile of 44 B.C.

3.75.1, Häussler, *Tac.* 368–9); here V. has varied the formula by applying it to Brutus' party, some of whose members have been mentioned in the preceding paragraph, rather than to Brutus himself. He does however proceed to an *epitaphion* for Brutus (and Cassius) immediately below.

M. Bruti ... XXXXII annum agentis Brutus died on 23 October 42 (EJ p. 54), and according to the paradosis he was then 'in his 37th year', i.e. 36 years old; this would place his birthday somewhere between 24 Oct. 79 and 22 Oct. 78 B.C. However, according to the paradosis of Cic. *Brut.* 324, Brutus was born ten years after Hortensius made his first speech ('annis ante decem causas agere coepit quam tu es natus'); and since we know that Hortensius' first speech belongs to 95 B.C. (ibid. 229 'L. Crasso Q. Scaeuola consulibus primum in foro dixit'), it follows from this evidence that Brutus was born in 85. Nipperdey proposed to resolve the discrepancy by emending *decem* to *sedecim* in Cicero's text. This simple emendation has won the support of A. E. Douglas ad loc. and would mean, when taken together with the evidence of V.'s paradosis here, that we could narrow down Brutus' birthday to late 79 B.C.; but E. Badian (*JRS* 57 (1967), 229) and G. V. Sumner (*Phoenix* 25 (1971), 365–6) have argued on historical grounds that such a late date is highly improbable. As it is unlikely that V., who was clearly attempting to give a precise date, would have been wrong by as many as six years, Mr J. J. Paterson suggests that we emend his text instead of Cicero's. It is certainly not difficult to suppose that *XXXXII* became *XXXVII*, a form of which is found in the paradosis; and if V. did indeed write that Brutus died 'in his 42nd year', that allows us to place his birthday in 85 B.C., the same year as that found in Cicero, at some point after 23 October.[1]
fortuna esse uoluit is Ciceronian (*Clu.* 22, 195, *Font.* 16).

diem quae illi omnes uirtutes unius temeritate facti abstulit Cf. Val. Max. 6.4.5 on Brutus: 'uno enim facto et illas [sc. uirtutes] in profundum praecipitauit'; also App. *BC* 4.133 ἐς ἀρετὴν ἀδηρίτω, χωρὶς ἄγους ἑνός (of Brutus and Cassius). Each statement is no doubt related to the topos *nemo sine uitio est*, for which cf. 119.4n. For *dies ... abstulit* cf. *TLL* 5.1.1046.78ff.; for Brutus' *uirtus*, which was proverbial, cf. Nisbet–Hubbard on Hor. *C.* 2.7.11, M. L. Clarke, *The Noblest Roman* (1981), 75–6. For *incorrupto animo*, above, cf. Cic. *TD* 1.43, Sall. *J.* 2.3, Val. Max. 2.1.3.

72.2 dux Cassius melior ... A similar *syncrisis* at App. *BC* 4.132–3. For the omission of *tanto* before *melior* cf. K–S 2.484, L–H–S 591, *TLL*

---

[1] Cornelissen (1887) had already proposed *III et XXXX annum agentis*. The birthday was also discussed by O. Seeck, *RhM* 56 (1901), 631–4, and P. Groebe, *Hermes* 42 (1907), 304–14 (also pp. 505–8, by Seeck). All three scholars wrote before the exact date of the battle of Philippi was known (cf. *Ann. Epig.* 1922, no. 96).

8.65.76–81; for *uis . . . uirtus*, below, cf. Wölfflin 280. For *malles . . . timeres* cf. 85.6n.

qui si uicissent . . . Though the sentence continues the preference for Brutus over Cassius, it also suggests that, had their side won, they would not have restored the republic but installed *principatus*. *libertas* is as conspicuously absent from the end of their story as it was from the beginning at 56.3–57.1.

72.3–73 SEXTUS POMPEIUS

Having mentioned those of Brutus' supporters who had died (71.2–3), and after an obituary notice for Brutus and Cassius themselves (72.1–2), V. now turns to the surviving remnants of Brutus' party. Many of them gravitated towards Sextus Pompeius (72.3–5), whose importance as an obstacle to Octavian over the next six years was such that V. devotes much of the present section to describing him in some detail (73). The sketch is hardly complimentary, V. being keen to underline, with some irony, the differences between him and his distinguished father; but we should remember that V. later pays tribute to the sanctuary which Sextus offered to various eminent refugees (77.2–3).

72.3 Cn. Domitius Cn. Domitius Ahenobarbus, son of L. Domitius Ahenobarbus (cos. 54 B.C.; cf. 50.1n., 3n.), had been an officer under Brutus (*MRR* 2.361, 365); for him cf. 76.2, 84.2; *RE* 5.1328–31 = Domitius 23 (Münzer), also *MRR* 2.332, 353, 373, 382, 421; *RRC* 1.527–8 nos. 519 and 521; 2.743. His son was L. Domitius Ahenobarbus (cos. 16 B.C.), who married Octavian's niece Octavia, was grandfather of the emperor Nero, and died in A.D. 25 – roughly the time when, in my opinion, V. started writing (cf. *nuper a nobis uisi*); for him cf. *RE* 5.1343–6 = Domitius 28 (Groag); *PIR*² 3.32–4 no. 128; Syme, *RR* 546 (index). Cn. Domitius' grandson was Cn. Domitius Ahenobarbus, the consul of A.D. 32; cf. *RE* 5.1331–3 = Domitius 25 (Groag); *PIR*² 3.30–2 no. 127. He evidently inherited his father's *nobilissima simplicitas*, according to V. at 2.10.2, and thus provided the ideal contrast with Sextus Pompeius below, who in V.'s opinion could hardly have been more different from his father Pompey the Great. The sympathy with which V. consistently treats the family of the Domitii (cf. also 2.11.3) contrasts strongly with Suetonius' extremely hostile comments at *Nero* 4–5 (cf. Syme, *RR* 421, 510); but Lana is perhaps right to conclude that 'in Suetonio il giudizio sfavorevole all'imperatore Nerone si ripercuote su tutti i membri della famiglia Domizia' (124).

For *sequi consilia* cf. *TLL* 4.453.60–2, adding Liv. 1.41.3; for *fortunae se committere* cf. Cic. *Verr.* 5.13.2 (F.), *Att.* 9.6.4, Liv. 7.12.11, Amm. 21.5.13; for *fugae se comm.* cf. Ap. *Met.* 7.24.

72.4 Staius Murcus ... Sex. Pompeium ... petit Murcus had been
in charge of a fleet for Cassius since 43 (*MRR* 2.349, 363), and continued
to patrol the Adriatic after Philippi (App. *BC* 5.2(8) with Gabba's n., Dio
48.18.3–4). A coin which testifies to his naval command has been variously dated to 44/43 B.C. (Weinstock 46) and 42/41 (*RRC* 1.519 no. 510).
For Murcus cf. 69.2n.; also Brunt, *IM* 486–9.

Sex. Pompeius (on whom see below, 73.1n.) had occupied Sicily late in
43 (*MRR* 2.362); V. briefly describes his earlier movements at 73.2 below
(see n.).

72.5 nullum habentibus statum The noun = 'political status' (cf.
L&S s.v. II.A.1), here with the extra connotation of 'permanency'. Cf.
2.2.3 'omnibus statum concupiscentibus'.

For *fortuna subduxerat*, above, cf. 103.1; *praesens periculum* is a cliché (cf.
OLD s.v. *praesens* 6b); *dux ... idoneus*, below, is also at Sall. *H.* 1.77.8
where the context, as here, is that of lacking a leader (cf. 125.2n.).

statio pro portu The former must be temporary, the latter per-
manent: cf. Sen. *Ot.* 7.4 'nobis haec statio non portus est' (Ruhnken);
also Lentul. in Cic. *Fam.* 12.15.2. The common political metaphors of
harbour and storms (for which cf. Pöschl 488 s.v. *Hafen*, 566 s.v. *Sturm*) are
particularly appropriate in the case of Sextus, the pirate king.

For *fortuna non electionem daret*, above, cf. Liv. 38.8.5 'electionem a
fortuna relictam'.

73.1 Hic adulescens ... The sketch of Sex. Pompeius is partly modelled on that of the troublesome politician Cethegus at Sall. *C.* 43.3–4
'seque ... impetum in curiam facturum. natura ferox, uehemens, manu
promptus erat, maxumum bonum in celeritate putabat', which also lies
behind the sketch at Liv. 3.11.6; in Liv. the narrative is resumed after the
sketch by the resumptive pronoun *hic* (7), just as here by *is* (3); on this
well known technique cf. Ogilvie ad loc., and 109.5n. For Sextus cf. *RE*
21.2213–50 = Pompeius 33 (Miltner); *MRR* 2.312, 329, 348–9, 362, 374,
382–3, 392, 397, 402, 408–9; Hadas.

V.'s use of *adulescens* hardly helps one decide whether Sextus was born in
76 B.C. (so Hadas 3–9) or between 68 and 66 (so *RE* 21.2214) or at some
other point (cf. J. Rougé, *REL* 46(1968), 180–93). Partly because he was
Pompey's son, and partly because *adulescens* (like μειράκιον) had suitably
pejorative overtones (see Ogilvie on Liv. 2.56.10), Sextus was conventionally described as 'young' by all our sources: see the collection of passages
in Hadas 5–6; also below, 79.5n.

studiis rudis, sermone barbarus We learn from Cicero (*Att.* 16.4.1)
that Sextus was literate but capable of solecisms and from Strabo
(14.1.48) that he was taught by the *grammaticus* Aristodemus. These passages are used by Hadas (10ff.) in an attempt to discredit V., who has
however simply inverted, in a conventional manner, the good qualities

which he habitually attributes to others (for *studia* cf. e.g. 1.12.3, 1.13.3, 94.1; for *eloquentia* cf. e.g. 2.6.1, 2.13.1, 2.18.5, 29.3). This is standard rhetorical practice (cf. e.g. Quint. 3.7.19ff. and Adamietz ad loc.): compare Cic. *Phil.* 13.43.

For the exprr. cf. 2.9.6 'uerbis rudem' (*arte r.* at Ov. *Tr.* 2.424, Stat. *Theb.* 6.437); Ov. *RA* 335 'barbara sermone', Cic. *Verr.* 4.112 'barbari lingua'; Cic. *Phil.* 3.15 'quam barbarus, quam rudis', Ap. *Apol.* 91. For *barbarus* + abl. cf. 108.2 and n.

cogitatione celer So Rhenanus. Heinsius' *cogitato* does not have the right nuance ('act of thinking'), the word being almost always found in the plur. = 'thoughts' (*TLL* 3.1475.35ff., but cf. Nep. *Dat.* 6.8, Quint. 4.5.2). Scheffer's *cogitatu* is almost equally unlikely since the word does not certainly appear until Apuleius (it is however a variant at Cic. *Off.* 1.27, and at Front. *Strat.* 2.5.30 the MSS are divided between *cogitatibus, cogitantibus* and *cogitationibus*). For *celer* cf. 118.2 and n.; for *manu promptus* cf., besides Sall. *C.* 43.4 (quoted above), *J.* 7.1, Liv. 2.33.5, 56.7, 3.11.7, Curt. 5.1.18, Quint. 12.1.23.

fide patri dissimillimus The *fides* of Pompey the Great was praised at 29.3: in underlining the difference between the two men V. is doubtless being ironical, since Sextus capitalised on his father's name, called himself Pius and generally made much of the concept of *pietas* (*RRC* 1.486–7 nos. 477–9, 2.739 and n. 1; Hadas 151–2; Syme, *RR* 157). More irony at 2–3 below (nn.). For V.'s constr. cf. Ov. *Tr.* 2.11.17 'dissimilis tibi . . . probitate'.

libertorum suorum libertus The *liberti* in question are Menas and Menecrates (3n.). The expr., like *seruorum seruus* below, is similar in form to those illustrated in L–H–S 55 (where the genitive is partitive, e.g. *rex regum*), but different in meaning (*libertorum* and *seruorum* are possessive genitives). For the idea Professor R. H. Martin refers to Sall. *H.* 1.55.2, Tac. *H.* 1.36.3 'omnia seruiliter pro dominatione'; cf. also 83.1n. For *humilis* as subst., below, cf. 126.3n.; I have found no parallel for *speciosus* similarly used of persons, but cf. 113.2n. (where add Curt. 5.1.8, Tac. *H.* 1.34).

73.2 senatus . . . post Antonii a Mutina fugam, eodem illo tempore quo . . . decreuerat The battle of Mutina took place around 21 April 43 (61.4n.); Antony fled immediately afterwards (ibid.) and senatorial sympathy swung in favour of the Pompeians (62.1). Brutus' provincial command in Macedonia was ratified at the same time as Cassius' in Syria, viz. 27 April 43 (cf. 62.2n.).[1]

---

[1] Note that Ellis, Halm and Stegmann are quite wrong to say that A here reads *Antonii*, which is the reading of B alone. Both A and P read *Antonianam*, thus providing further evidence of their common parent (R): see *TN* 12ff.

reuocatum ex Hispania 'having ⟨previously⟩ been recalled from Spain'. At some point during the summer of 44 (the date is disputed: see Hadas 62–4) Lepidus negotiated with Sextus that the latter should return from Spain on condition that he recovered his father's property; and Antony persuaded the senate to pass a decree to that effect (cf. Dio 45.10.6; App. *BC* 3.4 has a similar account but misdates the event, cf. *MRR* 2.326). Lepidus was rewarded by a senatorial *supplicatio* on 28 Nov. 44 (Cic. *Phil.* 3.23–4, 5.39; Frisch 153), but Sextus' journey from Spain took him no further than Marseilles (*MRR* 2.348).

clarissimum bellum The war took place in the summer of 44, but the evidence on its outcome is conflicting. According to Dio 45.10.3–6 Pollio was heavily defeated; Appian says that he and Sextus fought ὁμοίως (*BC* 4.84); and the impression given by V.'s phrase is that Pollio was successful. Most scholars have discounted V.'s version on the grounds that it is contradicted by that of Dio, which they accept; yet André (17–18), evidently followed by Haller (35), observed that the two accounts are not mutually exclusive. In 44 Pollio had only two (App. *BC* 3.46) or at best three (Brunt, *IM* 479, 491) legions, whereas Sextus had seven (Cic. *Att.* 16.4.2): it is therefore possible that Pollio's smaller force fought the splendid campaign which V. mentions but ultimately suffered the defeat which Dio records but about which V. is silent. André's thesis is perhaps given some support by the circumstances of Pollio's defeat, as described by Dio. We are told that Pollio's soldiers surrendered to Sextus on account of a trick of Pollio's which had misfired; and since it was evidently after this surrender that Sextus was first acclaimed *imperator* (cf. Hadas 58; *RRC* 1.486–7 nos. 477–9), V. perhaps believed that Sextus had achieved his success by default and that he would put the record straight by praising the campaign of his opponent Pollio. In so far as V.'s silence over Pollio's defeat resembles that of Appian, it is interesting to speculate whether both authors derive ultimately from Pollio's own work (see 76.2n. for a comparable case). Indeed it may be that ὁμοίως is Appian's rendering of *aequo Marte*, a standard historiographical euphemism for defeat which may well have been used by Pollio himself.

In 44 Pollio was probably proconsul of Hispania Ulterior (*MRR* 2.327), having been praetor in the previous year (G. V. Sumner, *Phoenix* 25 (1971), 358). For the expr. *clarissimum bellum* cf. Lucr. 1.475 'clara . . . certamina belli'.

(quem senatus) in paterna bona restituerat et orae maritimae praefecerat The hyperbaton, whereby Sextus' official title of *praefectus classis et orae maritimae* (*RRC* 1.520–1 no. 511) is delayed to the end of this long clause, is ironical in view of the criticisms of his character made in 1 above.

The date of Sextus' appointment as *praefectus* is calculated by scholars (e.g. Rice Holmes, *Arch.* 58 and n. 1, Frisch 291 and n. 97) as follows.

According to Dio 46.40.3 the appointment was made at the same time as Brutus and Cassius were granted their provincial commands, a synchronisation with which V. agrees (cf. *eodem illo tempore quo . . . prouincias decreuerat* above); and since we know that these commands were confirmed on 27 April 43 (cf. Cic. *Ep. Brut.* 1.5(9).1; above, 62.2n.), Sextus' appointment must have taken place that day too. It is admittedly strange that Cicero fails to mention the appointment in his letter to Brutus; but Rice Holmes observes that nowhere in all his writings does Cicero refer to Sextus as *praefectus*.

How does this date square with Sextus' being restored to his inheritance, V.'s other synchronisation here? It is clear from Cic. *Phil.* 13, the date of which was 20 March 43, that Pompey had by then not yet received the money which he had been promised as a result of Lepidus' and Antony's efforts in the previous year (cf. 13.10 'decreuistis tantam pecuniam Pompeio quantam ex bonis patriis in praedae dissipatione inimicus uictor redegisset', 12 'quod adulescenti . . . spopondistis . . . ut uideatur . . . in patrimonio suo collocatus'); nor had he received any of the actual property (cf. 13.10–12 'patebit . . . redimet . . . redimet . . . recuperabit . . . reddituros . . . retinere uero quis poterit clarissimo domino restituto? . . .' etc.). It may be that his appointment as *praefectus* coincided with a formal transfer of cash and/or property about which we have no evidence because it was never put into effect (Antony still occupied Pompey's house in 39 B.C., cf. 77.1, Dio 45.9.4); but I think the most we can safely say is that we have no evidence to contradict V.'s synchronisation of the two events. Indeed V. is supported by App. *BC* 3.4, although Appian misleadingly attributes the appointment as *praefectus* to the previous year, 44 B.C. (for a similar mistake by App. elsewhere see above, p. 132 n. 3).

73.3 ut praediximus   At 72.4 above.

in numerum . . . effecerat   'by receiving slaves and refugees into the ranks of his army he had created a large number of legions'. *modus* = 'number' occurs in a curious range of authors, e.g. Varr. *RR* 1.19.5, 1.19.1, *Il. Lat.* 904 'ingentemque modum . . . uirorum', Veg. *Mil.* 3.3, Eutrop. 2.6.1 'legiones . . . qui modus LX . . . armatorum milia efficiebat'. At 96.3 I was perhaps wrong to argue that *modus* there = 'type', although that is almost certainly its meaning in the passages of Virg. and Luc. which I quote there. For *effecerat* cf. such exprr. as *exercitum eff.* (Caes. *BC* 1.15.5, Liv. 23.25.6 etc.) and *magnum numerum militum . . . effecisse* (Cic. *Fam.* 11.10.3).

For Sextus' alleged retinue of slaves cf. Hor. *Epod.* 9.9–10, Dio 48.19.4. *seruitia*, commonly used = 'slaves' since Cic., is used of Menas and Menecrates (next n.) by Flor. 2.18.2.

Menam et Menecraten   Respectively *RE* 15.774–5 = Menas 3 (Modrze), *MRR* 2.389, 394, 405, 410 and *RE* 15.799–800 = Menekrates

15 (Münzer), *MRR* 2.384; also S. Treggiari, *Roman Freedmen during the Late Republic* (1969), 188–9, 265–6. V alone tells us that they were his father's *liberti*; and the fact that Sextus should use them for his own disreputable ends (cf. *per*), unlike his father who carried out his own good work himself, is, as Mr Seager points out to me, the first of the ironies of this passage.

rapto utebatur   The phrase is doubly ironic. Sextus was resorting to a way of life from which his father had sought to prevent others (cf. 32.6); and since such a life-style was conventionally imputed to foreigners (so E. Skard, *Sallust u.s. Vorgänger* (1956), 28), V. is perhaps also suggesting that Sextus' barbarousness is not restricted merely to *sermo* (1 above). Krause notes that Sextus scarcely needed to resort to piracy since he controlled Sicily, Sardinia and Corsica, from where Italy got much of its grain.

cum eum non depuderet ... infestare piraticis sceleribus   After *latrociniis ... infestato mari* above, the statement is of course repetitious; but V. is anxious to stress the περιπέτεια: Sextus employed the techniques of precisely those men whom his father had been empowered by the Gabinian law to eliminate (cf. 31.2). Cf. Manil. 1.920–1 'patrios armis imitatus filius hostes | aequora Pompeius cepit defensa parenti', Flor. 2.18.2 'o quam diuersus a patre! ille Cilicas exstinxerat, hic se piratica tuebatur', Luc. 6.420ff. For Sextus as a subject of declamation see Quint. 3.8.44, and for the popularity of pirates in general as a declamatory theme see Winterbottom, *Sen.*, General Index s.v. 'pirates'.

  If the text is right, *depuderet* is an otherwise unattested verb in which the prefix is intensive (as in *depudesco*) rather than negative (as in *dedecet*). On stylistic grounds E. J. Kenney has sought to question one of the two extant exs. of *depudesco*, viz. Ov. *Her.* 4.155, and in so doing also questioned *depuderet* here (*HSCP* 74 (1968), 175 and n. 23). He suggests V. perhaps wrote *dispuderet*, which is certainly attractive if the analogy of *dedecet* is worrying; but the presence of *depudesco* in the transmitted text of Ov. and in Ap. *Met.* 10.29 makes me hesitate to introduce changes here.

  For *armis ... ductu* cf. 115.4, where however the two are contrasted.

74–78   THE YEARS 41–39 B.C.

In this section the main historical narrative is treated in chh. 74 and 76.2–77, separated by a digression of events connected with Campania (75–76.1). Another digression (ch. 78) brings the section as a whole to a close and separates the present narrative from that which begins at 79.1. The technique, though characteristically Velleian (see above, p. 156), is perhaps not immediately obvious because each digression is introduced by a temporal phrase which at first sight appears to continue the main narrative (75.1 *per eadem tempora*, 78.1 *hoc tractu temporum*).

74 THE *BELLVM PERVSINVM* (41–40 B.C.)

74.1 Fractis Brutianis Cassianisque partibus   V. now resumes the narrative which he had suspended to elaborate on the character and career of Sextus Pompeius in ch. 73; with *substitit* we must therefore understand *in Macedonia, uel sim*. After Philippi Octavian and Antony made an unofficial pact dividing up the world between themselves and edging out their triumviral colleague Lepidus: see Syme, *RR* 206–7; *MRR* 2.358; Huzar 129–30.

For *fractis . . . partibus* cf. Sen. *D.* 11.9.8 and (diff. sense) Vell. 1.12.1;[1] for *obire prouincias* cf. 101.3n. *obiturus* expresses purpose (cf. 123.1 n.).

74.2 L. Antonius   For Mark Antony's brother, consul in 41 B.C., cf. *RE* 1.2.2585–90 = Antonius 23 (Klebs); *MRR* 2.370–1, 381. Note that V., as often, sharpens his portrait by alliteration and assonance: ' *cons*ul *ui*tiorum . . . *cons*ors sed *ui*rtutum . . . expers '; Acidalius wished to sharpen it further by reading *exsors*, but *uirtutum expers* is a recognised phrase (Cic. *De Or.* 3.55, *Fin.* 3.11, Virg. *Aen.* 10.752). Acidalius also wished to understand *interdum* as = *interim*, 'for the moment'; but this meaning, while perhaps supported by 82.4, seems not to be found until considerably later than V. (cf. *TLL* 7.1.2181.76ff.). Antony is thus being described as a 'mixed' character (cf. 88.2n.), a man of vices and occasional virtues.

apud ueteranos criminatus Caesarem   According to App. *BC* 5.19, L. Antonius joined himself to Octavian so that the latter should not enjoy too much favour with the troops, and then, on a pretext, took himself off to Mark Antony's colonies καὶ τὸν Καίσαρα τῷ στρατῷ διέβαλλεν ἐς ἀπιστίαν πρὸς ᾿Αντώνιον. See also Dio 48.6–8.

For *criminari apud* cf. *TLL* 4.1198.19ff.

qui instante diuisione praediorum . . . agros amiserant   On a matter as contentious as the redistribution of land, Ruhnken argued, V. is unlikely to have expressed either approval or disapproval;[2] Ruhnken therefore dismissed both the paradosis *iuste* and Lipsius' *iniuste* (or *-ta*), and himself proposed *instituta*, which provides a past part. parallel to *nominatis*. But is a past part. required here? Professor Goodyear writes to me as follows. 'The land distribution is at an early stage: Oct. returns after Philippi to carry it out, and finds it a thankless task. Announcements were made about the areas to be confiscated before the land was actually divided up and taken over by veterans: that is, I think, the picture envisaged in the *Dirae*, a "locus classicus" on this matter. Those whose land

---

[1] Compare also Hor. *C.* 2.7.11 ' cum fracta uirtus ' (of Philippi).

[2] Krause suggested that Ruhnken's objections would be met if Vascosanus' *iusta* = *satis ampla* (' liberal '); and indeed they would also be met if *iusta* = ' agreed ' (sc. by the pact between Oct. and Ant.). Yet neither of these meanings seems at all natural in the context.

was on the list of confiscated areas had, *de iure* at least, if not *de facto*, lost their property before the new owners arrived in Oct.'s train. One could get a perfect balance in sense with *nominatis* by a very small change, *instante* (*instāte*) for *iuste*. The division now being imminent and the new colonies named, the refugees had moved out.' I find this argument persuasive and have therefore printed *instante*, which had also occurred to E. Thomas.

Ruhnken also suggested *coloniis* for *colonis*; either word seems to me possible (compare App. *BC* 5.12 καταλέγοντι δ' αὐτῷ τὸν στρατὸν ἐς τὰς ἀποικίας with Dio 48.2.3 τήν τε χώραν . . . κατανεῖμαι), but *coloniis* marginally more suited to the context.

For the land distribution in general cf. Brunt, *IM* 328ff.

ad arma conciens magnum exercitum conflauerat The former phrase is Livian (31.3.5, 40.9, cf. 10.21.2 *in*), the latter Ciceronian (*Sull.* 33, *Phil.* 4.15; also Flor. 2.7.10). For *ad arma* in particular cf. Nisbet–Hubbard on Hor. *C.* 1.35.15. The size of the 'large army' is almost impossible to determine (Brunt, *IM* 495–6).

74.3 Fuluia *RE* 7.1.281–4 = Fuluius 113 (Münzer). This 'maligned lady' (Syme, *Sall.* 135 n. 56, cf. *RR* 208 and n. 1) was of course *M.* Antonius' wife.[1] The point of *nihil muliebre praeter corpus gerens*, below, seems to be that she resembled a man in every respect but her appearance (cf. Flor. 2.16.2 'Fuluia tum gladio cincta uirilis militiae'); she was therefore like Sempronia, 'quae multa saepe uirilis audaciae facinora conmiserat' (Sall. *C.* 25.1).

omnia armis tumultuque miscebat *omnia miscere*, with or without an accompanying abl. instr., is usually used in a context of revolution and is often found in the historians: see Landgraf on Cic. *Rosc.* 91, Vretska on [Sall.] *Ep. Caes.* 2.6.1, *TLL* 8.1094.29ff. For *tumultu* cf. Sall. *J.* 12.5, Virg. *Aen.* 2.487. An alternative phrase is *summa imis miscere* at 2.2.3, for which cf. Keller–Holder and Nisbet–Hubbard on Hor. *C.* 1.34.12.

For *belli sedem*, below, cf. Heubner on Tac. *H.* 1.65.2 (on 2.19.1 for *bello s.*).

Plancus . . . spem magis ostenderat auxilii quam opem ferebat Antonio V. consistently treats Plancus with irony or sarcasm (cf. 63.3nn., 83.1nn., 95.3n) and here he has mischievously separated the two terms *spem* and *opem* which are elsewhere almost invariably coordinated (as Plaut. *Capt.* 445, 517, *Rud.* 1145, Sall. *J.* 107.4, 114.4, Liv. 5.40.2, Front. p. 117 Naber = p. 112 van den Hout, Dictys 2.44). Cf. Cic. *Lig.* 30 'tu idem fer opem qui spem dedisti'. The *spes* which Plancus held out to

---

[1] A recent treatment of her is apparently to be found in B. Kreck, *Untersuchungen zur politischen und sozialen Rolle der Frau in der späten röm. Republik* (diss. Marburg, 1975), 152ff., which I have not seen.

Antonius is a reference to the fire signals at Fulginium, a stronghold some
distance from Perusia; those besieged in Perusia took heart at the sight of
the fires, unaware that Plancus had advised that no action should be
taken to aid them (App. *BC* 5.35).

Antonianarum partium, used of Mark Antony's followers at 84.2, is here
likely to refer to those of both brothers since Lucius professed to be fighting on his brother's behalf (Syme, *RR* 211); but the extent to which the
triumvir sympathised with his brother was probably minimal (E. Gabba,
HSCP 75 (1971), 149–50, whose paper is one of the latest studies of the
Perusine war).[1]

74.4 Perusiam expugnauit V. takes two words to deal with the
winter-long siege which became a byword for cruelty. By being able to
combine his own personal *fortuna* with *uirtus* Oct. is here depicted as the
ideal general, like Caesar before him and Tiberius afterwards (cf. 97.4n).
For *usus . . . fortuna sua*, above, cf. Liv. 25.35–1, 29.29.5, Curt. 7.9.1
(F.); *inuiolatum dimisit*, below, has a legal flavour; cf. Liv. 2.12.14 'iure
belli liberum te intactum inuiolatumque hinc dimitto'; *TLL*
5.1.1212.57ff.

in Perusinos . . . saeuitum For the immediate aftermath of the siege
cf. Syme, *RR* 211–12; Scott 27–8.

Macedonicus The anecdote about Cestius Macedonicus (*RE*
3.2.2007 = Cestius 12 (Groag)) is also at App. *BC* 5.49. For *subicere ignem*
cf. e.g. Cic. *Verr.* 1.69, *Rab. Post.* 13, Liv. 31.17.8; *subicere facem* is at 48.3.

75–76.1 CAMPANIAN CONNECTIONS (40 B.C.)

Taking advantage of Macedonicus' suicide which brought the Perusine
war to a dramatic end, V. now suspends his narrative of Plancus, Fulvia
and *Antonium inuiolatum* to deal with Campanian events. He resumes the
main narrative at 76.2, where the wording (*inuiolatam . . . Fuluiam
Plancumque*) echoes that of ch. 74 (ring composition).

For V. the present digression is important not only because it introduces three public figures whom he greatly admired (the emperor
Tiberius and his parents), but also because it provides an opportunity to
describe the heroic suicide of his own grandfather. 'Velleius has considerable pride of family and seizes any reasonable opportunity to advertise it
in his historical work . . . It would seem perverse to complain about his
lack of reticence, when the result is that we are unusually well informed on
his personal and family background and on his place in Roman society'
(Sumner 258).

---

[1] I have not seen P. Wallmann, 'Untersuchungen zu militärischen
Problemen des Perusinischen Krieges', *Talanta* 6 (1974), 58–91.

75.1 Per eadem tempora The series of tenses *exarserat–perdiderant–ciebat* implies that the Campanian war had been started by the dispossessed during the siege of Perusia and that it was subsequently kept alive by Ti. Claudius Nero, who managed to escape from Perusia after the end of the siege and take charge of a garrison in Naples (Suet. *Tib.* 4.2, Dio 48.15.3). There is a similar series of tenses at 54.2 'ingens partium eius fauor bellum excitauerat Africum, quod ciebat rex Iuba'.

For *exarserat* cf. 2.1.3, 48.1, 49.1, 104.2; *TLL* 2.1833.21ff.

qui perdiderant agros It has been suggested that V. means those 'who had been assigned lands under the law of 59' (Brunt, *IM* 317) or 'long-established residents with old ties with the family [of Nero]' (E. Rawson, 'More on the *clientelae* of the patrician Claudii', *Historia* 26 (1977), 345); but V.'s clause need not be restricted to either group since the dispossession was no doubt general. For *professus . . . patrocinium* cf. Liv. 6.15.8.

Ti. Claudius Nero He was praetor in 42, propraetor in 41/40, and pontifex in 46–33: see *MRR* 2.303, 359, 373, 381; also 94.1n. For *bellum ciere* cf. 129.3n.

magni uir animi doctissimique ingenii Ruhnken was the first of numerous scholars to object to *doctissimi*, on the grounds that Nero's intellectual accomplishment is not elsewhere attested. Yet this kind of detail is exactly what we should expect from V., with whose family Nero had such close ties. For *doct. ingenium* cf. Vitr. 10 *praef.* 3; F. quotes Mart. 9.77.4 'docto pectore'.

aduentu Caesaris sepultum atque discussum est In passages which V. clearly imitates (so Ruhnken) Cicero had praised Pompey for the effectiveness of his mere arrival on the scene of conflict: *Leg. Man.* 13 'cuius aduentu ipso atque nomine . . . impetus hostium repressos esse', 30 'quod bellum eius aduentu sublatum ac sepultum est'. The topos, which also occurs at 50.4, *Pan. Lat.* 4.25.3, 6.5.2, 6.19.4, 8.6.1, is closely related to those discussed at 92.2n., 94.4n., 103.1–4nn.

For *bellum sepultum* cf. 129.4n.; for *b. discussum* cf. Val. Max. 5.6 *ext.* 1.

75.2 quis . . . satis mirari queat? For variations on this formula cf. e.g. 1.16.2, Cic. *Fin.* 4.39, *Pan. Lat.* 3.12.1, 4.11.1, 9.6.1. *rerum . . . casus* is not 'an uncommon phrase' (E. Fraenkel, *JRS* 56 (1966), 150), cf. *TLL* 3.582.29ff.; and for *humanarum* cf. Tac. *H.* 1.3.2 'rerum humanarum casus'. For *dubios . . . casus* cf. Heubner on Tac. *H.* 3.66.3.

75.3 Liuia For her, her father, and V.'s fondness for her cf. 94.1n., 130.5n. The past tense *uidimus* is no doubt conditioned by the fact that Augustus was dead: it need not necessarily imply that when V. wrote this passage Livia was also dead. She had however died (in A.D. 29) by the time V. wrote 130.5.

Livia married Octavian in 38 B.C. (79.2n.) and was called *sacerdos diui Augusti* and Iulia Augusta after his death in A.D. 14; the latter nomenclature, which V. uses at 71.3, resulted from her having been adopted by Augustus as his *filia* in his will: see Dio 56.46.1, Tac. *A.* 1.14.1-2; Weber 57* n. 231, 92* n. 427; M. Grant, *Aspects of the Principate of Tiberius* (1950), esp. 116-18. To describe Augustus' death V. uses the expr. *ad deos* because, like Hercules of whom he uses the same expr. at 1.2.1 (cf. Cic. *TD* 1.32), the emperor became a god after his death (cf. 123.2n., 126.1n.). I can however find no parallel for *transgressus*.

fugiens . . . Caesaris arma, ⟨mi⟩nus bimum hunc Ti. Caesarem . . . gestans sinu Ruhnken chose to read *Caesaris manus, bimum*: the conceit of Livia fleeing from the grasp of her future husband is admittedly pleasing, but *arma* is firmly established in the paradosis and makes good sense; Ruhnken's explanation of how the alleged error occurred is, in addition, highly implausible. M. C. Gertz and (independently) Ellis kept the conceit by suggesting *arma ⟨ac ma⟩nus* ('armed grasp'):[1] certainly the two nouns are often combined (as at 115.4, see n.), but the mistake is less easy to suppose than if V. had written *arma manus*, and such an *asyndeton bimembre* is not, I think, in V.'s manner (cf. 100.3n., 125.5n.); Ellis was, in addition, no doubt led to the conjecture by an erroneous superscript in A. Vossius suggested *arma, ⟨mi⟩nus*: the alleged haplography is almost as easy as *arma manus*, and although we miss the conceit of Caesar's grasp, we gain the extra poignancy of Tiberius' being less than two years old; it does in fact diminish the drama of the episode to have the infant older than he was, and Tiberius' second birthday did not occur until 16 Nov. 40. Vossius' is thus the only conjecture which combines plausibility, pathos and precision. For *minus* used in this way cf. 1.17.1, 82.2; *OLD* s.v. 2a. For similar reflections on the ironies of Livia's career see Dio 48.15.4 (esp. ὥστε καὶ τοῦτο ἐν τοῖς παραδοξοτάτοις συμβῆναι, with which cf. 2 above).

uindicem . . . filium For *uindex* cf. 104.2n.; for Augustus' adoption of Tiberius in A.D. 4 cf. *TN* 132-6. *hunc*, above, = 'the present', as 1.13.5, 33.4, 43.4, 72.3, Catull. 24.2, Hor. *S.* 1.3.30, Cic. *Att.* 13.6.4, Liv. 1.56.2, 25.40.2 (reading *huius*). For *occultaretur fuga*, below, cf. Caes. *BG* 1.27.4 (F.).

76.1 Quod alieno testimonium redderem, [in] eo non fraudabo auum meum 'I will not deprive my own grandfather of a tribute which I would pay to someone else's'. The statement is nothing less than

---

[1] Gertz's suggestion is in his *Studia critica in Senecae Dial.* (1874), 149n. For the record, Burer's note here reads: 'exemp. uet. sic habet, ut legendum existimem, Caesaris arma, cuius bimum . . .'

the truth, cf. 2.12.6 'non tamen huius consulatus fraudetur gloria', 92.1 'praeclarum . . . factum . . . ne fraudetur memoria' (and n.), 120.3 'reddatur uerum L. Asprenati testimonium'. V. is in fact always keen to mention heroic deaths (cf. 87.1nn.) or write *epitaphia* (*TN* 43) or otherwise dispense praise where he thinks it is due (cf. 116.1–5nn.).

For C. Velleius Paterculus, V.'s paternal grandfather, cf. Sumner 262–4n; Nicolet 2.1065–6, no. 377; E. Rawson (next n. but one).

honoratissimo . . . lectus Under the *lex Pompeia de ui* of 52 B.C. Pompey established a board of 360 judges whose good character was supposed to be beyond question (Ascon. 38C 'numquam neque clariores uiros neque sanctiores') and whose purpose was to deal with Milo's murder of Clodius and subsequent disturbances (see Nicolet 1.620–2 for discussion). By belonging to this board C. Velleius was clearly reckoned 'one of the leading men of the equestrian order at that time' (Sumner 263).

V. here also tells us that his paternal grandfather had been *praefectus fabrum* to Pompey, Brutus and Ti. Claudius Nero. As Sumner (262) has observed, it is perhaps 'more than coincidence' that one Numerius Magius was also *praefectus fabrum* to Pompey in 49 B.C. (*MRR* 2.265, 271), since V. was related to the Magii (cf. the stemma in Wiseman 271) and may have been descended from this particular member of the family. Indeed it may be that N. Magius was V.'s maternal grandfather, as Dihle (639) suggests; but 'since we do not know at what stage the Velleii married into the Magii . . ., it would be impossible to decide whether the fact that both N. Magius and C. Velleius were *praefecti fabrum* of Pompeius resulted from, or led to, a marriage connection (if any)' (Sumner 262 n. 35). On the importance of the office of *praef. fabrum* at this period see Syme, *RR* 355–6.

uir nulli secundus in Campania That these words should be taken together and not separated by a comma after *secundus*, as in all editions, was rightly suggested by E. Rawson, *Historia* 26 (1977), 345–6. *nulli secundus* and equivalent phrases in both Latin and Greek seem always to be found with some qualifying word or phrase: cf. e.g. 2.11.1 'Q. Metellum, nulli secundum saeculi sui', Virg. *Aen.* 11.441 'haud ulli ueterum uirtute secundus', Curt. 5.10.3 'regio . . . armis uirisque et spatio locorum nulli earum gentium secunda', Sil. 7.54–5 'nulli quisquam uirtute secundus', 11.66 'nullique furore secundus', Stat. *Theb.* 2.573–4 'nec uertere cuiquam | frena secundus Halys', Soph. *Phil.* 181, Plato, *Tim.* 20A, Plb. 3.98.2, 4.8.2. In particular V. may have had in mind the description of Decius Magius, his own maternal ancestor (cf. 2.16.2), given by Livy at 23.10.7 'nulli Campanorum secundus'. If this is correct, it follows that, as Rawson says, V.'s paternal ancestors were Campanian also.

grauis ... corpore cum comes esse non posset This was the reason for C. Velleius' suicide, not the fact that 'all was lost' (Syme, *RR* 383).

There can be little doubt that Aldus' combination of the readings of B and PA, printed here, is correct. Though there are other possibilities, it is likely that (M) read both *cum* and *comes* and that (R) mistakenly omitted *comes* and B, when transcribing it from (M), mistakenly omitted to transcribe *cum* as well.

grauis corpore is unusual, but cf. Colum. 7.12.7 and esp. Plin. *Ep.* 6.20.12 'et annis et corpore grauem'; F. quotes Liv. 44.4.10 'praegrauis corpore'.

76.2–4 POLLIO'S EXPLOITS AND THE PEACE OF BRUNDISIUM (40 B.C.)

76.2 inuiolatam The attraction of the adj. into the gender of the nearest noun is not unusual (cf. 111.1n.) but is perhaps intended to be ironical in the case of Plancus, *muliebris fugae comes*.

nam Pollio Asinius ... As at 71.3 and 84.2 (see n.) *nam* explains the difference between items which are apparently similar: Pollio was an Antonian no less than Fulvia and Plancus, but he continued the struggle in person while they were forced by Oct. into exile.

The section on Pollio, which begins here, is noteworthy for its enthusiasm (*magnis speciosisque rebus*), unique detail (Altinum), defensive tone (3n., below) and relative length. Elsewhere too V. praises Pollio (most unexpectedly at 73.2: see n.) and appears to have special knowledge of his activities (86.3n.). It is therefore tempting to suppose that these passages derive, whether directly or not, from Pollio's histories. The matter is of course incapable of proof, but it is interesting to recall that in the opinion of E. Gabba Appian's history of the civil war, beginning with the Gracchi and continuing through the Social War, is based principally on Pollio's lost histories – and the nearest parallel to Appian's view of this whole period is acknowledged to be V. himself (see *Appiano e la storia delle guerre civili* (1956), esp. 47 n. 1; 'Italia e Roma nella "Storia" di Vell. Pat.', *Critica Storica* 1 (1962), 1ff.). It must be admitted, however, that Gabba's thesis has not found general acceptance (cf. e.g. E. Badian, *CR* 8 (1958), 159–62).

consiliis suis defectum [ac] fide data iunxit Antonio Since most edd. have accepted Gelenius' *illectum*, they have understood *consiliis suis* as referring to Pollio and *fide data* as an abl. instr.: 'he won Domitius over to the cause of A. by his counsel and by the pledge of immunity' (Shipley). Yet Damsté pointed out that at 72.3, to which *praediximus* (immediately above) refers, the phrase *consilia sua* is used of Domitius himself. Since V. is invariably precise with his cross-references, this makes it highly likely that *consiliis suis* is used also of Domitius here. On this view *illectum* is impossible, and Damsté himself conjectured *eiectum*: ‘Pollion le fit changer d’avis’ (H–W). I can however find no parallel for this use of the verb, and I think *defectum* is a more likely possibility, ‘having failed in his plans’: for the point cf. Dio 48.16.2 ὁ γὰρ Δομίτιος ἀπογνοὺς μηκέτι καθ’ ἑαυτὸν ἰσχύσειν, and for the expr. compare 120.5, Cic. *Clu.* 184, Val. Max. 3.1 *ext.* 1 ‘suo consilio defectus’.

What, then, of *ac fide data*? If we retain *ac*, the word will appear to link *fide data* with *consiliis suis* and suggest that both phrases are dependent on *defectum* (‘having failed in his plans and in the pledge he had given’); but hitherto no reference has been made to any pledge of Domitius’. If we delete *ac* (as Cludius proposed even when accepting Gelenius’ *illectum*), the resulting abl. abs. will refer to Pollio and go neatly with *iunxit Antonio* (‘after Dom. had failed in his own plans, Pollio issued a pledge and joined him to Antony’). I have therefore followed Cludius. For Domitius see further 72.3n.

76.3 non minus . . . esse conlatum Bosworth (463) rightly remarks that V.’s treatment of Pollio’s activities here ‘seems at least partially aimed at exculpating him from Antony’s charges of ingratitude’. The charges were presumably those which Antony made much later and to which Pollio replied in his pamphlet *contra maledicta Antonii* (mentioned by Charisius, p. 100.23 B). But Bosworth is wrong to add that V. presents the overtures to Domitius as ‘Pollio’s greatest service to Antony’ and that ‘this passage anticipates the famous *dictum* of 32 B.C.’: the former statement is not supported by the text here, and Bosworth has in my opinion misinterpreted the famous *dictum* (see 86.3n.).

V. emphasises the reciprocity of the two men by polyptoton, a form of paronomasia ‘quod uersatur in casuum commutatione aut unius aut plurium nominum’ (*Rhet. Herenn.* 4.30–1); Quintilian’s name for it is *antimetabole* (9.3.86). See Lausberg 2.119–23 §§ 643–7 and 219–21 § 801. *conferre* is of course the normal word for bestowing *beneficia*, cf. e.g. 53.1.

praeparatusque . . . Caesaris habuit belli metum Scholars have questioned *praeparatus* on the grounds that it is unusual; yet the word occurs at Gell. 10.11.7 ‘in praeparatu rei rusticae’, and I can see no real reason to change it. For *habere metum* cf. *TLL* 6.3.2404. 40–1.

pax circa Brundusium composita The date was late Sept. or early Oct. 40 B.C.: see Gabba on App. *BC* 5.64 (273). The western provinces were placed under Octavian’s control, Antony kept control of all provinces east of Scodra along the line of the R. Drin, and Lepidus continued in Africa. For reasons which will become clear later (at 78.2n.) I think it is important to emphasise the reconciliatory moves which Octavian and Antony made at this time. Antony revealed to Oct. the treachery of Salvi-

dienus Rufus (next n.), Oct. gave his sister Octavia to Antony in marriage
(78.1n.); coins were issued symbolising *concordia* (*RRC* 1.532–3, no. 529;
2.743; Weinstock 261ff.), both men shared the right to levy troops in Italy
(Plut. *Ant.* 30.2, App. *BC* 5.65, Dio 48.28.4), and both agreed on a joint
plan to attack Sextus Pompeius (Dio 48.29.1; Huzar 138). The atmosphere of this period, with its sense of hope and confidence as expressed in
Virg. *Ecl.* 4, is well described by DuQuesnay 34ff.

**76.4 per quae tempora Rufi Saluidieni ... consilia patefacta
sunt** Antony revealed the plans to Oct. on the occasion of the Peace of
Brundisium (App. *BC* 5.66). For the *nouus homo* Q. Salvidienus Rufus cf.
RE 1A.2.2019–21 = Salvidienus 4 (Münzer); Wiseman 258 no. 374;
Nicolet 2.1010–11 no. 310; D. R. Shackleton Bailey, *Two Studies in Roman
Nomenclature* (1976), 64 and 82; *MRR* 2.374, 383; Syme, *RR* 220 n. 6 ('We
possess only the "official version" of Salvidienus' treason'). The man's
obscure origins are mentioned also by Suet. *Aug.* 66.1 and Dio 48.33.2–3.
For the expr. *obscurissimis initiis*, below, cf. Tac. *A.* 3.66.3 (Fletcher).

parum habebat ... nisi in id ascendisset 'The use of a negative
conditional sentence after negative expressions like 'parum est' and the
like, where the strictly logical sequence of thought would rather require
an adversative coordinate clause, is peculiarly idiomatic' (Gudeman in
his American edn (1894) of Tac. *D.* 36.7, quoting *inter al.* Cic. *Rosc.* 49
(and Landgraf's n.), *Verr.* 5.157, Sen. *Ep.* 86.13, 89.20; the n. is slightly
modified in his German edn (²1914)). The meaning is: 'was not satisfied
with . . ., but would even have mounted to such a height . . .' (Watson).
parum habere is not common but cf. Sall. *J.* 31.9, Liv. 42.3.6, Val. Max.
5.1.3, and Krause quotes Lact. *Diu. Inst.* 5.9.10.

**proximus a Cn. Pompeio ipsoque Caesare ex equestri ordine
consul creatus esse** Salvidienus was designated consul for 39 B.C. (see
RRC 1.101; 528–9 no. 523; 743); for *proximus (-e) a,* = 'next after', cf.
124.4n. As Nicolet (2.986 n. 2) points out, V.'s statement is not absolutely
precise since *ex equestri ordine* could be used of every equestrian *nouus homo*
who became consul; V.'s statement 'signifie donc non pas seulement qu'il
était d'origine équestre, mais qu'il était passé *directement* de l'ordre
équestre au consulat, comme Pompée et Octave' (2.1010 n. 2 [on p.
1011], my italics). Even so, the only exact parallel for Salvidienus is
Pompey, whose rise from *eques* direct to consul was proverbial (cf. Vell.
30.2 'adhuc eques Romanus ante diem quam consulatum iniret'; Nicolet
2.986); Octavian was adlected into the senate on 1 Jan. 43 B.C. (*RG* 1.2)
and only became consul in August of that year after the *consules ordinarii*
(Hirtius and Pansa) had been killed (cf. 65.2); but V.'s comparison is not
unreasonable since Oct.'s time as a senator had been so short, and in any
case I do not think he had had an opportunity even to take up his seat.

For *ex equestri ordine consul* cf. 51.3 'ex priuato consularis' (*ex eq. ord.* is itself a common expr., e.g. Liv. 4.13.1, Suet. *Aug.* 63.2). For *summa*, above, cf. 60.2n.; for *infra se . . . uideret*, below, cf. Sen. *Thy.* 366 'infra se uidet omnia' (Ruhnken) (a similar idea at Vell. 2.15.2 'fastigium per quod homines . . . fastidire posset').

77 THE PEACE OF MISENUM (39 B.C.)

77.1 quem grauis urebat . . . annona The adj. seems to indicate that *annona* here, as at 126.3, = 'price of corn': for the price rise itself cf. App. *BC* 5.67, and for the expr. cf. Plaut. *Stich.* 632, *Bell. Afr.* 24.3, Suet. *Aug.* 25.2, *Vir. Ill.* 19.2. At first sight the adj. might also seem to support Cludius' *urgebat*, but cf. Hor. *Epist.* 1.13.6 'si te forte meae grauis uret sarcina chartae' and note that 'the *annona* . . . attracted colourful expressions' (Goodyear on Tac. *A.* 2.87, q.v.). For *consensus* as the subject of a verb, above, cf. 91.1n.; the phrase *expostulante populo* occurs on inscriptions (*CIL* 8.958, 11034, 12453). For *infesto mari* cf. 73.2n.

cum Pompeio quoque . . . pax inita Scholars place the Peace of Misenum in the first half of 39 B.C.: see e.g. Gabba on App. *BC* 5.71 (297) (intro.), Huzar 140–1. For the terms of the Peace see e.g. *MRR* 2.386–7.

Caesaremque et Antonium If the text is right (and no one has questioned it), this is the only indisputable ex. of *-que et* in V.: I think there is another ex. at 89.4 (see n.), and 2.3.1 is ambiguous but likely (' P. Scipio Nasica . . . nepos . . . filius . . . pronepos autem . . . priuatusque et togatus'). The usage occurs in Sall. *J.* (26.1, 55.1, 76.6, 91.2), Livy (cf. Ogilvie on 1.43.2, but incorrect on details) and Tacitus (cf. Goodyear on *A.* 1.4.1); also in poetry (D. O. Ross, *Style and Tradition in Catullus* (1969), 65–7; Brink on Hor. *AP* 196, 214, 444; K–S 2.37c). The precise tone of the usage is often difficult to catch; here Sextus is playing host to the very men who had been trying to eliminate him, and *-que et* is perhaps designed to underline the irony of the situation: Sextus suddenly had both his former enemies together under one roof.

Sextus' pun on 'Carinae' is also related in Flor. 2.18.3, Dio 48.38.2–3, *Vir. Ill.* 84.3, Plut. *Ant.* 32.3. For *haud absurde* cf. 83.3n.

77.2 animus inquies The same phrase was apparently used by Livy of himself in a preface now lost (fr. 68 Weiss. = Plin. *NH praef.* 16), though elsewhere he prefers the form *inquietus*; cf. also Sen. *D.* 9.2.9 and Just. 44.2.5. *ingenium inq.* is at Sall. *H.* 1.7, *inquies animi* ibid. 4.55, and *inquies animo* at Tac. *A.* 16.14.1. For *in (foedere) . . . manere* cf. Liv. 4.7.4.

id unum . . . salutare aduentu suo patriae attulit Ruhnken deleted *aduentu suo* on the strange grounds that Sextus did not come to Italy; he argued that the phrase was interpolated from 3 below (and cf.

COMMENTARY 2.77.3

79.1n., where a similar suggestion is supported). Yet Sextus certainly attended the meeting at Misenum, and since V. says at 78.1 that he returned to Sicily afterwards, it is quite natural (as Haupt 1.270 observes) that V. should think of him as arriving here. Halm conjectured *conuentu*, presumably on the grounds that it was Sextus' agreement rather than his arrival which was beneficial; yet *conuentus* = *conuentum* is rare (cf. *OLD* s.v.). For the pleonasm *unum tantummodo* cf. 117.1n.

For Sextus' service in offering asylum to refugees see esp. App. *BC* 5.143.

ex diuersis causis The 'various reasons' were adumbrated at 72.5. For *salutem pactus est* + dat., below, cf. Sen. *Suas.* 1.7.

77.3 Neronem Claudium . . . Titium According to Syme, V.'s list is 'partial in every sense of the term' (*RR* 227 and n. 1): the Peace of Misenum 'brought . . . to Octavianus an accidental but delayed advantage – prominent Republicans now returned to Rome, nobles of ancient family or municipal aristocrats. Here were allies to be courted.' For Ti. Claudius Nero cf. 75.1n., 94.1n.; for M. Iunius Silanus cf. *RE* 10.1.1095–6 = Iunius 172, cf. 171 (Münzer); *MRR* 2.353, 412, 416, 426; Syme, *RR* 551 (index); for Sentius Saturninus cf. 88.2n., 92.1n., 105.1n.; for L. Arruntius cf. *RE* 2.1.1262 = Arruntius 7 (v. Rohden); *MRR* 2.421; Syme, *RR* 537 (index); for M. Titius cf. 79.5n. Titius is the odd man out since in V.'s own terms he hardly qualifies as a *clarissimus uir* (cf. 83.2); but V. has perhaps added his name to the list to enhance the irony of 79.5–6, where Sextus is murdered by the very man whom he had saved (see n.).

aduentu suo I.e. in 42/41, cf. 72.4 (n.). For Murcus himself cf. 69.2n.

P. Thomas (1921) emended *celeberrimae*, below, to *celerrime*; but both Greek and Roman writers often attach appreciatory epithets to words like 'fleet' or 'ships' (e.g. 79.2 'speciosissima classe', Hom. *Od.* 13.149, 175; Sall. *H.* 4.69.13, Val. Max. 8.1 *abs.* 4, *Pan. Lat.* 10.12.3), and in any case, when Murcus brought over the survivors of Philippi, he thereby lent importance to Sextus' otherwise rather unimpressive following. This last point sharpens the irony of Menas' and Menecrates' attack on such a truly distinguished man (*talem uirum*), and Sextus, *libertorum suorum libertus* (73.1), has no more sense than to listen to them.

For *uires . . . duplicauerat* cf. *TLL* 5.1.2279.54–6; for *insimulatum falsis crimin(ation)ibus* cf. *TLL* 7.1.1912.13–16; for *fastidire* + double accus. cf. *TLL* 6.1.311.38–41. For Menas and Menecrates cf. 73.3n.

78 A SURVEY OF OTHER EVENTS (40–39/38 B.C.)

78.1 Hoc tractu temporum For the expr. cf. 94.1n.; for the nature of the section which it here introduces, see above, p. 179. Antony married Octavia towards the end of 40 B.C. after the Peace of Brundisium: see *MRR* 2.379 with full refs.

190

quas †magnis momentis† Labienus ... concusserat   This is Quintus, son of the T. Labienus mentioned at 40.4 and 55.4; cf. *RE* 12.1.258–60 = Labienus 5 (Münzer); *MRR* 2.363–4. His activity (fully described by Dio 48.24.4ff.) antedates the Peace of Brundisium. The text of this passage is problematic. Since *concutere* is regularly used with such nouns as *bello, tumultu* etc. (*TLL* 8.1393.59ff.), we might naturally expect the paradosis to mean 'with great disturbances'; yet despite Laurent, who compared 1.3.1 'Graecia maximis concussa est motibus' (cf. Curt. 4.14.20), *momentum* seems incapable of meaning 'disturbance'. One might suggest reading *motibus* here, but it is hard to see how the corruption would have arisen. Ruhnken proposed *mo⟨li⟩mentis*, 'with great efforts', but the plural use is extremely rare and does not occur before Fronto (*TLL* s.v.). According to Ellis, G. A. Koch defended the paradosis, but I do not know on what grounds: *momentum* can = 'effort' but this meaning seems restricted to the singular use and mainly to Livy (cf. *TLL* 8.1393.59ff.). Prof. Goodyear thinks V. may have written *magna moliens*: this is indeed attractive (cf. 2.14.1 'quod cum moliens reuertisset', 26.1 'multa . . . molitus', 129.2 'noua molientem'), but again it is hard to see how the corruption might have arisen. I have therefore obelised.

perducto eorum exercitu in Syriam   'having led their [the Parthians'] army right into Syria'. I have accepted Arntzenius' *perducto*: *per-* and *pro-* are often confused (cf. 128.4n.; W. M. Lindsay, *Notae Latinae* (1915), 175), and *producere* is a technical verb whose meaning is inappropriate here (cf. 85.1n.).

interfectoque legato Antonii   Viz. L. Decidius Saxa, who was evidently killed early in 40 B.C.: cf. *RE* 4.2.2271–2 = Decidius 4 (Münzer); *MRR* 2.365, 376, 384.

uirtute et ductu Ventidii   For P. Ventidus Bassus cf. 63.3n.; his exploits evidently lasted the two years 39/38 B.C. (cf. *MRR* 2.388, 393), in the latter of which he was awarded the triumph to which V. refers at 65.3. For *uirtus + ductus* cf. *SHA Gall.* 7.3.

celeberrimoque iuuenum Pacoro   For him cf. *RE* 18.2.2437–8 = Pacorus 1 (J. Miller); he was the son of King Orodes II (46.4n.), who had taken possession of the Roman standards after Carrhae (cf. 91.1). *celeberrimo* expresses not appreciation but plain fact: 'the most notable of their young men'.

78.2 interim Caesar per haec tempora   Such temporal pleonasm is found elsewhere in V. (2.4.1 'interim, dum haec . . . geruntur', 23.3 'ac deinde post', cf. 2.17.3, 122.2) and in other authors too (cf. E. Lindholm, *Stilistische Studien* (1931), 30–1; L–H–S 525). For the period which V. has in mind, cf. next n.

crebris in Illyrico Dalmatiaque expeditionibus   This phrase raises a number of difficult problems. It is attested by numerous other sources that Octavian campaigned in Illyricum in 35–33 B.C. (see *MRR* 2.407, 411, 415), and Wilkes has understandably assumed (47–58) that these are the campaigns to which V. refers here. It is however clear from *interim . . . per haec tempora* above and from *eadem tempestate* at 3 below that V. explicitly synchronises Octavian's campaigns with the actions of Ventidius and Calvinus, i.e. 39/38 B.C. This earlier period is thus, as W. Schmitthenner has rightly remarked, 'durch die chronologische Verknüpfung unbezweifelbar' ('Octavians militärische Unternehmungen in den Jahren 35–33 v. Chr.', *Historia* 7 (1958), 197 n. 5). Although no other source mentions a personal campaign by Oct. in Illyricum as early as this (Appian merely says that in 39 Octavian went to Gaul; *BC* 5.75), it is unlikely that V. has made a mistake since Appian later (5.80) produces the tantalising statement that in 38 B.C. Octavian recalled a 'large army' from Illyricum, the clear implication being that there had been military activity in the area. This implication may be corroborated as follows.

It is extremely interesting to note that V.'s sequence of events in the present chapter (Ventidius–Illyricum/Dalmatia–Calvinus) is precisely paralleled by Dio's account of 39 B.C. (48.39.2–42.2), except that Dio attributes the campaigns in Illyricum not to Octavian but to *Pollio* (48.41.7). Bosworth was persuaded by this striking coincidence of evidence to conclude that the campaigns of 39 B.C. in Illyricum were fought by Pollio on behalf of Octavian (467). Now such a conclusion makes good sense of the correspondence between V. and Dio since it was conventional to ascribe a subordinate's success to his commander-in-chief (cf. 96.2n.).[1] It also makes good sense of Appian's two statements, mentioned in the previous paragraph: Oct. himself *did* go to Gaul in 39 B.C., but despatched Pollio to Illyricum to conduct operations on his behalf. There is however a serious objection to Bosworth's hypothesis, namely the amount of evidence which links Pollio at this time, not with Octavian, but with Antony.

At the Peace of Brundisium in 40 B.C. it was agreed that Scodra, on the northern boundary of Macedonia, should divide Octavian's (Dalmatian) territory in the north from Antony's territory in the south (App. *BC* 5.65, Dio 48.28.4). Now we are told by Appian that Antony despatched στρατηγοί to various parts of his territory and sent an army against the Parthini (*BC* 5.75), by Dio that in 39 B.C. Pollio conquered the Parthini (48.41.7 ἐγένετο μὲν καὶ ἐν Ἰλλυριοῖς τοῖς Παρθινοῖς κίνησις, καὶ αὐτὴν ὁ Πωλίων μάχαις ἔπαυσεν), and by epigraphical evidence that Pollio triumphed *ex Parthineis* on 25 October 39 or 38 B.C. (*CIL* 1[2], p. 50). Since the Parthini are located 40 miles within Antony's territory, it was strongly argued by Syme that in 39 B.C. Pollio was proconsul of Macedonia for Antony ('Pollio, Saloninus and Salonae', *CQ* 31 (1937), 39–48).

---

[1] 'V.'s language is carefully chosen to allow for Oct.'s absence in person, without, of course, positively suggesting it' (Mr Seager writes to me).

COMMENTARY 2.78.2

Syme's view held the field more or less unchallenged until Bosworth produced his alternative version of events, and in further support of Bosworth we should note that there is considerable evidence linking Pollio with Octavian's Dalmatian territory about 200 miles to the north of the Parthini. The most important witness is Horace, who, in a famous ode to Pollio, credits him with 'Delmatico . . . triumpho' (2.1.16); and Florus, usually assumed to be based on Livy, says that 'hos [sc. Delmatas] . . . postea Asinius Pollio gregibus, armis, agris multauerat' (2.25.11).[1] More specifically, Porphyrio on Hor. C. 2.1.15 and Servius on Virg. Ecl. 4.1 both allege that Pollio captured the town of Salona(e) on the Dalmatian coast and named his son Saloninus in commemoration of the event. Admittedly Syme has impugned the credibility of the two latter witnesses (op. cit.); but Nisbet–Hubbard (on Hor. C. 2.1.16) rightly remark that 'there seem to be too many coincidences if Pollio had nothing to do with Dalmatia', and Bosworth, while accepting Syme's qualifications, uses the remainder of the evidence to argue that, so far from being proconsul of Macedonia for Antony, Pollio actually governed Illyricum for Octavian (463ff.).

Naturally the two sets of evidence seem almost impossible to reconcile, but J. André produced the suggestion that Pollio was given by *both* triumvirs, Octavian *and* Antony, a roving military commission to subdue the whole of the eastern Adriatic coastline (22–3, and earlier in *REL* 25 (1947), 142ff.). Now it cannot be denied that serious objections can be brought against this suggestion.[2] In the first place, a roving commission such as André describes seems to contradict the very notion of a dividing line at Scodra along the R. Drin between the triumviral spheres of influence which had been agreed at the Peace of Brundisium. Secondly, it was traditional practice that provincial governors should not in any case cross the boundary of their *prouincia*. Thirdly, it is unlikely that Octavian would have agreed to the pro-Antonian Pollio's being placed in charge of such a roving commission.

Yet these objections can perhaps themselves be countered. First, a roving commission, entrusted to a third party, well illustrates the atmosphere of reconciliation which surrounded the Peace of Brundisium. Worth comparison is the agreement between the two triumvirs at this time that

---

[1] The addressee of Virg. Ecl. 8 is represented as sailing past 'oram Illyrici . . . aequoris' (7). Until recently most scholars assumed that the addressee was Pollio and the year 39 B.C., in which case the poem would further corroborate Pollio's connection with Illyricum and hence with Octavian's part of the empire. G. W. Bowersock has however argued that the addressee is Oct. himself and that the year in question is 35 B.C. (*HSCP* 75 (1971), 73–80). Yet line 10 of the poem is hard to reconcile with Bowersock's view (cf. R. J. Tarrant, *HSCP* 82 (1978), 197–9), and it is almost certain that Ecl. 8 too links Pollio with Dalmatia.

[2] See I. M. LeM. DuQuesnay, 'Vergil's first *Eclogue*', Part 2 § IV, *Papers of the Liverpool Latin Seminar Fourth Volume 1983 (Arca 11, 1983)*.

they should both co-operate in attacking Sex. Pompeius (cf. 76.3n.). We must not be persuaded by the subsequent failure of the Peace of Brundisium to dismiss reconciliatory moves which the Peace produced. Secondly, although the convention of not crossing provincial boundaries cannot be denied, the Macedonian area had long been recognised as a special case in the *Lex de piratis persequendis* of the early first century B.C., according to which a magistrate could cross from Macedonia to Thrace in the interests of security (see K. M. T. Atkinson, *Historia* 9 (1960), 449, 451). Even Syme, who argued so strongly for Pollio's being Antony's man in Macedonia, said that 'one is not entitled to postulate over-sharp divisions of province or competence. And Pollio may well have crossed the Drin and operated in Montenegro' (*CQ* 31 (1937), 43: Syme's objection to Pollio's operating at Salonae was based on logistical, not constitutional, grounds).[1] Thirdly, since at this period Antony was Octavian's senior and more influential colleague, it is perhaps not surprising that Pollio was agreed as the man in charge of the commission. After all, Pollio had been one of those responsible for reconciling Antony and Octavian at Brundisium (App. *BC* 5.64).

Despite these points, it cannot be said that André's suggestion has found general acceptance.[2] But if he is correct, as I am nevertheless inclined to believe, the conflicting nature of the ancient evidence is resolved. If such a roving commission was agreed, each triumvir was presumably entitled to claim the credit for any success which their subordinate Pollio achieved; but given Antony's present seniority, it is not surprising that Pollio's triumph was awarded for his exploits against the Parthini in Antony's portion of the empire and that it was Antony who accepted an imperatorial salutation for Pollio's victory (cf. *MRR* 2.387, *CAH* 10.50). Besides, this was in keeping with Pollio's own pro-Antonian sympathies at the time (cf. 86.3n.). After Actium, however, Octavian may well have tried to reinterpret events by emphasising and claiming credit for Pollio's exploits in Dalmatia in the same way as Antony had done beforehand for the same man's exploits in Macedonia. On this hypothesis V. has here omitted Pollio's efforts on Antony's behalf and has, quite legitimately, ascribed to Octavian himself the exploits in Dalmatia which Pollio merely carried out on his behalf.

Yet some questions still remain. The preceding argument means that V. has not mentioned at all Oct.'s better known campaigns in Illyricum in

---

[1] As Mr Seager points out to me, the semi-dependent status which Illyricum often had during the republic, on occasion specifically on Macedonia (see above, p. 86 n. 1), may be relevant here as a factor which made operations across the dividing line easier to conceive of in this particular case.

[2] It is not even mentioned by G. Alföldy, *Bevölkerung und Gesellschaft der röm. Provinz Dalmatien* (1965 edn), 101–2. It is, however, accepted by Haller 72–6, for whom Pollio is 'ein Garant der Einigung der Triumvirn'.

35–33 B.C.[1] Why not? Writing before the appearance of Bosworth's article and assuming that the campaigns of 39 were carried out by Oct. in person, Schmitthenner proposed several possible answers to this question, none of them entirely satisfactory (op. cit. 197 and n. 7). (1) Perhaps V. planned to deal with the later campaigns in the future work mentioned at 96.3. Here Schmitthenner has assumed that V.'s future work would be a monograph on Tiberius' campaigns in Illyricum but containing some background material on Octavian's campaigns of 35–33; yet there is no evidence for this, nor indeed is it certain that V. really intended to write a future work at all (see 96.3n.). (2) Perhaps V. intended both the earlier and later campaigns to be subsumed under the present reference. It is true that V. here mentions 'crebris . . . expeditionibus', but the precise synchronisation of the passage with the events of 39/38 B.C. seems to rule out a reference to the campaigns of 35–33. The adj. crebris probably refers to the Blitzkrieg tactics which the brevity of the earlier campaigns demanded. (3) Perhaps V. thought it unnecessary to mention two very similar campaigns which had taken place in quick succession. Here we approach the crux of the problem. It is true that Dio (49.36.1ff.) adduces the same motive for the later campaigns as does V. here for the earlier ones (viz. ' ne . . . otium corrumperet militem'); but this does not explain why V. should choose to mention the earlier and lesser-known campaigns rather than the later and better-known ones. We should rather expect him to have done the opposite. The obvious inference to be drawn from his treatment of the earlier campaigns is that he wished to glorify Oct. as commander-in-chief at the expense of the subordinate Pollio; but why should V. wish to suppress Pollio, whom he elsewhere consistently admires, when he could have equally well have glorified Octavian by omitting the earlier campaigns of 39, in which Oct. took no personal part, and by mentioning those of 35–33, in which Oct. took command himself?

At this point in the argument we must introduce the false statement which V. makes at 86.3 to the effect that Pollio did not leave Italy at all after the Peace of Brundisium in 40 B.C. This distortion of events puts the passage here at 78.2 in an entirely different light: it suggests that here V.'s principal concern is not after all to glorify Octavian but rather to suppress entirely Pollio's association with the events which took place on the east coast of the Adriatic in 39 B.C. This would certainly explain why V. omits the better known campaigns and ascribes the earlier ones to Octavian himself; but why should he wish to suppress Pollio at all?

I have already suggested why some at least of our sources should associate Pollio with Dalmatia rather than with Macedonia (above, pp. 192–4); it is nevertheless remarkable that Pollio's association with Macedonia is disguised by precisely those sources with which he or his work has the closest links. Appian, the fifth book of whose Civil Wars is

---

[1] Recent studies of these campaigns are by M. Mirković, Živa Antika 18 (1968), 113–27, which I have not seen, and A. H. Malevanij, Vestnik Drevnei Istorii 2 (140) (1977), 129–42 (Eng. summary on pp. 141–2).

usually supposed to be based on Pollio's *Histories*, refrains from naming
Pollio as the στρατηγός sent against the Parthini (see above) and does not
mention Pollio's triumph over them. V. too, whose work is always favourable to Pollio if not actually based on his *Histories*, omits all mention of
Pollio's triumph.

Now Bosworth, whose main thesis is that Pollio abandoned Antony for
Octavian in 40 B.C., explains this common silence amongst our sources as
follows (468): '[It] may well mean that there was something discreditable about the triumph. Now, if Pollio had changed sides in 40 B.C. and
governed Illyricum for Octavian, he would have been highly vulnerable
to Antony's later charges of ingratitude . . . The best plan therefore was to
. . . slide over the triumph won in Octavian's service.' I cannot however
accept this argument because it is difficult to see how a triumph could be
per se 'discreditable', because I agree with André that in 39 Pollio was
working for Antony as well as Octavian (see above) and because I believe
that at this period Pollio's sympathies still lay with Antony (86.3n.).
Another explanation is called for.

It is clear from 86.3 that in the thirties Pollio rapidly became disillusioned with Antony, mainly but perhaps not entirely on account of his
association with Cleopatra, but that even as late as 32 B.C. he could not
bring himself to disown the man whose cause he had actively supported at
the start of the decade; nevertheless he promised Oct. that when the
impending struggle was over, he would not be disloyal to the victor (see n.
ad loc.). Antony's defeat at Actium and death at Alexandria released
Pollio from his obligations to the former triumvir and provided him with
an opportunity to disguise whatever service he had performed for Antony
from the moment when the latter's behaviour had become in his (Pollio's)
opinion intolerable. If V.'s work is any guide, Pollio in retrospect may
well have placed that moment earlier rather than later: V. goes out of his
way to emphasise Pollio's loyalty to Antony in 40 B.C. before the Peace of
Brundisium (cf. 76.3 and n.) but here at 78.2 and at 86.3 suppresses all
possible connection between Pollio and Antony in 39 B.C. Horace too,
who presumably knew Pollio personally and would wish to give pleasure
in an ode addressed to him, characteristically suggests that his triumph
was awarded for exploits, not in Macedonia, but in Dalmatia. Thus on
this hypothesis Pollio, who maintained his support for Antony with
increasing reluctance throughout the thirties, later sought to deny that
from 39 B.C. onwards he had ever given such support. In so doing he was
not in my opinion motivated by any recent enthusiasm for Octavian.

For *corrumperet militem* cf. Heubner on Tac. *H.* 1.53.3; for *patientia . . .
durabat* cf. Liv. 30.28.5, Val. Max. 8.7 *ext.* 1 (F.).

78.3 eadem tempestate *tempestas = tempus* (also at 1.2.3 and 1.8.6) is
ancient and commonly attested in historiography: see E. Fraenkel, *JRS*
41 (1951), 194 = *Kleine Beiträge* (1964), 2.135–6; Goodyear on Tac. *A.*
1.3.6 with refs.; Lebek 27–8, 367 (index). For the time in question see
next n.

Caluinus Domitius Cn. Domitius Calvinus, cos. 53 and 40 B.C., was sent in 39 by Oct. as proconsul to Spain, whence he celebrated a triumph in July 36: see *RE* 5.1.1419–24 = Domitius 43 (Münzer); *MRR* 2.388, 402; *RRC* 1.533–4, no. 532. The incident to which V. here refers is also mentioned by Dio 48.42.2, though there the centurion is not named; for the form of punishment cf. Plb. 6.37.1–39.11 and Walbank ad loc.

For *grauissimi . . . exempli* cf. Cic. *Hortens.* fr. phil. 5.27, Prop. 4.1.109 (Fletcher), Hor. *C.* 4.11.26; for *comparandi antiquis ex.* cf. Plin. *Ep.* 7.33.9 'exemplum . . . simile antiquis' (Ruhnken); for *auctor* cf. 119.4 and esp. Liv. 4.28.6 'auctor . . . saeui exempli' (F.). For V.'s fondness for comparisons with the past cf. 92.5n.; for *turpem . . . fugam* cf. 61.4n. On the text of *fusti* cf. 67.1n.

79–81 THE END OF THE *BELLVM SICVLVM* (38–36 B.C.)

This section consists of three parts, of which the first is designed to show that Octavian's *matura uirtus* could overcome a rival who claimed divine protection (cf. 79.3n., 5n.). Yet the spotlight inevitably falls more brightly on Agrippa, who was largely responsible for the victory over Sex. Pompeius (79.1, 4); and V. spends less time on the critical battle of Naulochus, which is dismissed in a single phrase, than on the behaviour of Titius and the reaction which it provoked (79.5–6). The disproportionate emphasis may be due to V.'s characteristic love of vivid anecdote; but it faithfully reflects the secondary role which Octavian played in the war against Sextus. Perhaps by way of compensation, V. in the next part devotes considerable space to Octavian's personal confrontation with Lepidus and his men, underlining the personal courage (*audacia*) of the former by contrast with the empty arrogance of the latter (cf. 80.3–4nn.). In the final part V. stresses Octavian's *liberalitas* and *munificentia*, essential qualities of the ideal autocrat (81.2–3nn.). After the elimination of Sextus and Lepidus, the only obstacle to that autocracy was now Antony, with whose deficiencies V. will deal in the following section (chh. 82–3).

79 DEFEAT OF SEX. POMPEIUS (38–36 B.C.)

79.1 molem belli . . . suscipere An unusual combination of the two regular phrases *moles belli* (cf. 95.1n.) and *bellum suscipere* (cf. *TLL* 2.1840.11ff.); cf. Tac. *A.* 13.6.2. For *crescente in dies . . . fama* cf. Liv. 4.6.5, 27.20.9, 35.41.1 (F.).

naualibusque adsuescendo certaminibus [atque exercitationibus] There are two reasons for suspecting the bracketed words. (a) *adsuesco* can be followed by either the dative or the ablative. Both nouns cannot be dat., because *exercitationes* cannot refer to manoeuvres during an actual battle; nor can both nouns be abl., because *certamina* cannot refer to practice battles. Thus one of the nouns would seem to be corrupt. (b) *exercitationibus* recurs at 2 below; and although V. regularly repeats words or phrases (as here: 1 *militem ac remigem . . . inuictus* ~ *militem remigemque . . .* [3] *inuictum*; cf. also 100.5n.), the repetition of *exercitationibus* seems to me different in nature from these other exs. and intolerably banal. I therefore think that *atque exercitationibus* has been interpolated from 2 below and that Bothe was right to delete it. The remaining noun *certaminibus* is dative: 'accustoming them to battle'.

For *adsuesco* (trans.) cf. *TLL* 2.909.60ff.; for *contraho* = 'assemble', a technical verb, cf. *TLL* 4.760.69ff. The collective singular *remex* (also at 2 below) occurs once in Cic. *Diu.* 2.114, Virg. *Aen.* 5.116, Prop. 3.12.34, Hor. *Epod.* 16.57 and Tac. *A.* 4.5.1, occasionally in Curt. (4.3.18, 5.18, 7.9.3: see H. Koskenniemi, *Der nominale numerus in der Sprache und im Stil des Curt. Ruf.* (Ann. Univ. Turk., Ser. B, Vol. 114, 1969), 106), and commonly in Liv. (e.g. 3.45.5, 5.40.9, 26.36.12, 37.10.9) (F.).

M. Agrippa, ⟨uir⟩ uirtutis nobilissimae   Kritz defended the paradosis on the grounds that such genitives often do not require the insertion of an extra noun; he quoted *inter al.* 128.2 'C. Marium ignotae originis', Tac. *A.* 6.31.1 'Abdus ademptae uirtutis', and some other exs. are Vell. 93.1, Curt. 6.7.2 'Dymnas modicae apud regem auctoritatis', 9.5.25, 10.3.6 (see too K–S 1.227). Yet the continuation of the expr. (*labore . . . inuictus* etc.) is difficult without *uir* (the same is true of 93.1), and *uir* is in V.'s manner, cf. 26.1 'uir animi . . . paterni', 34.3 'uir nouitatis nobilissimae', 72.3 'eminentissimae ac nobilissimae simplicitatis uiri', 75.1 'pater, magni uir animi', 125.5 'Dolabella quoque, uir simplicitatis generosissimae'. I therefore think that Ruhnken's simple insertion is likely to be correct.

Both *uirtutis* and *nobilissimae* have point when applied to the *nouus homo* Agrippa: cf. 96.1n., 128.1n. For the phrase itself cf. Tac. *Agr.* 1.1 (F.), where a comparable point is no doubt being made. For Agrippa in general see, in addition to 96.1n. and 127.1n., *MRR* 2.340–1, 375, 380, 383, 388–9, 393, 395, 403, 409, 413, 415, 419, 422–3; Reinhold.

labore uigilia periculo inuictus   These are all characteristic of the ideal general: cf. e.g. Xen. *Ages.* 5.2–3 (*uigilia* and *labor*), 6.1–3 (*periculum*); Liv. 21.4.5–6 (of Hannibal) 'plurimum audaciae ad pericula capessenda . . . nullo labore aut corpus fatigari aut animus uinci poterat . . . uigliarum somnique nec . . . discriminata tempora'; Tac. *Agr.* 18.5 'clarus ac magnus haberi Agr., quippe cui . . . labor et periculum placuisset'; Amm. 16.5.4–5; also above, 41.1 'patientia periculorum'; 105.1n., 114.1–3 intro. n.; Gutzwiller on *Pan. Lat.* 3.14.3. Syme has remarked that in our sources Agrippa's character 'seems to lack colour and personality . . . The picture is consistent – and conventional. It was destined for exhibition to a docile public' (*RR* 343, cf. also Grenade 466ff.). Sejanus later tried to be a second Agrippa (cf. *TN* 250–5), but he lacked the realism of his predecessor (on which see next n.).

parendique (sed uni) scientissimus, aliis sane imperandi cupidus The ancient sources are agreed on Agrippa's realistic unwillingness to rival Augustus (cf. Jos. *AJ* 15.361, Dio 53.23.4, esp. 54.29.2 ὅσον τε γὰρ τοὺς ἄλλους ἀρετῇ κατεκράτει, τοσοῦτον ἐκείνου ἐθελοντὴς ἡττᾶτο), something in which Tiberius later resembled him (cf. 99.1 and n.). V. has reconciled this trait with Agrippa's role as the ideal general (last n.) by means of the paronomasia *parendi/imperandi* which Livy had earlier used to describe Hannibal before he took over supreme command (21.4.3): 'numquam ingenium idem ad res diuersissimas, parendum atque imperandum, habilius fuit'. Minucius' speech at Liv. 22.29.7–11 on hierarchical command structure employs the same device (9 'dum imperare discimus, parere prudenti'), and cf. also Liv. 4.5.5, 7.18.7, Nep. *Att.* 3.2. For this general type of paronomasia cf. *Rhet. Herenn.* 4.30. For Agrippa's personality in general see Reinhold 149ff.

consultisque facta coniungens The distinction between intellectual (*consultis*) and practical (*facta*) qualities was conventional (see Vretska on Sall. *C.* 1.6, who refers to H. Fuchs, *MH* 4 (1947) 168), and normally the former were attributed to leaders while the latter were attributed to soldiers (cf. Sall. *C.* 20.16 'uel imperatore uel milite me utimini: neque animus neque corpus a uobis aberit'). But of course the ideal general combines the qualities of both leader and soldier (cf. 85.5n.), and so the combination of *consilia* and *facta* is conventional in portrayals of such men as Agrippa: cf. e.g. Enn. *Ann.* 222 'qualis consiliis quantumque potesset in armis', Sall. *J.* 85.47 'in agmine aut in proelio consultor idem et socius periculi uobiscum adero', Nep. *Them.* 1.4 'neque minus in rebus gerendis promptus quam excogitandis erat', Vell. 2.18.1 'consiliis dux, miles manu', Tac. *H.* 3.17.1, Herodian 2.9.2 νοῆσαί τε ὀξὺς καὶ τὸ νοηθὲν ἐπιτελέσαι ταχύς.

For V.'s form of expr. cf. Tac. *A.* 4.71.3 'tristibus dictis atrocia facta coniungere'; see also 110.5n. Phrases comprising *ponere* + *extra*, as above, are common; but V.'s expression, which presumably alludes to the ideal general's *celeritas bellandi* (cf. 41.1 and n.), seems rather different from those collected in *TLL* 5.2.2058.8off. For *per omnia* cf. 100.3n.

79.2 in Auerno ac Lucrino lacu Agrippa had made them into a single lake: see Reinhold 30–2 for the details. The resumptive use of *hic*, above, is a feature of portrait-writing (cf. 109.5n.). For *fabricare* of fleets, ships etc., below, cf. *TLL* 6.1.20.1ff. I can find no precise parallel for *speciosissima classe*, but cf. Cic. *Verr.* 5.86 'praeclara classis in speciem', *De Or.* 3.180 'hanc habent in specie uenustatem' and see further 77.3n.

cum prius . . . duxisset eam uxorem 'after he had first, when Nero (to whom she had previously been married) pledged Livia to him, . . . taken her as his wife': i.e. *ei* = Octavian; *despondente* governs *Liuiam*; and *uxorem* is in apposition to *eam* as at 44.3, 59.2, 78.1, 93.2. Heinsius wished to delete both *ei* and *eam*, but the redundant use of *is* is very common in V. (cf. 97.4n.). Oct. married Livia on 17 Jan. 38 B.C. (EJ p. 46); for various issues surrounding the marriage and its date see W. Suerbaum, *Chiron* 10 (1980), 337–53. Livia's first husband was Ti. Claudius Nero, father of the emperor Tiberius, cf. 94.1n.; for Livia herself cf. 75.3n. For *auspicatis* cf. *TLL* 2.1552.4ff.

79.3 sed uirum humana ope inuictum . . . fortuna concussit *inuictus* was a 'title' which had been borrowed from Alexander (called ἀνίκητος) by such Romans as Scipio Africanus (cf. Enn. *Var.* 3 V), Pompey (Cic. *Pis.* 34) and esp. Caesar (Cic. *Marc.* 12); subsequently it was attributed to Augustus by various authors (Hor. *S.* 2.1.10–11, Ov. *Tr.* 5.1.41, Manil. 1.925, Vitr. 1 *praef.* 1). See in general S. Weinstock, *HThR* 50 (1957), 211–40.

To such a man a severe reverse (*grauiter . . . concussit*) could only be the work of *fortuna*, and V., like Virgil in a similar connection at *Aen.* 6.174 (see Norden), underlines the unequal nature of the struggle by using *uirum* instead of *eum*; for this usage elsewhere cf. Bömer on Ov. *Met.* 3.731; Heubner on Tac. *H.* 2.68.4 and 3.80.2; Kuntz 98–9.

For *concussit* cf. 90.3n., for its use with *fortuna* cf. Sen. *D.* 8.5.7 (F.); for *humana ope* cf. Ogilvie on Liv. 3.19.10.

circa Veliam . . . uis Africi lacerauit ac distulit A three-pronged attack was launched against Sextus either in the spring (Dio 49.1.1) or at the beginning of July (App. *BC* 5.97) of 36 B.C., the latter date being generally accepted by modern scholars. Oct. and Agrippa set out from Puteoli, Lepidus from Africa, and Statilius Taurus from Tarentum. But a storm which blew up from the SW compelled Oct. and Agrippa to shelter at Velia, where many of their ships were nevertheless damaged (App. *BC* 5.98–9, Dio 49.1.3). Sextus however failed to capitalise on their disarray, content merely to call himself 'son of Neptune' (App. 5.100). This seems to be the storm to which V. here alludes, but he may have confused it with an earlier one off Sicily in 38 B.C. (see below, 4n.).

For *uis Africi . . . distulit* cf. Lucr. 1.272 'uenti uis . . . nubila differt': *differre* is the *mot juste* for storms etc. (*TLL* 5.1.1069.47ff.) and *dispulit* (Gelenius) should not be read here; for *adorta uis* cf. Liv. 2.36.5, 30.39.1 (F.); for *Africus* (abs.) cf. *TLL* 1.1255.45ff. For *lacerauit* of fleets etc. cf. Liv. 29.8.10, 18.5, 30.39.3, Sil. 4.246, Flor. 1.24.12, 1.40.18.

ea patrando bello mora fuit, quod . . . 'That delayed ending the war, which . . .' Oct. needed a month to repair his fleet (App. *BC* 5.99). For *bellum patrare* cf. 114.4n.; for the gerundive cf. Liv. 23.9.11

'restituendae . . . Capuae mora' (F.). In the rel. clause *dubia fortuna* (for which cf. Ter. *Hec.* 16, Cic. *Verr.* 2.38, Liv. 27.49.4) must be less critical than *ancipiti f.* (Cic. *Marc.* 15; Pease on Virg. *Aen.* 4.603), although elsewhere the adjj. appear to be synonymous (Luc. 4.770–1); the clause itself is precisely explained by *nam . . . ut . . . ita* below. For the expr. Krause compared 55.3 'plus quam dubio Marte'.

79.4 nam et classis eodem loco uexata est tempestate   No other source records a second storm during the campaigns of 36 B.C., whether at Velia or anywhere else. We are however told by Appian (*BC* 5.88–90) and Dio (48.48.1–4) that in 38 B.C. a storm had inflicted severe damage on an earlier fleet of Octavian at the promontory of Scyllaeum. It is therefore possible that V., perhaps misled by the fact that Sextus allegedly claimed the title 'son of Neptune' after this first storm too (Dio 48.48.5),[1] has confused the two storms and mistakenly attributed both of them to the same year and the same locality. See above, 3n.

For *classis . . . uexata* cf. Liv. 23.34.16, 30.39.3.

inopinato ⟨Pompeii⟩ classis aduentu   I agree with those who believe that *classis* alone is too obscure to have been written by V. In his app. crit. Stegmann mentions the unattributed conjecture ⟨*Pompeii*⟩, which I regard as most plausible: the word might easily have dropped out if it had been earlier abbreviated to *P.* (cf. 2.15.1 *Pompeio Rutilio* PA: *P. Rutilio* Gelenius, correctly). I have however been unable to trace the author of the conjecture.

For Agrippa's success at Mylae and Oct.'s disaster at Tauromenium cf. Reinhold 39–40 and Rice Holmes, *Arch.* 115–116, each with full refs. For *ut . . . ita* of contrasting actions cf. 125.4n.; for *inopinato . . . aduentu* (here almost suggesting that Sextus' tactic was unfair) cf. Liv. 42.54.7; for *sub ipsius Caesaris oculis* cf. Tac. *A.* 2.35.2; for *accepta clades* cf. 97.1n.

neque ab ipso periculum abfuit   Cf. Suet. *Aug.* 16.3 'nec temere plura ac maiora pericula ullo alio bello adiit'. For this use of *ipse* cf. 109.5n. Since the present and following sentences each refer to the same engagement at Tauromenium, it is tempting to suggest that the whole passage should be printed thus: '. . . circa T. accepta clades: neque ab ipso periculum abfuit ⟨et⟩ legiones, quae cum . . .'

Cornificio   For L. Cornificius cf. *RE* 4.1.1623–4 = Cornificius 5 (Münzer); *MRR* 2.393, 404; *PIR*[2] 2.373 no. 1503. *in terra*, below, is probably to be taken ἀπὸ κοινοῦ with *expositae* (used with *in* + abl. also at Virg. *Aen.* 6.416, Sen. *Ep.* 53.2, Liv. 28.44.10, Just. 18.1.3, and perh. Caes. *BC* 1.31.3; in general, Bell 254) and *oppressae sunt*.

---

[1] Sextus had in fact already used the Neptune motif on coins as early as 44/43 B.C.: see *RRC* 1.495–6 no. 483. Cf. also Dio 48.19.2 (40 B.C.), and Gabba on App. *BC* 5.100 (416).

79.5 sed ancipitis fortuna temporis matura uirtute correcta Ruhnken tentatively suggested *mature*, which has been adopted by most edd.; yet he acknowledged that the paradosis is supported by 125.3 'sed haec omnia ueteris imperatoris maturitas . . . sopiit ac sustulit', and I think it is further supported by Liv. 3.12.3 'neque in ciuitate Romana tantam indolem tam maturae uirtutis umquam exstitisse' (cf. Cic. *Cael.* 76 'uirtutis maturitas'). V. is portraying the conflict as one between a young brigand (73.1) who sometimes had fortune on his side (cf. 3–4 above) and a man whose *uirtus* and achievements belied his age (3 *uirum humana ope inuictum*). (Even on the latest date assumed for his birth (cf. 73.1n.), Sextus was in fact slightly older than Octavian; but the latter suffered as much as the former from accusations of being 'young': see Scott 17 and n. 7, referring to McCarthy, *CP* 26 (1931), 362–73.)

For *fortuna . . . correcta* cf. Sen. *Ep.* 98.3 'corrigit praua fortunae'; for *uirtute correcta* cf. Tac. *A.* 15.2.3 (F.); for *uirtus ~ fortuna* cf. 97.4n.; for *fortuna temporis* cf. 67.1n.

paene omnibus exutus nauibus V.'s brief description of the battle of Naulochus, which took place on 3 Sept. 36 B.C. (EJ p. 51; Gabba on App. *BC* 5.118 (490), Hadas 145–6). Sextus escaped with only seventeen ships (App. *BC* 5.121); for other details see Reinhold 40–1, Rice Holmes, *Arch.* 116–17. For *exutus nauibus* cf. Sall. *H.* 4.69.13 *classe* (Vell. 2.12.2 *exercitu*, 37.2 *copiis*); for *explicare naues* or *classes*, above, cf. *TLL* 5.2.1726.23ff.

dum inter ducem et supplicem tumultuatur Although there seems to be no exact parallel for this constr., no earlier ed. was troubled by it. *fluctuatur* was however proposed by Cornelissen (1877) and *multum luctatur* by Halm, who compared 63.3 'diu quarum esset partium secum luctatus ac sibi difficile consentiens'. Yet neither of these suggested verbs is essentially different in meaning from *tumultuatur*, which can be used of mental disturbance (e.g. Cic. *Cael.* 36) as can the noun *tumultus* (e.g. Sen. *Ep.* 56.5). Thus I do not consider these alternatives to be superior to the paradosis: V. does after all explain his meaning very clearly in what follows (*dignitatem retinet ~ ducem, uitam precatur ~ supplicem*).

dignitatem retinere is esp. Ciceronian (e.g. *Leg. Man.* 14, *Sull.* 80), and for *retinere* used of maintaining a quality in adverse circumstance cf. *OLD* s.v. 11; also *4b. iugulatus est* combines bluntness with the pseudo-legal flavour of 'executed' in modern 'newspeak' (for the word cf. Landgraf on Cic. *Rosc.* 13).

For M. Titius cf. *RE* 6A.2.1559–62 = Titius 18 (Hanslik); *MRR* 2.385, 401, 409, 420; Syme, *RR* 565 (index).

79.6 mox ludos . . . pelleretur The irony of this incident, for which V. is our only evidence, is underlined by alliteration and assonance ('*Pompeii . . . pop*uli'; '*sp*ectaculo quod *p*raebebat *p*elleretur'): Titius was expelled from the spectacle which he, the murderer of the popular Pompey who had earlier been his saviour (cf. 77.3), had had the insensitivity or callousness to provide in the theatre which carried the name of Pompey's father.

For *durauit . . . odium*, above, cf. 1.12.7, Sen. *Ag.* 522, Tac. *G.* 33.2; for *contractum o.* cf. *Rhet. Herenn.* 4.50 (F.), Just. 5.1.6 (+ abl.), *SHA Pert.* 13.9 (+ *unde*); for *in tantum . . . ut* cf. 30.6, 53.3; L–H–S 640.

80 LEPIDUS DISCARDED (36 B.C.)

80.1 exercitum Pompeii . . . sibi iunxerat While Oct. was still at Naulochus, Lepidus and Agrippa laid siege to Messana where Sextus' land forces, under L. Plinius Rufus, had taken refuge; when Plinius almost immediately sued for peace, Lepidus disregarded Agrippa's advice, accepted Plinius' proposal, and joined Sextus' forces to his own. See App. *BC* 5.122–3, Dio 49.10.2–11.2. Krause explains *sequentem . . . fidem* by saying that Sextus' army ' Caesari, non Lepido, se dedere voluit et putauit. Rem ambitiose in Octaviani gratiam narrat Velleius'. On the legionary strengths here and at 2 below see Brunt, *IM* 499.

For *fortunae indulgentiam*, above, cf. 2.1.4, 121.3n.; for *indulgentiam meritus* cf. *SHA Claud.* 13.7; *auctoritas* and *fides* are commonly combined, e.g. Cic. *Flacc.* 21, Liv. 41.24.9.

80.2 inflatusque . . . numero Cf. Suet. *Aug.* 16.4 ' M. Lepidum, quem ex Africa in auxilium euocaret, superbientem XX legionum fiducia . . .'; App. *BC* 5.122–3 specifies 22 legions. For *uictoriae comes*, below, cf. Caes. *BC* 3.80.3, Tac. *A.* 1.3.1 *u. socium*. At Sen. *Suas.* 7.6 Lepidus is called ' alienae semper dementiae accessio, utriusque collegae mancipium '.

(ut) totam uictoriam ut suam interpretaretur, audebatque . . . Kritz retained the paradosis *interpretabatur*, and his defence of the indic. is echoed by L–H–S 639: 'Anakoluthe infolge längerer Einschübe'. Ellis in his app. crit. suggested printing *in id furoris . . . dicendo* as a parenthesis, making *iunxerat* and *interpretabatur* co-ordinated main verbs. Yet neither of these explanations matches Gelenius' suggestion that *interpretaretur* was wrongly attracted into the mood of *audebat*, which immediately follows and appears at first sight to be joined to it by *-que*.

For *interpretari* + *ut* cf. e.g. Val. Max. 1.5 *ext.* 1 (*uelut*), Tac. *H.* 1.27.1, *A.* 4.38.4. For *in id furoris processerat ut*, above, cf. Sall. *J.* 5.2 'eoque uecordiae processit ut '; for *dissidere* with dat. cf. Hor. *C.* 2.2.18; with *in* + abl., Cic. *Att.* 7.6.2 (all F.).

denuntiare . . . excederet Cf. esp. Liv. 42.48.3 'denuntiatum . . . excederent ' (F.); see also K–S 2.228, adding Plin. *Ep.* 6.31.12.

80.3 non ab Scipionibus ... a Caesare This sentence, which is framed by the two significant proper names, introduces an episode which is designed to contrast the qualities of Octavian and Lepidus (cf. 4 *scires quid interesset inter duces*). On the one hand we have the former's true bravery and courage (*non ... quidquam ausum ... fortius* and *rapere ausus est*), on the other the latter's empty boasting (*inflatus* and *audebatque* above). The episode is heightened by fullness of expression (*inermis et lacernatus, et a militibus et a fortuna*), elegant variation (*cum ... , trahens, ingressus, euitatis, cum ...*), appealing to the reader (*scires*, cf. 85.6n.), paronomasia (*armati inermem*: see n.), and by the comparison with the past (cf. 92.5n.). Whether V. had any specific comparison in mind is difficult to say. Earlier edd. referred to Scipio Africanus' visit to Syphax (Liv. 28.17); Rockwood mentions the same man's bold deed after Cannae (Liv. 22.53). Among earlier incidents Livy chooses Mucius Scaevola's entry into Porsenna's camp as an example of *audacia* (cf. 2.12.3 *audaci facinore*, 14 *ausus*), and in Greek there is a comparable episode in the life of Agesilaus (Plut. *Ages.* 32.4, Polyaen. 2.1.14; Ag. is 'wearing a cloak' and 'unarmed').[1] At any rate, as Mr DuQuesnay points out, V. clearly wants us to see Oct. not as the defeater of the republican cause but as the inheritor of the *mos maiorum*.

praeter nomen nihil trahens The name is 'Caesar': V. turns to good account the point which Cic. had famously made in a hostile connection at *Phil.* 13.24 'o puer qui omnia nomini debes'; see also Schmitthenner, *Test.* 75. *nomen trahere* normally = 'to derive a name', but V. has used the verb on the analogy of *exercitum t.* or *manum t.* (cf. 112.4) *uel sim.* For the turn of phrase cf. 1.10.3 'nihil ... praeter speciem nominis ... retinenti', 40.3 'nihil praeter nomen imperatoris retinens', Licin. Mac. fr. 15 'nihil praeter nomina consulum suggerant', Laber. *prol.* 124 R 'nil nisi nomen retineo'. For *ausum patratumque*, above, cf. 61.1n.

euitatis quae ... tela in eum acta erant The omission of *tela* in A persuaded Orelli that the word was also omitted in (M) and that it had been inserted by Rhenanus in P but in the wrong place; Orelli himself preferred to insert *telis* after *euitatis* (the error would have arisen through homoeoteleuton). B's silence however implies that *tela* appeared in (M) and that its omission by A is without significance (for A's frequent omissions cf. *TN* 11 n. 2). Of course a reading of (M) is not necessarily identical with what V. himself wrote, and it must be admitted that the paradosis is unusual: when an antecedent is placed within a rel. clause it normally occurs second word or at least early in the clause (e.g. 26.2 'in qua ciuitate', 42.2 'quae nox'). Orelli's suggestion is therefore attractive, and one could argue that his hypothesised sequence of error simply took place at a previous stage in the transmission of the text. Yet the early placing of an included antecedent is not invariable (cf. L–H–S 564, K–S 2.310ff.) and I have, with some hesitation, retained the paradosis.

---

[1] I owe this last ex. to Mr J. F. Lazenby.

I have also retained *acta*, to which there is no linguistic objection (cf. *TLL* 1.1373.36ff.), despite the obvious attractiveness of Gelenius' *iacta*.

80.4 armati inermem secuti sunt The περιπέτεια of the incident is underlined by the paronomasia, a technique of which V. is fond (cf. Woodman, *EA* 6). For similar conceits cf. e.g. [Sall.] *Ep. Caes.* 2.2.4 'inimicorum arma inermis disiecit', Sen. *Ep.* 66.53 'confecit bellum inermis et mancus' (of Scaevola), *Pan. Lat.* 2.30.5 'ut ab inermibus uerterentur armati'.

[ad] in dissimillimam uitae suae potentiam peruenerat Quoting 91.4 'mortem dignissimam uita', Ruhnken proposed to retain *ad* and *uita sua* and emend to *indignissimam*: 'power too good for his life' (cf. *OLD* s.v. *indignus* 5 *b*). Yet Krause pointed out that Vascosanus' *ad dissimillimam uitae suae* produces an almost identical sense and that the phraseology is supported by 41.2 'dissimilemque fortunae suae ... habitum'. Bothe agreed with Krause, except that he deleted *ad* rather than *in*: before realising that *in* was the true reading, a scribe wrote *ad* and forgot to delete it. The meaning is: 'a position of power quite different ⟨in character⟩ from his general behaviour'. For the same idea cf. 85.3, where *uita* is used in the same sense.

Lepidus ... desertus Though alluded to in the phrase *iussu ... prauissimi* at 3 above, Lepidus actually 'appears for the first time only after he has been deserted by his soldiers' (Starr (1978), 165, who also points to the contrast in the two generals' clothing: Oct. is *lacernatus*, Lepidus *pullo uelatus amiculo*; so too Lepidus' desertion is contrasted with Oct.'s being the focal point of the crowd, cf. *armati ... secuti* above and *confluentium ... turbam* below). For *et a militibus et a fortuna desertus* cf. Caes. *BG* 5.34.2 'tametsi ab duce et a fortuna deserebantur'; also Sall. *H.* 2.47.2 'cuncta me cum fortuna deseruere', Tac. *A.* 2.21.1. For *inter ... turbam latens*, below, cf. Sen. *Thy.* 133f. 'liceat in media mihi | latere turba' (Ruhnken), Sen. *Suas.* 2.5 'ne in turba fugientium lateremus', 2.7; for *ultima ... turba* cf. Liv. 24.27.1; for *inter* rather than *in* cf. e.g. Liv. 3.45.5, 5.40.9, Val. Max. 1.7 *ext.* 6 (F.) and see M. González-Haba, *Glotta* 42 (1964), 191–213. For *genibus ... aduolutus est*, below, cf. *OLD* s.v. *aduoluo* 2; Goodyear on Tac. *A.* 1.13.6.

uita ... concessa ... spoliata ... dignitas Suet. once again agrees, cf. *Aug.* 16.4 'spoliauit exercitu supplicemque concessa uita ... relegauit'. After *dissimillimam ... potentiam* above, V. doubtless intends *uita* ironically here: the concession was hardly worth making. *spoliata dignitas* presumably refers to Lepidus' expulsion from the triumvirate and provincial command (*MRR* 2.400), though the event did not take place 'in the tenth year' after he had reached those heights (43 B.C., cf. 65.2); Krause explains *decimo* (above) as a round number, which perhaps it is.

For *spoliare dign.* cf. Caes. *BG* 7.66.5, Hirt. *BG* 8.50.3, Cic. *Cael.* 3; *tueri d.* is Ciceronian, cf. *Verr.* 3.9, *Clu.* 111 etc., and *dominium rerum* is a legal phrase, cf. *TLL* 5.1.1896.79ff.

81 OCTAVIAN'S GENEROSITY (36 B.C.)

81.1 contemplatus frequentiam suam V. here agrees closely with Dio 49.13.1 οὐκ ὀλίγοι ὄντες πρὸς τὴν ὄψιν τοῦ πλήθους σφῶν ἐθρασύνοντο. For the idea Popma quoted Luc. 5.259–60, Tac. *A.* 1.25.2 'quotiens oculos ad multitudinem rettulerant, uocibus truculentis strepere'; cf. also 4.2.1. For the contrast *cogere*~*rogare*, below, cf. Liv. 32.21.32 'quod rogant, cogere possunt'; for *sustinere* + infin. cf. 86.2n.

partim seueritate partim liberalitate discussa principis The combination of severity and generosity is characteristic of the ideal general (cf. 114.3n.). For details of Oct.'s donatives on this occasion cf. Dio 49.14.2–3, App. *BC* 5.128–9; it is interesting that V. seems to have slipped into the almost technical expression *liberalitas principis* here (cf. 100.2n.; Kloft 73). For *seditio . . . discussa* cf. Front. *Strat.* 1.9.2.

81.2 supplementum Campanae coloniae, cuius ⟨agri⟩ relicti erant publici Scholars have long recognised that the deficiencies of V.'s text at this point can be clarified by reference to Dio 49.14.4–5, which here is very close to V.: καὶ τὸ μὲν ἀργύριον [*liberalitate*] αὐτοῖς αὐτίκα, τὴν δὲ χώραν οὐ πολλῷ ὕστερον [*per id tempus*] ἔδωκεν. ἐπειδὴ γὰρ οὐκ ἐξήρκεσεν ἡ ἐν τῷ δημοσίῳ ἔτι τότε οὖσα, προσεξεπρίατο [cf. *adiectum*] ἄλλην τε καὶ παρὰ Καμπανῶν τῶν ἐν τῇ Καπύῃ οἰκούντων συχνήν [cf. *speciosum*] (καὶ γὰρ ἐποίκων ἡ πόλις πολλῶν ἐδεῖτο), καὶ αὐτοῖς τό τε ὕδωρ τὸ Ἰούλιον ὠνομασμένον, ἐφ᾽ ᾧ καὶ τὰ μάλιστα διὰ πάντων ἀγάλλονται, τήν τε χώραν τὴν Κνωσίαν, ἣν καὶ νῦν ἔτι [*hodieque*] καρποῦνται, ἀντέδωκε [cf. *pro his*]. Dio's statement that the Campanian colony required a large number of settlers is at first sight strange in view of the law which Caesar had passed in 59 'ut ager Campanus plebei diuideretur' (Vell. 44.4, cf. 45.2). But 'since 44 (or 49) land may have become vacant as a result of war losses, proscriptions, and confiscations', suggests Brunt; 'doubt must arise whether any considerable distribution of the Ager Campanus took place as a result of Caesar's law in 59' (*IM* 317). If Brunt is right,[1] it may be that V. wrote *cuius ⟨agri⟩ relicti erant publici* ('whose public land had been abandoned'), a reading which would at least help to explain Dio's statement that more settlers were needed. If we accept this suggestion (Runken's ⟨*agri*⟩ *eius*

---

[1] He takes into account Vell. 75.1, where the context (cf. 74.2) suggests that residents in the area had lost their land to a previous group of settlers round about the time of the *bellum Perusinum.*

relicti is similar in meaning but less neat), it obviates the need for any of the more extensive supplements that have been proposed.[1] For the plural form of *ager publicus* cf. Cic. *Leg. Agr.* 1.10, 2.10, Liv. 2.61.2 etc.

pro his . . . ornamentum est We learn from Dio (last n.) that the revenue of 1,200,000 sesterces came from Cnossos and that the water-supply was the Aqua Iulia, not to be confused with the aqueduct of the same name built at Rome in 33 B.C. *hodieque* (on which cf. 98.1n.) attests to V.'s continuing interest in the region of Capua (see above, pp. 182 ff.).

Cludius' *instrumentum* is an attractive proposal for the paradosis *instar*: the noun is liable to such abbreviations as *instr* (see *TLL* 7.1.2010.66–7; A. Cappelli, *Lexicon Abbrev.* s.v.), and the antithesis *instrumentum ~ ornamentum* is found e.g. at Cic. *Dom.* 62, *Ac.* 2.31. For the combination of *salubritas* and *amoenitas*, a standard pair in eulogistic accounts of places etc. (cf. Quint. 3.7.27 'est et locorum (laus) . . . in quibus similiter speciem et utilitatem intuemur, speciem in maritimis, planis, amoenis, utilitatem in salubribus, fertilibus'; I. M. LeM. DuQuesnay, 'Vergil's first *Eclogue*', *Papers of the Liverpool Latin Seminar Third Volume 1981* (*Arca* 7, 1981), 71–3), cf. esp. Plin. *Ep.* 10.90.2 'si tu, domine, hoc genus operis [an aqueduct] et salubritati et amoenitati ualde sitientis coloniae indulseris'; also Cic. *Leg.* 2.3, Suet. *Tib.* 11.1. For the importance of water-sources in the Roman world see Gutzwiller on *Pan. Lat.* 3.9.4, who quotes Vitr. 8.1.1 'est enim [sc. aqua] maxime necessaria et ad uitam et ad delectationes et ad usum cotidianum', 8.3.28, Front. *Aq. praef.* 1, 2.88 (an interesting ex. of environmental concern, with the water-supply illustrating *cura principis*), Rut. Nam. 1.97ff. (see Doblhofer ad loc.). *aqua* first = 'aqueduct' in Cic. *Leg.* 3.7, thereafter in Frontin. (F.); for *uberiores reditus*, above, cf. Colum. 3.3.2 (F.).

81.3 insigne coronae classicae . . . meruit Agrippa is represented as wearing this crown in Virgil's description of Actium, *Aen.* 8.683–4: 'cui, belli insigne superbum, | tempora nauali fulgent rostrata corona'. Although most other writers (Dio 49.14.3, Liv. *per.* 129, Sen. *Ben.* 3.32.4) agree with V. that Agrippa was the first to be so honoured, Pliny (*NH* 16.7) says that the antiquarian Varro had previously won the crown in 67 B.C.: see Reinhold 42–3 n. 101 for discussion.

uictor deinde Caesar reuersus in urbem The date was 13 November 36 B.C. (EJ p. 34). There was tremendous jubilation, and honours were voted to Octavian, including an inscription bearing the words 'pax terra marique parta' (Dio 49.15, App. *BC* 5.130; S. Weinstock, *JRS* 50 (1960), 47).

---

[1] E.g. . . . *coloniae*; ⟨*concessi enim ueteranis agri, qui ciuibus coloniae*⟩ *eius relicti* (Haase); . . . *coloniae*, ⟨*ueteranis in agros deductis, qui coloniae*⟩ *eius relicti* (Halm).

contractas emptionibus complures domos ... facturum promisit The emperor's various houses and their relationship both to one another and to the temple of Palatine Apollo are extremely confusing. Octavian had originally lived near the Forum Romanum in a house which had belonged to the orator Licinius Calvus, but at this time he was living on the Palatine in a house which had belonged to Hortensius (Suet. *Aug.* 72.1). This latter house was evidently not noted for its spaciousness (*neque laxitate ... conspicuis*: Suet. loc. cit.); it is therefore not surprising that, as V. says, Oct. had engaged estate agents to buy up several adjacent properties in order that he could extend his own property (*quo laxior fieret ipsius*; for the expr. cf. Sen. *Ep.* 56.7, Plin. *Pan.* 50.6).[1] Before work could start, however, lightning struck precisely that area where the extensions were planned; on the advice of the *haruspices*, therefore, Oct. abandoned his personal development and instead declared the area to be public property on which he would build a temple to Apollo (Suet. *Aug.* 29.3, Dio 49.15.5). Thus in V.'s account *publicis se ... professus est* is explained by *templumque Apollinis ... promisit* and *-que* is therefore epexegetic (for which cf. K–S 2.25–6). When the temple was eventually completed it was one of the glories of Augustan Rome, with its famous porticoes and Greek and Latin libraries (*RG* 19.1, Suet. *Aug.* 29.3). For bibliography on the temple cf. Nisbet–Hubbard on Hor. *C.* 1.31.1, adding O. Richmond, *JRS* 4 (1914), 193ff., G. Carettoni, *JRS* 50 (1960), 201–2, J. M. Carter on Suet. *Aug.* 29.3 and 72.1. Such public building projects were taken as a sign of the emperor's *munificentia* (cf. 126.4n.; Kloft 80).

circa is of course adverbial. The omission of *se* in *facturum promisit*, though unusual for V. (cf. 125.2n.), is nevertheless hardly felt in view of *se ... professus est* immediately above, esp. since *-que*, as we have seen, is epexegetic.

82–83 THE YEARS 36–32 B.C.

In this section V. switches from praise of Octavian to criticism of Antony, thereby avoiding the issue which has exercised numerous modern scholars, viz., Octavian's status in 32 B.C. when all Italy swore allegiance to him personally in an extra-constitutional oath of loyalty (*RG* 25.2).[2]

---

[1] Dio 49.15.5 τόπον ... ὥστ' οἰκοδομῆσαί τινα ἐώνητο is translated by the Loeb ed. as ' ... bought for the purpose of erecting a building upon it', which cannot be right since it implies that Oct. did not already have a residence there, an implication which is contradicted by Suet. *Aug.* 29.3. Dio's phrase means 'area which he had bought for building purposes', and his account agrees with that of V. Unfortunately Weinstock 277 follows the Loeb ed.

[2] Cf. e.g. H. W. Benario, *Chiron* 5 (1975), 301–9; E. W. Gray, *PACA* 13 (1975), 15–29.

Yet the avoidance is unlikely to have been intentional. V. took for granted the morality of Octavian's cause (below, p. 219; in general Syme, *RR* 270–1) and is here more concerned simply to vilify Antony's behaviour in a series of characteristically vivid vignettes (82.3, 4, 83.2).

82 ANTONY'S ORIENTAL CAMPAIGNS (36, 34 B.C.)

82.1 Qua aestate Caesar tam prospere †Libium in Sicilia bene† fortuna ... titubauit ad orientem In my opinion the problems of this desperate passage centre round the three words *Libium*, *bene* and *militauit* in the paradosis. Some scholars have believed that V. is linking success in Sicily with good fortune in the East, the latter consisting in Antony's Parthian defeat and alliance with Cleopatra, both of which eventually led to Actium and hence to the final victory of Augustus. It was this belief which led to Haupt's proposal (1.271–2 *fortuna, in Caesare et re p. mitis, saeuiit ad orientem*), which has had some popularity; and on this view *bene*, or something very like it, might be retained to balance *prospere*. Yet Krause rightly condemned this view as 'indigna ciui Romano et ipso Velleio', himself agreeing with Ruhnken and Kritz that V. is contrasting success in Sicily with misfortune in the East (cf. 97.1 'dum in hac parte imperii omnia geruntur prosperrime, accepta in Germania clades'). On this view *bene* is unlikely to be correct as it stands, since it merely echoes *prospere*.

Two questions now present themselves: to what precise success in Sicily is V. referring? and how did he express the statement concerning misfortune in the East? The questions are linked, as will be seen, by the problem concerning *bene*, which some scholars have seen as concealing a verb or the object of a verb itself concealed by *Libium*, while others have taken it as concealing an adj. with *fortuna* or an adv. with *militauit*.

The *aestas* is that of 36 B.C., the period when Sex. Pompeius was defeated (79.4–5), Lepidus thwarted (80.2–4), and the mutinous troops calmed (81.1–2). Many scholars, from Rhenanus onwards, have emended *Libium* to *Lepidum*, e.g. ... *tam prospere Lepidum in S. uicit, fortuna* ... (J. F. Christ); but despite V.'s keen dislike of Lepidus, I do not think Octavian's outmanoeuvring of him merits recapitulation here: V. recognised that Lepidus was an unimportant figure, and Octavian's action, however courageous, was essentially bluff. Besides, *prospere* is not the right word to denote an individual's success. Heinsius toyed with emending *Libium* to *Lilybaeum*, but acknowledged that that port played only a minor role in the early stages of the campaign against Pompeius. On second thoughts he suggested *tam prospere ⟨pro re⟩ ciuium in Sicilia* [sc. *militauit*], and indeed several scholars have proposed a generalised reference to 'the war in Sicily': e.g. *tam prospere finiuit in S. bellum, fortuna* ... (Kritz, followed by Hellegouarc'h), *tam prospere bellum finiuit in S. ... ⟨minus⟩ bene ...* (Laurent), *t. p. ⟨rem⟩ ciuium in S. tenet, fortuna* ... (Huth). Yet none of these suggestions is altogether convincing, and I have decided to obelise.

The problem of *militauit* has proved equally intractable in the past. In classical Latin *fortuna militauit* can only mean 'fortune soldiered', which does not make sense in the context and is unparalleled as an expression. We need a word indicating change or deterioration, and Sauppe (in Orelli's edn) suggested *inclinauit* (accepted by Kritz, who compared Liv. 3.61.4 'si fortuna belli inclinet'), while Ruhnken had earlier proposed *mutauit*. Yet neither of these seems to me superior to *titubauit*, which Prof. Goodyear has suggested to me and which I have printed. For the expr. cf. Sen. *D.* 5.25.1 'magnorum uirorum titubare fortunam', Sil. 11.4 'f. titubante', Amm. 28.5.14 'si sub eo fortuna titubauerit belli'.

Finally, note that although some scholars have objected to *in Caesare et republica*, the expr. is Velleian (cf. 76.4 'et Caesarem . . . et rem p.', 83.1) and is an ex. of his 'urbana adulatio' (so Kritz).

cum XIII legionibus ingressus Armeniam ... habuit regem eorum obuium   Since Flor. 2.20.10 gives the figure as 16 legions, Freinsheim ad loc. proposed to emend *XIII* to *XVI* here. Yet still other figures are given by other authorities (see e.g. Rice Holmes, *Arch.* 223, Bengtson 18, and Brunt, *IM* 503–4, all of whom support Florus); and in such circumstances, and given the notorious unreliability of MSS in transmitting numerals, I can see no point in altering V.'s figure. Gelenius' *ingressus* must however be accepted, despite Ellis 170, as the phrase *per eas regiones . . . petens* makes clear (so Krause).

habere obuium is a common expr. (e.g. Liv. 10.32.4, 31.37.2, Tac. *A.* 1.34.1, *H.* 3.59.2). Strictly speaking Antonius was not confronted by the Parthian king (Phraates IV), who never fought in person (Plut. *Ant.* 44.2), but by his commander-in-chief Monaeses (*RE* 16.1.43–4 (Modrze)); Phraates however naturally took credit for the victory (cf. *CAH* 10.74–5). For the whole campaign see Bengtson, who, however, has little to say about V.'s account.

82.2 Statiano   Oppius Statianus, *RE* 18.1.747 = Oppius 34 (Münzer); *MRR* 2.404–5.

For *cum . . . discrimine*, below, cf. Liv. 25.24.12, 37.53.16; for *discrimen* + genit. cf. *TLL* 5.1.1361.8off.; for *adire pericula* cf. *TLL* 1.627.16ff. I have adopted Kreyssig's ⟨*a*⟩ *quibus*: *a* is more likely than *e* to have dropped out after *pericula*, and for *seruare* + *a* cf. Claud. Quadr. 7, Plin. *NH* 7.104 (quoted in *OLD*), to which F. adds Pallad. 5.8.7. I have also printed *desperaret* (Haupt 1.274): *ea* requires that the verb be in the subjunc. (it introduces a consecutive clause), and the impf. seems to me to give better sense and to be more idiomatic than Bothe's *desperauerit*.

captiui cuiusdam (sed Romani) consilio ac fide   The story is told in more detail, with neo-Livian rationalising, by Florus (2.20.4ff.), who like V. says that the man was a survivor of Carrhae. Plutarch however attributes the credit to ἀνὴρ τῷ γένει Μάρδος, πολλὰ τοῖς Πάρθων ἤθεσιν ἐνωμιληκώς (*Ant.* 41.1). Some (e.g. Tarn in *CAH* 10.74) believe the former story to be wrong, arguing that V. has confused *Marsus*, mentioned by Horace as a generic survivor of Crassus' army (*C.* 3.5.9), with *Mardus*. Freinsheim, on the other hand, argued that the confusion was Plutarch's, whose text he emended to Μάρσος. In favour of Freinsheim, as Krause noted, is the fact that Plut. would hardly have said πολλὰ . . . ἐνωμιληκώς if the man had really been a Mardian: they were local people. *Contra* Bengtson 34.

consilium and *fides* are commonly collocated, cf. *TLL* 4.452.82ff.

diuerso siluestrique peruaderent Sc. *itinere*. Ellis wished to insert *loco* because Amerbach wrote the word both before and after *peruaderent*, although he deleted it on each occasion (Stegmann wrongly implies that it is deleted only once). There is a similar passage at 105.2, where I followed A (see n.); but there *ingenio* makes sense and was retained by A, whereas neither of those conditions obtains here.

82.3 fugam . . . uictoriam uocabat So too Flor. 2.20.10 'ferocior ali-quando factus est, quasi uicisset, quia euaserat' and Dio 49.32.1–2, who adds that Octavian was not deceived by Antony's misleading reports: though appearing publicly to accept them, he allowed rumours of the truth to circulate. Perhaps Oct. capitalised on the irony of Antony's describing his flight from the Parthians as a victory: the Parthians' own technique of fighting (*Parthica fuga*) was proverbially successful.

Gruter observed that V.'s phrase is like Sall. *J.* 98.6 'ipsi duces feroces quia non fugerant, pro uictoribus agere' (where Koestermann quotes Curt. 4.16.28), also comparing Hor. *C.* 4.4.51–2 'quos opimus | fallere et effugere est triumphus'.

tertia aestate . . . Artauasden fraude deceptum I.e. 34 B.C.; for Octavian's propagandist portrayal of the victory cf. Goodyear on Tac. *A.* 2.3.1 (esp. Dio 50.1.4 there quoted), Scott 37; for the Armenian king himself cf. *RE* 1.2.1308–9 = Artavasdes 1 (Baumgartner); for the expedition see Bengtson 44–6.

catenis . . . aureis The occasion was Antony's 'triumph' in Alexandria late in 34, described by V. below (4n.). Gold or silver chains were a conventional mark of respect (e.g. Just. 5.11.4, Prop. 2.1.33, Sil. 17.630, Amm. 27.12.3; other exs. quoted in Ruhnken, vol. 2, ad loc.). For *ne quid honori deesset* cf. Cic. *Fam.* 13.77.1 'ut honori tuo deessem' (F.).

82.4 crescente deinde et amoris in Cleopatram incendio . . . bellum patriae inferre constituit V. clearly states that Antony, on account of his relationship with Cleopatra, decided to attack his country. He dates the decision after the triumph over Artavasdes (cf. *deinde, cum . . . uectus esset Alexandriae*), which took place in late 34 B.C., but before the defection of Plancus (cf. 83.1–2 *Inter hunc . . . transfugit ad Caesarem*), which took place after Antony had divorced Octavia in May/June 32 B.C. (Dio 50.3.2). Exactly the same sequence of events is given by the epitomator of Livy, who dates the decision more precisely after the end of the triumvirate in Dec. 33 B.C. but before Antony's divorce (*per.* 132 'cum M. Antonius ob amorem Cleopatrae . . . finito triumuiratus tempore . . . bellumque moliretur quod urbi et Italiae inferret, ingentibus . . . copiis ob hoc contractis remissoque Octauiae . . . repudio'). The period of time in question is thus the spring of 32 B.C.

Now it seems to be an axiom of modern scholarship that Octavian wished to disguise the true nature of his struggle with Antony and/or to avoid the charge that he was renewing the civil wars which his recent victory over Sex. Pompeius was alleged to have stopped (cf. App. *BC* 5.130). Octavian's propaganda therefore depicted Antony as being completely under the malign influence of Cleopatra (cf. e.g. Dio 50.5.3, Hor. *Epod.* 9.11ff., Plut. *Ant.* 60.1, Serv. on *Aen.* 8.678, 696): it was she who posed the threat to Rome and Italy, while Antony, if at all possible, 'must not be mentioned' (Syme, *RR* 275; so too Scott 43–4; Grant, *Cleo.* 198). In this way, it is said, Oct. cleverly prepared the way for the moment when, late in 32 B.C., he declared war against Cleopatra alone (cf. Dio 50.4.4–5, 6.1, Plut. *Ant.* 60.1).

However, this hypothesis creates more problems than it solves. For example, it does not explain why the end of the civil wars was celebrated by Octavian in 29 B.C. when Antony had been defeated (cf. 89.3n.). It does not explain how Oct. could depict Antony as Cleopatra's slave yet at the same time contrive 'not to mention' him. It does not explain Suetonius' statement that Antony was declared a public enemy (*Aug.* 17.2 'hostis iudicatus'), which many scholars conveniently omit to record. And above all it takes no account of Antony's decision to attack Italy, a decision which is attested by most ancient authorities but which several modern scholars seem again not to mention (e.g. Syme, *RR* 271–95; *CAH* 10.95–9; Grant, *Cleo.* 289ff.). There are several possible explanations of this last omission,[1] but I suspect that scholars have simply extrapolated on the basis of what actually did happen late in 32 (viz. Oct. declared war on Cleopatra) rather than think themselves into circumstances as they actually were earlier that year.

That Antony had decided to attack Italy is stated not only by V. and Livy but also by Florus (2.21.1–3) and Dio (50.3.2); Plutarch implies as much (*Ant.* 56.1–2, 4, 57.3, 58.1), and adds the interesting observation (without giving any reason for it) that Antony postponed the attack and that this was reckoned to be one of his greatest mistakes (58.2). These authors no doubt inferred Antony's intention from the fact that in the spring of 32 he moved the whole of his army from its winter quarters in

---

[1] E.g. fashionable denigration of Oct. and corresponding sympathy for Ant.; the difficulty of reconciling the ancient evidence with the modern theories of Oct.'s propaganda, mentioned above.

Asia Minor to the west coast of Greece, an action which does indeed suggest that such was his intention. We also possess the texts of contemporary documents which state or imply that Cleopatra would conquer Rome (cf. W. W. Tarn, *JRS* 22 (1932), 135–48): the documents need not of course reflect official policy, but they are excellent evidence, quite independent of Oct.'s propaganda, for oriental opinion at the time. Now if Oct. and Italy, on the basis of Antony's troop movements across the Adriatic and other evidence, concluded that an invasion was imminent, the notorious oath of allegiance (see above, p. 208) becomes far more comprehensible than it is in the accounts of those historians who omit to mention Antony's decision to invade.[1] To this period may also belong the declaration that Antony was a public enemy, which Suetonius records.

As it was, of course, the invasion was postponed. We cannot now know why, but the most likely reason would seem to be a compromise by Antony between the various rival pressure groups within his camp (cf. Dio 50.3.2, Plut, *Ant.* 56.2–3). If the invasion had gone ahead as planned, it would have been a mixed blessing for Octavian. He might have had some difficulty in repelling it (this is the clear implication of Plut. *Ant.* 58.2), but at least Antony would have appeared unequivocally as the aggressor. The postponement, on the other hand, left Octavian in a superior military position for the following year (cf. Plut. *Ant.* 58.2), but it also meant that he now had to take the initiative. He was therefore 'compelled', as a result of circumstances which had changed radically since the spring and early summer, to declare war on Cleopatra late in 32 B.C. That he declared war on her alone is not surprising, if, as suggested, Antony had already been declared an enemy earlier in the year.

Whatever the truth may be, it seems to me that we cannot simply dismiss the evidence of the ancient authorities who, like V., state that Antony decided to attack Italy.

For *amoris incendio* cf. Cic. *Fin.* 5.70 'cupiditatum incendiis'; for *uitiorum . . . aluntur* cf. 102.3n.

cum ante Nouum se Liberum Patrem appellari iussisset *ante* probably refers to 39 B.C., when Antony visited Athens with his wife Octavia and ordered people to address him as Dionysus (cf. Socrates of Rhodes, a contemporary, fr. 2, *FGrH* 2.2, p. 928 = Athen. (4) 148c (ἐκέλευσεν); Sen. *Suas.* 1.6–7 'uellet se L. P. dici et hoc nomen statuis suis subscribi iuberet'). At roughly the same time he issued *cistophori* depicting himself as Dionysus (cf. A. Bruhl, *Liber Pater* (1953), 128; Michel 130–1; Taylor 109, 122 fig. 15; *CRR* 193 nos. 1197–8). Antony's first attested connection with Dionysus, however, goes back to 41 B.C., when he was greeted as the god at Ephesus and likened to the god at Tarsus (Plut. *Ant.* 24.3, 26.3); and the relationship between god and man was continued in

[1] The oath is usually placed later in the year by historians, but I do not know what their evidence is. Rice Holmes (*Arch.* 144–5) seems to place it early, but before any decision by Antony to invade.

Antony's triumphal entry into Alexandria in 34 B.C., described by V. just below (see n.), and on other indeterminable occasions (for the evidence see the excellent survey of J. L. Tondriau, 'Romains de la république assimilés à des divinités', *SO* 27 (1949), 130–2). Plutarch rightly describes Dionysus as the god 'to whom Antony always likened and attached himself most' (*Ant.* 75.4). The prefix *Nouus* (= *Néos*) was used in many such titles to indicate that the man reproduced the qualities or achievements of the god concerned: see Nock 1.144ff., esp. 148–9 = *JHS* 48 (1928), 30ff., esp. 34–6; but Nock is wrong to imply (148 = 34) that Antony did not himself seek the title (see above).

Antony was able to derive two particular advantages from calling himself Nouus Liber Pater (or *Néos Διόνυσος*). First, he reinforced the connection with the Ptolemaic dynasty which he already enjoyed through his relationship with Cleopatra. There had long been a connection in Alexandria between the Ptolemies and the Dionysiac cult (see P. M. Fraser, *Ptolemaic Alexandria* (1970), 1.201–5, 2.342–50), and Cleopatra's father had actually been called Ptolemy XII Neos Dionysos. In Egyptian texts her father is 'New Osiris', since Osiris was identified, at least in part, with Dionysus (see *RE* Suppl. 9.509–10; Hdt. 2.42.2; Plut. *De Is. et Os.* 35). The same identification naturally applied to Antony also, and we find that statues were erected to him as Osiris and to Cleopatra as Isis, Osiris' mythical 'wife' (Dio 50.5.3; Grant, *Cleo.* 275–7). The fact that the name Osiris means 'Occupier of the Monarchy' (*RE* (as above) 469–70) no doubt bound Antony all the more tightly to Cleopatra's cause; but it clearly left him open to attack from Octavian's propaganda.

The second advantage, not unconnected with the first, was that the title Nouus Liber Pater linked Antony with Alexander the Great. There seems little doubt that at some point during his career (the exact date is problematic) Alexander established a relationship between himself and Dionysus which was considerably elaborated on after his death: see Nock 1.134–44, esp. 136ff. = 21–30, esp. 22ff. (142–4 = 28–30 on the link with the Ptolemies). Antony's own relationship with Dionysus represents only one element in a fairly long list of correspondences between himself and Alexander. For example, after the battle of Philippi in 42 B.C. he had covered Brutus' body with his purple cloak (Plut. *Ant.* 22.4), as Alexander had done in the case of Darius (Plut. *Alex.* 43.5); Antony's attempted conquests of the east in 36 and 34 B.C. are parallel to those of Alexander;[1] Antony's pamphlet *De Ebrietate Sua* (on which cf. K. Scott, *CP* 24 (1929), 133–41) doubtless quoted *inter alia* examples of earlier outstanding men who were reputed to drink heavily, among whom Alex. was conspicuous (cf. Vell. 41.1); both Antony and Alex. represented themselves as descendants of Hercules (cf. Michel 114ff.); and the triumphal ceremony which

---

[1] Of the campaign in 36 Bengtson says 'der Traum des Ant. von der Nachfolge Alexanders d. Gr. war ausgeträumt' (47), comparing, perhaps mistakenly, the campaign of 34 with that of Hitler against Russia.

Antony conducted in Alexandria in 34 B.C. has striking parallels with celebrations attributed to Alexander (see below). It could of course be argued that Antony's behaviour was hardly special since Alexander-imitation had long been conventional among Roman politicians: on this see Weippert (pp. 193ff. on Antony); G. Wirth, 'Alexander und Rom', and E. Schwarzenberg, 'The portraiture of Alex.', in *Alexandre le Grand: image et réalité* (Entretiens Hardt 22, 1976), 181ff., 223ff. Yet here again the image of an all-conquering hero can hardly have pleased Octavian, who desired that role for himself and after Actium proceeded to adopt it (cf. D. Kienast, 'Augustus und Alexander', *Gymn.* 76 (1969), esp. 441ff.).

The scholarly literature on all aspects of this subject is vast; on Alex. in particular see also 41.1n. and 94.2n. (where the title of Michel's work should be corrected), and D. Gillis, 'Imitatio Alexandri', *CRDAC* 11 (1977-8), 45-65.

cum redimitus hederis ... uectus esset Alexandriae The occasion was the victory over Artavasdes in the later part of 34 B.C.: see Huzar 182, 296 n. 28, with full refs. According to Grant (*Cleo.* 243-4), V. has 'correctly indicated the special religious character which Antony gave to the procession' and has not assumed, as did contemporary Romans, that Antony sacrilegiously held a proper Roman triumph outside Rome. See also Syme, *RR* 270 and n. 1. For the similarly Bacchic celebrations of Alexander cf. Curt. 8.10.15ff., 9.10.24ff.

For *corona uelatus* cf. Ov. *Ex P.* 4.14.55 'tempora sacrata mea sunt uelata corona' (Krause); I can find no exact parallel for *cothurnis succinctus*, but the verb is used with nouns of such variety (see L&S s.v.) that I am disinclined to question the text.

83   THE ANTICS OF PLANCUS (32 B.C.)

83.1 Inter hunc apparatum belli By making *hunc* agree with *apparatum* rather than *belli* V. intends us to infer that Antony's bizarre appearance as Dionysus constituted preparation for war. The intention is of course wickedly humorous, but the inference is itself illogical since the Dionysiac incident is explicitly stated to have taken place before Antony decided on war (*cum ante . . . cum . . .*). The true meaning of the phrase, as H–W saw, can only be: 'during the preparation for this war [i.e. the one I have just mentioned]'. *hunc* stands for *huius* and is an example of enallage (cf. 91.3n.).[1] V.'s sleight of hand is aided by the fact that *apparatus belli* (*TLL* 2.256.71ff., 1842.68-73) and *app. luxuriae* (*TLL* 2.258.11ff.) are both quasi-technical expressions, and he appears at first glance to have used the former when he really ought to have used the latter.

---

[1] If at 82.4 V. had said 'Antony declared war and entered Alexandria dressed up as Dionysus', then *inter hunc apparatum belli* would have meant 'during this preparation for war' and would have been an example of straightforward irony.

COMMENTARY 2.83.2

non iudicio . . . sed morbo proditor   The contrast *iudicium/morbus* is
fairly common (cf. Cic. *Off.* 1.49, [Sall.] *In Cic.* 1.1 'iudicio magis quam
morbo animi', Sen. *Contr.* 1.6.9 'iudicio . . . non . . . furore aut morbo',
2.1.6) and indicates that mental illness or madness is in question. Charges
both of dementia and of treachery are extremely frequent in political
invective (Opelt 269, 279: index s.vv. *demens, proditor*), but V.'s phrase is
particularly memorable. For *morbo* + substant. cf. D. R. Shackleton
Bailey's suggested punctuation at Hor. *C.* 1.37.9–10 'turpium, | morbo
uirorum' (*Proc. Leeds Philos. Soc.: Lit. and Hist. Section* 10.3 (1963), 113);
Krause compares φύσει προδότης at Xen. *Hell.* 2.3.30.
    For L. Munatius Plancus and V.'s treatment of him cf. 63.3nn., 74.3n.,
95.3n.; Bosworth 449–51. For *amor rei p.* cf. *TLL* 1.1969.53ff.; for *amor*
used of persons in a political context cf. 62.6n. and Hellegouarc'h, *VL*
146–7, there quoted.

humillimus adsentator reginae . . . auctor et minister   Most of
the expressions in this passage can be paralleled in political invective: cf.
e.g. Cic. *Caec.* 14 'mulierum adsentatoris', Liv. 31.25.10 'a. regios',
39.27.8; Sall. *H.* 1.55.21 'pessimis seruorum', Cic. *Mil.* 87 and Ascon.'s
n., *Pis.* 11, Vell. 73.1, *SHA Aurel.* 38.3 'ultimus seruorum'; Cic. *Verr.* 3.21
'ministri cupiditatum', Ov. *Met.* 9.577 'uetitae scelerate libidinis
auctor', Vell. 19.1 'auctores nouarum pessimarumque rerum', 33.1
'semper uenalis et alienae minister potentiae', Tac. *H.* 4.27.1 'illum auctorem sceleris, hunc ministrum uocant', *A.* 6.48.4 'stuprorum eius
ministri'. Some of these exs. derive from Opelt's work, q.v. For *infra seruos*
cf. Tac. *A.* 13.2.2; for *obscenissimarum rerum* cf. Sen. *Contr.* 1.2.13 (F.).

83.2 in omnia et [in] omnibus uenalis   'venal to all men and for all
purposes' (Watson). *in omnia* may be taken closely with *uenalis* (cf. e.g.
Tac. *H.* 2.56.1 'in omne fas nefasque . . . uenales', *A.* 12.46.1), but the
expr. is otherwise common in V. and elsewhere (cf. 97.1n.). I can find no
parallel for *uenalis* + dative; but without Gelenius' deletion *in omnibus*
might be understood as simply repeating *in omnia*, as Lipsius observed
when making the same correction himself.

caudam trahens genibus innixus   The first phrase explains the
second: Glaucus' appearance was that of a 'merman' (cf. Ov. *Met.*
13.962–3 'caerula bracchia uidi | cruraque pinnigero curuata nouissima
pisce'; also 915 'ultima . . . tortilis inguina piscis'). Accusations of
dancing or miming were conventional in political invective (cf. Opelt
158–9; Cic. *Pis.* 18 with Nisbet's n.; e.g. Cic. *Deiot.* 26 'ait hac laetitia D.
elatum uino se obruisse in conuiuioque nudum saltauisse', and cf. also
Tac. *A.* 11.31.2). Cicero had long ago accused Antony of including *mimi*
in his retinue (*Phil.* 2.67), and Antony in his propaganda later accused
Oct. of holding an impious banquet similar to that described by V. here
(Suet. *Aug.* 70): see in general on this aspect of propaganda K. Scott (as
above: 82.4n.), M. P. Charlesworth, *CQ* 27 (1933), 175.

216

caeruleatus occurs only here but is formed on the analogy of many similar words (cf. J. André, *Etude sur les termes de couleur dans la langue latine* (1949), 210–11). *saltare* + accus. is the normal expr. for ' to dance the ~ ' (see e.g. K–S 1.278).

ob manifestarum rapinarum indicia Cornelissen (1887) proposed *manifesta*, but cf. Cic. *Fam.* 15.2.6 'indicia manifestarum insidiarum'. *refrigeratus* here = ' cold-shouldered by '; for the constr. with (*ab* +) abl., cf. e.g. Suet. *Claud.* 41.1, Quint. 5.7.26; metaphorical uses of ' cold ' are very common, e.g. the elaborate joke in Catull. 44.

The moment when Plancus and his nephew Titius (below) defected seems to have been mid-32 B.C. (Plut. *Ant.* 58.2, Dio 50.3.1ff.; Carter 193). They were responsible for revealing to Oct. the contents of Antony's will (Plut. Dio. locc. citt.), which he in turn revealed to the senate. The question whether all or part of the will was forged is debated (cf. Syme, *RR* 282–3; J. Crook, *JRS* 47 (1957), 36–8), but most modern scholars seem to agree with Dio (50.3.5–4.1) that its contents, once revealed, had a decisive effect on public opinion: people inferred, from the clause which said that Antony wished to be buried in Alexandria alongside Cleopatra, that he intended to transfer the capital thither from Rome. Yet, as Syme admits (*RR* 283 n. 3), Plutarch attaches far less importance to the will (*Ant.* 58–9) and V. does not mention it at all. It seems to me that people were probably far more worried about Antony's troop movements across the Adriatic, to which V. does refer (cf. 82.4n.); the will simply confirmed what they knew already.

dictitans id probatum a Caesare cui ille ignouerat ' insisting that Octavian had approved what he had (only) forgiven '. *id* = ' uitam priorem Planci et facinora ' (Krause); for the omission of a word = ' only ' cf. 68.5n. For the contrast *probatum/ignouerat* Gruter quoted Liv. 36.35.11 ' ueniam impetrasse non causam probasse uideri ', Curt. 7.1.6 ' supplicio magis quam crimini . . . exemptus '. For *clementiam . . . interpretabatur*, above, cf. Tac. *H.* 1.52.4 'ipsa uitia pro uirtutibus interpretabatur ', Front. *Strat.* 1.10.3, Ap. *Apol.* 73 (noted by G. B. A. Fletcher, *Latomus* 30 (1971), 384). For Oct.'s *clementia* cf. 86.2n.

mox autem hunc auunculum It is clear from BA that (M) read *mox autem hunc mox auunculum.*[1] Rhenanus, realising that the repeated *mox* was an error, deleted it in certain copies of the *ed. pr.* such as those used by Kritz and Haase (see his p. v.). My own copy of P, however, and Burer's lemma therein, both read simply *hunc mox auunculum*. Though the case is admittedly not clear-cut, it seems to me that *mox autem hunc auunculum* is more correct than *hunc mox auunculum*, from which it ought to follow that my copy of P is earlier than those of Kritz and Haase (see 67.1n.). Yet

---

[1] At *TN* 7 n. 7 I wrongly stated that (M) read *mox autem hunc auunculum.*

according to Kritz and Haase, their copies of P also read *non* instead of *homo* at 35.2: the latter is undoubtedly correct and is read in my copy of P, from which it ought to follow that my copy is *later* than those of Kritz and Haase! The conflicting nature of this evidence will come as no surprise to those who have read my long n. at 67.1; and I can see no way of resolving the conflict (i.e. of placing the various copies of P in some sort of chronological order) without a great deal more evidence being available.

For Titius cf. 79.5n.

83.3 Coponius . . . P. Silii socer   For Coponius cf. *RE* 4.1.1215 = Coponius 3 (Münzer); *MRR* 2.257, 276. For P. Silius (Nerva) cf. 90.4n. I have assumed, with Kritz and others, that the paradosis *pater* arose through a misinterpretation of *P*. There is a comparable error at 102.3 (see n.).

haud absurde (-*um*) is also at 38.1, 77.1, Sall. *C.* 3.1, 25.5; *non a.* at Val. Max. 2.4.5, Tac. *A.* 12.9.1, 13.14.1. The adjj. *grauissimus* here and *recens* below both add to the humour of the scene.

pridie quam tu illum relinqueres   Some scholars (e.g. Shipley) have thought that *pridie quam* here = *priusquam*; but there seems to be no other ex. of this meaning in Latin, with the possible exception of Marcell. *Dig.* 40.5.10.2.[1] I therefore assume that *pridie quam* has its normal meaning and that the irony lies, not in an insinuation that Plancus must inevitably have been implicated in the *nefanda* with which he charges Antony, but in the feigned assumption that Antony must have been irreproachable until the day before Plancus left him, since otherwise an honourable man like Plancus would not have supported him for so long.

84–87 ACTIUM AND ITS AFTERMATH
(31–30 B.C.)

When V. was born, in 20/19 B.C.,[2] the battle of Actium was already more than a decade past and Virgil's glorification of it was becoming known to the Roman world (*Aen.* 8.671ff.).[3] Other poets to celebrate the battle were Horace (*C.* 1.37), Propertius (3.11, 4.6) and ps.-Rabirius (*Bell. Act.* in *PLM* 1.212ff.).[4] Every five years Actium was commemorated by games 'pro salute et uictoria' which continued throughout the empire even after

---

[1] I am most grateful to the Secretariat of *TLL* for information on this point. None of the exs. of *pridie* = 'in the time preceding', as given in *OLD* s.v. *b*, seems to me to require this meaning but rather the normal meaning (incl. Liv. 9.11.4). See also above, 65.2n.

[2] For the date see Sumner 275 n. 111.

[3] See esp. G. Binder, *Aeneas und Augustus* (1971), 213ff.

[4] Cf. Nisbet–Hubbard on Hor. *C.* 1.37; M. L. Paladini, *Latomus* 17 (1958), 240ff., 462ff.

Augustus' death (Weinstock 315–16), and the fiftieth anniversary of the battle in A.D. 20 was marked by coin issues (Grant, *RAI* 57–8, 61, 164–5). Thus throughout V.'s life Actium was kept in the public eye, and the sixtieth anniversary in A.D. 30 coincided with the date when he published his work.[1] It is therefore not surprising that, despite the summary form of his work, V. has devoted considerable space to the battle and its sequel.

V. dramatises his account by reflecting briefly on what might have happened if Antony had won (85.6, 86.1n.), by indulging in ornate sentence structure[2] and complex alliteration (85.5nn.), and by elaborating the actual encounter almost (but not quite) to the point of illogicality (85.3n.).[3] These dramatic devices help to emphasise the significance of the battle, which in V.'s opinion was that it brought to an end the civil wars (87.1).[4] Just as he began his account of the civil wars with a *syncrisis* of Pompey and Caesar (49.1–3 *alterius . . . alterius, hic . . . illic, illa . . . haec*), so he now begins his account of Actium with a *syncrisis* of Antony and Caesar's adopted son (84.1 *in hac parte . . . ⟨in⟩ illa, hinc . . . illinc, haec . . . illa, hinc . . . illinc*). By repeating the technique (ring composition) V. invites a comparison between the *syncrises* themselves, i.e. between present circumstances and those then. Whereas in 49 B.C. Caesarians displayed *prudentia* but did not follow the *causa melior* (49.1 'alterius ducis causa melior uidebatur', 3 'uir antiquus et grauis Pompeii partes laudaret magis, prudens sequeretur Caesaris'), now almost twenty years later the *prudentia* of Octavian's supporters was matched by the excellence of their cause (84.2 'meliora et utiliora'). They now had right on their side not only because Antony had alienated popular sympathy but also because Octavian himself was avenging the murder of his adoptive father, something of which V. reminds readers at the beginning and end of the Actian narrative. At 84.1 he uses the phrase *Iulianae partes* to emphasise the link between Octavian and Caesar (cf. also 85.2), and at 87.3 he observes that Cassius Parmensis was 'the last of Caesar's assassins to die, as Trebonius had been the first'. The reference to Cassius occurs in a retrospective section (87.2–3) in which V. reflects on those who died not only in the campaign immediately past but also in earlier years of the civil wars and which thus forms an effective and appropriate conclusion to his narrative of the civil wars as a whole.

---

[1] For the date of publication of V.'s work see Woodman (1975), 273–6.

[2] Analysed in *Latomus* 25 (1966), 564–6.

[3] V.'s account is of little help in elucidating the many strategic and tactical problems with which modern scholars, most recently Leroux and Carter, have been occupied. But we could hardly expect him to be as helpful as he is when describing campaigns in which he took part himself (cf. *TN* 153–4).

[4] So too Liv. *per.* 133, Suet. *Aug.* 9.1, Flor. 2.22.1, and 'il est évident qu'elle fut sentie comme telle par le peuple romain' (Jal 152 n. 2). By 'civil wars' V. means those which began in 49 B.C. (see 48.3n., 89.3n.); but Suet. (loc. cit.) means those which began with Mutina in 44/43.

84 BEFORE THE BATTLE

84.1 Caesare... Coruino consulibus 31 B.C. Consular dating of this type 'is used almost exclusively to highlight important events' (Starr (1978), 80 n. 1; cf. e.g. 1.12.3–6, 1.13.1, 2.2.2, 2.4.5, 2.15.1, 27.1 etc.). For Corvinus cf. 71.1n. For *apud Actium* cf. Tac. *H.* 1.1.1 'bellatum apud Actium' and Fletcher (1964), 54.

exploratissima Iulianarum partium ... uictoria 'The battle of Actium was decided before it was fought' (Syme, *RR* 296). V. explains why in the following sentences, although his explanation involves an apparent contradiction with 85.3–4 below (see n.).

As Mr Seager points out to me, the use of the phrases *Iulianarum partium* here (cf. also 85.2) and *Antonianarum partium* at 2 below 'not only emphasises the continuity with Caesar but implies that only Octavian had any claim on any level to be considered Caesar's successor, which was after all the original bone of contention between him and Antony'. For the link with Caesar cf. also Virg. *Aen.* 8.680–1, where Oct. fights under the Julian star, and Prop. 4.6.59, where Caesar actually looks down on the battle. For *Iulianus* cf. also 63.3n.; for *exploratissima ... uictoria* cf. Cic. *Fam.* 6.1.3, 6.6.12, 11.14.1 and regularly in Caes. *BG.*

uigebat in hac parte miles atque imperator, ⟨in⟩ illa marcebant omnia The contrast is no doubt standard (cf. Marcellus' speech in Liv. 23.45.2 'qui pugnent marcere Campana luxuria, uino et scortis omnibusque lustris per totam hiemem confectos. abisse illam uim uigoremque, delapsa esse robora corporum animorumque'). Yet Octavian's troops had in fact been hardened by recent campaigns in Illyricum in 35–33 (cf. 78.2n.), whereas Antony's were slack both because they lacked similar training and also because they included oriental recruits (Dio 50.6.5; Syme, *RR* 294–5) whom the Romans traditionally regarded as soft (cf. Balsdon 60ff., 68ff.). Antony's sojourn in Egypt with Cleopatra had invited charges of effeminacy against him and his army (cf. 82.3–4nn.; Hor. *Epod.* 9.11–16), and Carter 188–90 believes that Cleopatra's presence in Antony's camp in 32 had a deleterious effect on his troops' morale. For the troops available to each side cf. Carter 202–3.

P omits *in*, which Vascosanus supplied. Since the clause does not make sense without *in*, P's reading, if correct, would require the preposition to be understood from the preceding clause and would thus be an example of ἀπὸ κοινοῦ. This construction, which is to be distinguished from *uariatio*,[1]

---

[1] *uariatio* occurs where the sense of a clause or phrase does *not* require a preposition to be understood from elsewhere: since *summouere*, for ex., is often constructed with the simple abl., there is no need to understand *ex* ἀπὸ κοινοῦ with *campo* and *curia* at 126.2 'summota e foro seditio, ambitio campo, discordia curia' (see n. ad loc.). Another ex. is Quint. 3.8.7 'emolumentum non utilitate aliqua sed in sola laude consistit', which Adamietz is wrong to call ἀπὸ κοινοῦ (ad loc.).

occurs very frequently in verse (e.g. Lucr. 3.622–3 'neque flamma creari | fluminibus solitast neque in igni gignier algor' and Kenney ad loc.; esp. Clausen on Pers. 1.131), but seems to be more controversial in prose, where editors do not have the metre to guide them. E.g. at Liv. 37.7.16 'inde non per Macedoniam modo sed etiam Thraciam prosequente . . . Philippo' neither Weissenborn–Müller nor Madvig print ⟨per⟩ *Thraciam*, whereas at 45.8.4 'quorum et uim bello et fidem in pace expertus esses' they all print ⟨in⟩ *bello*. In the latter case their reason is doubtless that *in* could so easily have been omitted after *uim*; yet Drakenborch did not insert it and cf. Tac. *D*. 6.6 'nam ingenio quoque, sicut in agro' where Winterbottom (unlike Gudeman and Peterson) does not print ⟨in⟩ *ingenio*. The present case in V. is similarly difficult. Baehrens (235ff.) has a very long discussion of the phenomenon in many authors and defends P's reading here on the grounds that ἀπὸ κοινοῦ is particularly common in sentences which involve two contrasting elements and in which there is also an ellipse of the substantive in the second element, as here (pp. 295–6). In his Addenda (p. 534) Baehrens parallels Cic. *Acad*. 1.39 'cum alia in parte animi cupiditatem, alia rationem collocarent' and remarks: 'Die beiden Stellen stützen sich gegenseitig auf immer!!' (cf. also Liv. 28.12.10 'res quadam ex parte eandem fortunam, quadam longe disparem habebant'). These passages suggest that V. could have dispensed with *in* here had he wanted to, but his rhetoric makes it likely that he included it since this is the beginning of a series of contrasts which are otherwise exactly balanced. I have therefore followed Vascosanus. *in* might easily have been omitted by a scribe in an attempt to 'correct' *illam arcebant*, which, as we know from BA, was the reading of (M). For ἀπὸ κοινοῦ with *in* cf. *TLL* 7.1.804.11ff.; with prepositions in general, L–H–S 835; Bömer on Ov. *Met*. 6.190; A. E. Housman, *CQ* 10 (1916), 149 = *CP* 938; E. J. Kenney, *CQ* 8 (1958), 55; Brink on Hor. *Epist*. 2.1.31.[1]

hinc re⟨mi⟩ges firmissimi Octavian's fleet had gained valuable experience in the naval war against Sextus Pompeius (above, ch. 79). In preferring the adj. *firmus* to *ualidus*, V. resembles Cic. Caes. and in general Liv. (Adams (1974), 59–60).

illinc inopia adfectissimi Agrippa's victory at Leucas (see below) had interfered with Antony's supply-routes (Dio 50.13.6, 14.4) and forced

---

[1] The work of E. Ramach (*De figurae, quae dicitur ἀπὸ κοινοῦ, usu et de praepositionum repetitione et omissione apud rerum scriptores argenteae Latinitatis: Tractantur Vell. Pat., Curtius Rufus, Iul. Florus, Iun. Iustinus*, unpubl. diss. Vienna, 1930) is disappointingly unhelpful. His definitions of ἀπὸ κοινοῦ are extremely broad and include some phenomena which we would not normally call ἀπὸ κοινοῦ at all and others which we would call by different names (e.g. hyperbaton). He merely lists exs. without any discussion or comparative material.

COMMENTARY 2.84.1

his army to raid the surrounding countryside (Plut. *Ant.* 68.4–5). A colourful account of the area's unpleasantness today is provided by Carter (211).

The superl. form *adfectissimus* is apparently found only here; for *inopia adf.* cf. Cic. *Att.* 6.3.2 (F.).

nauium haec magnitudo modica nec celeritati aduersa, illa specie [et] terribilior   The contrast between the speed and manoeuvrability of Octavian's ships and the size and weight of Antony's became a feature of the battle legend (cf. Hor. *Epod.* 1.1–2, Dio 50.23.2–3, 32.2–3, Plut. *Ant.* 65.4–66.2, Flor. 2.21.5–6 'urbium specie'). 'But whether there was any significant difference in size or speed is open to question. In any case, both sides intended to employ the tactics that had served Octavian and Agrippa so well in their decisive victory over Sextus Pompeius five years earlier' (Grant, *Cleo.* 310; also Carter 215). Propertius makes a similar point to V. but refers it to the threatening decoration of Antony's ships (4.6.49–50). For the number of ships involved see Leroux 31ff.

Heinsius proposed *hac . . . illac*, but *haec . . . illa* is an ex. of enallage (i.e. = *harum (nauium) . . . illarum*, 'the size of these ships . . . of those . . .'): for enallage in general cf. 91.3n., and with *hic* in particular cf. e.g. Cic. *Tim.* 33 'hos siderum errores' (where the Greek is τὰς τούτων πλάνας, Plato, *Tim.* 39c8); *TLL* 6.3.2741.75ff. On the other hand I think Rhenanus was right to delete *et*:[1] either a scribe wrote *et* in the mistaken expectation of a double contrast with *nec* immediately above or else (and more likely) it is a simple case of dittography (so Kreyssig). For similar wrong insertions cf. 76.2, 107.2, 110.6. E. Thomas defended *et* (= *etiam*); Burer conjectured *species t.*; others have suggested a lacuna after *et* (e.g. ⟨*turribus*⟩ Burman); others still have supplied a word meaning 'only' (e.g. *illa* ⟨*sola*⟩ *specie t.* Bothe; but cf. 68.5n.).

For *magnitudo modica* cf. Varro, *RR* 2.7.4, *Rhet. Herenn.* 3.31, Sen. *NQ* 5.12.3.

illinc ad Caesarem cotidie aliquis transfugiebat   No doubt an exaggeration, and perhaps a conventional motif (cf. Caes. *BC* 1.78.2 'magnus eorum cotidie numerus ad Caesarem perfugiebat', 3.61.2 'cum paene cotidie a Pompeio ad Caesarem perfugerent', *BG* 7.44.2, *Bell. Afr.* 32.3); yet Dio tells us that there were frequent desertions from Antony in the spring of 31 (50.11.2), and V.'s testimony is accepted by Leroux 30. Titius and Plancus had already crossed over (83.2n.), and others who fled were M. Iunius Silanus, M. Licinius Crassus, Cn. Domitius Ahenobarbus, Q. Dellius, C. Geminius, and the kings Amyntas, Rhoemetalces and Deiotarus Philadelphus (cf. Plut. *Ant.* 59.3, 63.3, Dio 50.13.5–6, 51.4.3). For

---

[1] In his personal copy of the *ed. pr.* (see von der Gönna 239), having originally conjectured *erat* in P. Later *et* was also deleted by Gelenius.

222

the timing of some of these desertions see below, 2n. We are also told that Q. Postumius and king Iamblichus, suspected of treachery, were executed *pour encourager les autres* (Dio 50.13.7).

Heinsius noted that *s* and *d* are confused at 76.4.

denique in ore atque oculis . . . classis hostium superata   For the three named victories see also Dio 50.13.5; Carter 209–10. The reference of *bis ante ultimum discrimen classis hostium superata* is much more difficult to determine (Liv. *per.* 132 merely mentions 'pugnae nauales'). The possibilities are as follows. (a) Dio seems to draw a distinction between the actual capture of Patrae and the naval victory which preceded it (50.13.5 Πάτρας εἷλε Κύιντον Νασίδιον ναυμαχίᾳ νικήσας). We infer from Plutarch, on the other hand, that Corinth soon returned to Antony's possession and thus its seizure by Agrippa was not a genuine victory at all (*Ant.* 67.7). It is therefore possible that V., having discounted the temporary success at Corinth, is doing the same as Dio but with reference to both Patrae *and* Leucas: in that case *bis . . . superata* would constitute a 'summing-up' of the two genuine naval victories. (b) At 50.12.2 Dio tells us that Octavian took Corcyra 'with his ships' after its garrison had deserted and that subsequently the enemy refused to fight a sea-battle 'through fear'. An imaginative historian might well represent this success as a naval victory.[1] (c) It is well known that somewhat later Agrippa defeated Sosius in a naval battle (Dio 50.14.1–2) after the latter had attempted a break-out coinciding with a joint mission by Dellius and Amyntas to Macedonia for Antony (Carter 211–12). This victory, together with (b) above, may explain the phrase *bis . . . superata*. Alternatively V. may be referring to any two of the successes mentioned in (a)–(c) above. It is impossible to know.

For the common combination of *os* and *oculi* cf. Wölfflin 268–9; the expr. is regularly used of things, e.g. Cic. *Verr.* 2.81 'in ore atque oculis prouinciae'.

84.2 rex Amyntas meliora et utiliora secutus   For this king of the Galatians cf. *RE* 1.2.2007–8 = Amyntas 21 (v. Rohden); *PIR*[2] 1.94–5 no. 572. On the significance of *meliora et utiliora* see above, p. 219.

Haase transposed the present sentence *rex . . . transmisit ad Caesarem* to follow *transfugiebat* at 1 above. The suggestion is extremely attractive because it produces a homogeneous section on deserters in which the general statement *illinc . . . transfugiebat* is followed by the three specified examples of Amyntas, Dellius and Domitius. Yet there are two reasons why I am not convinced. (a) The three named deserters constitute a most effective ending to the pre-battle narrative. Amyntas' desertion was not

---

[1] Compare how Hor. in *Epod.* 9 describes the inactivity of the enemy (19–20) as a victory (27 *marique uictus hostis*). On this poem see also next fn.

only thought worthy of celebration by Horace in *Epode* 9 (lines 17–18)[1] but was also regarded by Servius as the reason why Oct. was victorious (*uictoriam consecutus: Aen.* 6.612); Dellius was responsible for actually revealing Antony's battle plans to Oct. (Dio 50.23.3); and Domitius, debilitated but defiant, is a splendidly dramatic figure. The flight of these three was 'the final straw'. (b) Chronology may also tell against Haase's transposition. If V. did *not* intend the sentence *bis . . . superata* at 1 above to include the victory over Sosius (see n.), Haase's transposition would disrupt the chronological order of events, in which all three desertions took place after the successes at Corcyra, Leucas, Patrae and Corinth.[2] If however V. *did* intend *bis . . . superata* to include the victory over Sosius, Haase's transposition would indeed place Domitius' desertion before that victory, where it belongs, but would still misrepresent the timing of Amyntas' and Dellius' desertions, both of which took place well after the victory over Sosius (Carter, loc. cit.). On the whole, therefore, I think it is safer to keep the order of the sentences as found in the paradosis.

nam Dellius, exempli sui tenax *nam* is used to explain the difference between listed items which are apparently similar (see Pease on Cic. *ND* 1.27). Here the difference is one of motive: Amyntas and Dellius both deserted, but in so doing the former was prudent and high-minded (cf. *meliora et utiliora*) whereas the latter was simply a chronic traitor (*exempli sui tenax*). (A similar contrast, but applied to a single person only, is at 83.1.)

For *exempli sui* cf. Sen. *D.* 12.19.4, Tac. *H.* 4.59.3 (F.); for *exempli . . . tenax* cf. Sen. *Ep.* 120.6 (F.). For Dellius cf. *RE* 4.2.2447–8 = Dellius 1 (Wissowa); Nisbet–Hubbard on Hor. *C.* 2.3.

ut a Dolabella * ad Caesarem** The sense, if not the content, of the lacuna may be supplied by Sen. *Suas.* 1.7 '(Dellius) ab Dolabella ad Cassium transiturus salutem sibi pactus est . . . , a Cassio deinde transit ad Antonium, nouissime ab Antonio transfugit ad Caesarem' (quoted by Lipsius). For Dolabella cf. 60.4n.

numquam reginam nisi nomine salutauit I.e. he refused to acknowledge her title, cf. Suet. *Vesp.* 15 'solus priuato nomine Vespasianum salutauerat', to which Krause adds Dio 49.40.4 (also of Cleopatra)

---

[1] The dramatic moment of this poem is, in my opinion, a drinking party which takes place in Rome after the news of Amyntas' desertion but before the final victory (which the revellers proceed in lines 27ff. to visualise): see esp. R. Miles, *The Epodes of Horace* (diss. Newcastle, 1980), 115–33; also A. E. Housman, *JP* 10 (1882), 194–6 = *CP* 7–8, Wistrand 24ff. Williams (212ff.) and Leroux (38ff.), however, believe that the poem describes the actual aftermath of the battle.

[2] Thus reconstructed by Carter 210–14, based closely on Dio and accepted by Grant, *Cleo.* 304–7.

ἀλλ' ὀνομαστί ἐ προσαγορεύσαντες. Dio tells us (50.13.6) that Domitius, who had a grudge against the queen, died of disease soon after his desertion, a circumstance to which V.'s *maximo et praecipiti periculo* perhaps refers; alternatively V. may simply mean that Domitius ran the risk of being put to death by Oct. as a suspected assassin of Julius Caesar. For *praecipiti periculo* cf. Cels. 2.11.6 'si incisa uena praeceps p. est' (F.); for Domitius himself, 72.3n.

85   THE DAY OF THE BATTLE

85.1 maximi discriminis dies   2 Sept. 31 (EJ p. 51). For the emphasis on the 'actual day', a well known dramatic technique, cf. 86.1 and n.; for *aduenit . . . dies* cf. Cic. *Verr.* 2.37, Virg. *Aen.* 7.145, 11.687 (F.), Liv. 29.1.5 (9.5.11 'hora . . . aduenit'); for *discriminis* cf. perhaps *discriminis hora* at Luc. 6.415, Val. Fl. 5.311.

productis classibus   'having led out their fleets' (a technical verb, cf. *Bell. Alex.* 14.3, *SHA Did.* 6.4). We are told by Dio 50.31.5 that Octavian's fleet adopted a crescent-shaped formation; and Prop. 4.6.25 implies (perhaps fancifully, but accepted by Leroux 48) that Antony's did the same. It is therefore just possible that *producere* here has its other meaning of 'extend, draw out' (cf. *cornu* below), which appears to be the interpretation of Huzar 219.

pro salute alter, in ruinam alter terrarum orbis dimicauere   By the middle of the second century B.C. the Romans were regarded by Polybius as rulers of the whole world (cf. Plb. 1.1.5, 1.2.7 with Walbank's n., 1.3.10, 15.10.2 with Walbank's n., 21.16.8, 21.23.4; also P. A. Brunt on 'The conception of world empire' in P. D. A. Garnsey and C. R. Whittaker (edd.), *Imperialism in the Ancient World* (1978), 168–9 with n. 34), but Tib. Gracchus in 133 B.C. was said to be the first Roman to have voiced the same conclusion (Plut. *Tib. Gracch.* 9.5; cf. Harris 126). The earliest extant Latin text to refer to the Roman dominion over the *orbis terrarum* is *Rhet. Herenn.* 4.13, after which the concept becomes increasingly common, with reference both to contemporary or earlier times, in numerous authors (e.g. Lucr. 3.836–7, Nep. *Att.* 20.5, Liv. 29.17.6, 30.32.2) but esp. in Cicero (cf. Vogt 156). It also appeared on the coinage of 76–74 B.C. (*RRC* 1.407 no. 393, 409 no. 397) and of course Octavian himself later claimed that 'orbem t. imperio p. R. subiecit' (*RG init.*).[1] It is therefore not surprising that V. too regarded Rome as ruler of the world, evidently as early

---

[1] Hence arose two other topoi: that the *urbs Roma* is the centre of the *orbis* (cf. 100.1n., adding Vogt 160 n. 30, Otto 358–9, F. Christ, *Die röm. Weltherrschaft in der antiken Dichtung* (1938), 81–3); and, under the empire, that the emperor rules the whole world 'from east to west' (cf. 126.3n.). The topos of there being (an)other world(s) to conquer, as in the case of e.g. Caesar (cf. 46.1 and n.), is clearly connected with, if somewhat contradictory to, the present concept.

as the mid-second century B.C. (cf. 1.12.7 'iam terrarum orbi superato') and certainly by the late republic (cf. 31.1–3; Lana 220 n. 6). It was thus equally natural that he should regard Actium as deciding who should rule the *orbis terrarum* (cf. 86.1, 89.1–2): so too e.g. Prop. 4.6.19 'huc mundi coiere manus'. In general on this topic see the works already cited, esp. Harris 108–12 and 126–30; add A. N. Sherwin-White, *The Roman Citizenship*[2] (1973), 438–40; Weinstock 50–3.

The claim that one's own side was fighting *pro salute* was conventional in dismissing charges of expansionist imperialism (cf. Cic. *Off.* 1.38, Liv. 10.16.7, 21.41.14, Curt. 4.3.19); such charges were of course hardly applicable in the case of Actium, but if the enemy was alleged to be bringing *ruina* (so too Hor. *C.* 1.37.6–8 'dum Capitolio | regina dementes ruinas | . . . parabat'), then *salus* was a natural counter-claim: so too Prop. 3.11.49–50 'Roma . . . salua', 4.6.37 'mundi seruator . . . Auguste', *IGRRP* 4.316 'pro salute' (of the victory at Actium). For the general contrast cf. Curt. 10.9.2–3 'imperium . . . dum a pluribus sustinetur, *ruit* . . . populus Romanus *salutem* se principi suo debere profitetur'.

For *dimicare pro salute* cf. also Cic. *Har. Resp.* 41; for *dimicare in ruinam* cf. Manil. 5.210 'dimicat in cineres'; for *ruina orbis* cf. 124.1 and n.; for *salus* in general cf. 103.5n.

85.2 M. Lurio *PIR*[2] 5.110 no. 425; *RE* 13.2.1853 = Lurius 1 (Miltner); *MRR* 2.421; Wiseman 239 no. 238. For Arruntius below cf. 77.3n. For *cornu . . . commissum* cf. Liv. 32.30.9; for *Iulianarum* cf. 84.1n.

Publicolae Sosioque The names were correctly restored by Rhenanus in his personal copy of the *ed. pr.* (von der Gönna 239). For L. Gellius Publicola cf. *RE* 7.1.1003–5 = Gellius 18 (Münzer); *MRR* 2.421; according to Plut. *Ant.* 65.1 he held the right wing along with Antony himself. Publicola was the half-brother of Messalla Corvinus (Liv. *per.* 122, Dio 47.24.5), the consul of 31 B.C. (84.1) and someone admired by V. (cf. 71.1n.); Lana rightly thinks it significant that V. does not mention the relationship (126 n. 402). For C. Sosius, defeated by Agrippa in the attempted break-out before the battle (cf. 84.1n.), cf. *RE* 3A.1.1176–80 = Sosius 2 (Fluss); *MRR* 2.417, 422.

Taurus . . . Canidius For T. Statilius Taurus cf. *MRR* 2.403, 422; also 127.1n. For P. Canidius Crassus cf. *RE* 3.2.1475–6 = Canidius 2 (Münzer); *MRR* 2.401, 421.

85.3 in altera nihil praeter milites This statement is substantiated in 4–5 below: *in longum fortissime pugnandi durauit constantia, in mortem dimicabatur, cum diu . . . dimicassent, aegre summissis armis*. The tenacity of Antony's soldiers, and the ferocity of the fight to which they contributed, are at variance with the impression created in 84.1 that Antony's resources were generally weak and powerless. The discrepancy is doubtless attributable

to Octavian's propaganda, which denigrated Antony and his party before
the battle (84.1n.) in order to encourage desertions, but which elaborated
the unspectacular conflict itself in order that it should play a worthy role
in history (Syme, *RR* 297).[1] Yet the discrepancy remains only an impression. The only specific group that V. criticised at 84.1 were the rowers;
although *uigebat in hac parte miles atque imperator* clearly invited a contrasting judgement on Antony's *milites*, V. avoided it by using the vague word
omnia. He is thus relatively free to commend Antony's soldiers, and hence
the fierce struggle, in the present passage.

prima occupat fugam Cleopatra   So too Flor. 2.21.8 'prima dux
fugae regina', but most modern scholars agree that the flight was a pre-
arranged manoeuvre on Antony's part (Carter 223-4, Leroux 50-1,
Grant, *Cleo.* 313). V. makes 'flight' the leitmotiv of 3-6 (*fugientis, desertor,
fugisse, absente, fugacissimi, fugam*), but this was one *fuga* which Antony
could not claim as a victory (cf. 82.3, anticipating Actium by ironic
contrast). For *occupat fugam* cf. Flor. 1.46.9 (diff. sense); for the jibe *desertor
exercitus sui*, below, cf. Liv. 21.43.15, Just. 22.8.12.

85.4 pugnandi durauit constantia   *durauit constantia* is pleonasm of a
type similar to those mentioned in L–H–S 793–4: it helps to emphasise the
persistence involved. For *constantia* + gerund(ive) cf. Val. Max. 1.1.15,
Plin. *Ep.* 5.1.4, [Quint.] *Decl.* 19.7; for *capite* (metaphorical, above) cf.
101.2n.; for *detracto capite* (non-metaph.) cf. Plin. *NH* 29.76, 141.

uerbis mulcere cupiens   For the contrast with *ferro . . . interimere* cf.
117.3; for the expr. cf. Pacuv. 395, Sall. *H.* 4.58, Virg. *Aen.* 1.153, 197,
5.464, Ov. *Met.* 1.390-1, Tac. *H.* 1.85.1.

85.5 cessere uictoriam   Heinsius proposed to make the noun abl., but
cf. Just. 22.7.4, 32.4.7 (in both cases there is also a dat., however). V.'s
whole sentence seems to reply on complex alliteration: '*d*iu . . . *d*imicass-
ent *d*uce [aaa] *c*essere *u*ictoriam *c*itiusque *u*itam *u*eniamque *C*aesar
[bcbccb: parallel + chiastic] *p*romisit . . . *p*recarentur *p*ersuasum [ddd]'.
For *summissis armis*, above, cf. Amm. Marc. 26.7.17 'aquilisque
summissis'; for *uitam ueniamque*, below, cf. Ov. *Ex P.* 2.1.45 (F.), Claud. *IV
Cons. Honor.* 86 (Burman).

---

[1] Paladini, op. cit. (above, p. 218 n. 4) 470, remarks that Prop. uses
exactly the opposite technique: 'un solo giorno fu sufficiente ad ottenere
tanto grande victoria' (cf. 86.1n.). She also points out (p. 217 n. 2) that
V. does not mention the firing of Ant.'s ships by Oct.: 'per non sminuire
l'azione vittoriosa di Ottaviano . . . e per non oscurare la gloria della
sua clemenza verso i nemici'. But whether Dio is right about the firing
at all (50.34.1ff.) is doubtful (Carter 225).

milites optimi imperatoris, imperatorem fugacissimi militis functum officio   Though there were naturally thought to be differences between the responsibilities of a general and those of a common soldier (cf. Xen. *Anab.* 1.3.15, 3.1.25, Sall. *C.* 20.16 'uel imperatore uel milite me utimini', Tac. *H.* 4.66.2), the ideal general conventionally shared in the hazards of a soldier's life (cf. *TN* 174) and combined the qualities of both leader and fighter (cf. 79.1n., Hom. *Il.* 3.179, Sall. *C.* 60.4 'strenui militis et boni imperatoris officia simul exsequebatur', Caes. *BG* 5.33.2, Liv. 9.1.2, Plin. *NH* 7.140, Curt. 3.11.7, Suet. *Aug.* 10.4, Tac. *H.* 3.17.1, 5.1.1, Plin. *Pan.* 19.3, Amm. 28.3.2). On this occasion Antony did none of these things, and it was left to his soldiers to make up for their leader's incompetence (another conventional idea, for which cf. 112.5n., adding Liv. 3.61.2 and Ogilvie 510). Complex alliteration again helps to sharpen the point of V.'s antithesis: 'milites *o*ptimi *i*mperatoris, *i*mperatorem *fu*gacissimi militis *fu*nctum officio'.

85.6 ut dubites   In *TAPA* 105 (1975), 99–121, K. Gilmartin discusses the use of the indefinite second person subjunctive in Latin historical writing and finds that it is used (on average) more frequently by V. than by any other historian except Florus (p. 107). She argues that historians use it mainly in three contexts: (a) to heighten a description, although V. uses it thus less than one would expect (only once, at 25.1 *putares*); (b) to emphasise a characterisation, by far the commonest use in V. (1.11.6 *inueneris*, 72.2 *malles . . . timeres*, 105.2 *diceres*, 122.2 *nescias . . . mireris* (see my n. ad loc.), and 125.5 *nescias*); (c) to suggest interpretations, as at 69.6 *reperias* and 80.4 *scires*. Gilmartin places the present instance *dubites* in category (c). S. A. Handford (*The Lat. Subjunc.* (1947), 143) notes that 'in many consecutive clauses . . . the requirements of sense override the sequence-habit very frequently'; I assume that this explains the tense of *dubites* here.

suo   an   Cleopatrae   arbitrio   uictoriam   temperaturus fuerit   Octavian in his propaganda depicted Antony as completely dominated by Cleopatra (see Serv. on *Aen.* 8.678 and 696: 'Aug. in commemoratione uitae suae refert Antonium iussisse ut legiones suae apud Cleopatram excubarent et eius nutu et iussu parerent'), a picture which V. follows in much of this ch. (see also 86.1n.).

I have printed Burer's excellent emendation of the paradosis but have followed Vossius in deleting *-ne* after *suo*: *-ne*, which Burer doubtless inserted because it is the 'normal' construction, is often omitted 'in knapper Gegenüberstellung zweier Begriffe' (K–S 2.525). (*-ne* is not supported by A, which merely represents Amerbach's misreading of *-uo*, which, we infer from P, is likely to have been the reading of (R). Thus, while I have thought Ellis' emendation worthy of inclusion in the app. crit. on general grounds, it must be remembered that he was almost certainly led to it by the appearance of *ne* in A, an apograph in which he had a completely unjustified confidence.)

For the tense of *temperaturus fuerit* (and of *facturus fuerit* at 86.2 below) cf. E. C. Woodcock, *A New Latin Syntax* (1959), 139–40. The paradosis reads *fuerat*,[1] as a result of which a scribe may well have 'corrected' *direxerit* to *direxit* below; I think Halm was right to prefer the subjunc. because the *qui*-clause is part of the indirect question and is also a disguised causal clause. I have however preferred the form *derexerit* to *di-*: see *TLL* 5.1.1232.34–1233.46.

For *uictoriam* (*-ae*) *temperare* cf. Sall. *C*. 11.8, Cic. *Marc*. 8, Tac. *H*. 3.31.3, 4.1.3; for *se . . . fuga rapuisset*, below, cf. Curt. 5.13.15, 7.7.36, Ap. *Met.* 5.21.1, 8.21.4, 9.23.4 (F.); for *se rapere + ad* cf. Cic. *Phil.* 13.18, Hor. *S.* 2.7.117–18, Ov. *A*. 3.5.29 (*illuc*) (F.); for *praecipiti fuga* cf. *TLL* 6.1.1472.61–3 (Liv. Sen. *Ep.* Luc. Amm.). *locatus in terra exercitus* recurs from 2 above; for such repetitions cf. 100.5n.

86–87 AFTERMATH AND *CLEMENTIA* (31–30 B.C.)

86.1 Quid ille dies terrarum orbi praestiterit   Prop. also looks back on the effects of that day: 'tantum operis belli sustulit una dies' (3.11.70); cf. also 85.1, 103.4 'temptemus id unum dixisse, quam ille [sc. dies] omnibus fauerit' (and n.), Mayer on Luc. 8.332. The precise sense of *dies* here is presumably that given in *OLD* s.v. 4, 'a day in respect of its events, achievements, etc.'; in this sense the gender is usu. masc. For *terrarum orbi* cf. 85.1n.

ex quo in quem statum peruenerit fortuna publica   The precise reference of this phrase is impossible to determine since V. is being deliberately imprecise (cf. next n.) in order to heighten the suggestiveness, and hence also the eulogy, of his sentence. The immediate contrast is between the turmoil of the civil wars and the stability which resulted from Octavian's victory; but V. is also inviting speculation, as he did with *suo an Cleopatrae arbitrio* at 85.6 above, on what might have happened if Antony had won (cf. Hor. *C*. 1.37.6–12, Prop. 3.11.29ff.; Syme, *RR* 287–8): Lana (257) notes similar speculation, with ref. to Pompey, at 48.2 and says that 'Velleio vuol far capire ai Romani che devono essere riconoscenti ai principi: a Cesare . . . ed a Ottaviano'. We must remember too that *status* developed into a political term (131.1n.): V. may be contrasting the political system under the triumvirs with that which obtained under Augustus. Later writers, hostile to emperors, saw this as a contrast between republic and empire, with Actium as the watershed (e.g. Tac. *H*. 1.1.1, App. *Hist. pr.* 14, *BC* 1.5, Dio 51.1.1–2); but V. regarded it as a return to political normality (89.4n.).

For *fortuna publica* cf. Liv. 1.27.1, Val. Max. 5.3.3, Sen. *Contr.* 4.7, Sen. *Ira* 1.11.5, Tac. *A*. 14.11.2. Its meaning tends to vary between 'public

---

[1] Corrected by Rhenanus in his personal copy of the *ed. pr.* (von der Gönna 239).

good' and 'fate of the state', the reason being that Rome had a protective goddess Fortuna Publica, whose temple was on the Quirinal (Ov. *Fast.* 5.729–30, *CIL* 1^2.397 and pp. 211, 319) and whose role was to ensure that the fate of the state was synonymous with its success. In some cases the phrase *fortuna publica*, like its equivalents *f. rei pub.* (Sall. *C.* 41.3) and *f. pop. Romani* (*RRC* 1.460 no. 440), can allude to the goddess; but Lana's suggestion that that is so here is excluded by the wording of the rest of the clause (227).

quis in hoc transcursu tam artati operis exprimere audeat? V. praises the effects of Octavian's victory by means of the 'inexpressibility topos', which he excuses on the grounds that his work is only a summary: so too at 89.1, where see n. By contrast (*uero*, 2 below), he *will* illustrate Octavian's *clementia*.

V. refers to his work by the word *transcursus* also at 55.1 and 99.4, an expr. which (like *iustum opus* at 96.3, 99.3 (see n.) and 103.4) seems to be paralleled only in Plin. *NH* (3.39, 18.126, 19.154). The pleonasm with *artati* is characteristic (cf. 1.16.5 'artatum angustiis temporum', 116.5n., 177.1n., 118.1n.); cf. also Sidon. *Ep.* 4.3.8 'artati carminis breuitas'. For *artare* used of books, writings etc. cf. Mart. 1.2.3 and Howell and Citroni ad loc., and their refs. to Birt and Roberts. *audere* and its derivatives are commonly used of authors, usu. in contexts of originality or inventiveness (e.g. Enn. *Ann.* 216, Catull. 1.5, Virg. *G.* 4.565, Hor. *Ep.* 1.19.11, 2.1.166–7, 182, 2.2.111, Claud. *Rapt.* 1.3).

86.2 uictoria … clementissima *clementia* was the virtue which Augustus singled out at the start of *RG* (3.1–2, see below) and which accompanied *uirtus, iustitia* and *pietas* on the golden shield given him by the senate and people (*RG* 34.2). References to this *clementia* are collected by Shackleton Bailey 96–7; see also 87.2n., 100.2n., 4–5nn.; Wickert 67–8; A. Wallace-Hadrill, *Historia* 30 (1981), 298–323.

nec quisquam interemptus est ⟨nisi⟩ paucissimi et ii qui … 'nor was anyone killed except a very few and in particular those who …' I find it slightly easier to assume that *nisi* was omitted by mistake (so Heinsius) than that *est* was written wrongly in its place (so Gelenius). I have however adopted Gelenius' *ii* for *hi*: the latter was retained by Heinsius, and it is true that *hic* is often used where we might expect *is* (e.g. 80.2); but where *et* is used to introduce a qualification, as here, it seems always to be followed by *is* (K–S 1.619). *ii* and *hi* are of course very often confused.

A quite different approach has been followed by some others, e.g. *pauci summoti qui* (Baiter in Orelli's edn), *paucissimi eiecti* (Halm, but not in his edn); I can however see no reason why V. should be so guarded about the few executions which took place (see Syme, *RR* 299–300), esp. in view of his remarks on the proscriptions and on Philippi below.

qui ⟨ne⟩ deprecari quidem pro se [non] sustinerent V. echoes almost exactly *RG* 3.1 'uictorque omnibus *ueniam petentibus* ciuibus peperci'. I have adopted Heinsius' emendation because the required sense is *ne . . . quidem* (cf. 71.3 'ne temptata quidem hostis misericordia'), to which *quidem . . . non* is not equivalent; it is likely that *ne* dropped out and *non* was wrongly inserted. On *sustinere* + infin., first found in Liv. 23.9.7, see Fletcher (1964), 61.

qu⟨em fin⟩em . . . uictoriae suae facturus fuerit After *fuerit* Rhenanus inserted *modum*, which has been widely accepted; but it is difficult to see why the word should have been dropped out. I much prefer Professor Goodyear's suggestion that we insert *finem* after *quem*: the error will have occurred through homoeoteleuton, *finem facere* is an extremely common phrase (e.g. Sall. *J.* 31.7, numerous times in Cicero's speeches, Liv. 36.45.4), and for *finis uictoriae* cf. 2.17.1 'uir qui neque ad finem uictoriae satis laudari . . . potest' (a not dissimilar context).

si sic licuisset In the case of the proscriptions, according to V., Octavian was simply outnumbered by his colleagues (66.1 'furente deinde Antonio simulque Lepido . . . repugnante Caesare sed frustra aduersus duos'); as for Philippi, V. at 71.1 does not mention the vindictiveness which he here excuses, but cf. Suet. *Aug.* 13.1 'nec successum uictoriae moderatus est sed . . . in splendidissimum quemque captiuum . . . saeuiit'.

at Sosium . . . seruauit incolumem 'Sosius' peril and Sosius' rescue may have been artfully staged', suggests Syme (*RR* 297); certainly the clemency he received was well known (Dio 51.2.4, 56.38.2 τίς οὐκ οἶδε τὸν Σόσσιον . . .;), although we do not know the role played by Arruntius. For Sosius cf. 85.2n.; for Arruntius, 77.3n. For *prisca grauitas* cf. 116.3n.; I have adopted Lipsius' ⟨cum⟩ because that is the constr. used by V. elsewhere (63.3, 115.2); for the idea cf. Sen. *Clem.* 1.2.1 'bonitatem tuam cum fortuna tua litigantem' (Ruhnken): the picture of Oct. wrestling with his conscience emphasises the admirableness of his decision to be merciful.

86.3 non praetereatur Asinii Pollionis factum et dictum memorabile V. is fond of reporting the epigrammatic remark which illustrates a person's character: cf. e.g. 2.14.3, 70.3, 83.3. In this he is following a recognised belief which was associated esp. with Socrates (cf. Cic. *TD* 5.47 '(Socrates) disserebat, qualis cuiusque animi adfectus esset, talem esse hominem; qualis autem homo ipse esset, talem esse eius orationem; orationi autem facta similia, factis uitam'; Solon ap. Diog. Laer. 1.58), was favoured greatly by Plutarch (e.g. *Alex.* 1.2 πρᾶγμα βραχὺ πολλάκις καὶ ῥῆμα . . . ἔμφασιν ἤθους ἐποίησε), and generally found expression in many other ancient writers (see refs. in Otto 257; Häussler, *Nachträge* 40, 114, 195; Bramble 23–4). Now Pollio's remark here has been

231

used by modern scholars as indicating his political sympathies in 32/31 B.C. (see below), but we should remember that the technique of 'speaking in character' (*prosopopoeia, ethopoeia*) was a common exercise in the schools of rhetoric (cf. S. F. Bonner, *Education in Ancient Rome* (1977), 267–70), was regularly deployed in the courts of law (cf. *Rhet. Herenn.* 4.65–6; Lausberg 2.237–8, 241–2, §§ 822, 826), and was one of the recognised resources of the writer of history (Quint. 3.8.53). It is thus at least worth asking the question whether examples of attributed speech are genuine. Naturally the question cannot be answered with any certainty. The remark reported by V. at 70.3 looks fictional, yet a similar version of it is quoted by Val. Max. (see ad loc.); *bons mots* such as those at 2.14.3 and 83.3 do tend to be remembered, yet the former at least bears a striking similarity to the topos mentioned at Sen. *Ep.* 43.4 (where see Summers' nn.). The *dictum memorabile* which V. here attributes to Pollio could well be genuine, since no doubt much of his life was known either through his own works or those of others;[1] yet this *dictum* too is not without its parallels elsewhere (see below).

namque cum se post Brundisinam pacem continuisset in Italia For the meaning of this sentence see Shipley's translation (quoted below). Contrary to what V. says here, Pollio campaigned west of the Adriatic immediately after the peace of Brundisium and was awarded a triumph: for a full discussion of the campaign and a suggestion why V. should here seek to disguise Pollio's participation in it see 78.2nn. (pp. 192–6).

This is the only occasion on which V. uses *namque* instead of *nam*: in this preference for *nam* he resembles Cic. Caes. Liv. and Tac. *A.*; Sall. by contrast uses *namque* often except in *J.* (see Adams (1974), 60).

eneruatum . . . animum As Ov. *RA* 753, Liv. 23.18.12; when the word is used in sexual contexts it usually refers to physical exhaustion (cf. Hor. *Epod.* 8.2; V. Grassmann, *Die erotischen Epoden des Horaz* (1966), 50–1). For *partibus . . . se miscere* below cf. Tac. *A.* 4.44.2 'donec Antonii partibus . . . misceretur'.

'mea . . . praeda uictoris' A similar epigram is attributed to Atticus apropos of an earlier struggle: 'noli, oro te, . . . aduersum eos me uelle ducere cum quibus ne contra te arma ferrem, Italiam reliqui' (Nep. *Att.* 4.2). The parallel (cf. also Sen. *Med.* 517–18, Luc. 9.241 'dominum, quem clades cogit, habebo') might suggest that the sentiment is conventional and was attributed indiscriminately to a variety of people (see above); but most modern scholars assume that in Pollio's case the *dictum* is genuine.

---

[1] Noting that V.'s introductory phrase *factum et dictum memorabile* is the singular equivalent of the title of Val. Max.'s work, Lana suggests (90 n. 129) that V. may have derived the Pollio anecdote and others from a collection of 'deeds and sayings' not unlike that of Val. Max.

On that assumption, Bosworth has recently used the *dictum* to support his thesis that at this period Pollio, so far from being the aloof and neutral figure portrayed by Syme (*RR* 291, *Tac.* 136), was in fact working for Octavian (447–8):

> 'When Octavian invited him to join his staff, he retorted that his services to Antony were the greater, Antony's benefactions to him the more celebrated; therefore he would withdraw himself from the struggle and become the spoil of the victor. The whole tone of the *dictum* is exculpatory. One is led to infer that because of Antony's benefactions Pollio seemed obliged to take his side in the crucial struggle. The riposte was that, despite appearances, the debt to Antony was squared, and there were no remaining obligations of *pietas*. This remark can be set in its context. In the prelude to the Actium campaign it seems that Antony was canvassing his former [*sic*] partisans and issuing pamphlets accusing of ingratitude those who failed to take his side. At any rate Pollio produced a pamphlet *contra maledicta Antonii* [Charis. p. 100.23 B]. The contents are unknown, but it is a reasonable assumption that in it Pollio rebutted charges of ingratitude and made counter-accusations of his own . . . Pollio moreover uttered a public statement, disassociating himself from his former benefactor. Such statements would have been encouraged by Octavian . . . He [Pollio] had disavowed and attacked his old patron, which was all Octavian could have wished from him. Pollio's "neutrality" in 32 certainly does not prove his independence. Rather it indicates that he had some share in the manufacture of Octavian's propaganda, and that by 32 he was working for the eventual victor.'

Is this novel interpretation, which I have been compelled to quote at length, correct?

The context in which V. mentions Pollio's *dictum* is that of Octavian's *clementia* after Actium towards those who had supported Antony before the battle. We should thus expect Pollio, like Sosius just mentioned, to be an illustration of that *clementia*.[1] V. must therefore be describing an incident which exemplifies Pollio's continuing allegiance to Antony (or, at the very least, his non-allegiance to Octavian) prior to Actium. And this is exactly what V. is doing, as Shipley's Loeb translation makes perfectly clear (my italics): '*Although* he had remained in Italy after the peace of Brundisium, and had never seen the queen nor taken any active part in Antony's faction after this leader had become demoralised by his passion for her, when Caesar asked him to go with him to the war at Actium he replied: " My services to Antony are *too* great, and his kindness to me *too* well known; accordingly I shall hold aloof from your quarrel and shall be the prize of the victor." ' Pollio was certainly disillusioned by Antony's behaviour (*neque . . . uidisset umquam reginam, post eneruatum amore eius Antonii*

---

[1] Sen. *Clem.* 1.10.1 also takes Pollio as an ex. of Octavian's *clementia*, but gives no indication of any date.

animum) and took no active steps to assist his cause (*neque . . . partibus eius se miscuisset*); but he was still too closely involved with Antony, both emotionally and politically, to join Octavian.[1] The pamphlet mentioned by Charisius no doubt made precisely that point (so too *CAH* 10.94 n. 1), which is the opposite of that supposed by Bosworth. The incident described by V. cannot therefore mean that by 32 Pollio 'was working for the eventual victor', as Bosworth argues; on the contrary, he was the aloof figure portrayed by Syme, and as such became a splendid example of Octavian's *clementia*.

A more general issue. Bosworth supports his argument by saying that Pollio 'cannot have belonged to the Augustan opposition' since V.'s 'high praise excludes him as an opponent of the new dispensation' (451). Not so. V. never mentions Pollio again in his account of Augustus' reign, a silence which *could* be interpreted as V.'s refusal to mention the continuing dissidence of someone whom he otherwise admired.[2] As it is, however, V.'s judgement on individuals is usually independent of political considerations (cf. 112.5n., 120.5n.) and is more often based on their moral worth or *uirtus* (see Hellegouarc'h (1964)).

For *praeda uictoris* cf. Liv. 32.21.34, Val. Max. 5.6.7, Tac. *H.* 4.76.1, Just. 41.1.4.

87.1 Proximo deinde anno . . . imposuit manum Although Oct. celebrated a separate triumph for it (89.1n.), V. regards the Alexandrian campaign in 30 as a mere 'mopping up' operation: see Wistrand 52–5. For *ultimam . . . manum* see 117.1n., and cf. Ov. *RA* 114, *Met.* 8.200–1, Sen. *Ep.* 12.4, Plin. *NH* 36.16, Gell. 17.10.5 (F.).

se ipse non segniter interemit For Antony's death on 1 Augustus 30 (EJ p. 49) see Huzar 226, 300 nn. 40, 41, with full refs. For similar phraseology cf. 1.6.6, 35.5, 69.2, Liv. 40.4.14, Tac. *A.* 14.58.4, 16.16.2.

multa desidiae crimina morte redimeret Roman writers liked to note if a death was in keeping with the victim's life (91.4n.), or if a splendid life was marred by a shameful death (as 87.3 below), or if, as here, a

---

[1] Bosworth has mistakenly assumed that the comparatives *maiora . . . notiora* mean 'more . . . more' and that *illius in me beneficia notiora* is cancelled out by *mea in Antonium maiora merita sunt*. But these two phrases are simply complementary and refer to the reciprocity of political *amicitia* (on *merita ~ beneficia* see Hellegouarc'h, *VL* 163–70), the comparatives mean 'too . . . too', and you must supply the thought 'quam ut discrimini uestro pro te [Augusto] intersim' or, in Krause's formulation, 'quam ut honeste ad bellum aduersus eum [Antonium] proficiscar'. Such an ellipse is readily intelligible in the light of the sentence which immediately follows (*itaque . . .*).

[2] Lana (90) thinks that at 86.3 V. 'intende biasimare la neutralità di Pollione', but I can see no evidence for this.

shameful life was redeemed by a noble death (cf. also Sen. *Suas.* 7.8 'P. Scipionem a maioribus suis desciscentem generosa mors in numerum Scipionum reposuit', Suet. *Otho* 12.2, Tac. *H.* 2.31.1 'exitum quo egregiam Otho famam (meruit)', 2.50.1 'duobus facinoribus, altero flagitiosissimo, altero egregio, tantundem apud posteros meruit bonae famae quantum malae', *A.* 1.53.5 'constantia mortis haud indignus Sempronio nomine; uita degenerauerat'). For the Roman attitude towards suicide, which varied according to circumstances, see next n.; Pease on Virg. *Aen.* 4.475; Tarrant on Sen. *Ag.* 590ff.; Balsdon 249–52, each with further refs. There is a full bibliography on the subject, plus a long list of Roman suicides (not absolutely reliable), in Y. Grisé, 'De la fréquence du suicide chez les Romains', *Latomus* 39 (1980), 17–46. A good bibliog. on death and its descriptions in Latin literature is in H. Raabe, *Plurima mortis imago* (1974).

For *crimina . . . redimeret* cf. Sen. *NQ* 6.23.2 (F.); for *desidiae crimina* cf. Prop. 1.12.1, Hyg. *Astr. praef.*, *Anth. Lat.* 433.4, Aug. *Ciu. Dei* 3.17 (Fletcher).

in morsu sane eius expers muliebris metus For the varying accounts of her death see Grant, *Cleo.* 329–37. The Romans were addicted to describing heroic suicide by women: e.g. 26.3 (Calpurnia), 88.3 (Servilia), Liv. 1.57–9 (Lucretia), 30.15.6–8 (Sophoniba), Hor. *C.* 1.37.22–3 'nec muliebriter expauit ensem' (Cleopatra), Sen. *Suas.* 2.2., *Contr.* 2.2.1, 2.5.8, 10.3.2, Plin. *Ep.* 3.16 (Arria). A list of female suicides is given at Hyg. *Fab.* 243. See too last n.

Some edd. have believed that the appearance of *sane* in the paradosis, so close in form to *sanies* and in a context of snakes, is hardly coincidental: they have therefore emended (e.g. *morsu et sanie eius*, Burman). Though there is something to be said for this argument, I do not think it is correct. It is at first sight strange that this sentence contrasts with its predecessor (cf. *at*) since Antony and Cleopatra both committed suicide. But the contrast resides in the manner of the two deaths: Antony's was straightforward and positive (*se ipse non segniter interemit*), whereas Cleopatra's was devious (*frustratis custodibus*) and relatively passive (*inlata aspide . . . spiritum reddidit*).[1] Yet, whatever the manner of her suicide, her courage in actually accomplishing the deed was admirable, a reservation which *sane* very neatly expresses (cf. *OLD* s.v. *sane* 8). I am therefore inclined to believe

---

[1] I owe this explanation to Mr Seager. The only alternative I can think of is that V. regarded Cleopatra's death as unfortunate (and hence as contrasting with Antony's) since Octavian had not intended that she should die (cf. *frustratis custodibus*); but this explanation has less point and does not square well with 87.2 immediately below. [In implying that Oct. did not wish Cleopatra dead V. follows the majority of ancient witnesses (e.g. Plut. *Ant.* 78.3, Suet. *Aug.* 17.4, Dio 51.13.1–4), but many modern scholars disagree (e.g. Huzar 227, Grant, *Cleo.* 332, Nisbet–Hubbard on Hor. *C.* 1.37 p. 409). In support of the ancient evidence is W. R. Johnson, *Arion* 6 (1967), 93–7.]

that *sane* is correct. Now P's reading *morsu sane eius* implies that *morsu* is abl. instr. with *reddidit*; this leaves *sane* very oddly placed and Acidalius transposed it with *eius*. It is however clear from BA that (M) read *in morsu sane eius*, which I think Vossius and Kritz were right to defend: the preposition either indicates the moment at which the biting took place, as they suggested, or is an example of '*in* concessivum' (cf. *TLL* 7.1.782.3ff.): the two are often difficult to distinguish, cf. e.g. Cic. *Sest.* 72 'in luctu inridentes', *TD* 2.50 'non immoderate magno in dolore', Hor. *Ep.* 1.5.20 'contracta . . . in paupertate solutum', Prop. 1.16.32 'surget et inuitis spiritus in lacrimis', Stat. *Silu.* 5.1.18 'adhuc in uulnere primo', *Theb.* 2.640 'adhuc in uulnere uires'.

For *muliebris metus* cf. Liv. 1.13.1 *m. pauore*, 2.40.1 *m. timor*. For *frustratis custodibus*, above, cf. Liv. 2.13.6 (where the deponent form is used).

87.2 nemo ex his . . . ab eo iussuue eius interemptus 'Flatterie évidente' (H–W); 'Vell. says that Octavian killed no one' (Huzar 301 n. 47). Such statements take no account of the clear meaning of V.'s words, which is: 'none *of the following* . . . was killed by him or at his command', viz. D. Brutus, Sex. Pompeius, Brutus and Cassius, and Antony and Cleopatra, all of whom, as V. proceeds explicitly to say, either committed suicide or were killed by Antony.[1] With the possible exception of Cleopatra (see above, p. 235 n. 1), all these individuals, had they lived, would have put a severe strain on the *clementia* to which Oct. had already laid claim after Actium (86.2); their not surviving was thus a stroke of luck, which could well be attributed to his personal *fortuna* (97.4n.). Hence V.'s phrase *fuitque et fortuna et clementia Caesaris dignum*.

On the function of 87.2–3, which forms a retrospective survey denoting the end not only of the Actium campaign but also of the civil wars as a whole, see above, p. 219.

D. Brutum Cf. 64.1–2.

cum dignitatis quoque seruandae dedisset fidem *quoque* = 'in addition to his life'; for the episode in question cf. 79.5–6. For *fides* + gerundive cf. e.g. Liv. 37.10.4; for *dignitatem seruare* cf. Cic. *TD* 2.48.

87.3 Brutus et Cassius Cf. 70.5 and 2. For the notion *antequam . . . animum* cf. 71.3 'ne temptata quidem hostis misericordia'; for *experiri animum* cf. Liv. 2.25.3, 27.13.8, 34.13.4, Sen. *Ben.* 2.3.2, Quint. 5.7.20, Just. 14.1.11.

---

[1] I.e. *his* looks forward to the list of names which begins with D. Brutus and Sex. Pompeius and ends with those of Antony and Cleopatra. Syme (1978), 51, mistakenly says that D. Brutus and the rest are mentioned 'in parenthesis' and thus misinterprets the passage in the same way as the scholars quoted above.

fuisset For the tense edd. quote Cic. *Att.* 1.14.1 'qualis fuisset, scripsi ad te antea'.

professioni ei, qua semper usus erat Canidius is described by Oros. 6.19.20 as fiercely hostile to Oct., but no record has survived of 'his habitual boast'. On him see 85.2n.

ultimus ... Parmensis Cassius morte poenas dedit 'Cassius was not in fact the last of the assassins to suffer condign punishment, as stated by Velleius. There was Turullius, not omitted by Valerius Maximus' (Syme (1978), 52, cf. Val. Max. 1.1.19, who does not in fact say that Turullius was the last to die). It is true that Turullius did not die until shortly before Antony (cf. Dio 51.8.2–3), and it is possible that V. has confused him with Cassius, as suggested by Shackleton Bailey (intro. n. to Cic. *Fam.* 12.13(419), a letter evidently written by Cassius Parmensis and mentioning Turullius in § 3). But since we do not know the date of Cassius' death, it is equally possible that V. may be right. For Cassius cf. *RE* 3.2.1743–4 = Cassius 80 (Skutsch); *MRR* 2.341, 360; for the grim nightmares which preceded his death see Val. Max. 1.7.7.

For Trebonius' death see 69.1; most edd. supply *primus* either before or after his name here.

88–89.1 HOME AFFAIRS AND OCTAVIAN'S RETURN (30–29 B.C.)

This brief section provides an effective interlude between the victory at Actium in 84–7 and the summary of Augustus' reign at 89.2–6. Its purpose is twofold: to commend Maecenas and his *modus uiuendi* (88.2n.) and to contrast the reception planned for Octavian by Lepidus (88.1) with that which he actually received (89.1). For such transitional sections in V. see above, p. 156.

88.1 Dum ultimam ... imponit manum The similarity in wording to 87.1 indicates that the same year is here being dealt with as there: V. thus places the conspiracy in 30 B.C., which is also the date implied by all other authorities except App. *BC* 4.50, who says 31. Modern scholars have floundered around amidst this conflicting evidence, but there seems no doubt that Appian is mistaken: see Wistrand 1–16 for full discussion and a possible explanation of Appian's error. See also next n. but one.

M. Lepidus *PIR*² 1.60 no. 368; *RE* 1.1.561 = Aemilius 74 (v. Rohden); for his father cf. 63.1n. For his mother Iunia cf. *PIR*² 4.359 no. 850; *RE* 10.1.1110–11 = Iunius 193 (Münzer); for her brother cf. 62.2n.

consilia inierat   The tense of the verb has provoked comment. According to Fraenkel (71 n. 6) the pluperf. indicates the anteriority of the earlier stages of the Lepidus affair compared with its later stages (*poenas exsoluit* at 3 below). According to Wistrand (40–2, cf. 8–9) the pluperf. represents a 'state': comparing *inter al.* Cic. *Verr.* 5.91 'haec dum aguntur, interea Cleomenes iam ad Pelori litus peruenerat', he says 'the pluperf. of the principal sentence clearly denotes a state, whose simultaneity with the goings on described in the preceding clause is indicated by *dum* and stressed by *interea*'. I am not sure that either of these explanations is precisely correct – and in V.'s passage there is, in any case, no *interea*.

In the preceding ch. Octavian finished off the civil wars (87.1 *ultimam bellis ciuilibus imposuit manum*), Antony and Cleopatra committed suicide (ibid.), and Canidius and Cassius Parmensis died (3). These events are over and done with, but now V., in the present transitional ch. (see above, p. 237), wishes to mention an episode which evidently precedes the deaths of Canidius and Cassius and is explicitly synchronised with the first of the events in ch. 87 (cf. 88.1 *Dum ultimam bello . . . Caesar imponit manum*). I therefore believe that V. wrote *inierat* to indicate the relationship of the Lepidus affair to the events of the preceding ch.; and having once given this indication, he is able to continue the story of Lepidus in the normal perfect tense (3 *restinxit . . . exsoluit*).

Wistrand's interpretation of the pluperf. tense did not prevent his proposing (9) the emendation *consilia ini⟨t⟩. erat tunc . . . praepositus*; but this destroys the chronological precision which I think V. desired, and the supposed corruption is less easy than that suggested by Madvig (next n.).

88.2 ⟨erat⟩ tunc urbis custodiis praepositus   Madvig rightly observed (1.35–6) that if we retain the paradosis, i.e. if we understand *est* with *praepositus*, the suggestion will be that Maecenas was appointed specifically to meet the present crisis. It is, however, generally agreed that Maecenas was in office before the crisis broke;[1] I have therefore adopted Madvig's easy supplement. It should be noted, however, that this is not a comparable use of the pluperf. to that which I suggested in the case of *inierat* above: ⟨*erat*⟩ . . . *praepositus* is an ex. of the pluperf. denoting a state, used very commonly with the passive form of verbs (cf. Wistrand

---

[1] How long before is less generally agreed. Syme (*RR* 292) takes for granted Dio's statement (51.3.5) that in 31 Octavian had left Maecenas in charge at Rome; but Wistrand (15ff.) argues strongly in favour of *Eleg. Maec.* 1.45ff., which states that Maecenas accompanied Oct. to Actium in that year, and concludes that Maecenas did not return to Rome until shortly after the battle. The problem is certainly tricky, esp. in view of Hor. *Epod.* 1.1ff., but on the whole I agree with Fraenkel (71 n. 6, 72) that Syme's interpretation 'stands to reason' and that the *consolatio* is an ex. of panegyrical licence (so too H. Schoonhoven in his edn of *Eleg. Maec.* (1980), pp. 62–4). (Madvig's point about V.'s text of course remains true on either interpretation.)

40), and is to be translated in English accordingly ('At that time C. Maecenas was in charge . . .'). It is the word *tunc* which indicates the chronological relationship between Maecenas' tenure of office and Lepidus'
embarking on his conspiracy.

The plural *custodus* suggests that the word is to be taken in a concrete
sense: 'police force' (so *TLL* 4.1558.69–70; Shipley);[1] for Maecenas'
position as Octavian's 'unofficial but influential representative' at this
time see T. J. Cadoux, *JRS* 49 (1959), 153.

C. Maecenas   For Augustus' celebrated minister cf. *RE* 14.1.207–
29 = Maecenas 6 (Stein and Kappelmacher); Nicolet 2.932–3 no. 209;
Fraenkel, index s.v.; Nisbet–Hubbard on Hor. *C.* 1 and 2, indexes s.v.

equestri sed splendido   *splendor* and *splendidus* are applied almost technically to *equites*: see Hellegouarc'h, *VL* 458–61, and Nicolet 1.213–24;
the latter remarks, apropos of Maecenas, that the words apply only to
'une très petite minorité, et toujours en rapport avec des activités
publiques' and that they indicate only 'les plus haut placés des
chevaliers' (pp. 223–4).

uir, ubi . . .   The following character sketch requires consideration at
some length.

(1) One of the two key points which V. makes about Maecenas is that
he lacked political ambition. This was a characteristic for which
Augustus' minister was famous (cf. Hor. *S.* 1.6, Prop. 3.9.27–30, *Eleg.
Maec.* 1.31–2) and it took the form of remaining within the *equester ordo*.
Though there were no doubt individuals of a similar inclination under the
republic, of whom Atticus is the most notable example (cf. Nep. *Att.* 6.2
'honores non petiit, cum ei paterent propter uel gratiam uel dignitatem';
in general Nicolet 1.699–722), the phenomenon is particularly symptomatic of the imperial age: cf. Annaeus Mela (Tac. *A.* 16.17.3 'petitione
honorum abstinuerat per ambitionem praeposteram'), Cornelius Fuscus
(*H.* 2.86.3 'quietis cupidine'; cf. R. Syme, *AJPh* 58 (1937), 7), Minicius
Macrinus (Plin. *Ep.* 1.14.5 'nihil altius uoluit . . . honestam quietem huic
. . . dignitati . . . praetulit'), Arrianus Maturus (ibid. 2.11.1 'quietis
amore'), Terentius Iunior (ibid. 7.25.2 'otium').[2] Lack of political ambi-

---

[1] Although it seems to be the case that the *Vigiles* were not properly
organised by Augustus until 23 B.C. (see *OCD* s.v.), other similar groups
evidently existed before that date and could have been detailed to help
in a crisis (see A. W. Lintott, *Violence in Republican Rome* (1968), 105).
According to App. *BC* 5.132, the *Vigiles* were organised as early as
36 B.C., but this is generally thought to be an error.

[2] In a ch. entitled 'Der *otium–negotium* Konflikt' H.-P. Bütler remarks on
the number of men in Pliny's letters who removed themselves from
public life (*Die geistige Welt des jüngeren Plinius* (1970), 51 n. 43); but
otherwise he has nothing to say on the subject.

tion is not however restricted to *equites* but extends to senators also (cf. Syme, *Tac.* 27): cf. M. Vinicius, V.'s dedicatee (Dio 60.27.4 τὴν ἡσυχίαν ἄγων), Memmius Regulus (Tac. *A.* 14.47.1 'quiete defensus'), Galba (Tac. *H.* 1.49.3 'segnitia'; Suet. *Galba* 9.1 'paulatim in desidiam segnitiamque conuersus est ne quid materiae praeberet Neroni et, ut dicere solebat, quod nemo rationem otii sui reddere cogeretur').

(2) The second key point which V. makes about Maecenas is that he was a 'mixed' character, balancing efficiency by the *otium* and *luxuria* for which he was famous (cf. Sen. *Ep.* 114.4, 120.19, *Dial.* 1.3.10, Mart. 10.73.3–4, Juv. 12.39). His two aspects are contrasted by means of *sane . . . uero* (= μέν . . . δέ) and by the corresponding temporal clauses *ubi . . . simul . . .* Now 'mixed' characters are commonly described in historiography (cf. Häussler, *Tac.* 330–2; J. Lucas, *Les obsessions de Tacite* (1974); also 119.4n.), and the particular type to which Maecenas belongs may perhaps be traced back as far as Alcibiades (cf. J. Griffin, *JRS* 67 (1977), 20–2). The most notable republican example is Sulla (Sall. *J.* 95.3 'cupidus uoluptatum sed gloriae cupidior; otio luxurioso esse, tamen ab negotiis numquam uoluptas remorata'), but, as with (1) above, this type of person is especially symptomatic of the imperial age: cf. Sentius Saturninus (Vell. 105.2 'uirum multiplicem uirtutibus, nauum, agilem, prouidum, militariumque officiorum patientem ac peritum pariter, sed eundem, ubi negotia fecissent locum otio, liberaliter lauteque eo abutentem, ita tamen ut eum splendidum ac hilarem potius quam luxuriosum aut desidem diceres'), L. Piso (Vell. 98.3 'esse mores eius uigore ac lenitate mixtissimos, et uix quemquam reperiri posse qui aut otium ualidius diligat aut facilius sufficiat negotio'; Sen. *Ep.* 83.14 'urbis custos, ebrius . . . fuit. maiorem partem noctis in conuiuio exigebat. usque in horam fere sextam dormiebat . . . officium tamen suum . . . diligentissime administrauit'), Sallustius Crispus (Tac. *A.* 3.30.2–3 'ille, quamquam prompto ad capessendos honores aditu, Maecenatem aemulatus sine dignitate senatoria multos . . . anteiit, diuersus a ueterum instituto per cultum et munditias copiaque et adfluentia luxu propior. suberat tamen uigor animi ingentibus negotiis par, eo acrior quo somnum et inertiam magis ostentabat'), Petronius (ibid. 16.18.1–2 'ille dies per somnum, nox officiis et oblectamentis uitae transigebatur; utque alios industria, ita hunc ignauia ad famam protulerat . . . sed erudito luxu . . . pro consule tamen Bithyniae et mox consul uigentem se ac parem negotiis ostendit. dein reuolutus ad uitia . . .'), Licinius Mucianus (Tac. *H.* 1.10.2 'luxuria industria, comitate adrogantia, malis bonisque artibus mixtus: nimiae uoluptates cum uacaret, quotiens expedierat magnae uirtutes').

Thus Maecenas is seen to be characteristic of his age. But why is lack of ambition so often described, as in (1) above, by the terms *otium, segnitia* or *quies*? And is it sufficient to say (as does O. Seel, *Römertum und Latinität* (1964), 252) that the type of 'mixed' personality described in (2) above is merely 'einen Gemeinplatz charakterologischer Beschreibung'?

(3) In the days of the republic the ideal Roman was the politician who sought *dignitas, gloria* and *fama* through the consulship, taking advantage

of a constitutional system which was theoretically open to all (cf. D. Earl, *The Moral and Political Tradition of Rome* (1967)). Such men were described by a familiar series of nouns and adjectives, among which the following are particularly noteworthy: *industria* (e.g. Cato, *ORF*² 51, fr. 128; *Rhet. Herenn.* 4.27, 34; Cic. *Verr.* 3.7–8, 4.81, 5.181, *Font.* 42, *Phil.* 13.24, *Rep.* 1.1; *Comm. Petit.* 29; Sall. *J.* 1.3; Liv. 23.14.1); *uigilantia* (e.g. Cic. *Leg. Agr.* 2.77, *Phil.* 7.20, 8.30; Sall. *C.* 52.29, 54.4); *strenuus* (e.g. Cato, *Orig.* fr. 73; Cic. *Mur.* 20, *Mil.* 96, *Phil.* 8.11; Liv. 4.35.9, 5.12.8, 10.8.3, 22.35.7, 28.40.4); *intentus* (cf. Syme, *Sall.* 268 and n. 169); *promptus* (e.g. Sall. *H.* 1.77.1 'rem publicam . . . in periculis a promptissimo quoque defendi'; Liv. 22.59.11 'nobis etiam promptioribus pro patria'). Opposite qualities, such as *somnus*, were unforgivable (e.g. Cic. *Att.* 1.14.6, *Fam.* 7.30.1; Sall. *C.* 2.8). Now almost all of those good qualities are military in character, the reasons for this being: (i) that political leaders were in fact generals as well and military glory was an almost universal ambition and the highest prize (see Harris 10–41); (ii) that politicians often likened their relationship with their citizens to that of a caring general or *dux* (Hellegouarc'h, *VL* 324ff.); (iii) that the metaphorical language of popular philosophy, under Stoic influence, saw life itself as a military campaign and the 'good man' (and hence also the politician *par excellence*) as a soldier (cf. Sen. *Ep.* 96.5; D. Steyns, *Les métaphores et comparaisons de Sénèque le philosophe* (1907), 1–38; A. Oltramare, *Les origines de la diatribe romaine* (1926), 56 and n. 4, 280–1). In the socio-political world described by such vocabulary, *otium* has no place. *otium* was conventionally inimical to the military life (e.g. Enn. *Scen.* 234–5 V = 195–6 J; Liv. 2.58.7 and Ogilvie ad loc.; Vell. 78.2 'res disciplinae inimicissima, otium') and to the 'good life' of the popular philosopher (Sen. *Ep.* 51.6); it was regarded as incompatible with a free and competitive society (Sall. *H.* 1.55.25–6 'accipite otium cum seruitio . . . potior uisa est periculosa libertas quieto seruitio', 3.48.13 'otium pro seruitio'),[1] and above all with the life of the active politician, who, if he indulged in *otium*, was required to defend his indulgence (e.g. Cato, *Orig.* fr. 2; Sall. *C.* 4.1, *J.* 4.4; Cic. *TD* 1.5, *Off.* 3.1–5, there quoting the famous *dictum* of Scipio Africanus: 'numquam se minus otiosum esse quam cum otiosus'; J. P. V. D. Balsdon, *CQ* 10 (1960), 47 and n. 1; W. A. Laidlaw, *GR* 15 (1968), 44ff.).[2] Since *luxuria* was a natural partner of *otium*, it too was suspect and not advertised; yet many successful politicians undeniably indulged in *luxuria*, which thus, though paradoxically, became 'linked with the pursuit of *dignitas* tradi-

---

[1] Milton echoed these passages of Sallust, his favourite historian, in *Samson Agonistes* 268–71. Bishop Thomas Newton noted the parallels in his edn (1752).

[2] The notion of 'active leisure' has survived almost continuously to the present day: see e.g. R. R. Bolgar (ed.), *Classical Influences on European Culture A.D. 500–1500* (1971), 225–38, K. Gross, *AuA* 26 (1980), 122–37. Add W. Cowper, *The Task* 6.928–9; John Keats, *Letters* (ed. H. E. Rollins, 1958), 1.231, 2.175; H. Wilson in *The Times*, 18 Jan. 1971.

tional among the Roman upper class' (A. W. Lintott, 'Imperial expansion and moral decline in the Roman republic', *Historia* 21 (1972), 632).

(4) In the days of the empire everything was changed. The openly competitive system for political honours was replaced by imperial patronage in the form of *commendatio* (cf. 124.3n., 4n.), and the ultimate prize was no longer the consulship but the position of *princeps*, for which there could be no competition at all except through military revolution. The existence of the *princeps*, and the almost total dependence of political life on his favour, meant that men behaved differently and adopted different sets of values. Unable to do everything himself, the *princeps* required subordinates to administer provinces and command armies. But this was to place power in the hands of others, and, as Dio remarked, 'most *principes* do not wish anyone to be superior to themselves . . . they do not wish their subordinates to be completely successful and thus win glory . . . The man who expects to survive should relieve his masters of undertakings which involve great difficulty, but reserve for them the successes' (49.4.2–4). The best way of avoiding 'complete success' was to demonstrate that one was a man of *otium, quies,* or *segnitia,* since these were traditionally antithetical to political freedom, political ambition, and the kind of military success which might pose a threat to the *princeps*: see above in (3). Agricola's career as described by Tacitus is an object lesson in this *modus uiuendi*. Tacitus continually stresses his *quies* and *otium* (*Agr.* 6.3), his *inertia pro sapientia* (6.3), and his *tranquillitas* and *otium* (40.4): it seems that he 'is deliberately putting forward for praise qualities which would hitherto [i.e. during the republic] have been thought unworthy of the dignity of a senator' (W. Liebeschuetz, 'The theme of liberty in the *Agr.* of Tac.', *CQ* 16 (1966), 130). There were thus powerful reasons why during the empire men described their lack of ambition in terms of *otium*, as we have seen in (1) above: *otium* aptly denoted the opposite of everything that the ambitious politician stood for.

(5) There is a difference between the *otium* of those in (1) above and that of those mentioned in (2). The *otium* of the latter group involved *luxuria* and *uoluptas*, and consequently would seem to be less easily defensible; yet Tacitus approves of Petronius, Crispus and Mucianus no less than V. approves of Maecenas, Saturninus and Piso. A partial explanation for this approval is no doubt that these men at least balanced their *luxuria* by administrative efficiency. They were thus, in a way, balanced characters; and indeed Tacitus' obituary of Piso, another of the group, approvingly singles out precisely his *moderatio* and *temperamentum* (*A.* 6.10.3). Yet this is only a partial explanation. More important is a feature of autocratic societies which Sallust put into words as follows (*C.* 7.2): 'regibus boni quam mali suspectiores sunt, semperque iis aliena uirtus formidolosa est'. The feature may be illustrated from any such society: for some ancient examples see Collard on Eur. *Suppl.* 446, Vretska on [Sall.] *Ep. Caes.* 1.1.5; a modern ex. is Nazi Germany, where the autocrat is recorded as having said that honest men are dangerous: 'Men liable to corruption are less dangerous' (*Hitler's Table Talk 1941–44* (ed. H. R. Trevor–Roper,

[2] 1973), 234). Under the imperial system at Rome it was the emperor who through propaganda appropriated all the traditional (i.e. republican) virtues for himself (cf. Grenade 465–7, Béranger 216). As Pliny said, 'sunt quidem cuncta sub *unius* arbitrio, qui pro utilitate communi *solus* omnium curas laboresque suscepit' (*Ep.* 3.20.12). The emperor was the *custos* (cf. 104.2n.); he took charge of the *tutela imperii* (105.3n.); above all, he was *optimus* (126.5n.). Anyone thought to be displaying these or equivalent qualities risked being considered a usurper of the emperor's role and hence also, perhaps, of his position as *princeps*. Thus Nero 'uirtutem ipsam exscindere concupiuit' (Tac. *A.* 16.21.1; cf. W.-R. Heinz, *Die Furcht als politisches Phänomen bei Tac.* (1975), 75); Domitian was 'infensus uirtutibus' (*Agr.* 41.1, cf. 31.3 'uirtus . . . subiectorum ingrata imperantibus'), and during his reign 'promptissimus quisque saeuitia principis interciderunt' (3.2). The full effect of this last statement, and of the contrast with republican times, can only be appreciated when it is compared with the sentence of Sallust which it echoes (*H.* 1.77.1, quoted in (3) above). If *uirtus* was so dangerous, the natural alternative was, in Roman terms, *luxuria* or *otium*: as Pliny again put it, 'cum suspecta uirtus, inertia in pretio' (*Ep.* 8.14.7). Hence there arose men like Maecenas, Crispus and the rest, who practised *otium, luxuria* and *somnus* because these denoted their incompatibility with, and hence disinclination for, the position of *princeps*. As for the nobility in particular, 'their mode of living stood if possible at a higher level than ever before. This was the only way in which social distinction could find expression' (M. Gelzer, *The Roman Nobility* (1969), 159). It is a far cry from the days of the republic, when *luxuria* denoted the pursuit of political success (see (3) above).

(6) Naturally some modifications will need to be made to the admittedly general picture presented in (4) and (5) above. For example, the distinction made in (5) between the two types of *otium* is somewhat artificial. *otium* is a particularly multivalent word, and no doubt it was claimed by men in (1) precisely because of its connotations of *luxuria* which it had in the case of those in (2). Again, not all emperors were as repressive as Domitian, and many of them presumably wished their citizens to be *boni*: it was after all another convention that the *princeps* should be an example to his subjects (cf. 126.5n.). Tacitus most realistically portrays Tiberius as incapable of deciding whether to favour men of *uirtus* or not: 'neque enim uirtutes sectabatur et rursum uitia oderat: ex optimis periculum sibi, a pessimis dedecus publicum metuebat' (*A.* 1.80.2).[1] Under Tiberius a *promptus homo* like L. Arruntius was regarded with suspicion (Tac. *A.* 1.13.1), but not eliminated. By and large, however, the general picture is

---

[1] A nice parallel has come out of modern Yugoslavia, where the authorities were worried about the effects of a pornography boom on the country's citizens and their morale. But one pornographer is reported as having said: 'Tito should be grateful to us. It is safer for the Croats and Serbs and the rest of us to look at photos of pretty girls than to hatch political plots' (*Sunday Times* 14 January 1973).

in my opinion true enough. It is significant that in V.'s description of Maecenas he defends the minister's *uigilantia* and *prouidentia* (traditionally good qualities) by mentioning his *otium* and *luxuria* (traditionally bad qualities), not the other way round. So too with Saturninus at 105.2. The opposite technique is however found in Tacitus, where, as in Sallust's description of Sulla (see (2) above), the *otium* of Crispus and Petronius is defended by reference to their *negotium*. But the explanation lies not in any intrinsic difference between Maecenas and Saturninus on the one hand and Crispus and Petronius on the other, but rather in the different attitudes of the two historians describing them. V. supported the imperial system: he therefore suspected qualities which might threaten emperors, and approved of those which precluded revolutionary ideals. It is significant that, to judge from his description of Sejanus as merely 'otiosis *simillimum*' (127.4 and n.), he had Tiberius' henchman marked down as a potential threat. Tacitus however affected to support the republican system of government: he therefore described men in republican terms, and his approval of *otiosi* and *luxuriosi* stems not from their *otium* as such but from their ability to achieve a kind of political success within (or despite) the imperial system (cf. Syme, *RR* 104–5, *Tac.* 538).

(7) The general point that *otium* was regarded differently under the empire from under the republic has of course often been made before (cf. e.g. F. Tietze, *RhM* 88 (1939), 258; O. Skutsch, *Studia Enniana* (1968), 164–5), and it is hardly surprising if V., as I have argued, illustrates the difference in outlook. Yet J.-M. André, whose *L'otium dans la vie morale et intellectuelle romaine, des origines à l'époque augustéenne* (1966) is the standard work, has written an article arguing the contrary thesis, that V.'s history marks 'le retour des préjugés ancestraux contre l'*otium*' ('L'*otium* chez Valère-Maxime et Vell. Pat. ou la réaction morale au début du principat', *REL* 43 (1965), 294–315; the quotation from p. 313). His argument would be remarkable if it were true, and there are indeed some small pieces of evidence in its favour: V. admires *industria* at 22.2, 43.4 and 97.2 (cf. Hellegouarc'h (1964), 676ff., but too enthusiastic in my opinion), and *uigilantia* or *uigilia* at 34.3 and 79.1; he deplores the onset of *otium*, *luxuria* and *somnus* at 2.1.1, and defends Scipio Aemilianus' *otium* along Ciceronian or republican lines at 1.13.3. Yet most of these cases are drawn from the republican portion of V.'s narrative, when moral and political values were of course different from those of imperial times. The significant evidence, I believe, lies in the character sketches of Maecenas here at 88.2, of Piso at 98.3, and of Saturninus at 105.2;[1] and that evidence supports the thesis which I have been illustrating here.

---

[1] André is compelled to explain V.'s treatment of Maecenas by alleging that 'l'historien a proposé une morale très "hierarchisée" qui légitime pleinement l'*otium* des princes et de leurs grands serviteurs' (op. cit. 311); and he naturally gets into considerable difficulties when dealing with the case of Saturninus (313), whose description by V. he seems anyway to have misunderstood (see 105.2n.). André has subsequently repeated his general thesis in *REL* 49 (1971), 238.

For *agendi sciens* cf. Cic. *De Or.* 1.214 'regendae rei publicae scientissimus' (F.).

otio ac mollitiis paene ultra feminam fluens   For *mollitiis . . . fluens* cf. 1.6.2, Cic. *TD* 2.52; for *otio . . . fluens* cf. *luxu fl.* at Liv. 7.29.5, 32.7, Curt. 10.3.9, Sen. *Ep.* 78.25, and *luxuria fl.* at Tib. 2.3.51. *mollitia* was a particularly feminine attribute (e.g. Plaut. *Pseud.* 173–4 'uos quae in munditiis, mollitiis deliciisque aetatulam agitis . . . inclutae amicae', Sen. *Contr.* 1 *praef.* 8 'mollitia corporis certare cum feminis', Sen. *D.* 9.17.4 'ultra muliebrem mollitiam'), and for *otium* in such contexts cf. Sen. *Ep.* 82.2 '"mollis est"'; paulatim enim effeminatur animus atque in similitudinem otii sui . . . soluitur'. For *ultra feminam* cf. Tac. *H.* 2.63.2 'ultra feminam ferox', *SHA Tyr. Trig.* 30.16 'ultra femineum modum'; on effeminacy in general see H. Herter, *RAC* 4.620–50.

angusto clauo †pene contentus   More emendations have been suggested for this phrase than for almost any other in V., the majority of them directed towards producing an abl. noun from the paradosis *pene* (see Stegmann 175). Yet since *i* is very often written wrongly for *o* in V.'s text (Kritz lxxxix; several exs. involve terminal letters), I think that the required abl. with *contentus* is provided by *angusto clauo* and that *pene* hides an adverb. Lipsius' *bene* is perhaps a little too colloquial, but there is little to choose between that, his alternative *plane*, and Salmasius' *plene*.

nec minora consequi potuit sed non tam concupiuit   'and had the ability to achieve no less distinction but did not have the same desire for it'. The connective element in *nec* goes with *potuit*, the negative element with *minora*; and with *minora* we must understand *quam Agrippa*. The expr. is certainly awkward, but I do not think emendation is called for.

88.3 noui ac resurrecturi   At first sight these adjj. appear contradictory, in which case we would be compelled to take *ac* in a corrective sense, 'or rather'; yet I can find no good parallel for *ac* used in such a contradictory expr. (see Hand, *Turs.* 1.466–7, *OLD* s.v. *atque* 4a, in both of which the nearest case is Cic. *TD* 5.45 'hebeti ingenio atque nullo'). I am therefore persuaded to agree with Freitag that the adjj. are virtually synonymous, in which case *noui* must refer to the 'repetition or resumption of an action' (*OLD* s.v. 7a, quoting *Bell. Alex.* 33.2 'ne qua rursus noua dissensio . . . nasceretur', Virg. *Aen.* 6.820 'natosque . . . noua bella mouentis'). Herel deleted *noui ac*.

For *speculatus . . . consilia*, above, cf. Sall. *J.* 108.1, Liv. 42.17.1, Just. 18.2.4 (F.); for *summam . . . dissimulationem*, 97.1n.

ille quidem male consultorum poenas exsoluit   We do not know the circumstances of his death (but see next n. but one). It can be inferred from App. *BC* 4.50, as interpreted by Wistrand 11–16, that after the detection of his conspiracy by Maecenas he was sent to Octavian in

Egypt; but if so, we do not know whether he ever arrived. R. A. Bauman, on the other hand, has argued that Lepidus was dealt with by Maecenas on the spot (*The Crimen Maiestatis in the Roman Republic and Augustan Principate* (1967), 180).

For *male consultorum* cf. Tac. *A.* 1.78.2, 6.6.2, Plin. *Pan.* 70.7, Dictys 2.21; for *poenas exsoluit* cf. Catull. 66.77, Liv. 26.40.15, 28.25.6, Val. Max. 1.1 *ext.* 3, Tac. *A.* 1.10.3.

aequetur . . . Lepidi uxor 'Lepidus' wife Servilia deserves comparison with Antistius' ⟨wife⟩ already mentioned'. The cross-reference is to 26.3, where Calpurnia, the wife of P. Antistius, 'iugulato . . . uiro gladio se ipsa transfixit'. According to Appian (*BC* 5.93) a marriage had been arranged between Lepidus and Mark Antony's daughter Antonia; whether the marriage was called off, or whether Antonia died after marrying Lepidus, is uncertain (*PIR*² 1.60). For heroic female suicides cf. 87.1n.

uiro igni deuorato The paradosis reads *uiuo igni deuorato*, which is normally taken as an abl. abs. = 'by swallowing live coals'; but this raises a number of serious problems.

(1) This method of committing suicide, as Vossius observed, is almost beyond belief. In the whole of Roman history (see Grisé, quoted on 87.1n.) there is only one parallel for it, viz. Brutus' wife Porcia, whose case became extremely famous (cf. Val. Max. 4.6.5, Mart. 1.42, Dio 47.49.3, App. *BC* 4.136).[1] Yet V. does not compare Servilia with Porcia, who (to make matters more poignant) was actually the young Lepidus' aunt, but with Calpurnia at 26.3, who (as we have seen: last n.) killed herself with a sword. That V. fails in these circumstances to make a comparison with Porcia seems to me an extremely strong argument that Servilia's manner of suicide was different from hers. One cannot argue that V. omits to mention Porcia because he has not mentioned her hitherto in his work: her case was clearly so celebrated that he could easily have drawn the comparison even without having mentioned her earlier.

---

[1] According to Flor. 2.9.15, Q. Lutatius Catulus killed himself *ignis haustu* in 87 B.C., but all other authorities, including V., make it clear that he died from suffocation (cf. 22.4, Val. Max. 9.12.4, App. *BC* 1.74, Plut. *Mar.* 44.8). Seneca mentions dying by *haustus ignis* (*Prou.* 6.9) and by *flamma ore rapienda* (frag. 124 H), but, as Howell on Mart. 1.42 observes, he was no doubt thinking of Porcia's case. Whether Porcia herself so died was queried but accepted by Plut. *Brut.* 53.5–7; Fabricius on Dio 47.49.3 suggested that she too suffocated, and more recently it has been thought she may have died from plague (see Howell, loc. cit.). But it is the generally accepted ancient view which concerns us here. Another case of suffocation was perhaps Jovian (cf. Eutrop. 10.18.1).

246

(2) It is very doubtful that *ignis* can ever = 'coal(s)'.[1] The usual expr. for 'live coals' is *carbones uiui* (Petron. 135) or *ardentes* (Val. Max. 4.6.5, of Porcia) or *candentes* (Cic. *Off.* 2.25). Thus *igni* here almost certainly = 'fire'; but in that case *uiuo igni deuorato* is a very odd phrase. Although one can apparently say *ignem haurire* = 'to swallow fire' (as we have seen: above, p. 246 n. 1),[2] and although one can also say *ignis uiuit* = 'the fire is burning [as opp. to not burning]' (cf. Plaut. *Aul.* 93, Ov. *Fast.* 3.427), it must be extremely doubtful whether one can say 'she swallowed burning fire'.

(3) Some of these problems were raised by E. Hohl ('Ein Strafgericht Oktavians und ein Gnadenakt des Augustus', *Würzb. Jahrb. f. d. Altertumsw.* 3 (1948), 107–10), who proposed to understand *uiuo . . . deuorato* as a dative 'abhängig von pensavit' and as referring not to Servilia but to her husband Lepidus: 'consumed by fire while still alive'. However, this proposal raises difficulties of its own. It is very awkward to understand *uiuo* as referring back to Lepidus: we should expect V., who frequently uses pronouns even when they are not needed (97.4n.), to have added *ei*. In addition, the relationship of *pensauit* to the alleged dative is tenuous and obscure. These awkwardnesses are well illustrated in Hohl's attempt at translating the clause: 'Durch ihr eigenes vorzeitiges Sterben hat diese Frau das unsterbliche Gedächtnis ihres Namens dem lebendig Verbrannten "dargewogen"' (p. 109).[3]

(4) Most of the above difficulties would be removed if we adopted the emendation *uiro* for *uiuo*, proposed by H. van Herwerden (*Mnem.* 32 (1094), 103), who interpreted the phrase as an abl. abs. = 'after her husband's body had been cremated' (i.e. following his execution for treason). Although I do not think the Latin is capable of this interpretation, there is in my opinion a good deal to be said in favour of Herwerden's suggestion if *uiro igni deuorato* is given the more natural meaning 'after

---

[1] At *C.* 2.1.7–8 *incedis per ignes* | *suppositos cineri doloso* Horace has strikingly combined the two common exprr. 'walk through fire' and 'fire under ash'. When each expr. occurs in isolation, it is clear that the word 'fire' should be given its normal meaning (see Nisbet–Hubbard ad loc., E. K. Borthwick, *CQ* 19 (1969), 312). But it might be argued that Horace's combination of the two will not make sense unless *ignes* = 'burning coals/embers'; in which case we are dealing with a metonymical extension of meaning which is due to Hor.'s *callida iunctura* in this particular passage but is not, I think, relevant to the passage of V.

[2] *ignem haurire* is commonly used metaphorically for drinking in the fire of love: see Lyne on *Ciris* 163.

[3] Hohl feels obliged to explain his translation further, for he continues: 'mit anderen Worten: die ebenso harte wie schimpfliche Todesstrafe der vivi crematio . . . erhielt ihr Gegengewicht, ihre "Kompensation" in dem unsterblichen Ruhm, den seine schuldlose Witwe sich dadurch errang, dass sie dem Gerichteten in freiem Entschluss in den Tod nachfolgte'.

her husband had been burned to death': cf. *Aetna* 621 'cunctantes deuorat ignis' (the verb also used of a volcano at Sen. *Ep.* 79.2), Sulp. *Chron.* 2.5.2 'illi deuorari ignibus . . . maluerunt' (it may be relevant that Sulp. often imitates V.). Admittedly the phrase leaves vague the precise circumstances of Lepidus' death: it is not clear whether Octavian ordered him to be burned alive, a punishment normally reserved for low-class arsonists but enthusiastically suggested by Hohl apropos of his own interpretation, or whether Lepidus committed suicide. Yet such vagueness is exactly in V.'s manner (cf. his account of Canidius' death at 87.3) and the phrase would make good sense. I have therefore, after considerable hesitation, adopted Herwerden's conjecture.

praematura morte immortalem nominis sui pensauit memoriam It is extremely difficult to decide between this text, which is Burer's suggestion in the light of his reading of (M), and that of P, which is *praematuram mortem immortali . . . memoria*. (A makes both pairs of noun + adj. accusative, which is of course impossible.) If we follow Burer, the clause will mean 'who . . . bought eternal memory for her own name by a premature death' and the use of *pensare* will be the same as that at 115.5 'numquam . . . ulla opportuna uisa est uictoriae occasio quam damno amissi pensaret militis' and Tac. *D.* 40.4 'nec bene famam eloquentiae Cicero tali exitu pensauit'. If we follow P, the clause will mean 'who . . . compensated for her premature death by the eternal memory of her own name' and the use of *pensare* will be paralleled by numerous passages in which a disadvantage in the accus. is compensated for by an advantage in the abl.: e.g. Liv. 27.40.2 'aduersa secundis pensando', 37.1.2, fr. 50 'si quis tamen uirtutibus uitia pensauit', Ov. *Her.* 2.143 'stat nece matura tenerum pensare pudorem', Germ. *Arat.* 92 'Icarus ereptam pensauit sidere uitam', Tac. *Agr.* 22.3 'damna aestatis hibernis euentibus pensare', Quint. *Decl.* 272 (p. 116.17–18) 'pensauimus omnia ista uictoria', [Quint.] *Decl.* 3.16 'uulnera laude pensabimus'. I have sided with Burer, but only after much hesitation. For V.'s use of *repensare* cf. 2.12.5 (where the text is again in doubt) and 21.3.

For paronomasia of the type *morte immortalem* cf. *Rhet. Herenn.* 4.29 ('addendis litteris'); Verhaak (70) compares Quint. 9.3.71 'emit morte immortalitatem'. For *nominis memoria* cf. Heubner on Tac. *H.* 1.67.1.

89.1 Caesar autem reuersus in . . . urbem Oct. returned to Italy in the summer of 29 (Dio 51.21.1), entering the city in mid-August (next n. but one).

⟨qu⟩o concursu, quo fauore omnium hominum, aetatium, ordinum There is very little to choose between Damsté's conjecture, printed here, and Lipsius' ⟨*quo*⟩ *occursu*, since each noun is used regularly in accounts of *aduentus* (see *TLL* 9.2.405.1ff. for *occursus*, and 103.4n. for *concursus*): V. uses the latter at 103.4, the verb *occurrere* at 59.6. I have sided with Damsté; the error perhaps arose through abbreviation (e.g.

c̄cursu) and for the combination with *fauor* cf. Liv. 27.45.6 'quo concursu
. . . quo fauore hominum iter suum celebretur'. Vascosanus also wished
to restore *concursu* (see app. crit.), but he fails to produce the parallelism of
the two pairs of interrog. adjj. (cf. *quae . . . quae* below).

Halm wished to read *hominum omnium ⟨generum⟩, aetatium, ordinum*, comparing the *aduentus* at Cic. *Pis.* 96 which contains those three genitives and
to which could be added the parallel passage at § 52, and also *Att.* 2.19.2.
Yet *genera* does not always accompany the pair *aetates ordines* (cf. *Sest.* 109,
Har. Resp. 11, *Dom.* 90, *Att.* 4.1.4, prob. *Cat.* 4.14, Curt. 3.11.22), and I
can see no real need for its insertion here: 'of all men, ages and ranks'
makes unexceptionable sense.

magnificentia triumphorum . . . munerum   Oct. entered the city
to three days of triumphs, 13–15 August (cf. *RG* 4.1, EJ p. 50, Dio
51.21.5–9): the first day's was for his victory in Illyricum in 34–33, the
second for Actium, and the third for Alexandria (87.1n.). Games were
also celebrated the same year (Dio 51.22.4ff., *RG* 22), as well as in the
following year (Dio 53.1.4ff.).

For *magnificentia triumphorum* cf. 121.3; for *m. munerum* cf. Cic. *Fam.* 2.6.3,
Off. 2.56 and (diff. sense) Tac. *H.* 2.81.2.

**ne in operis quidem iusti materia, nedum huius tam recisi digne
exprimi potest**   It was a panegyrical convention to profess one's inability to deal with the subject under discussion (cf. 6 below, 104.4n.,
126.1n.): sometimes V. promises to return to the subject in a future, more
elaborate, work (cf. 96.3n.); sometimes, as here, he says that even in a
more elaborate work he could not deal properly with the subject (cf. 103.4
'uix in illo iusto opere abunde persequi poterimus, nedum hic implere').
All these *recusationes* are useful devices for inflating the importance of one's
theme; but whether V. ever really intended to write a *iustum opus* (also at
99.3) or *iusta uolumina* (48.5, 114.4, 119.1) must remain doubtful: see
Woodman (1975), 287–8 for full discussion.

As Professor D. A. West has remarked to me, the combination *in . . .
materia . . . exprimere* tempts one to see in this *recusatio* a metaphor drawn
from sculpture (cf. the *recusatio* at 6 below *imaginem . . . oculis . . .
subiecimus*). Certainly *exprimere in* is so used (e.g. Cic. *De Or.* 3.15 'libros
Platonis . . . in quibus omnibus fere Socrates exprimitur'; for the literal
use cf. Plaut. *Pseud.* 56 'expressam in cera . . . imaginem'), and it is also
true that *opus* can be used of a sculptor's product (*TLL* 9.2.845.17ff.) and
that *recidere* can be used of stone (Hor. *C.* 2.18.4). Thus it may well be that
V. intended the sustained metaphor: '. . . cannot be properly expressed even
in the material ⟨available to⟩ a full-scale work of art, still less in that of
the present hewn-down one'. But some readers might still prefer to understand *materia* merely = 'scope' *uel sim.* (*TLL* 8.461.39ff., 464.53ff.). *recido*
is also used of literary material at Plin. *Ep.* 1.20.8, but there the image is
drawn from horticulture. For *exprimere* + ind. question cf. 124.1n., *TLL*
5.2.1794.37ff.; for *ne . . . quidem . . . nedum* cf. K–S 2.67.16.

89.2–93 THE REIGN OF AUGUSTUS

Although V. continues to treat the events of Augustus' reign until ch. 123 (Augustus' death), it has been generally observed that it is Tiberius who dominates the narrative from ch. 94 onwards (see *TN* 46–55). Thus the present section in effect brings to a conclusion V.'s narrative of Augustus himself.

The structure of this section seems to have been misunderstood by most scholars, who, unaware of V.'s characteristic alternation between chronological reporting and 'survey-writing', have believed that in 89.2–6 he is dealing with the years immediately after Actium and in particular with the 'settlement' of 27 B.C. This is not the case. In 89.2–6 V. explicitly puts forward a 'survey of the *whole* of Augustus' principate' (89.6 '*uniuersam imaginem principatus eius*': see n.), which he follows in 90–3 with a more detailed account of the first two decades of Augustus' reign. Similarly in the Tiberian narrative a general survey of Tiberius' reign (ch. 126) is followed by a more detailed account of the first sixteen years of his reign (129–30).

89.2–6 A GENERAL SURVEY OF AUGUSTUS' REIGN

V. describes Augustus' reign as a period of 'restoration' (*repraesentauerit, reuocata, restituta, redactum, reuocata, rediit*), a conventional technique which he also adopts at the corresponding place in the Tiberian narrative (viz. ch. 126: see *TN* 234).[1] An emphasis upon restoration naturally accorded well with the propaganda of Augustus himself, who wished his principate to be seen as a period of return to moral, social and political excellence (e.g. *RG* 8.5 'multa exempla maiorum . . . reduxi'; cf. Syme, *RR* 440ff.); and indeed the similarities between *RG* and V.'s history at this point are noteworthy.[2] Yet these considerations should not persuade us that V.'s remarks are without historical foundation, which is not the case (see nn. below).

89.2 Nihil . . . nihil . . . nihil . . . nihil . . . quod non Augustus . . . repraesentauerit The first two cola contrast with each other (*optare ∼ praestare, homines ∼ dii, a diis ∼ hominibus*) and as a pair correspond exactly to the third and fourth cola (*optare ∼ uoto concipi, praestare ∼ felicitate*

---

[1] Starr (1978), 60, following E. Cizek ('L'image du renouvellement historique chez V.P'., *Stud. Clas.* 14 (1972), 89–90), sees the section 89.3–4 as ending the 'epoch of immorality' which on his thesis began at 2.1.1. See above, p. 51 n. 1.

[2] This has of course long been realised by the various edd. of *RG*; see, most recently, Hellegouarc'h–Jodry 807, 811–13.

consummari), which also contrast with each other (*uoto concipi* ~ *felicitate consummari*). This elaborate arrangement suggests that *ab hominibus* should be understood with *uoto concipi*, and *a diis* with *felicitate consummari*; and since this last phrase corresponds to *dii hominibus praestare*, as we have just seen, it follows that Augustus is being placed on the same level as the gods. It was common to ascribe divinity to a benefactor (see esp. I. M. LeM. DuQuesnay, 'Vergil's first *Eclogue*', *Papers of the Liverpool Latin Seminar Third Volume 1981* (*Arca* 7, 1981), 102–6), precisely the role in which Augustus is seen here.

The above analysis also suggests that the abll. *uoto* and *felicitate* are comparable: just as one can say either *uotum concipere* (e.g. Liv. 41.21.11) or *uoto concipere* (cf. Plin. *Pan.* 4.4, Amm. 26.7.16), so one can also say either *felicitatem consummare* (Sidon. *Ep.* 1.2.1, cf. Sen. *Ep.* 39.6 'consummatae infelicitatis') or, apparently, *felicitate consummare* (but I can find no parallel). Cf. *spe(m) concipere* at 103.4n. and 106.2n.

Given the emphasis on restoration in the next sentence (*reuocata* etc.), I believe that *repraesentauerit* here = 'restored' rather than simply 'bestowed'. It is clear from *OLD* s.v. that the verb is capable of a wide variety of meaning depending on its precise context; but the idea of restoration does seem to me to be present also at Cic. *Phil.* 2.118 'si repraesentari morte mea libertas ciuitatis potest'.

Thus the sentence means: 'Thereafter (*deinde*) there was nothing which men can desire from gods, nothing which gods can bestow on men, nothing which ⟨can⟩ be conceived of ⟨by men⟩ in their wishes, nothing which ⟨can⟩ be brought about in happiness ⟨by gods⟩, which Augustus . . . did not restore . . .' For somewhat similar statements Ruhnken quoted Cic. *Leg. Man.* 48 'qui ab dis immortalibus tot et tantas res tacitus auderet optare quot et quantas di immortales ad Cn. Pompeium detulerunt', Liv. 35.31.16 'nihil quemquam a diis immortalibus precari posse quod non Magnetes ab illis haberent'.

89.3 finita uicesimo anno bella ciuilia, sepulta externa On 11 January 29 (cf. EJ p. 45), twenty years almost to the day since Caesar initiated the civil wars by crossing the Rubicon on 10 January 49, Octavian closed the temple of Janus, an act which indicated that 'per totum imperium p. R. terra marique esset parta uictoriis pax' (*RG* 13). It seems to me inconceivable that Octavian should have gone through this elaborate and historic ritual if, as Grenade has argued (52–3), the civil wars were not formally ended until the following year, 28 B.C. No significance should be attached to the fact that V. here appears to distinguish between *bella ciuilia* and *bella externa*, since the antithesis between the two is merely conventional (cf. Jal 23 and n. 4). At *RG* 34.1 ('in consulatu sexto [28 B.C.] et septimo [27], postquam bella ciuilia exstinxeram, . . . rem p. ex mea potestate . . . transtuli') the pluperfect tense indicates that the action of the main clause is later than that of the *postquam*-clause and hence that the end of the civil wars antedated 28 B.C. Thus the views of V.

and Augustus on this point coincide (cf. also 48.3n.). Liv. *per.* 133 ('imposito fine ciuilibus bellis altero et uicesimo anno') is presumably to be explained by inclusive reckoning from an earlier starting-point (viz. 50 B.C., when the senate took measures against Caesar).

For *sepulta* (*bella*) cf. 90.1 and 129.4n.

reuocata pax   On the Augustan cult of peace, a positive response to the absence of war which culminated in the construction of the *ara pacis* in 13–9 B.C. (see below, 4n.), cf. S. Weinstock, *JRS* 50 (1960), 47–50.

For *sopitus . . . furor* below cf. *Pan. Lat.* 10.5.1 (V. uses the verb also at 125.3); for *armorum furor* cf. Val. Max. 4.6.4, Sen. *Contr.* 1 *pr.* 11, Flor. 2.9.5; for *furor* as an almost technical description of civil war cf. Jal 421ff.

restituta uis legibus, iudiciis auctoritas, senatui maiestas; imperium magistratuum ad pristinum redactum modum   In 57 B.C. Cicero had equated his own exile with the disappearance of senatorial authority, fruitful harvests, religious reverence and other items, and he had suggested that with his return all these desirable things would return also (*Red. Sen.* 34): 'cum uiderem me non diutius quam ipsam rem p. ex hac urbe afuturum, neque ego illa exterminata mihi remanendum putaui et illa, simul atque reuocata est, me secum pariter reportauit. mecum leges, mecum quaestiones, mecum iura magistratuum, mecum senatus auctoritas, mecum libertas, mecum etiam frugum ubertas, mecum deorum et hominum sanctitates omnes et religiones afuerunt', cf. 36 'in rem publicam sum pariter cum re publica restitutus'.[1] Similarly V. here says that senatorial *maiestas* and other items, among which he later includes agriculture and religious reverence (4 below), were restored in the years after 29 B.C., a restoration for which he has already said that Augustus was solely responsible (2 above). So too he greets Tiberius' accession with a comparable list of items at 126.2 ('accessit magistratibus [Gelenius] auctoritas, senatui maiestas, iudiciis grauitas'). There can thus be little doubt that such emphases on 'restoration' were conventional in marking a new régime or new state of affairs (cf. 126.2n.); on the other hand, it should not be thought that the items in the present passage are simply conventional and have no relevance to the circumstances which obtained in the years after 29 B.C. (See also below, 4nn.)

Sattler has rightly remarked on the significance of V.'s words here at 89.3. 'Gesetze, Gerichte, Senat und Magistrat sind diejenigen Institutionen, welche nach der traditionellen Auffassung das Gemeinwesen zu einer Republik machen, ohne sie gibt es keine Republik' (40–1 with n. 95). Now while it may be true that 'the institutions of the *res publica* themselves persisted throughout the Triumviral period', it is certainly no less true that 'the Triumviral period was profoundly marked by violence, illegality and the arbitrary exercise of power' (Millar (1973), 54 and 50, with appropriate evidence). Thus the phrase 'restituta *uis* legibus', rather than

---

[1] I owe this excellent parallel to Mr Seager.

(say) 'restitutae leges', is an accurate reflection of what happened when the triumviral period was over. Similarly during the triumvirate the courts existed but lacked *auctoritas* (see e.g. Millar (1973), 59–61) and the senate continued to exist but lacked *maiestas* (see e.g. Syme, *RR* 196–201). *iudiciis auctoritas* in particular no doubt refers to the personal interest which Aug. took in the *iudicia* in general (see A. H. M. Jones, *The Criminal Courts of the Roman Republic and Principate* (ed. J. Crook, 1972), 91ff.) and which was expressed in concrete form in the *leges Iuliae iudiciorum publicorum et priuatorum* of 17/16 B.C. and A.D. 7 (see J. Crook, *Law and Life of Rome* (1967), 70–1, with further refs.). *senatui maiestas* refers to the *lectiones senatus* which are mentioned specifically by V. below (4n.) and by Suet. *Aug.* 35.1 'senatorum affluentem numerum deformi et incondita turba . . . ad modum pristinum et splendorem redegit duabus lectionibus' (in fact there were three: see below); but the phrase presumably includes the other measures which Augustus took to enhance the dignity of the senate (see Jones, *Aug.* 91–3).

imperium magistratuum ad pristinum redactum modum is a more difficult sentence to pin down, as various scholars have found. Premerstein (227–8) believed that V. is referring to Octavian himself, who, *potitus rerum omnium* by 28/27 B.C., contented himself merely with the archetypally republican magistracy of the consulship from then on (cf. *RG* 34.3 'post id tempus . . . potestatis . . . nihilo amplius habui quam ceteri qui mihi quoque in magistratu conlegae fuerunt'). E. T. Salmon takes a rather similar view, though he makes no reference to Premerstein (*Historia* 5 (1956), 462–3). In H. Siber's view V. is referring to the replacement of nomination, under the triumvirate, by election (*Das Führeramt des Augustus* (1940), 80, cf. R. Syme, *JRS* 36 (1946), 157–8). Grenade (166–7) suggested that V. means 'le retour à la règle des deux consuls annuels'.

I think it is important to remember that in phraseology such as this *redigere* simply means 'restore something to its former state' (cf. 98.2 'in pristinum pacis redegit modum' = 'restored them to their former peaceful state'; *OLD* s.v. 2a); the verb can certainly imply 'reducing' or 'limiting', as Premerstein and Salmon believe (cf. *OLD* s.v. 7a), but can equally well imply 'increasing' or 'strengthening' (cf. 109.1 'corpus . . . custodientium . . . perpetuis exercitiis paene ad Romanae disciplinae formam redactum'): the meaning depends upon the context, Here, I believe, *both* implications are applicable; I therefore think there is some truth in each of the scholarly suggestions mentioned in the last paragraph. Under the triumvirate the triumvirs themselves had enormous powers which they used regularly and arbitrarily to appoint magistrates who in their turn valued their offices not *per se* but simply as stepping-stones to lucrative provincial commands (cf. Dio 48.53.1–3; Millar (1973), 52). Thus power was wielded excessively by the few *principes uiri* and inadequately by the plethora of *magistratus*. V.'s sentence simply means that this situation no longer obtained and that a return was made to pre-triumviral days. Since there were now fewer *magistratus*, they were compelled to take their responsibilities more seriously; and the *principes uiri* such as Agrippa and even Augustus himself had (arguably, at least) no more *potestas* or *imperium* than in the old days (cf. *RG* 6.1 'nullum magistratum contra morem maiorum delatum recepi', 34.3 quoted above). That this is V.'s meaning would seem to be confirmed by his statement about praetors, immediately following (next n.).

tantummodo octo praetoribus adlecti duo   There had been eight praetors under Sulla; Caesar had occasionally doubled this number (Dio 43.49.1, 51.4), and in 38 B.C. there had been as many as sixty-seven praetors (Dio 48.43.1)! According to Dio (53.32.2) Augustus fixed the number at ten in 23 B.C., which later rose to twelve (Dio 56.25.4).

89.4 prisca illa et antiqua rei publicae forma reuocata   *rei publicae forma* is an almost technical expr. = 'system of government' or 'form of government' (cf. Cic. *Ep. Brut.* 1.15.10 'nullum enim bellum ciuile fuit ... in quo ... non ... aliqua forma esset futura rei publicae; hoc bello uictores quam rem publicam simus habituri non facile adfirmarim'; *TLL* 6.1.1076.31ff.). The whole phrase sums up *restituta uis legibus ... adlecti duo* and refers simply to the dissolution of the triumvirate (the precise date of which is uncertain) and the consequent return to the earlier form of administration.

Scholars used generally to believe that Augustus claimed to have 'restored the republic' in 27 B.C., as a result of which they assumed either that V. was here faithfully echoing Augustus' deceitful claim (see the scornful remarks of Syme, *RR* 324) or that he used the word *forma* to express some scepticism about the claim (so Lana 230, S. Commager, *The Odes of Horace* (1962), 213 n. 102). Yet neither view is necessary or justified since it has now been shown (esp. by Millar (1973), 61-7, but see also E. T. Salmon, *Historia* 5 (1956), 457, and E. A. Judge, *Polis and Imperium: Studies in Honour of E. T. Salmon* (ed. J. A. S. Evans, 1974), 279-311) that Augustus did not make the claim which had long been attributed to him.[1]

The word-order found here, two adjectives separated by *ille et*, occurs in a wide variety of authors (e.g. Catull. 22.9 'bellus ille et urbanus', Cic. *Lael.* 99 'callidus ille et occultus', *TD* 2.38, Liv. 38.17.12 'dura illa et horrida', Val. Max. 2.7.1 'acrem illam et animosam', Tac. *D.* 40.2 'magna illa et notabilis', *A.* 4.61 'canorum illud et profluens') and regularly elsewhere in V. (1.16.3 'priscam illam et ueterem', 2.14.1 'immensa illa et incondita', 28.3 'primus ille et utinam ultimus', 110.6 'stabilem illum ac formatum'). It will be seen from these exs. that such phraseology usually combines two adjj. of the same or similar meaning: for V.'s love of such synonyms cf. 97.2n.

---

[1] Despite his careful examination of the phraseology used by various sources, Judge (pp. 304-5) seems nevertheless to have misinterpreted our passage of V.; contrast Millar (1973), 64.

rediit cultus agris   Agriculture as a symbol of peace under an ideal ruler is a topos as old as Hom. *Od.* 19.109ff. (the famous passage discussed by Philodemus, *On the Good King According to Homer*: see O. Murray, *JRS* 55 (1965), esp. p. 169 'Homer really believes that good harvests go with a benevolent and just ruler'); cf. also Hes. *WD* 228–32 εἰρήνη δ' ἀνὰ γῆν . . . | . . . θαλίης δὲ μεμηλότα ἔργα νέμονται. | τοῖσι φέρει μὲν γαῖα πολὺν βίον (and M. L. West on 225–47), Hor. *C.* 4.5.17–18 'tutus bos etenim rura perambulat, | nutrit rura Ceres almaque Faustitas' (where Heinze quotes Menand. rhet. 377.13 on the good king: γεωργεῖται μετ' εἰρήνης ἡ γῆ, also EJ 98a), 4.15.4–5 'tua, Caesar, aetas | fruges et agris rettulit uberes', Plin. *Pan.* 32.1 'princeps qui terrarum fecunditatem . . . referret', *Pan. Lat.* 3.10.1 and Gutzwiller ad loc., 5.13.3ff., 6.9, 9.18.4–5, 11.15.4. See in general Cairns 109–15; DuQuesnay 61ff.

Yet V. does not simply repeat the topos unthinkingly: after all, he omits it from the comparable panegyric of Tiberius at ch. 126. The fact is that twenty years of civil war had considerably affected the Italian countryside: peasant farmers were drawn from it for recruitment into the army (cf. P. A. Brunt, *JRS* 52 (1962), 73ff.), and the armies themselves, through their various depredations up and down Italy, did violence both to the land and to the livelihood which it provided (see Brunt, *IM* 289–93). It was doubtless this bleakness and devastation which prompted Virgil during the thirties to compose his *Georgics*. After the civil wars, on the other hand, and most notably in 30 and 14 B.C., many thousands of veteran soldiers were settled on the land by Augustus, as he proudly records (*RG* 3.3, 16.1: see Brunt, *IM* 332–44). This policy, to which there was in fact no alternative, could be capitalised on by propaganda and represented without difficulty as a rejuvenation of agriculture and hence also as a general return to a rural way of life, with all the attendant moral qualities which that life symbolised (see Syme, *RR* 449ff.). It is doubtless significant that on the *ara pacis augustae* the goddess Italia appears in a context of rural prosperity normally associated with a 'golden age' (see, conveniently, Earl, *Aug.* 113–16, with bibliog. on p. 202).

sacris honos   As apposite an item as agriculture above, since indifference to religion could be represented as a cause of the civil wars (e.g. Hor. *C* 3.6), and Aug., after he had terminated those wars, embarked on an ambitious programme of religious reforms (see e.g. Latte 294–311, Liebeschuetz 56ff.). So too *securitas* immediately below, while a familiar political slogan (cf. 103.4n.), was self-evidently appropriate to the new age. For *certa cuique . . . possessio*, below, cf. Cic. *Amic.* 55 'amicitiarum sua cuique permanet stabilis et certa possessio', Sen. *Ben.* 6.3.3 (F.).

leges emendatae utiliter, latae salubriter   The same point is made, with somewhat confusing detail, by Suet. *Aug.* 34.1: 'leges retractauit et quasdam ex integro sanxit, ut sumptuariam, et de adulteriis et de pudicitia, de ambitu, de maritandis ordinibus. hanc, cum aliquanto seuerius

quam ceteras emendasset, prae tumultu recusantium perferre non potuit
...' It is not clear from the context whether Suetonius' *ut* introduces
examples of both revised and new laws or only the latter; but since it is
thought that Sulla in 81 had passed a *lex Cornelia sumptuaria* and others *de
adulteriis et de pudicitia* and *de ambitu* (see G. Rotondi, *Leges publicae populi
Romani* (repr. 1962), 354–5, 359–60, 361; *MRR* 2.75), Suetonius seems not
to be illustrating only new laws.[1] Yet there was no previous law *de maritandis ordinibus*, from which it appears to follow that this law must be new
to Augustus; yet this is the only one of the four mentioned which Suet.
specifically says that Augustus 'revised' (*hanc cum ... emendasset*). The
apparent discrepancy may be resolved if we assume, as do many scholars
(see 93.2n.), that around 28 B.C. Augustus introduced a new marriage law
which he was compelled to withdraw but which, on this hypothesis, he
reintroduced as the *lex Iulia de maritandis ordinibus* in 18 B.C. However, this
revised law was itself too severe (*seuerius ... emendasset*)[2] and required
immediate modification before it was acceptable ('perferre non potuit nisi
adempta demum lenitaue parte poenarum et uacatione trienni data auc-
tisque praemiis'). But in time this re-revision too proved unacceptable
(Suet. *Aug.* 34.2 'sic quoque abolitionem eius ... pertinaciter postulante
equite'), as a result of which Augustus in A.D. 9 caused the *lex Papia
Poppaea* to be passed.

This discussion, while incidentally clarifying (it is hoped) the passage of
Suetonius and indicating the difficulties surrounding the evidence for
Augustan legislation, at least suggests some of the individual laws to
which V. may be referring. On Aug.'s new laws in particular see *RG* 8.5
'legibus nouis me auctore latis'; cf. also 6.1 and Suet. *Aug.* 27.5 'recepit et
morum legumque regimen ... perpetuum'; A. Watson, *Law Making in the
Later Roman Republic* (1974), 96–9. *emendare*, used by both V. and Suet., is a
technical legal term (*TLL* 5.2.461.24ff.); hence Horace's verbal play at
Epist. 2.1.2–3 'res Italas ... | legibus emendes'.

senatus ... lectus 'senatus ter legi' (*RG* 8.2); the dates were 29, 18
and probably 11 B.C. (Dio 52.42.1–3, 54.13–14, 54.35.1 with Jones, *Studies*
22–3). *nec* here = 'but not', for which cf. *OLD* s.v. *neque* 5, L–H–S 481;
for *lego* = 'revise (the senate)' cf. *OLD* s.v. 6*b*.

**principes uiri ... hortatu principis ad ornandam urbem inlecti
sunt** Whether or not the polyptoton *principes ... principis* is intentional,
V.'s choice of phraseology provides an interesting sidelight on how the
Augustan principate was viewed (cf. Premerstein 114).

---

[1] On other such laws revised by Aug. see also *CAH* 10.147–8; one mentioned there is the *lex de maiestate*, on which see the detailed discussion of
Bauman, op. cit. (at 88.3n.), 266ff.

[2] Cf. Dio 54.16.1 τοῖς τε ἀγάμοις καὶ ταῖς ἀνάνδροις βαρύτερα τὰ ἐπιτίμια
ἐπέταξε, where the comparative adj. suggests that there had indeed been
marriage legislation before 18 B.C.

Since the *principes uiri* mentioned by Suetonius were all *triumphatores* (*Aug.* 29.4 'ceteros principes uiros saepe hortatus est ut pro facultate quisque . . . monimentis . . . urbem adornarent', viz. Marcius Philippus, L. Cornificius, Asinius Pollio, Munatius Plancus, Cornelius Balbus, Statilius Taurus and Agrippa; cf. also Dio 54.18.2 τοῖς τὰ ἐπινίκια πέμπουσιν ἔργον . . . προσέταξε, Tac. *A*. 3.72.1), and since *-que et* joining two nouns is found elsewhere in V. (77.1n.), I think that *triumphisque . . . functi* simply defines the *principes uiri* and does not refer to a separate group of people.

For Augustan buildings in general see Earl, *Aug.* 99ff., with bibliog. on p. 202; those for which the *princeps* was himself responsible are listed in *RG* 19ff. For *inlicere* in a neutral or favourable sense, as here, see Goodyear on Tac. *A*. 2.37.1.

89.5 †consulatus tantummodo usque ad undecimum quem continuaret Caesar cum saepe obnitens repugnassset impetrare potuit† The text of this passage has in general not received from scholars the discussion which its exceptional obscurity deserves; even Kritz's note is surprisingly inadequate. Since the paradosis (though printed by Stegmann and Hellegouarc'h) is ungrammatical, some emendation is required.[1] A simple change to *impetrari* would produce correct grammar but also almost impossible sense and Latinity; in my opinion, therefore, more extensive emendation is required.

It will be as well to recall the facts about Augustus' consulships. (1) He held the consulship in 43 and 33 and then continuously from 31 to 23 inclusive (cf. Suet. *Aug.* 26.2 'sequentes [sc. consulatus] *usque ad undecimum continuauit*'): in 23 he resigned the office more or less permanently (Dio 53.32.3–4). (2) In 22 he was offered the consulship for life, but refused (*RG* 5.3 'consulatum quoque tum annuum et perpetuum mihi delatum non recepi'). (3) In 21 and again in 19 he was offered the year's consulship, but refused (Dio 54.6.2, 10.5; cf. Suet. *Aug.* 26.2 '*multisque* mox, cum deferrentur, *recusatis*'); in the latter year he did however accept *consulare imperium* for life (Dio 54.10.5 with Jones, *Studies* 13–17). (4) Augustus asked for the consulship for himself in 5 and 2 B.C. in order to honour his grandsons (Suet. *Aug.* 26.2 'duodecimum . . . et rursus tertium decimum . . . *ultro petiit* ut C. et Lucium filios . . . deduceret in forum').

In the light of this evidence, the key questions concerning V.'s passage seem to me to be these. (a) Does the verb *continuare* refer to the successive consulships which Augustus actually held between 31 and 23, as in (1) above; or (b) does it refer to the annual consulship which he was offered in 23 but refused, as in (2) above? (c) Does *impetrare potuit* make some reference to the popular lobbying of 22, 21 and 19 B.C., as in (2) and (3)

---

[1] 'Le sens est clair, mais l'expression est fort alambiquée', remarks Hellegouarc'h 2.234, who translates the paradosis thus: 'Malgré sa résistance énergique et répétée, tout ce que César put obtenir fut de ne pas exercer sans discontinuer le consulat au-delà du onzième.'

above; or (d) does it refer to Augustus' own requests for the consulship in 5 and 2 B.C., as in (4) above?

If we answer questions (b) and (c) in the affirmative, the latter part of the sentence can be emended as Burman suggested: . . . *quem ⟨ut⟩ continuaret Caesar, cum saepe obnitens repugnasset, impetrari ⟨non⟩ potuit*, 'but the request that he should continue it was unsuccessful, since he had often strenuously refused it'. Burman's suggestion, curiously ignored by Kritz, seems to provide a plausible reading of the passage; but, like the few other proposals which have been made, it does not eliminate all the difficulties. First, the logic of the *cum*-clause is rendered inept, and the timing of *repugnasset* is wrong: Augustus' refusals came *after* 23 B.C., not before (cf. Suet. 'multisque *mox* . . . recusatis', i.e. in 22, 21 and 19). The proposals of Gelenius (*consulatus tantummodo usque ad undecimum ut continuaret . . . impetrari potuit*), Krause (who supplied *ut* after *consulatus* and deleted *quem*), and Madvig 2.308 (*consulatus tantummodo usque ad undecimum quin continuaret Caesar . . . impetrare ⟨non⟩ potuit*), in each of which *cum* must be given a concessive force, avoid the inept logic of Burman's suggestion but still do not avoid the chronological objection.[1] Secondly, while it is unlikely that on any reading *nam* at the start of the next sentence will have its normal meaning 'for', it is virtually certain, as we shall see below, that it should perform its idiomatic function of distinguishing between two items which are otherwise similar; but since Burman's ⟨*ut*⟩ *continuaret . . . impetrari* ⟨*non*⟩ *potuit* is equivalent to, not distinct from, *repulit* in the next sentence, it follows that *nam* cannot on this interpretation perform its idiomatic function. Thirdly, Burman rather optimistically hoped that *gessit (uel sim.)* should be understood by zeugma in the first part of the sentence (with *consulatus* presumably changed to *consulatum*); but this is impossible, as Ruhnken pointed out, because Augustus did not hold the consulship *usque ad undecimum* – he was consul twice more in 5 and 2 B.C. The only thing Augustus did *usque ad undecimum* was to hold the consulship *continuously*, which means that *continuare*, not *gerere*, must be supplied in the first part of the sentence: e.g. *consulatum* ⟨*continuauit*⟩ *tantummodo usque ad undecimum, quem* ⟨*ut postea*⟩ *continuaret Caesar . . .* This seems to me highly unlikely. It therefore looks certain that *continuaret* is required to govern *consulatus . . . usque ad undecimum*, in which case we should evidently give an affirmative answer to question (a) above. But can we go further?

It seems to me, as I have already implied above, that the logical relationship between this and the following sentence is expressed principally by *nam* below, but also by *tantummodo* here, and that *nam* is performing its idiomatic function of drawing a distinction between items

---

[1] It is of course true that the *recusatio imperii* is a eulogistic topos (see 124.2n. and 125.1, in which latter *impetrare* occurs); but why should V. be made to distort the facts of history when he is able to make the eulogistic point quite adequately without so doing? It should perhaps be noted that Grenade (252) uses Madvig's conjecture as evidence that Aug. refused the consulship *before* 23 B.C.

which are in most respects similar (cf. 71.3, 76.2, 84.2n.). The items in question here are the consulship and the dictatorship, the two highest magistracies in the state, either of which Augustus, in virtue of his position, was evidently considered by the people entitled to hold indefinitely. To this extent the two magistracies are directly comparable. The distinction between them can only be that whereas Augustus was successfully prevailed upon to hold the consulship continuously, similar entreaties were fruitless in the case of the dictatorship. We therefore require an emendation which will bring out this distinction, and that of Gelenius, mentioned above, will do admirably, provided we also change *repugnasset* to avoid the chronological objection to which, as we saw above, it was open. I thus suggest: *consulatus tantummodo usque ad undecimum ut continuaret Caesar, cum saepe obnitens repugna⟨turus e⟩sset, impetrari potuit: nam dictaturam quam pertinaciter ei deferebat populus, tam constanter repulit* ('Only in the case of the consulship was there a successful request that he should hold it continuously eleven times, although ⟨later⟩ he was often to refuse it strenuously: for the dictatorship he rejected as consistently as the people stubbornly offered it to him.').[1] None of the proposed changes is particularly violent (*repugnaturus esset* was perhaps corrupted through being written compendiously), the passive use of *impetrari* is easily paralleled (cf. 107.2; *OLD* s.v. 1*b*), and the concessive *cum* constitutes a typically Velleian reminder of Augustus' refusals of the consulship in 22, 21 and 19. But while I find the text, thus emended, extremely attractive, it perhaps involves too many changes over all to print. I have therefore, and with some reluctance, obelised.

nam dictaturam . . . constanter repulit   Cf. *RG* 5.1 'dictaturam et apsenti et praesenti mihi delatam et a populo et a senatu, M. Marcello et L. Arruntio consulibus [22 B.C.], non recepi'. V.'s *pertinaciter ei deferebat populus* is presumably to be explained by Augustus' own words *et apsenti . . . mihi delatam* (i.e. when he was away in the East); V.'s *constanter repulit* is to be explained by Suetonius' story that Augustus refused the dictatorship 'genu nixus deiecta ab umeris toga nudo pectore' (*Aug.* 52, cf. Dio 54.1.4).

89.6 pacatusque uictoriis terrarum orbis   Cf. *RG* 13 'cum per totum imperium p. R. terra marique esset parta uictoriis pax'; on this characteristically Augustan way of regarding *pax* cf. 126.3n. For *pacatus uictoriis* cf. Cic. *Prou. Cons.* 4 (F.); for *opera* = 'political works/ achievements', below, cf. 123.2n.

---

[1] Gelenius' change of *quem* to *ut* is simpler than those of Madvig and superior to Krause's placing of *ut* after *consulatus*, since on my interpretation *tantummodo* is required to qualify *consulatus*. A variation on Krause's proposal would however eliminate this objection (*consulatus tantummodo ⟨ut⟩ usque ad undecimum [quem] continuaret . . . impetrari potuit*), and some readers may feel that this form of emendation represents a more plausible explanation of the corruption of the paradosis than does Gelenius'.

**omne aeui sui spatium impensurum in id solum opus scripto-
rem fatigent** 'would exhaust a writer (even) if he were to devote his
whole lifetime to this one task'. The logic of this statement is that death
would find the writer exhausted by his labours and so unable to complete
them – a rather obscure way of saying that it would take more than a
lifetime fully to describe Augustus' achievements. The statement is an
example of the panegyrical 'inexpressibility topos', for which cf. 104.4n.,
126.1n. Since V. has promised to write only a brief history (as he reminds
himself in the next clause: *memores professionis*), he cannot of course be
expected to deal in detail with all of Augustus' achievements: he thus has
a perfect excuse for presenting only an *imago* of the Augustan principate
(see further 96.3nn.).

While perf. participles are used often to express a conditional clause
(e.g. Cic. *De Or.* 3.179 'haec tantam habent uim, paulum ut immutata
cohaerere non possint') and future partt. are regularly used as the apod-
osis of a conditional sentence (e.g. Tac. *H.* 4.39.3 'haud defutura conscio-
rum manu, ni . . . abnuisset'), the use of a future part. to express a
conditional clause seems rare; M. Ruch ('Le participe futur en -*urus* dans
la conditionnelle', *LEC* 37 (1969), 152–61) cites two exs., Plin. *Ep.* 9.33.1
'auctor cui bene uel historiam scripturus credidisses', Tac. *Agr.* 1.4
'quam (ueniam) non petissem incusaturus'. The use of such a part. here
seems to me to support Acidalius' simpler change to *fatigent* rather than
Vossius' to *fatigarent*.

For *aeui . . . spatium*, a variant on the commoner *aetatis spatium* (F. cites
Plaut. *Stich.* 81, Cic. *Senec.* 60, *Top.* 73, Lucr. 2.1174, 3.774, Sen. *Ep.* 92.28,
Curt. 9.6.18), cf. Ov. *Met.* 15.874, Tac. *Agr.* 3.2. For *memores professionis*,
below, cf. 55.1n.

uniuersam imaginem principatus eius . . . subiecimus An
example of enallage (91.3n.): 'a survey of the whole of his principate'.

Scholars have generally believed that this sentence is *pro*spective, anticipating the account of Augustus' reign which follows in chh. 90ff.; Acidalius even emended to *subiiciemus*. Yet at the corresponding point in the
Tiberian narrative the equivalent sentence (129.1 'proposita quasi
uniuersa principatus Ti. Caesaris ⟨ ⟩') is indisputably *retro*spective and
refers to 126.1–5, to which the equivalent section in the Augustan narrative is 89.2–5 just preceding.[1] I am therefore of the opinion that *uniuersa
imago* refers to the survey of Augustus' reign which V. has just presented
and that this is confirmed by the relatively wide span of dates and events
which the survey embraces. (At 129.1 V. expresses enthusiasm to discuss
the details of Tiberius' reign (see n.), even though 126.1–5 was intended
to stand in lieu of such a discussion (126.1n.); here, however, at the point
corresponding to 129.1 in the Tiberian narrative, V. expresses no such

---

[1] I do not consider the Tiberian parallel to be nullified either by the
lacuna at 129.1 or by the discussion of Sejanus which intervenes
between ch. 126 and 129.1. See in general *TN* 234.

enthusiasm and the greater part of 90–93 is devoted to the unhappy domestic scene. Whether the contrasting treatment of the two reigns is intentional it is impossible to say. See in general above, p. 115 and n. 1, pp. 118f.)

V.'s phraseology is here extremely interesting. *imago* suggests that he is speaking metaphorically in terms of painting (cf. Flor. *praef.* 3 'quia ipsa sibi obstat magnitudo rerumque diuersitas aciem intentionis abrumpit, faciam quod solent qui terrarum situs pingunt: in breui quasi tabella totam eius imaginem amplectar'), but *oculis . . . subiecimus* suggests that he may be making a simultaneous allusion to the rhetorical technique of *sub oculos subiectio* (Cic. *Orat.* 139 'rem dicendo subiciet oculis', Quint. 9.2.40–1 'illa . . . sub oculos subiectio', referring to Cic. *De Or.* 3.202 and quoting 'haec, quae non uidistis oculis, animis cernere potestis' from one of Cic.'s lost works), variously known also as *demonstratio (Rhet. Herenn.* 4.68), *euidentia* (Quint. 8.3.61ff.) and ὑποτύπωσις (Quint. 9.2.40): see in general Lausberg 2.224–31 §§ 810 and 813; G. Zanker, *RhM* 124 (1981), 297–311. Although the technique usually involved detailed description (Quint. 9.2.40 'sub o. subiectio tum fieri solet cum res non gesta indicatur sed ut sit gesta ostenditur, *nec uniuersa* sed per partes') and precise events (e.g. a siege, cf. Quint. 8.3.67ff.; Lausberg 2.227), whereas in the preceding passage V. has expressed himself in general terms, I think there is some evidence that he may be making the allusion. Unlike some writers (e.g. Sen. *Ep.* 94.21), V. believed that general surveys were a means of achieving vividness (cf. 1.14.1 'cum facilius cuiusque rei in unam contracta *species* quam diuisa temporibus *oculis animisque* inhaereat', 38.1 'ut quae partibus notauimus, facilius simul uniuersa conspici possint'); his account at 2–5 above, while not detailed, is certainly vivid and expressive; and finally, an allusion to *sub oculos subiectio* would give additional point to the transference of the adj. *uniuersus* from its natural partner *principatus* to *imaginem* (see above): it would be a way of indicating that V., in contrast to most writers, has aimed to achieve the effect of *s. o. subiectio* but *without* resorting to detailed description. Note that V. makes a similar allusion to a different rhetorical technique at 117.1 (*mora*; cf. Woodman (1975), 284 n. 1), and that Horace makes a comparable reference precisely to *sub oculos subiectio* at *AP* 181 (with Brink's n.). Similar phraseology to V.'s is also at Val. Max. 4.6 *init.* 'quasdam imagines . . . contemplandas lectoris oculis subiciam', but in his case there is perhaps less evidence that he is making such an allusion. For *oculis subicere* in its primary sense, of an actual view being subjected to one's gaze, cf. e.g. Liv. 3.69.2, 25.24.11, 37.26.6, 44.3.7 'omnis regio . . . oculis subicitur', Curt. 3.2.12.

90–93 AUGUSTUS' FIRST TWO DECADES

The section is divided into two parts, foreign successes (90–91.1) and domestic reverses (91.2–93), each of which is subdivided into three further parts in its turn.

COMMENTARY 2.90.1

90–91.1   Foreign successes (26–9 B.C.)

Most of this section is devoted to an excursus on Spain (90.2–4) which is 'sandwiched' between fleeting references to the northern frontier (90.1) and to Parthia (91.1). Spain, which had been allotted to Augustus as part of his *prouincia* by the settlement of 27, was the first area he visited in the aftermath of that settlement, and his campaign there in 26–25 was the last in which he personally commanded an army on active service in the field. The *princeps*' Spanish campaign was thus a natural choice for a historian in the twenties A.D. who wished to celebrate a foreign success from the early days of the principate.

At least, Augustus' campaign was represented as a great success at the time: Augustus called himself *imperator* (cf. Barnes 21), and closed the temple of Janus as a sign that 'per totum imperium . . . terra marique esset parta uictoriis pax' (*RG* 13, cf. Dio 53.26.5); Livy went out of his way to record both the closing of the temple and Augustus' military victory (1.19.3, 28.12.12); and Horace welcomed the *princeps* as a second Hercules whose exploits had guaranteed peace (*C.* 3.14.3–4, 14–16 'Caesar Hispana repetit penates uictor ab ora . . . ego nec tumultum nec mori per uim metuam tenente Caesare terras', on which see Cairns 179ff.). Yet persistent trouble in Spain in later years showed up the hollowness of Augustus' victory, which he attempted to disguise by refusing the appellation *imperator* on the occasions when his other generals were successful there (see Barnes 21).

V.'s excursus, though written roughly fifty years afterwards, exactly reflects the Augustan propaganda of the twenties B.C. Its main theme is the *pax* which Augustus brought to Spain after two centuries of conflict and danger, the contrast between 'then' and 'now' being emphasised by the frequent insertion of dates (see further 49.1n.), by the elaborate anaphora of *illae . . . illae* etc., and finally by the grandiloquent – but misleading – concluding sentence: *has igitur prouincias . . .*

90.1   The North and West (26–9 B.C.)

90.1 Sepultis (ut praediximus) bellis ciuilibus . . . armorum series lacerauerat   The cross-reference is to 89.3 above.

The notion that the state is a body with limbs is extremely ancient (W. Nestle, *Klio* 21 (1927), 350ff.) and very common in Latin, particularly imperial, literature (A. Momigliano, *CQ* 36 (1942), 117–18; Béranger 218ff.). V. touches this almost moribund metaphor into life by the imagistic context into which he places it: the body of the state has been badly injured (*lacerauerat*) by the attacks of the civil wars, but now that its adversary is dead and buried (*sepultis*), its limbs can start to recover from their wounds and co-ordinate again (*coalescentibus*). For *sepulta . . . bella* cf. 129.4., adding Val. Max. 6.9.5 (F.); for *series armorum* cf. Tac. *H.* 4.54.3 'continuae ciuilium bellorum series'; for *coalescere . . . membra* cf. *Pan. Lat.* 2.36.4 'sub uno capite diuersa r.p. membra coalescunt'.

COMMENTARY 2.90.1

Many attempts have been made to emend the paradosis *et coram aliero* (see Kritz's long n.). Some scholars have favoured emendations which produce a repetition of the preceding verb (thus *et coaluere*, Rhenanus):[1] a rhetorical repetition of this kind is certainly in V.'s manner (cf. 109.1n., 110.1n.), but the emendation fails to produce the antithesis to *rei publicae* which is evidently required by the following sentences on distant places. Recognising just this point, Purser proposed *erat cura alienorum* (or *aliorum*), to which Kreyssig's earlier ⟨*habita*⟩ *est cura alienorum* is very similar: *cura* or a derivative is extremely appropriate in the context of illness metaphors, as several scholars seem to have realised (e.g. *et curante eo*, Lipsius); but neither *alienorum* nor *aliorum* strikes me as particularly convincing. One could perhaps persist with emendations belonging to this latter category (e.g. ed. Bipont.'s could be improved to: *egit curam ulteriorum*), but there is no hope of recovering what V. actually wrote: I have therefore obelised.

Dalmatia, XX et CC ⟨annos⟩ rebellis, ad certam confessionem parata est imperii Heinsius objected to the paradosis *pacata* because *pacatae* quickly follows at the end of this paragraph; but Kritz rightly notes that such subconscious repetitions are in V.'s manner (cf. my n. on 100.5). A much more serious objection is to *pacare + ad*: the meaning would presumably be 'pacified to the point of acknowledging our empire', but I know of no exact parallel for the expression. We should perhaps expect something like *perducta* (cf. Sen. *Ep.* 82.19), but Bothe suggested *parata*, which implies that Augustus merely prepared Dalmatia for its final submission (*certa confessio*) at some later date. Can the implications of Bothe's simple change be defended?

V. tells us that the action of the main verb, whatever it was, took place 220 years after Dalmatia first 'rebelled': he is therefore referring to the conclusion of the *Bellum Pannonicum* in 9 B.C., which took place exactly 220 years after Rome first came into conflict with Illyricum in 229 (on which see N. G. L. Hammond, *JRS* 58 (1968), 1ff.). Now however conclusive this war might have seemed at the time (cf. *RG* 30.1 'Pannoniorum gentes ... deuictas per Ti. Neronem ... imperio p. R. subieci'), it had to be seen in a different light after the great revolt of Dalmatia and Pannonia in A.D. 6–9. To a man of V.'s time the war of A.D. 6–9 was the *certa confessio imperii*, to which the campaigns of 13–9 B.C. had been only the prelude. And whereas Augustus claimed the credit for the earlier campaign despite its having been waged by Tiberius (*RG* loc. cit.), his failure to record the later war in *RG*, for whatever reason, allowed Tiberius rightly to be seen as its main architect. Certainly these were V.'s own views, as is clear from his own account. At 96.2 (see n.) he respectfully acknowledges Augustus'

---

[1] Made by Rhenanus in his own copy of *ed. pr.* (von der Gönna 240) and then independently by Bergk 300 years later in 1835. Halm's refinement *etiam coaluere* is mistakenly attributed by Bolaffi to himself and by Stegmann and Hellegouarc'h to Novák (1906), who himself ascribes *etiam* to Ellis.

responsibility for the *Bellum Pannonicum* by echoing the wording of *RG*; but he regards the later war as Tiberius' exclusive achievement, as is clear from his whole narrative of the event (see 110–115nn.). The same also seems clear from 39.3 'at *Ti. Caesar . . . certam . . .* parendi *confessionem . . .* Illyriis Dalmatisque extorsit', a passage which strongly suggests that in V.'s view the final submission of Dalmatia did not take place till A.D. 9.[1] I therefore believe that Bothe's excellent emendation, made initially on stylistic grounds, is vindicated both by the facts of history and by V.'s own stated beliefs.

For the notion of *confessio imperii* Ruhnken on 39.3 quoted Enn. *Ann.* 493V 'qui uincit non est uictor nisi uictus fatetur', Liv. 3.28.10 and Hegesipp. 1.32; Vahlen on Enn. quoted Liv. 4.10.3, 36.45.6, 42.47.8, to which add 38.37.5, Caes. *BG* 1.36.1, Virg. *Aen.* 12.568, 936–7, Curt. 4.5.7, Just. 30.3.9.

feris incultisque nationibus   The paradosis *multisque* is nonsense. Heinsius, seeing that V. wrote *incultisque*, noted rightly that the word is common in ethnographical contexts (cf. *TLL* 7.1.1070.31ff.), but not that V. is imitating Sall. *J.* 80.1 'Gaetulos, genus hominum ferum incultumque' (so too Mela 1.110). On Augustan activities in the Alps cf. 95.2 and n., *RG* 26.1, Dio 53.25.3–5.

nunc ipsius praesentia, nunc Agrippae   Augustus campaigned in Spain in 26–25 (see Dio 53.25.5–8), but his achievement (to which V. refers also at 38.4 and 39.3) was short-lived: further trouble in Spain ultimately demanded the attention of Agrippa in 19 (Dio 54.11.2–6). For Augustan activities in Spain cf. D. Magie, *CP* 15 (1920), 323–39; R. Syme, *AJPh* 55 (1934), 293–317; C. H. V. Sutherland, *Coinage in Roman Imperial Policy* (1951), 33ff., *The Romans in Spain* (1939), 132ff. and *The Emperor and the Coinage* (1976), 22–3; A. Brancati, *Augusto e la guerra di Spagna* (1963); W. Schmitthenner, *Historia* 11 (1962), 54ff.; Syme (1970) = *RP* 825ff.; R. F. J. Jones, *JRS* 66 (1976), 46.

See also 92.2n. for the panegyrical tone of *praesentia*, which here has additional point in Augustus' case: his Spanish campaign was the last in which he personally commanded an army. *ipsius* = 'of the general himself', for which sense cf. 109.5n.

amicitia principis   Augustus' *amicitia* for Agrippa is implicit at 127.1 (See n.) and Suet. *Aug.* 66.3. On Augustus' *amici* in general see J. Crook, *Consilium Principis* (1955), 31–6 and also p. 189 (no. 347). Agrippa's third consulship was in 27; he received *trib. pot.* in both 18 and 13.

For *uario Marte* below cf. Quint. 8.6.24.

---

[1] The wording of this passage in my opinion points to A.D. 9; it is true that in the next sentence the refs. to Raetia, Vindelicia and the Scordisci suggest an earlier date, yet that same sentence also contains the words 'Pannoniamque . . . nouas imperio nostro subiunxit prouincias', which again seems to refer to A.D. 8/9.

COMMENTARY 2.90.2

90.2–4   Excursus on Spain (218–25 B.C.)

90.2 abhinc annos CCL   *abhinc* = 'from A.D. 30', the year of the consulship of M. Vinicius, the man to whom V. dedicated his history: for this
method of dating, which is common in V., see in general 100.2n. V. here
adds two other indications of date (the names of the consuls and the out-
break of the Second Punic War), a·practice he usually reserves for solemn
occasions (cf. 103.3n.). The year in question is 218 B.C., which is not quite
250 years from A.D. 30; but V. is doubtless using *CCL* as a round number,
a perfectly legitimate technique when such large spans of time are
involved; but more recent events demand more precise criteria (see
93.1n.).
  For Cn. Cornelius Scipio Calvus, the uncle of the hero of Zama
(Africanus), see *RE* 4.1.1491–2 = Cornelius 345 (Henze); *MMR* 1.232–3,
239, 274; for his expedition to Spain in 218 see J. F. Lazenby, *Hannibal's
War* (1978), 125ff.

per annos CC   Agrippa's victory in 19 (above, 1n.) is precisely 200
years from 218, the date which V. has just mentioned; but whether he
actually means 19 rather than 25, the date of Augustus' victory, must
remain doubtful (see below, 4n.).
  For *multo . . . sanguine*, below, cf. 95.2n.; for *mutuo s.* cf. Petron. 80.3 (F.)
and (rather diff. sense) Tac. *A.* 12.47.2 *mutuo cruore*; for *contumelia . . . periculum* cf. Liv. 2.48.7 (F.).

90.3 Scipiones consumpserunt   These were Cn. Scipio and his
brother P. Cornelius Scipio, the consul of 218, both of whom V. has
already mentioned: on the former see above, 2n.; on the latter see *RE*
4.1.1434–7 = Cornelius 330 (Henze); *MRR* 1.237–8, 274. For their
deaths in Spain in 211 see Lazenby, op. cit. 130ff.
  For *consumo* used thus cf. Sall. *H.* 1.55.5 'quos fortuna bello
consumpserat'; F. adds Hor. *S.* 1.9.33.

contumelioso XV annorum bello   See 2.1.3 'triste deinde et contu-
meliosum bellum in Hispania duce latronum Viriatho'. The Lusitanian
War (as it is known) lasted from 154 to 139 and produced a Spanish
national hero in Viriathus, who was its leader from 147 until his death in
139. Neither the period of the war itself (15 years) nor that of Viriathus'
own career (8 years) squares well with *XX annorum bello sub duce Viriatho*
which is found in the paradosis. More recent edd. either obelise *XX* (Ellis,
Bolaffi) or accept Lipsius' *X* (Krause, Kritz, Haase, Halm), without
paying sufficient attention to Vossius' *XV*, which he defended as follows:
'Tot enim annis circiter duravit bellum, quod Viriatho potissimum duce
gestum . . . videtur Vell. de duratione belli potius quam annis imperii
Viriathi loqui.' Vossius pointed out that this is exactly what is done by

265

Liv. *per.* 54 ('Viriathus . . . per XIV annos, quibus cum Romanis bellum gessit') and Florus (1.33.15), and he could have added Oros. 5.4.14 ('Viriathus . . . per XIV annos Romanos duces atque exercitus protriuisset'). It seems to me altogether probable that V. belongs to the same tradition.

On Viriathus see *RE* 9A.1.203–30 (Gundel); A. E. Astin, *Scipio Aemilianus* (1967), 374 (index). For *bello . . . exercere* cf. Liv. 45.30.7, Claud. Caes. *ILS* 212, col. 2, ll.33–4. For the metaphorical use of *sub* in *sub duce* see 89.6 and Brink on Hor. *Epist.* 2.1.99 (Appendix 7, pp. 426–7).

Numantini belli 143–133, with which V. dealt at 2.1.3–4. *concutio* is a favourite verb of V. (1.3.1, 78.1, 79.3, 121.1): for its use with *terrore* cf. Sulp. *Chron.* 1.47.4 (not in Klebs), and F. compares Virg. *Aen.* 12.468 'hoc concussa metu mentem', Curt. 8.2.24 'pauor . . . concusserat': see too Cic. *TD* 4.19 and E. Skard, *Ennius u. Sallustius* (1933), 29.

in illis turpe Q, Pompeii foedus turpiusque Mancini . . . 'Here occurred the disgraceful surrender of Quintus Pompeius, whose terms the senate disavowed, and the more shameful capitulation of Mancinus, which was also disavowed, and its maker ignominiously handed over to the enemy' (Shipley). These treaties, with which V. dealt at 2.1.3–5, were in 139 and 137: see in general Astin, op. cit. 127–8 and 148–9 (Pompeius), 131–3 (Mancinus). *dediti* alludes to the formal surrender of Mancinus (*deditio*, cf. 2.2.1). For the men involved see *RE* 21.2056–8 = Pompeius 12 (Miltner); *MRR* 1.477; and *RE* 8.2508–11 = Hostilius 18 (Münzer); *MRR* 1.484.

For *ignominia* + gen. see *OLD* s.v. 2a.

illa ** tot . . . absumpsit duces Unlike most edd., I find it impossible to believe that V., who elsewhere uses the plural throughout this ch. (*Hispaniae, in quas prouincias, illae enim prouinciae, illae, illae, in illis, has igitur prouincias, eae*), changed to the singular on this occasion. *Pace* Krause, the rhetoric is impaired rather than improved by the change; and I can see no historical reason why the singular should be more apposite here. Cludius simply changed the offending singulars to plurals, but this is a fairly radical step; more convincing, to my mind, is the assumption that a word has fallen out: lacunae are common in V.'s text (*TN* 26–7), and here I would suggest *illa⟨rum⟩* folowed by such a word as *acies, iuuentus* or *miles*. Professor Goodyear proposes *illa ⟨natio⟩*; but it is of course impossible to know exactly what the truth is.

Sertorium On this *fax belli* (2.15.3) see *RE* 2A.2.1746–53 = Sertorius 3 (Schulten). His rebellion evidently lasted from 80 to 72 (*MRR* 2.77, 118), so V.'s *quinquennium* looks like a considerable underestimate; yet the word 'could be defended as a round figure for the period 79–74, 79 being the

first year anything was done about him, while Pompey and Pius started winning in 73' (Mr Seager writes).
patrum aetate, above, is a Livian phrase (1.30.2, 8.37.12, 36.7.10, 45.7.2); for *diiudicari* + indir. question, below, cf. Heubner on Tac. *H.* 2.39.2.

90.4 has igitur prouincias ... For this use of *hic* to 'sum up' see 109.5n. The panegyrical tone of this sentence as a whole may be illustrated by its comparison with two others: Cic. *Leg. Man.* 31 'hoc igitur bellum tam turpe, tam uetus, tam late diuisum atque dispersum quis umquam arbitraretur aut ab omnibus imperatoribus uno anno aut omnibus annis ab uno imperatore confici posse?', *Pan. Lat.* 8.13.1 'hoc igitur bellum tam necessarium, tam difficile aditu, tam inueteratum, tam instructum ita, Caesar, aggressus es ut, statim atque illo infestum maiestatis tuae fulmen intenderas, confectum omnibus uideretur'.

abhinc annos ferme L perduxit Caesar Augustus ut ... latrociniis uacarent Is V. referring to Augustus' own much acclaimed victory in 25, or to Agrippa's more decisive victory in 19 (see above, 1n.)? The numeral *L*, if correctly transmitted, would seem to indicate the latter date, which is almost exactly 50 years from A.D. 30 (i.e. *abhinc*, cf. 2n.). Yet V. also says that, as a result of the victory (*ut*), peace reigned in Spain under C. Antistius, who was governor in Spain *before* 19 (cf. G. Alföldy, *Fasti Hispanienses* (1969), 3–5).[1] It would therefore appear that V. is referring to Augustus' own victory in 25, which is quite in keeping with the tone of this section as a whole (see above, p. 262) but which means that V. has misrepresented the facts: 'not even brigandage in Spain after 25, that is a tall story' (Syme (1970), 103 = *RP* 848, also (1978), 53, and *AJPh* 55 (1934), 314; see Dio 53.29.1–2, 54.5.1–3, 11.2–7, 20.3). V. cannot of course be accused of falsifying the date, which he has qualified by his use of *ferme*; but whether, by using a date which is exactly true if calculated on the basis of 19 B.C. (as also at 2 above), he wished to create an impression of overall truth, it is impossible to say.

On C. Antistius Vetus see further 43.4n. On P. Silius Nerva see *RE* 3A.1.92–5 = Silius 21 (Nagl); Alföldy, op. cit. 7; he was the father of the P. Silius mentioned at 101.3 (n.) and of A. Licinius Nerva Silianus mentioned at 116.4 (n.).

The contrast between *bellum* and *latrocinium* is standard, though usually put to different purposes (cf. e.g. 31.2, Sall. *J.* 97.5, Liv. 38.32.2, Tac. *A.* 12.29.3).

---

[1] Alföldy assumes that *abhinc* = 'from the *Bellum Sertorianum*', mentioned in the preceding sentence; but this would be contrary to V.'s customary use of the word (see above, 2n.), and in any case does not obviate the problem under discussion.

91.1   The East (20 B.C.)

91.1 ab oriente ac rege Parthorum signa Romana ... Augusto remissa sunt   'The Roman standards ... were returned to Augustus from the Parthian king in the East.' The date was 12 May 20 (B. Levick, *Tiberius the Politician* (1976), 234 n. 38); the Parthian king was Phraates IV, to whom V. refers elsewhere in this sentence. Suetonius (*Tib.* 9.1) tells us that it was Tiberius who received the standards in person, but the truth of this has been doubted: see in general *TN* 98 n. 2; R. J. Seager, *LCM* 2 (1977), 201–2 (with whom I agree that 94.4 is the more natural place for V. to mention Tiberius' role, if any; anticipation here at 91.1 would spoil the effect of ch. 94 as a whole). For Orodes cf. 46.4n. The contrast *occidens* ~ *oriente*, as Mr DuQuesnay points out, suggests that V. is here praising Augustus by an allusion to the ' East ~ West' topos (for which see 126.3n.).

Crasso presso ... Antonio pulso   In 53 (cf. 46.2–4) and 36 B.C. (cf. 82.1–3) respectively.

P's *presso* was altered by Gelenius to *oppresso*, yet there is one occasion in Virgil (*Aen.* 9.329–30 'tris iuxta famulos temere inter tela iacentes armigerumque Remi premit') and others in Tacitus (*H.* 3.77.2 'reliquae (naues) in litore captae, aut nimio ruentium onere pressas mare hausit', 4.2.3 'paucos erumpere ausos circumiecti pressere', and possibly *A.* 14.5.1, 15.53.2, 16.9.2: see N. Eriksson, *Studien zu den Annalen des Tac.* (1934), 123 n. 1) where *premere* evidently = *opprimere*. The use of simple verbs for compounds is favoured by ' den raffinierten Stilkünstlern' (S. Lilliedahl, *Florusstudien* (1928), 72), and so also by V. elsewhere (Bolaffi xvii). Why not here too?

quod cognomen illi uiro ... indidit   16 January 27 (EJ p. 45). ' The name Augustus is given as a culminating tribute for all the good works detailed in the preceding chapters (even though some of those good works were done long after 27 B.C.) ' (Starr (1978), 102).

Doubts have been cast over *uiro*, yet there is nothing intrinsically wrong with *ille uir* used to refer to someone just mentioned (cf. 2.8.1, 53.3). Besides, it is clear from accounts of this same event in other authors (e.g. Suet. *Aug.* 7.2 'ampliore cognomine quod loca quoque religiosa et in quibus augurato quid consecratur augusta dicantur', Flor. 2.34.66 'sed sanctius et reuerentius uisum est nomen Augusti, ut scilicet iam tum, dum colit terras, ipso nomine et titulo consecraretur', Dio 53.16.8 Αὔγουστος ὡς καὶ πλεῖόν τι ἢ κατὰ ἀνθρώπους ὢν ἐπεκλήθη) that the name *Augustus* was recognised as having some 'superhuman' connotation: Livy emphasises this by frequently contrasting the adjj. *humanus* and *augustus* (e.g. 1.7.9 with Ogilvie's n.; L. R. Taylor, *CR* 32 (1918), 158–62; H. Erkell, *Augustus, Felicitas, Fortuna* (1952), 9–25), and it would seem that V.'s *uiro* is here aimed at a similar effect (so too 79.2–3 'hac classi Caesar ... bellum intulit; sed uirum humana ope inuictum ... fortuna concussit'). On 'Augustus' in general see Taylor 158ff.; Erkell, op. cit. 36ff.

Aldus and Lipsius, understanding *sententia* to be the subject of *indidit*, altered *consensus* to *consensu* (intrusive final -*s* is a common error: see Kritz xciv); others take *sententia* as abl., making *consensus* the subject of *indidit*. Whether either of these interpretations is right is questionable. *indo* is most often used passively, with *nomen uel sim.* as its subject (cf. *TLL* s.v.), and is so used invariably by V. himself elsewhere (cf. 1.11.2, 2.10.2, 2.11.2); when it is used actively it normally has a person as its subject (but cf. Liv. 1.49.1). Additionally, in the present instance, we should expect the pluperfect tense since the event took place seven years before the action of the main verb *remissa sunt*. Yet I doubt whether these considerations justify altering the text, and for *consensus* as the subject of a verb elsewhere cf. 77.1, Cic. *Leg.* 1.47, *Fam.* 10.12.4, Sen. *D.* 1.3.14, Plin. *NH* 2.160, 7.120, Tac. *H.* 1.30.2 (F.).

For Plancus see 63.3nn., 74.3n., 83.1nn., 95.3n.

91.2–93   Domestic reverses (23–19 B.C.)

V. now turns aside from foreign affairs to deal with three episodes of domestic reverses, the first two of which end with some general truth or reflection (91.4, 92.5). He begins with plots against the régime (91.2–4), which are described in language deriving straight from the turmoil of late republican politics: the antitheses of *bonus . . . pessimus* and *uis . . . ius*; the accusations of thuggery, revolution and culpable penury (*gladiator, ausus, res familiaris*); and the notion of *publica ruina*. Some of the same ground is also covered in the second episode (92), although viewed from the point of view of law and order: V. is thus able, at the expense of some repetition (91.3 *collecto in aedilitate fauore populi . . . ut ei praeturam continuaret* ~ 92.4 *florentem fauore publico . . . praeturam aedilitati . . . iuncturum*), to spotlight his hero C. Sentius Saturninus, who was later to play a prominent part in Germany alongside Tiberius in A.D. 4 (105.1–2nn.). The third and final episode (93) is devoted to the death of Marcellus, who is given an obituary notice.[1] By collecting this gloomy material into one place, V. is able to throw into sharper relief the bright picture of Tiberius' youthful promise which is drawn in ch. 94 (see *TN* 95–9; also 238–9 on the technique of contrasting rulers).

91.2–4   Plots against Augustus (23/22–19 B.C.)

91.2 Erant   tamen   qui   hunc   felicissimum   statum odissent *felicissimus status* was Augustus' own description of his régime (reported at Gell. 15.7.3); but V. perhaps also echoes Cic. *Sest.* 46 'cum

[1] Compare Tacitus' employment of concluding obituary notices (Syme, *TST* 79–80), and see also *TN* 43, 153–4.

alii rem ipsam publicam atque hunc bonorum statum . . . odissent'. On
status as a political term cf. 131.1n.; and on *felix (felicitas)* see 106.3n.[1] On
opposition in general to Augustus see Syme, *RR* 333–48, 476–89; Sattler
72ff.; Yavetz 92–7.

L. Murena et Fannius Caepio, diuersis moribus   The nomenclature of the former conspirator is reported variously in our sources and has
been considerably debated. He is called 'Licinius Murena' by Dio
(54.3.3–5), 'Varro Murena' by Suetonius (*Aug.* 19.1, *Tib.* 8), and simply
'Murena' by Strabo (14.5.4). We also learn from Dio (loc. cit.) that his
sister was Terentia, the wife of Maecenas, which means that he was also a
Terentius (originally, at least: see G. V. Sumner, 'Varrones Murenae',
HSCP 82 (1978), 192).

Now it is an interesting coincidence that according to the *Fasti Capitolini*
the consul of 23 was 'A. T[erentius . . . Var]ro Murena' (EJ p. 36), the
same man as is called 'Terentius Varro' elsewhere by Dio (53.25.3) and
Strabo (4.6.7). Yet this man's name is missing from all the other *Fasti* for
that year, a discrepancy which scholars have explained by assuming that
the consular Murena was identical with the conspirator Murena and that
his name was removed from all but one of the *Fasti* because he suffered a
damnatio memoriae in the aftermath of the conspiracy. If this assumption is
correct, the man's full name is likely to have been 'A. Terentius Varro
Licinius Murena' (Syme, *RR* 325 n. 5), in which case we are required to
make the further assumption that the 'L.' in V.'s text is either an error
(whether by a scribe or by V. himself) or a scribal abbreviation for
'Licinius'. This series of assumptions has been strongly urged by R.
Hanslik (*RhM* 96 (1953), 282–7) and D. Stockton (*Historia* 14 (1965),
21–2), although K. M. T. Atkinson has argued equally strongly against
the identification of the consul with the conspirator (*Historia* 9 (1960),
469–73).[2] Which view is correct? The question is of considerable importance because of its implications for the dating of the conspiracy itself (see
below).

Now if the consul and the conspirator were the same person, why is it
that none of our literary sources makes the identification? Strabo, being
our only contemporary witness, was in a position to do so but did not;
Dio, writing for a third-century A.D. audience, ought to have done so for
their clarification but did not; and V., who would certainly have wel-

---

[1] Mr DuQuesnay has pointed out to me that the *caduceus*, the symbol of
felicitas, occurs earlier than I implied at 106.3n.: it appears on the
coinage of 83 and 44 B.C. (see *RRC* 1.372 no. 357, 1.489 no. 480.6, 494).
A recent study (L. Zieske, *Felicitas* (1972), 259–60) has nothing of significance on V.'s use of the word.
[2] Atkinson in fact goes further, arguing that Dio has wrongly identified
the Licinius Murena who defended Primus (54.3.2–3) with the Murena
who conspired against Augustus (ibid. 4–5).

comed the irony and περιπέτεια of a perverted statesman (cf. esp. *Murena sine hoc facinore* . . . *bonus*), also made no connection between the conspirator and the consul. In view of this remarkable unanimity among our sources, I believe that the conspirator was a different individual from the consul of 23. If this conclusion is correct, why is the consul's name missing from all the *Fasti* with the exception of the *Capitolini*? This question has already been answered by M. Swan (*HSCP* 71 (1966), 235–47), who has demonstrated that such a discrepancy characteristically occurs when a consul, though elected, fails to take up office. It cannot of course be argued that in the present case the reason why the consul failed to take up office was that he conspired; for that would place the conspiracy in 24 B.C., a date which is at variance with all our other evidence. (G. V. Sumner, loc. cit., also concludes that the conspirator and the consul of 23 were different persons, arguing that the former was called L. Licinius Varro Murena who as a child had been adopted by L. Licinius Murena, cos. 62. Sumner has a full bibliog. of the problem on p. 185 n. 1, and a stemma of the Varrones Murenae on p. 194. See also Nisbet–Hubbard on Hor. *C.* 2.10.)

For what is known of Caepio, the other conspirator whom V. mentions and who was prosecuted by Tiberius (Suet. *Tib.* 8), see *RE* 6.2.1993–4 = Fannius 16 (Kappelmacher); *PIR²* 3.118 no. 117. V. contrasts him with Murena in a *syncrisis* introduced by the phrase *diuersis moribus*, as at 1.13.3–4 and Sall. *C.* 53.6; see also *TN* 42 and n. 3.

bonus ... pessimus These were familiar republican labels for those who supported or attacked the status quo (cf. Hellegouarc'h, *VL* 484–93 and 526–8); but whether *bonus* actually = 'Caesarian' here (so Jones, *Aug.* 7) must remain extremely doubtful; certainly *pessimus* is unlikely to mean 'republican' (so Syme, *RR* 334): V.'s judgement is here more likely to be moral than political, as often (see Hellegouarc'h (1964), 673–4).

sine hoc facinore perhaps alludes to the topos *nemo sine uitio est* (cf. 119.4n.).

occidendi Caesaris consilia The date of the plot is extremely controversial: in favour of 23 are Millar, *CD* 88–90; Stockton (above), pp. 18–40; S. Jameson, *Historia* 18 (1969), 204–29; L. J. Daly, ibid. 27 (1978), 83–98; in favour of 22, Dio's date (54.3.4–8), are Hanslik; Atkinson, pp. 440–69; Swan and Sumner (all referred to above); and R. A. Bauman, *Historia* 15 (1966), 420–32. If the conspirator and the consul of 23 are different persons, as argued above, then the latter date is presumably preferable.

91.3 Rufus Egnatius On M. Egnatius Rufus cf. *RE* 5.1999–2000 = Egnatius 36 (Groag); *PIR²* 3.72 no. 32; P. Badot, *Latomus* 32 (1973), 606ff.

271

per omnia gladiatori quam senatori propior This acute vignette, which (as Verhaak 101 remarks) is sharpened by homoeoteleuton, is characteristically Velleian: for *per omnia* + *quam* + compar. adj. cf. 35.2, 130.5; for *per omnia* in general cf. 100.3n. The derogatory use of *gladiator*, of which Cicero was particularly fond (see Opelt 136), is of course originally a metaphor from sword-fighting: Seneca interestingly retains the metaphor when he says 'Egnati . . . in eum [sc. Augustum] mucrones acuebantur' (*Breu. Vit.* 4.5).

collecto in aedilitate fauore populi Rufus' career as a fire-fighting aedile, and the popularity he thereby incurred, are described by Dio 53.24.4–6 under 26 B.C. However, Dio's account concludes with the words τοῖς δ' ἀγορανόμοις παραχρῆμα ἐπιμελεῖσθαί τε ὅπως μηδὲν ἐμπίμπρηται, κἂν ἄρα τι τοιοῦτο συμβῇ, κατασβεννύναι τὸ πῦρ προσέταξε [sc. ὁ Αὔγουστος], to which very similar wording is found at 54.2.4 under 22 B.C., where no mention is made of Egnatius: τοῖς δ' ἀγορανόμοις . . . τὴν τῶν ἐμπιμπραμένων κατάσβεσιν ἐνεχείρισεν [sc. ὁ Αὔγουστος]. Millar (*CD* 87–8) and most modern scholars follow H. A. Andersen's suggestion that Dio has reported the same events twice and that 22 is the true date both of Rufus' aedileship and of Augustus' reaction to it (*Cassius Dio und die Begründung des Principates* (1938) = id. and E. Hohl, *Studies in Cassius Dio and Herodian* (repr. 1975), n. 74 [pp. 29–31]). See too next n.

For *collecto . . . fauore* cf. Suet. *Claud.* 12.3; the verb is used with *beneuolentiam* at Cic. *Lael.* 61, Caes. *BC* 2.31.3 (F.).

in tantum quidem ut ei praeturam continuaret, mox etiam consulatum petere ausus . . . Dio 53.24.5 implies that Egnatius was elected praetor while still aedile, which on Andersen's hypothesis (last n.) would mean that he held the praetorship in 21. We know from 92.4 below that Egnatius was canvassing for the consulship in 19: thus, since his praetorship, a whole year will have intervened, which makes good sense of V.'s *mox* here.

V.'s choice of the word *ausus* indicates that Egnatius was now *audax*, already showing the revolutionary spirit which will lead him to plot against Augustus when his consular venture fails. On this sense of *audax* see 48.3n., and see also next n. but one. For *continuare* + accus. and dat. cf. K–S 1.318.

cum esset omni flagitiorum scelerumque conscientia mersus Heinsius proposed *ceu sentina mersus*, quoting (among others) Flor. 1.47.8 'mersamque uitiis suis quasi sentina rem publicam'; but Krause and Kritz rightly defend *conscientia* by quoting Cic. *Pis.* 39 'conscientia oppressus scelerum tuorum': true, *mersus* is not quite the same as *oppressus*; but *conscientia scelerum* (-*is*) is a set phrase: see next n., Heubner on Tac. *H.* 4.56.1, and id. on 4.41.1 for *c. flagitiorum*. On *conscientia* in general cf. McGushin on Sall. *C.* 15.3–5.

omni is an instance of enallage, defined as 'the transfer to a governing substantive of an adjective which by logic, or at least by convention, belongs with an expressed dependent genitive' (V. Bers, *Enallage and Greek Style* (1974), 1, cf. also pp. 70–1): so too with *uetere* at 92.2 below (*cuilibet* at 92.5 is not dissimilar), and cf. Cic. *Pis.* 21 'ex omni scelerum importunitate'. There is thus no call for Burman's proposed change to *omnium*. For discussion of the phenomenon in Latin cf. Löfstedt, *Synt.* 2.110–11; L–H–S 159–60.

nec melior illi res familiaris quam mens foret Cf. 68.1 'quippe peior illi res familiaris quam mens erat' (of Caelius Rufus), and, more generally, 48.3 'suae alienaeque . . . fortunae . . . prodigus' (of Curio). V.'s hostile attitude to the impoverished circumstances of these men is due to the close connection between poverty and revolution (*egestas/inopia* and *audacia*): e.g. Thuc. 3.45.4 ἡ μὲν πενία ἀνάγκῃ τὴν τόλμαν παρέχουσα, Tac. *A.* 14.57.3 'inopem, unde praecipuam audaciam'. This connection was made especially often in Rome of the late republic (e.g. Cic. *Leg. Agr.* 1.22, *Sest.* 85, Sall. *C.* 18.4 'summae audaciae, egens, factiosus, quem ad perturbandam r. p. inopia atque mali mores stimulabant', 28.4 'egestate . . . nouarum rerum cupidam'), and the particular passages which V. seems to have in mind are Sall. *C.* 5.7 'agitabatur . . . animus ferox inopia *rei familiaris* et *conscientia scelerum*', *H.* 1.77.7 'ad eum concurrere homines . . . corruptissimi, flagrantes inopia et cupidinibus, *scelerum conscientia* exagitati'. In general see pp. 17–18 of Wirszubski's article quoted at 48.3n.

interimere Caesarem statuit Egnatius presumably decided on this course of action after Saturninus had blocked his bid for the consulship (92.4, below): thus a date of 19 seems certain for this *scelus*. For the following *saluo saluus* cf. 49.3n.

91.4 ⟨ut⟩ publica quisque ruina malit occidere quam sua proteri The idea is a commonplace (e.g. Liv. 2.24.2, 45.26.6 'hi conscientia priuatae noxae, . . . ut communi ruina patriae opprimerentur', Sen. *Contr.* 9.6.2, Luc. 7.654–5 'nec, sicut mos est miseris, trahere omnia secum | mersa iuuat gentesque suae miscere ruinae', Sen. *Tro.* 1014–17, *Ag.* 202 and Tarrant ad loc., Tac. *A.* 4.1.3, Claud. *Rufin.* 2.17–20 with Levy's good n.), but especially in evidence in the literature of the late republic: Cic. *Sest.* 99 'qui propter implicationem rei familiaris communi incendio malint quam suo deflagrare', *Cat.* 2.21, 4.14 'qui cum sibi uiderent esse pereundum, cum omnibus potius quam soli perire uoluerunt', Sall. *C.* 31.9 'incendium meum ruina extinguam', cf. Cic. *Mur.* 51, Flor. 2.12.7.

Burer's ⟨ut⟩ is guaranteed by *malit* and by 118.4 'quippe ita se res habet ut . . .'.

in occultando   Herel added *scelere*, but for *occultare* used absolutely cf. e.g. Cic. *Verr.* 2.91, Stat. *Theb.* 2.535. I have accepted Krause's *carcere* for *carceri* below: cf. 129.3n.

mortem dignissimam uita sua obiit   For the topos 'he died according as he lived' cf. 63.2 (and n.), Sall. *C.* 55.7 (cf. also 61.4 with Vretska's n.), Cic. *Phil.* 9.15, Ov. *A.* 2.10.38, Just. 6.8.10, Plut. *Mar.* 12.4. For its opposite cf. 87.1n. For *mortem obire* cf. 102.1n.

92   Consulship of Sentius Saturninus (19 B.C.)

92.1 Praeclarum excellentis uiri factum C. Sentii Saturnini . . . ne fraudetur memoria   By displaying the virtues of *seueritas* and *constantia* (2 below) Saturninus achieved *gloria* (5) which V. intends to hand down to posterity (*ne fraudetur memoria*). No doubt the episode, which is typically Velleian (cf. 76.1n.), is intended to convey an implicit moral; but we should note that the method is quite different from the explicit moralising of Polyb. (e.g. 1.35.6–7) and Diod. (e.g. 1.1.4ff.) on the one hand and of Liv. (*praef.* 10 'hoc illud est praecipue in cognitione rerum salubre ac frugiferum, omnis te exempli documenta in inlustri posita monumento intueri: inde tibi tuaeque rei p. quod imitere capias, inde foedum inceptu, foedum exitu, quod uites') and Tac. (*A.* 3.65.1) on the other. Indeed it is interesting that the closest parallels for V.'s approach seem to belong to the formative periods of Greek and Roman narrative literature respectively. Thus Herodotus claimed to be writing history 'in order that the memory of men's actions should not be erased by the passage of time and that great achievements . . . should be glorified' (1.1, cf. H. Immerwahr, *AJPh* 81 (1960), 261–75), in this resembling the earlier writers of Greek epic whose aim was to retell the κλέα ἀνδρῶν (H. Strasburger, *Homer und die Geschichtsschreibung, SBAW* (1972), 1.33). And Cicero tells us of 'illa carmina quae . . . in epulis esse cantitata a singulis conuiuis de clarorum uirorum laudibus' (*Brut.* 75: see Harris 25 and n. 2, whose lack of scepticism on the matter is most welcome). What significance, if any, is to be attached to this similarity, I do not know.

For Sentius Saturninus, one of V.'s heroes, cf. 88.2n., 105.1–2nn.; for discussions of the moral dimension of classical historiography see e.g. P. Scheller, *De hellenistica historiae conscribendae arte* (1911), 74–8; Avenarius 22–6; Herkommer 128ff.

92.2 circumferens terrarum orbi praesentia sua pacis suae bona   'distributing to the whole world by his very presence the benefits of his own peace'. Ruhnken's deletion of *sua* deprives us both of the effective polyptoton and of the panegyrical commonplace whereby the ruler confers benefits merely by being present: cf. 90.1 'Hispaniae nunc ipsius praesentia . . . pacatae', Curt. 7.8.4 'tanta erat apud eos ueneratio regis ut facile periculi . . . cogitationem praesentia eius excuteret', *SHA Marc. Aur.* 8.5. 'quae omnia mala Marcus et Verus sua cura et praesentia temperarunt', *Max.* 26.4, *Au. Cass.* 13.4, *Commod.* 19.8. This topos (which is closely related to those discussed at 75.1n., 94.4n., and 103.1–4nn.) is doubtless intended to hint at the divinity of the ruler, *praesens* being the technical description of an efficacious god: cf. Hor. *C.* 3.5.2–3 'praesens diuus habebitur | Augustus', *Epist.* 2.1.15; K. Scott, 'Emperor worship in Ovid', *TAPA* 61 (1930), 58–63. For *pacis bona* cf. 110.2n.

Augustus seems to have been away from Rome between 21 and 19 (cf. Dio 54.6.1–10.7, though his account is not without its obscurities).

It is a nice question whether to follow Heinsius in deleting *in* before *ordinandis*. There seem to me to be two approaches to the problem. (a) According to *TLL* 7.1.790.32–791.28 *in* + abl. is frequently used 'ubi directionem (sc. dat. vel *in* c. acc.) indicari expectes'. To this general class belongs '*in* expressing purpose' ('*in* finale'), in which *in* is found either with a simple noun (e.g. Curt. 6.7.7 'fidem in parricidio dedisse') or with a gerund(ive) (e.g. Curt. 4.4.17 'in quibus occidendis defecerat rabies'). Interestingly, most of the exs. with a simple noun are classed as 'exempla certa' in *TLL* (790.57ff.), whereas most of the exs. with a gerund(ive) are classed under 'exempla usus nondum perfecti vel incerta' (790.38ff.). The reason for this imbalance is presumably that the dat. gerund(ive) is regularly used to express purpose and edd. have therefore doubted the genuineness of the preposition. No doubt this procedure is justifiable in those cases where textual corruption is likely on other grounds, but this does not seem to be the case in most of the 'exempla incerta' in *TLL* (cf. esp. Cic. *Parad. Sto.* 17, Liv. 21.2.7 'mirae artis in sollicitandis gentibus imperioque suo iungendis fuerat', Val. Max. 1.7.2 'naturalem animi in omnibus rebus subtiliter perspiciendis uigorem'), and among the 'exempla certa' are Curt. 4.14.6 'in illis colendis . . . usurpare uictoriae praemia', Plin. *NH* 22.129 'in aluo sistenda torretur'. I am reluctant to believe that such a wide range of texts can be in error over the same construction: the evidence suggests to me that *in* + abl. gerund(ive) can be used as indicated in *TLL* and that our passage of V. may be an ex. of the usage.

(b) Alternatively, we may be dealing with an extension or conflation of construction. On the one hand one can say 'qui tum procul in Gallia prouincia . . . aberat' (Liv. 22.31.9, cf. *TLL* 1.206.65ff.); on the other, *in* + abl. is regularly used to express being 'engaged or occupied in an activity' (see *OLD* s.v. 39): it may be that V. has simply combined the two and said 'Caesar was away ⟨engaged⟩ in ordering the affairs of . . .'. It has to be admitted that according to the evidence of *TLL esse* with *in* + gerund (as opposed to a simple noun) is not common in the sense of 'to be engaged in' (one ex. in Cato, Ter. Cic. Gell.: 7.1.771.31–8), and exs. with the gerundive are less common still (only a sacral text in Macrob. 3.9.11 'qui in his rebus gerundis sunt', Gell. 3.1.4 'longe iamdiu in eo ipse quaerendo fui', cf. Cic. *Rosc.* 39 'qui . . . in agro colendo uixerit'). Yet this evidence, slender though it is, makes me reluctant to deny that V. could have written *in* with this meaning.

The most likely hypothesis, I believe, is that V. had neither of the above usages of *in* precisely in mind, since they belong principally to the classifications of grammarians, but that he nevertheless used the preposition here to express an area of meaning which falls somewhere between the two of them. For a case which is perhaps comparable cf. 116.4n.

et solus et absente Caesare consul The other consulship was kept open for a time in the hope that Augustus himself would take it, as he had 31–23; but in the end he appointed Q. Lucretius to the job, doubtless later than the events which V. describes here (cf. Dio 54.10.1–2). Saturninus himself resigned late in 19, whereupon M. Vinicius, grandfather of V.'s dedicatee (see 101.3n., 104.2n.), became suffect consul.

uetere consulum more ac †seueritate Although V. often indulges in the close repetition of a word or phrase (cf. 100.5n.), I do not believe that he repeated *seueritate* so soon after its appearance seven words earlier. Are we then to delete *ac seueritate* (so Ruhnken)? I think not. As Freitag among others has noted, V. likes also to repeat himself by the use of synonyms (e.g. 63.3 'secum luctatus ac sibi difficile consentiens', 113.2 'maiorem quam ut temperari posset, neque habilem gubernaculo', and also 92.5 below), and I believe he did so here: we cannot however know what the synonym was, since the transmitted *seueritate* has been caused by assimilation to the same word's earlier appearance in the sentence. The scribal error is mental, not visual (for which cf. M. L. West, *Textual Criticism and Editorial Technique* (1973), 23–4; also below, next n. but one).

It will be noticed how, in his story of Saturninus, V. twice proceeds from the general to the particular (*cum alia . . . tum in comitiis . . .: nam et quaesturam petentes . . . et Egnatium . . .*). For *prisca seueritas*, above, cf. 127.4n.; for *seueritas* and *constantia*, above, cf. Cic. *Sull.* 45.

protraxisset . . . fraudes 'he had brought out into the open the frauds of the *publicani*': for other exs. of the verb in this sense see Liv. 27.3.1 'nouum . . . per indicium protractum est facinus'; *OLD* s.v. 2. For *publicanorum fraudes* cf. Liv. 25.5.1; for *punisset auaritiam* below cf. perhaps Cic. *Mur.* 67 'puniui ambitum' (and see *OLD* s.v. *punio 1b*); for *fraus* and *auaritia* cf. Cic. *Mur.* 14, Liv. 44.24.8.

redegisset in aerarium pecunias publicas Stanger's *redegisset* restores a technical expression which is guaranteed by such parallels as Cic. *Diu. Caec.* 56, *Phil.* 13.10, Liv. 2.42.2, 4.53.10 'uenditum sub hasta consul in aerarium redigere quaestores iussit', 6.4.2, 7.27.9 'magnam pecuniam in aerarium redegit', 21.15.2 etc. The erroneous *regessisset* was doubtless caused by the proximity of *gessisset* above.

For *egit consulem*, below, cf. 109.2n., *OLD* s.v. *ago* 26.

92.3 profiteri A technical verb = 'to register one's name' (*nomen* being understood), i.e. 'to be an electoral candidate': cf. *OLD* s.v. 2*b*. Another technical expr. in this section is *in campum descendere* below (*TLL* 3.217.13ff.). For *perseuerare* = 'persist ⟨in saying⟩', below, an unusual sense, cf. Cic. *Amic.* 24, to which F. adds Gell. 1.21.2.

92.4 florentem fauore publico Cf. Cic. *Rep.* 2.60 'summa apud populum gratia florentem'; for *fauor publicus* cf. Ov. *Ex P.* 4.14.56. *renuntiare* below is another technical verb, = 'declare someone elected': cf. L&S s.v. IBi: *OLD* s.v. 4.

92.5 quod ego factum cuilibet ueterum consulum gloriae comparandum reor V. elsewhere praises an action by comparing it favourably with what happened in the old days: 78.3 'grauissimum comparandumque antiquis exemplum', 80.3 'non ab Scipionibus aliisque ueteribus Romanorum ducum quidquam ausum patratumque fortius'. Various considerations no doubt led him to this method of bestowing approval. The *mos maiorum* was habitually stressed by Romans of all periods, but particularly by those of Augustan times (cf. *RG* 8.5 'multa exempla maiorum exolescentia iam ex nostro saeculo reduxi'; Syme, *RR* 442); and historians traditionally viewed the course of Roman history as a decline from some earlier 'golden age' with which the present age could effectively be compared (e.g. Liv. *praef.* 9 with Ogilvie's nn., and Luce 245 and n. 31, 250ff.; also Earl 41ff. and Williams 619ff.). More generally, men are always accustomed τὰ ἀρχαῖα μᾶλλον θαυμάζειν (Thuc. 1.21.2), as V. proceeds to acknowledge in the following clauses. Note the alliteration and assonance of: '*u*isis *l*audamus *l*ibentius . . . *p*raesentia *in*-*ui*dia, *prae*-terita *u*eneratione *p*rosequimur . . . obr*ui* . . . *i*llis *in*strui'.

audita uisis laudamus libentius We have just observed V.'s habit of repeating himself in different words (above, 2n.): the present expression is another example, being merely an alternative form of the epigram which follows (*audita* ~ *praeterita*, *uisis* ~ *praesentia*).[1] Contrasts between *audire* and *uidere* are very common (e.g. *TLL* 2.1274.10ff.), though I have found no exact parallel to V.'s meaning here; Horace does however come half-way to it at *C.* 3.24.31–2 'uirtutem incolumem odimus, | *sublatam ex oculis quaerimus inuidi*'.

---

[1] If this were not the case, V. would be denying, as does Isoc. *Panath.* 150, the proverbial belief that *homines amplius oculis quam auribus credunt* – a belief to which he subscribes and which he uses for praise of Tiberius at 121.3 (see n., adding Cic. *Arch.* 8, Nep. *Att.* 13.7, Tac. *D.* 8.2; Fraenkel 393 n. 3).

praesentia inuidia, praeterita ueneratione prosequimur The sentiment is of course a topos, of which V.'s is 'die knappste lateinische Fassung' (Häussler, *Tac.* 233, quoting innumerable other exs.: see also e.g. Nisbet–Hubbard on Hor. *C.* 2.20.4). *inuidia* of the present is a regular hazard for historians (116.5n.), but in the immediate context V. is more concerned to apologise for his personal *ueneratio* of the past.

his . . . illis Bothe wished to transpose these words on the grounds that often *hic* = 'the latter' and *ille* = 'the former'; yet *hic* . . . *ille* regularly mean 'the one . . . the other', their precise reference being understood from the context (e.g. Ov. *Tr.* 1.2.23–4 'nihil est nisi pontus et aer, | fluctibus hic tumidus, nubibus ille minax', Plin. *Ep.* 5.8.9–10; *OLD* s.v. *hic* 13). For *obruo* used metaphorically of persons see Val. Max. 1.1.9, Sen. *Contr.* 4 *praef.* 4, Stat. *Ach.* 1.294 (F.).

93 Death of Marcellus (23 B.C.)

93.1 Ante triennium fere . . . M. Marcellus . . . decessit We know from Plut. *Marc.* 30 and Serv. *Aen.* 6.861 that Marcellus died during his aedileship, and from Plin. *NH* 19.24 that his aedileship fell in 23, the year implied also by Dio for Marcellus' death (53.30.4). It therefore seems undeniable that Marcellus died in 23; but how does this date square with the four indications of chronology given in V.'s text here?

(1) *Ante triennium fere quam Egnatianum scelus erumperet.* The *scelus* is attributed with certainty to 19 (cf. 91.3n.): exactly 'three years before' would thus take us to 22, but V. is being explicitly imprecise, as his use of *fere* shows. (2) *circa Murenae Caepionisque coniurationis tempus.* The *coniuratio* has been variously dated to 23 or 22 (cf. 91.2n.); but for our purposes this controversy is less important than the fact that here too V. is being intentionally imprecise, as his use of *circa* shows. It does not therefore seem to me that the true date of Marcellus' death, 23, is incompatible with the inexact indications of date given in (1) and (2).

The same cannot however be said for (3) *abhinc annos L*, the reading of the paradosis. *abhinc* = 'from A.D. 30' (cf. 90.2n.); yet 'fifty years' from A.D. 30 take us no further than 21 B.C. It seems to me unlikely, *pace* Massauer, that V. is here giving a round number (see my arguments at 100.2n., where a very similar problem occurs); nor does he qualify the numeral by *fer(m)e*, as he does at 90.4. I believe that V. originally wrote *abhinc annos LII M. Marcellus*: the corruption is entirely credible before *M*.

(4) *magnificentissimo munere aedilitatis edito.* Most scholars assume that this spectacle is the same as that to which Propertius allegedly refers in his lament for Marcellus (3.18.19–20 'Attalicas supera uestis, atque omnia magnis | gemmea sint ludis: ignibus ista dabis' with Butler–Barber's nn.) and that both authors are therefore referring to the *Ludi Magni*. These games were organised by the curule aediles and took place annually on 4–19 September: thus, if the above hypothesis is true, Marcellus' death

could be dated with more precision to some point after mid-September
23 B.C. Yet Propertius' lines are extremely controversial, and Shackleton
Bailey (199) has raised some significant objections to the paradosis (in
particular that '*ignibus ista dabis* should apply to private possessions, not to
the decorations of a public festival'). In my opinion we cannot be certain
that Propertius refers to the *Ludi Magni*; we therefore cannot be certain
that these are the games to which V. is here referring. We know from the
elder Pliny (loc. cit.) that Marcellus was still alive on 1 August 23, and
although we have no reason to assume that V.'s phrase here contradicts
him, we equally have no justification, on present evidence, for assuming
that it improves on him. See also Swan, op. cit. (at 91.2n.), 242.

It will be noticed that the text reads *fere* here but *ferme* at 90.4, the latter
being the form for which V. indicates a preference (14:9, according to the
statistics in *TLL* 6.1.492.15ff.). Adams (1974), 57, observes that there was
a stylistic difference between the pair from the late republic onwards.
'*Fere* was the current term, *ferme* (which, however, is used by Plautus) an
archaism. *Ferme* is avoided completely or used rarely by Cicero, Caesar,
Seneca the Elder, Celsus, Quintilian and others. The historians show a
taste for the archaism. Tacitus has *fere* only in the minor works and once
in the *Histories*. Curtius uses *ferme* 14 times, though it is outnumbered by
fere (29 times). Livy has a slight preference for *ferme* . . . [with] a marked
increase in the incidence of the archaism in the third decade.'

scelus erumperet Cf. 100.2n.; Liv. 40.20.5 (F.), Val. Max. 1.6.13
'erupit . . . parricidium'.

ut tamen id . . . posse contingere non existimarent 'mais l'on
pensait aussi que M. Agrippa ne l'en laisserait pas jouir en toute
tranquillité' (Hellegouarc'h). Agrippa was, after all, 'parendi (sed uni)
scientissimus, aliis sane imperandi cupidus' (79.1). For the rivalry
between him and Marcellus see Reinhold 78–83; also below, 2n.

admodum iuuenis Marcellus died 'in his twentieth year' according
to Prop. 3.18.15, but in his eighteenth year according to Serv. *Aen.* 6.861:
is Prop. merely giving a round number *metri gratia*, or is Servius (or his
text) wrong? Since we do not know exactly when Marcellus was born,
there is no means of knowing; but most scholars assume the latter, in
which case Marcellus would have been born in 42.

Since the phrase *admodum iuuenis* concludes the *decessit*-colon (cf. 2.2.3),
the following genitives seem awkwardly 'in the air'; yet cf. 128.2 'C.
Marium ignotae originis' and the exs. quoted at 79.1n. The phrase *magnificentissimo . . . aedilitatis* is Ciceronian: *Fam.* 11.17.1.

sane (ut aiunt) ingenuarum uirtutum . . . *ut aiunt* is placed here,
rather than after *ingenuarum* (so Rhenanus) or *uirtutum*, because V. wishes
it to apply to the whole phrase *ingenuarum . . . capax*. Marcellus is hardly

the 'golden boy' for V. that he was for Virgil (*Aen.* 6.868ff.) or Sen. (*Marc.* 2.3 'adulescentem animo alacrem, ingenio potentem . . . sed et frugalitatis continentiaeque in illis aut annis aut operibus non mediocriter admirandae, patientem laborum, uoluptatibus alienum')—naturally, in view of what is said about Tiberius at ch. 94 below.

For *laetus animi* cf. Tac. *A.* 2.26.1 (*animo* at Ap. *Met.* 5.6.7); for *l. ingenii* cf. *l. ingenio* at Vict. *Epit.* 44.3, Serv. *Aen.* 11.73; for *fortunae . . . capax* cf. Tac. *H.* 2.1.2; for *in quam alebatur* cf. Cic. *Att.* 8.3.3 'istum in rem p. ille aluit' (F.), Val. Max. 2.10.4, 9.3 *ext.* 2.

93.2 (ut fama loquitur) It is clear from the position of this clause that it refers to *qui . . . se subduxerat tempori* as a whole (see on *ut aiunt* above): thus V. is circumspect about a motive which Suet. regards as certain (*Aug.* 66.3 'quod Marcellus sibi anteferretur, Mytilenas se relictis omnibus contulisset [sc. Agrippa]', cf. *Tib.* 10.1). According to Plin. *NH* 7.149, Agrippa's departure was a form of banishment ('pudenda Agrippae ablegatio'), but 'a political suspect is not placed in charge of provinces and armies' (Syme, *RR* 342).

For *principalis* = 'imperial' cf. 124.3n.; for *fama loquitur* cf. Luc. 4.574, Flor. 2.20.7, [Sen.] *Herc. Oet.* 206, Mart. 1.8, Just. 18.4.7, Min. Fel. 9.3, Amm. 21.15.5 (cf. also Vell. 102.1, 121.3); for *praesenti se subduxerat tempori* cf. 72.5; for *tacitas . . . offensiones* cf. Tac. *A.* 13.19.2 'occultis inter eas offensionibus' (Krause).

filiam Caesaris Iuliam . . . duxit uxorem Julia, who had previously married Marcellus in 25, married Agrippa in 21: on her see 100.3–5nn.

On the phraseology here cf. 79.2n. The word-order *filiam Caesaris Iuliam*, and *filia eius Iulia* at 100.3, indicate that I was wrong to prefer Haase's correction to Gelenius' at 96.1 (*TN* 60, 105).

feminam neque sibi neque rei publicae felicis uteri In view of the precariousness of birth and survival, the Romans, whose society depended upon manpower for its military and economic success, had always set great store by children (cf. J. P. V. D. Balsdon, *Roman Women* (1962), 190–203, 209–10). It was conventional to praise parents by saying that 'adferunt laudem liberi parentibus' (Quint. 3.7.18, where Adamietz quotes Hermog. 16.23 Rad.), and it was a topos of panegyric that under a good ruler there is *spes liberorum parentibus* (cf. 103.5n.). In epithalamia in particular it was conventional to pray that parents should produce 'praeclaros Latio . . . nepotes, | qui leges, qui castra legant' (Stat. *Silu.* 1.2.266–7 with Vollmer's n.; cf. also A. L. Wheeler, *AJPh* 51 (1930), 211–15, P. Fedeli, *Il carme 61 di Catullo* (1972), 113–15).

Now at several points during his reign Augustus turned his attention to moral and social legislation: as early as 28 B.C. (cf. P. Csillag, *The Augustan Laws on Family Relations* (1976), 29–30), in 18 B.C. (the *Lex Iulia de maritandis ordinibus*), and in A.D. 9 (the *Lex Papia Poppaea*): see further

89.4n., and *ANRW* 2.13.278–339. Many scholars have believed that the purpose of this legislation was precisely demographic and aimed at increasing the birthrate (see e.g. *CAH* 10.448ff.), but it has been shown that there are serious objections to this view (see Brunt, *IM* Appendix 9). More recently other interpretations have been advanced: the legislation was an intrinsic and essential element in Augustus' attempt at regenerating Roman morality (K. Galinsky, *Philol.* 125 (1981), 126–44), or it was aimed at encouraging the family 'in order to stabilise the transmission of property, and consequently of status, from generation to generation' (A. Wallace–Hadrill, *PCPS* 27 (1981), 58–80). Whatever the truth, the important fact for our purposes is that Augustus' legislation was seen by contemporaries as being aimed at increasing the birthrate and assuring the state's military manpower (cf. G. Williams, *JRS* 52 (1962), 28–46; Liebeschuetz 90–100; F. Cairns, *Grazer Beitr.* 8 (1979), 185–204). The attitudes of the Augustan age are reflected in the so-called *Laudatio Turiae*, a husband's eulogy for his dead wife, in which he records that, since as a couple they failed to have the children they desired, his wife offered to divorce him so that he could marry again and have children by someone else (EJ 357, lines 35ff. = pp. 26–7 in E. Wistrand's (1976) edn).

It is against this kind of background that V. pronounces the present verdict on Julia. Doubtless he would have preferred to bestow on her the kind of praise which Claudian gives to the mother of Probinus and Olybrius ('o duplici fecundam consule matrem | felicemque uterum', *Prob.* 2.202–3, cf. also Sil. 4.356–7); but Julia's record as a mother made this impossible. By her marriage to Agrippa she produced the following sequence of unfortunate children: Gaius and Lucius Caesar (cf. 96.1n.), both of whom were destined by Augustus to play a part in his succession but who died premature deaths (see 102.2–3); the younger Julia, banished by Augustus in A.D. 8 for adultery; Agrippina, attacked by Tiberius in A.D. 29 (cf. 130.4nn.) and herself described by Tac. as 'infelici fecunditate fortunae totiens obnoxia' (*A.* 2.75.1, where Goodyear compares Cic. *Phil.* 2.58 'o miserae mulieris fecunditatem calamitosam', Ap. *Apol.* 85 'o infelix uterum tuum'); and Agrippa Postumus, widely regarded as unstable and even mad (112.7n.), and killed on Tiberius' accession to the principate in A.D. 14.

Julia herself was banished in 2 B.C. for adultery. It is somewhat ironical that another topos of epithalamia was that children should resemble their parents (see Wheeler and Fedeli, quoted above, also West on Hes. *WD* 235 and Nisbet–Hubbard on Hor. *C.* 2.4.20).

INDEXES

1 GENERAL

ablative absolute, 'Tacitean' type of, 81, 125

accusative, in apposition to sentence, 57, 154, 167

aduentus, of general on the field of battle, 90; of great man in a city, 118–19, 121, 248–9

Agricola, 242

Alexander, prototype for Caesar, Antony, etc., 53, 71, 200, 214–15

alliteration, 75, 81, 98, 113, 138, 180, 202, 219, 227–8, 277

Amerbach's apograph, 1–2, 87, 112–13, 118, 141, 153, 176 n. 1, 204, 211, 228

ἀπὸ κοινοῦ, 76, 201; of prepositions, to be distinguished from *uariatio*, 220–1

apostrophe, 146

Appian, 80, 132; *see also* Velleius Paterculus (c) as historical source

asyndeton bimembre, 184

audax, 65, 78–9, 111

Burer, J. A., appendix of, 1–2, 151–3, 186, 217, 228

character: elements of, 167; and physical appearance, 166; illustrated by epigrammatic remarks, 231–2: 'mixed' characters, 180, 240; acting out of caracter, 162, 167–8; character sketches, 52, 156

chiasmus, 57, 72, 82, 88, 138

chronology, problems of (all dates B.C.): Caesar as *flamen Dialis* (87), 59; Caesar's actions on behalf of the children of the proscribed (63), 61; length of the civil wars, 78, 117, 219, 251–2; events of January 49, 81 and n. 1, 85–6; Pompey's birthday (106), 103; Pompey's marriage to Cornelia (52), 105; Octavian's age, 127–8; Brutus' Macedonian command (27 Apr. 43), 132–4, 177–8; Octavian's first consulship (43), 143; Brutus' birthday (85), 173; Sex. Pompeius' appointment as *praefectus classis* (27 Apr. 43), 177–8; campaigns in Illyricum (39/38), 192–6; oath of allegiance to Octavian (32), 278–9; victory in Spain (25 or 19?), 267; Murena's plot (23 or 22?), 270–1; Marcellus' death (23), 278–9

Cicero: echoed by V., 52, 60, 65, 67, 68, 69, 73, 75, 76, 79, 82, 84, 114, 115, 124–5, 127, 131, 138–9, 145, 146, 148–50, 167, 173, 181, 202, 206, 259, 269–70; *Phil.* 11.27, interpretation of, 133

clausulae, 152

colloquial language, 146–8, 169

comparatio compendiaria, 54–5, 128

conquestio: requires detailed treatment, 101; questions in, 100; topoi of: untimely death, 78, 'no loyalty is shown to the unfortunate', 99–100, 'unburied in a foreign field', 102, *commutatio fortunae*, 101

consolatory literature, 145–50; topoi of: *indignatio*, 147, 'Is the world governed by providence?', 149, *opportunitas mortis*, 78, 82,

uariatio of prepositions, 110; different from ἀπὸ κοινοῦ, 220–1

Velleius Paterculus

(*a*) his methods of writing: attention to dates, 75, 101–2, 103, 127–8, 130, 143, 173, 262, 265, 278–9; methods of dating, 65, 83, 220, 265, 267; biographical divisions of his work, 51 and n. 1, 123 n. 1; methodical writing, 138, 155–6, 186–7, 201, 231, 250; separates one section of his work from another, 81–2, 139, 156, 179, 237; writes general surveys, 250, 261; writes colourfully or dramatically, 65, 91, 104–5, 108, 112–13, 123, 139, 145, 170, 179, 184, 197, 204–5, 209, 216, 219, 225, 227, 229; autopsy, 130; uses epigrams to illustrate a person's character, 231–2; promises to write future work(s), 70–1, 82, 195, 249

(*b*) his attitudes: caution and scepticism, 80, 84, 86–7; conservative temperament, 86; abhors political violence, 156; admires *otium* and *otiosi* at the expense of *industria* and *strenui*, 239–44; sees the continuity of history, 65, 83, 262; likes comparisons with the past, 197, 204, 277–8; moral dimension of his work, 274; is generous in dispensing praise, 184–5, 274, 277–8; criticises other writers, 103; sees things from a soldier's point of view, 136, 165, 197; is sensitive to *militaria uerba*, 96–7, and to *uerba sordida*, 55–6; preoccupied with Campania, 64–5, 179, 182–6, 206–7; is realistic on 'power politics', 90

(*c*) as historical source: as unique or almost unique source, 69, 113, 132–4, 179, 183, 186, 201–2, 215; errors, 69, 77, 95, 104–5, 107, 109–10, 130, 140, 143, 171, 195, 200–1, 232, 267; reliability, 59, 61, 69, 72, 80, 81 n. 1, 92, 93, 103, 108, 119, 124–5, 132–4, 160–3, 164–5, 171, 175–6, 177–8, 210–11, 215, 217, 222, 236, 237–8, 250, 252–4, 255, 272; in conflict with other sources, 54 (Suet. Plut.), 59 (Suet.), 69–70 (Cic.), 73 (Plut. Dio), 80 (App.), 94–5 (Plut. App.), 99 (Plut. App. Dio), 105 (Plut.), 117 (Plut.), 125 (Dio), 135 (Liv.), 165 (Cic.), 169 (App.), 170 (Plut.), 174 (Suet.), 207 (elder Plin.), 210 (Plut.); in agreement with other sources, 59 (Suet.), 61 (Dio), 67 (Dio), 73 (Dio), 74 (Plut.), 77 (Dio), 80 (App.), 98 (Plut. App. Dio), 102 (Plut.), 103 (App.), 110 (Plut.), 121 (Nic. Dam.), 124 (Plut. Cic. Nic. Dam.), 125 (App.), 132 (App. Dio), 135 (Liv. App.), 136 (Plut.), 137 (Plut. App.), 142 (Suet. Dio), 159 (Caes. Dio), 165–6 (Dio), 170 (Plut. App.), 172 (Dio), 173 (Cic. App.), 177 (App. Dio), 178 (App.), 183–4 (Dio), 187 (Dio), 192 (Dio), 199 (Jos. Dio), 203 (Suet.), 205 (Suet.), 206 (Dio), 207 (Liv. Sen. Dio), 208 (Dio), 211 (Flor. Dio), 211–13 (Liv. Flor. Plut. Dio), 222 (Dio); *see also* chronology, problems of verbs: compound for simple, 91, 170; simple for compound, 268

word-order, 161, 254; inverted, 74, 147; interlaced, 81, 82, 167, 172 word play (paronomasia), 78, 84, 93, 103, 105, 108, 116, 136, 140, 155, 180, 187, 199, 204–5, 248, 272

zeugma, 75, 94; differs from syllepsis, 96 n. 2

2 LATIN WORDS

a + abl. + gerundive, 77
adulescens, derogatory, 175
aequaliter ('equidistant from all points'), 120
animaduertere + accus. and inf., 64
annum egredi ∼ annum ingredi, 127–8
arcus ('halo'), 120
artare, of books and writings etc., 230
auctoramentum, 147
audax, derogatory, 65, 78–9, 111; appreciatory, 56–7, 197, 204
audere, of literary invention etc., 230
Augustus, 268

caeruleatus, 217
caninus, 140
cauere + dat. of a thing, 81
causa, civil war jargon, 83–4; *causam habere* + *ut* or *quod*, 62
clementia + *aduersus*, 107
concordia, 81, 188
creare = cooptare, 59
cum, inverted, 74–5, 126, 163 n. 1; causal, with noun as antecedent, 89

depudet ∼ dispudet, 179
deuorare, 246–8
dies, dramatic use of, 225, 229
dignatio, 116
dignitas, 75, 162, 240–2
dinotare ∼ denotare, 169–70
discingere, 55–6
dissimilis + *quam*, 107

et, transposition of, 142; = *et quidem*, 123; *et . . . -que*, 91–2; *et . . . -que . . . -que*, 142

excalceare, 55–6
expedit + dat. + accus. and inf., 114
experientiā ('in the light of experience'), 112
explicare = tractare fusius etc., 71
exprimere, 249
exsistere ∼ exstare, 158

fatalis + dat. ('destined for'), 94
fere ∼ ferme, 279
firmus + abl., 138; *∼ ualidus*, 221
forma rei publicae, 254
fortuna, as travelling companion, 168; as deserter, 168; personal, 106, 108, 236; public, 229–30; personal ∼ public, 102; *uirtus* and, 182, 202; *fatigata*, 168
fulgor and *fulgens*, of lightning, 90, 139–40
furere + *in* + accus., 76
fusti ∼ fuste (abl.), 151–2

genitus, 116

hercules!, 94
hic, resumptive, 52, 62, 199, 267; = 'the present ∼', 62, 184; *hic . . . ille*, 'the one . . . the other', 278
humanus, 123

iacere mentionem, 141
iam, 163 and n. 1
igitur, position of, 142
ignis, cannot = 'coal(s)', 247 and n. 1
imago, 261
immanis ('very great' etc.), 71, 118–19, 167

tumultuari + *inter*   ('oscillate between one role and another'), 202

uir, in apposition, 72, 198; used instead of a pronoun, 200; used with a pronoun, 268

ullus ex + abl., 74

umbra ('outline'), 157

uox, metaphorical, 146

3 NAMES

Note. All dates are B.C. unless otherwise stated.

Printed in Great Britain
by Amazon